W9-BIN-502

HIGH RISE

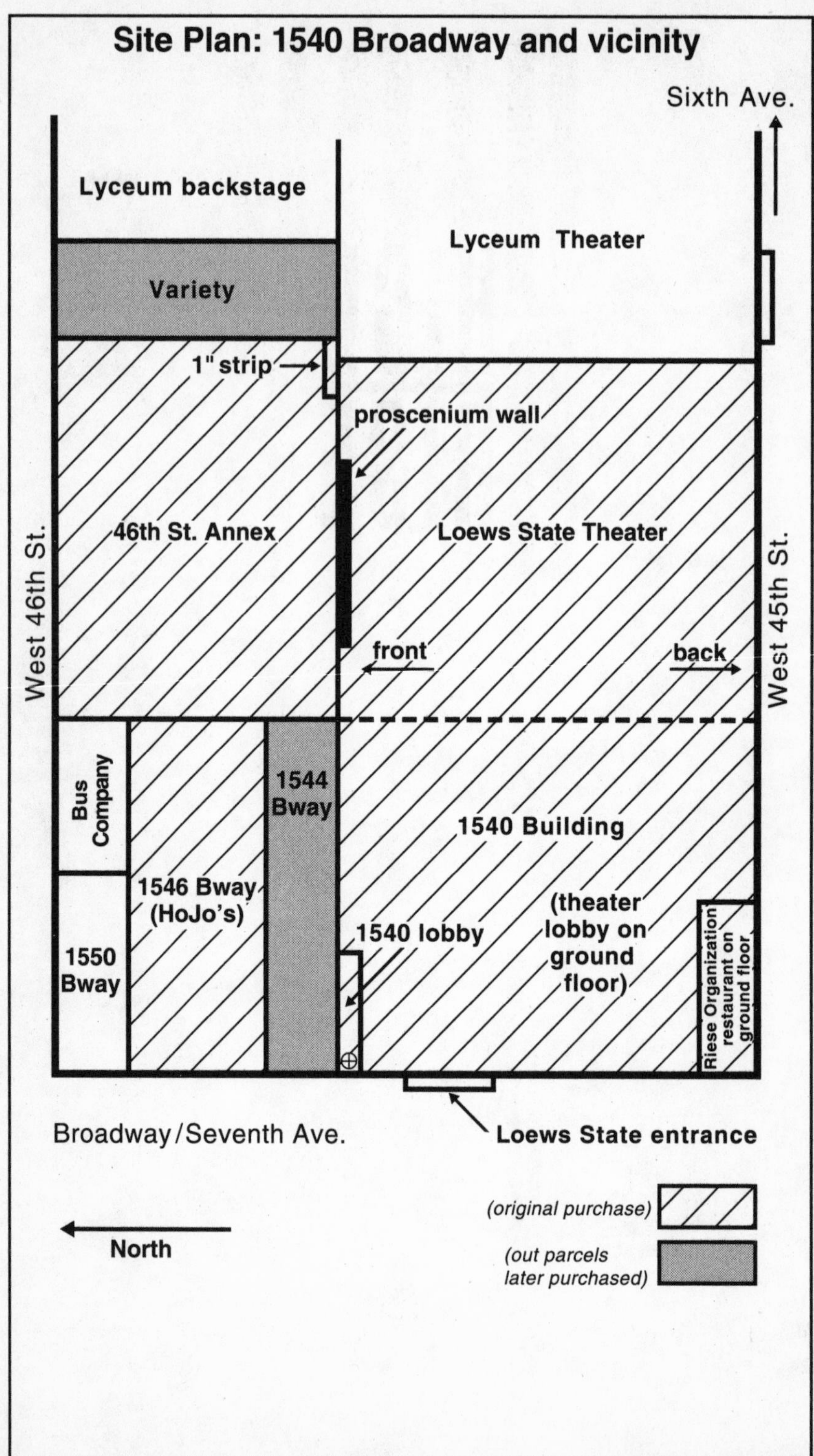
Site Plan: 1540 Broadway and vicinity
Sixth Ave.
Lyceum backstage
Lyceum Theater
Variety
1" strip
proscenium wall
46th St. Annex
Loews State Theater
West 46th St.
West 45th St.
front
back
Bus Company
1544 Bway
1540 Building
1546 Bway (HoJo's)
1550 Bway
1540 lobby
(theater lobby on ground floor)
Riese Organization restaurant on ground floor
Broadway/Seventh Ave.
Loews State entrance
(original purchase)
(out parcels later purchased)
North

HIGH RISE

How 1,000 Men and Women Worked Around the Clock for Five Years and Lost $200 Million Building a Skyscraper

JERRY ADLER

HarperCollins*Publishers*

Photographs and illustrations follow page 118.

HarperCollins books may be purchased for educational, business, or sales promotional use. For information please write: Special Markets Department, HarperCollins Publishers, Inc., 10 East 53rd Street, New York, NY 10022.

FIRST EDITION

Designed by C. Linda Dingler

Library of Congress Cataloging-in-Publication Data

Adler, Jerry

High rise : how 1,000 men and women worked around the clock for five years and lost $200 million building a skyscraper / Jerry Adler.—1st ed.

p. cm.

ISBN 0-06-016701-7

1. Real estate development—New York (N.Y.)—Manhattan—Case studies. 2. Skyscrapers—New York (N.Y.)—Manhattan—Case studies. 3. Eichner, Ian Bruce. I. Title

HD268.N5A43 1993 92-53320

333.77'15'097471—dc20

---

93 94 95 96 97 ❖/RRD 10 9 8 7 6 5 4 3 2 1

PREFACE

It was one of the more fatuous observations about the 1980s—I know, because I used to go around saying so myself—that it was the decade in which real estate replaced sex as the venue for the everyday fantasies of most Americans. In the course of writing this book I learned that this was never the case, even for people in the real estate business. But clearly the ownership of real property excited the imagination and greed of Americans in the 1980s as it never had before. The country had discovered a new principle—actually, one that has been rediscovered approximately every other decade since the beginning of capitalism—the Law of Perpetual Motion of Real Estate Prices. It was literally true, for a few years in the middle of the decade, that people who owned their own homes could make more money over the course of a year sleeping in their beds at night than they did at work during the day. And if that was true of the occupant of a $75,000 condominium apartment, how much more so of the person who built the apartment house? Or the office building down the street?

While it lasted, it was great. Fortunes were made in a few years, and fortunes already made grew many times larger. The same was true, naturally, of contemporaneous booms in securities, precious metals, and art. But unlike the others, the real estate boom didn't merely reallocate value among existing assets; it had a profound impact on the landscape and built environment of America. Estimates are that nearly a third of all the office space ever built in this country was built between 1980 and 1990. New neighborhoods were colonized by builders who in places like New York had used up every available square foot of the old business districts. After a long period of esthetic dormancy, the office building became again an important vehicle for architectural expression. "Landlords," those humble foot-soldiers of entrepreneurship, content to sit back and collect a 6% return on equity, became "developers," dashing patrons of art and influential arbiters of taste. Vast enterprises employing thousands were organized to wring the profits of development from the stubborn pavement, and the banks fueled it all with their inexhaustible billions.

Of course, everyone knew this ride couldn't continue forever. But it was so much fun that no one was willing to acknowledge a crash until his nose actually hit the windshield. By 1990 vast tracts of new office space had come into a market desolated by recession. A deflation of commercial real estate values estimated at around 30 percent set in, enough to wipe out a good part of the fortunes made just a few years earlier, and also to threaten the prosperity—and for a time, it seemed, the very existence—of some of the nation's largest banks. By early 1992, Olympia & York, the $5 billion real estate empire whose profoundly Orthodox owners were assumed to have a direct pipeline to the real estate secrets of the Almighty, was in serious if not mortal trouble. This was a particularly nasty turn of events for New York, whose leaders often spoke of real estate as one of the foundations of its economy, as if the exiguous nature of an economy founded on constructing empty buildings had not occurred to them. Empty the buildings were and empty they remained—touching in their emptiness, monuments to vast ambitions unrealized and to the sweat and genius of the men and women who made them.

This is the story of one such building, and the people who conceived and built it. Architects, engineers, bankers, real estate brokers, demolition workers, ironworkers, lawyers, and city planners all have roles in it. Foremost among them is the developer, Ian Bruce Eichner, without whom there would have been no building, and also no book. There have been other books about real estate, and about office buildings, but none that affords such an intimate glimpse of the way in which a developer goes about his business. This was not an exercise in vanity on Eichner's part. He undertook his role in this project for the intellectual satisfaction of analyzing and explaining what he does. Eichner became a developer for the same reason anyone does—to make money—but he is unique in his belief that the unexamined dollar is not worth making. For the chance to see how fortunes are made, and lost, in the high-stakes game of commercial real estate, I—and everyone who reads this book—owe him a debt of gratitude. And if nothing else, this book should lay to rest the canard that all profits in real estate are unearned. At the outset of the Broadway State project, Eichner anticipated making tens of millions of dollars for about four years' work. At the conclusion ... well, the conclusion speaks for itself, but any fair-minded reader would have to agree that Eichner worked hard for every dollar he didn't make from the project, as well as those he did.

High Rise would not have been possible without the cooperation, assistance, and invaluable guidance of Bruce Eichner. But all of the opinions expressed in these pages are my own. If there are errors of fact or judgment, I alone am responsible.

The building at the corner of Broadway and West 45th Street is the product of the labor of literally thousands of people, some of whom never even saw the site. In telling the story of this building, I have presumed on the time and patience of more people than I care to recall, and I am grateful to each and every one of them, including those whose names I never knew or have filed away and forgotten. But there are some whose cooperation stands out in my mind, and I would be remiss if I failed to thank by name the following:

Howard Hornstein, above all, for his wisdom and faith in me.

At Eichner Properties: Luk Sun Wong, Mitchell Mailman, William Tung, Henry Miller, Alice Hoffman, Scott Lewis, Lydia Robinson, Nancy Goshco, and Marie Globus, and especially Andrea Kremen.

At Skidmore, Owings & Merrill: David Childs, Bill Hellmuth, Audrey Matlock, Terry Bell, and Phil Murray.

At Turner Construction Company: Sal LaScala, John Ellis, Gary Negrycz, and Bob Fee.

At VMS: Steve Berini.

I am also grateful for the friendship, support, and advice of the following during the five years that this book took to write: Steven Adler, Susan Bonhomme, Kris Dahl, Ralph DiBart, Martin Gottlieb, Neal Hirschfeld, David Hirshey, Richard Kot, Mickey Lebowitz, Charles Leerhsen, Aric Press, Gil Schwartz, and Berthe Small. My original editor on this project was Harriet Rubin, and I am grateful for her confidence in me. During this entire period I was employed as a writer by *Newsweek* magazine. The reader is entitled to wonder how it was possible for me to hold a full-time job and still be present for all the events described in this book. That is a secret I share with a few of my immediate editors. They know who they are. I have been very lucky to work for a company that stands by its workers as loyally as does *Newsweek*, and I salute it here.

I also must thank my parents, Harry and Hilda Adler, for teaching me the difference between right and wrong, which is very important knowledge for someone writing about the real estate industry. And above all my wife, Beth Lebowitz, who almost always laughed in the right places.

This book is dedicated to my sons, Ben and Max, in hopes that they will grow up to be men as good as some of those who built 1540 Broadway. Some, but not all. By the end of the book the reader should be able to tell the difference.

WHO'S WHO

At Eichner Properties:

Bruce Eichner, president

Development

- Luk Sun Wong
- William Tung
- Alice Hoffman

Legal

- Howard Hornstein
- Andrea Kremen
- Karen Kasner

Finance

- Henry Miller
- Lydia Robinson

Construction

- Mitchell Mailman
- Pat Rafter
- Scott Lewis (owner's representative at site)

Leasing

- Leslie Eichner

At Skidmore, Owings & Merrill:

- David Childs, design partner
- Bill Hellmuth, design associate
- Audrey Matlock, design associate and senior designer
- Duncan Reid and Steve Dynia, senior designers
- Lisa Gould, designer
- Tom Fridstein, management partner
- Susanne Churchill and Dale Peterson, project managers
- Joe Blanchfield, senior technical coordinator
- Terry Bell, job captain, technical coordinator
- Bob Halvorson, structural engineering partner
- Phil Murray, senior structural engineer

At Turner Construction Company:

- Bob Fee, head of New York office
- Gary Negrycz, project executive
- Sal LaScala, project manager
- John Ellis, project supervisor
- Michael Danberg, assistant to Ellis
- Pradeep Mehra, project engineer
- Lee Tsangeos, estimating engineer

At VMS:

- Steve Berini
- Maria Cheng

At The Hahn Company:

- John Gilchrist, president
- Vernon Schwartz, executive vice president
- Al Corti, director of leasing
- Rick Froese, project manager
- Jack Illes, New York leasing officer

1

The street was deserted when the big flatbed trailers began arriving before dawn on a Saturday morning in late June of 1988. Twenty-two of them had driven through the night from Allentown, Pennsylvania, east on Interstate 78, through the Lincoln Tunnel, and then across the streets of midtown Manhattan to the block of West 45th Street between Sixth Avenue and Broadway; and there they parked. The crane arrived alongside the excavation on the western end of the block at around eight o'clock, a 100-ton FMC Link-Belt, a battered and graffiti-scarred veteran of the Bronx, and then two men closed off the street at the eastern end, because the crane took up the whole width of it, from sidewalk to sidewalk.

Michael Danberg, an engineer with the Turner Construction Company, had drawn the assignment of announcing the street closing to all the businesses along the block. There were scores of them filling a dozen grubby old West Side commercial buildings. Unlike some of the other nearby streets, which are known all over the world as the homes of particular trades (diamonds on 47th Street; musical instruments on 48th; women, or rather pictures of women, on 42nd), there was nothing to distinguish this block of 45th Street. A theater, the Lyceum, built in 1902 and now most often dark, was the first building to the east. Hamburger

Harry's. A parking lot, unnamed. The Cabana Carioca, a Brazilian restaurant. A branch of 47th St. Photo, a discount store run entirely by young Orthodox Jews. At the far end, just before another construction site, in the shadow of the silver shoeboxes of Sixth Avenue, was the St. James Hotel, unknown to travel agents or tour guides, offering "colored television"; and the hotel's newsstand, whose sign grandiloquently but cryptically proclaimed the "Ghinie Charms Discount Stationery and Smoke Shop." The sidewalk in front of the St. James was home to a number of young men whose employment appeared to consist of eyeing hungrily the cartons of goods delivered all day long to 47th St. Photo under the nervous gaze of several large bushy-bearded Hasidim. It was outside this hotel, a few months earlier, that a developer who was showing the area to a prospective tenant was approached by two skinny young women with a different kind of space to rent. The tenant drew back in fastidious horror. "And that," the developer added indignantly, in recounting this outrage to a representative of the mayor's office of midtown development, "was the *chief executive officer of a Fortune 500 company!*" Now a prominent placard on the entrance to the St. James said, in large letters, "Restraining Order." The text of the order prohibited, in the law's magisterial redundancy, "prostitution and all acts prohibited by Chapter 230 New York Penal Law."

Mike Danberg thought the distribution of circulars about the street closing was beneath the professional dignity of someone who had been out of school for practically a whole year.

"What kind of engineering do you call this?" he grumbled to John Ellis, the project superintendent.

"Applied engineering," Ellis replied dryly. He was an immensely tall, soft-spoken, omnicompetent Englishman who had built buildings for Turner in Kenya and Kuwait and all over the world before he was deemed ready for the challenge of midtown Manhattan. On his first job in New York, a woman who objected to a building going up that would block her view across Third Avenue threw eggs out her window at the crane. He had come to regard the legendary hardships of high-rise construction in midtown Manhattan as overrated. Worse than Kenya, certainly, but at least you could get a beer at lunch, which was more than you could say for some of the places he'd worked.

The crane traveled with its eighty-foot boom folded over on itself, like an ingeniously articulated insect limb, and it had to be unhinged and pinned into place, and the cables run through sheaves, and outriggers extended onto steel bearing plates on the street, and the whole thing tested and adjusted before it could do any useful work. The truck drivers, whose problem this wasn't, slumped in their cabs, lost in the peaceful reveries of those who make eighteen dollars an hour while everyone else works. Not that their job was without its hardships. One man left for a few minutes to get some breakfast, and when he got back discovered that his cab had been broken into and his radar detector was missing. The other drivers thought this was very funny.

"Hey, kid, better check your load," one called to him. The driver instinctively looked back at his trailer, on which rode a single steel beam, approximately twenty feet long.

"Fucking junkies would steal it if it wasn't chained down, too," he muttered.

Most of the trucks carried only one piece of steel. The largest of them was on the first truck. It was a thirty-foot-long member with the cross section of an **H**, bristling with flanges, ears, gusset plates, and miscellaneous other welded and bolted protrusions for the purpose of making connections to the adjoining girders. Each of the arms of the **H** were more than two feet long and eight inches thick. This was the bottom section of one of the major columns of the building that was to be constructed at this corner. It was to bear the weight of forty-five floors and their human occupants, and transmit it to a steel baseplate ten inches thick, sitting atop a large cube of concrete, which would disperse the load onto the ancient and infinitely resilient schist of midtown Manhattan.

After a couple of hours a man named Bobby Sasso drove up in a silver Lincoln. Sasso was the Working Teamster Foreman on the job. "Working Teamster Foreman" is a contradiction in terms. A Working Teamster Foreman does not perform any construction work, drive a truck, or supervise any workers. The general contractor pays him an average of $75,000 a year in wages and fringes, including overtime for hours when he is not even present at the construction site. He is assigned by the Teamsters to check that all drivers making deliveries are dues-paying members of the local. The main requirement of the job, therefore, is to be able to recognize a Teamster, and for this Bobby Sasso was unusually well qualified, since his father was president of the local.

Sasso was a muscular, brutishly handsome young man with a short black beard. In the winter he came to work in a leather jacket with an astonishing array of zippers, snaps, tabs, epaulets, flaps, and patches, but in the warm weather he would sometimes go shirtless, showing off a chest only slightly less impressively decorated with tattoos, and a medallion on a gold chain the thickness of a clothesline. He stood on the sidewalk for a while with a group of men who were also working, and admired the column on the truck.

"That's a pretty big piece of steel," one man said after a while.

"What are you talking about?" Sasso said, heatedly. "I've been on plenty of jobs, and that is a *big fuckin' piece of steel.*"

"You got any idea what it weighs?" he asked after a moment.

"Around thirty, thirty-one tons."

Pause.

"That's a fuckin' big piece of steel," Sasso repeated, appreciatively.

Pause.

"Aaaah … how much is that in *pounds*, anyway?" he asked.

Not counting the drivers, there were perhaps twenty-five people at work on the site this day—foremen, superintendents, engineers, mechanics, and assorted supernumeraries, as well as a handful of iron-workers who would actually perform the labor. However, no building was really taking place at all. The job was to unload the twenty-two trucks and move their cargo some sixty feet, sixty vertical feet, to the bottom of the excavation. The end product of all that labor would be twenty-two pieces of steel lying on their sides in a hole, and the trucks would drive away, and everyone would go home until Monday. It was eleven-forty-five in the morning, fifteen minutes before lunchtime, before cables were slung around the first piece of steel and the crane began lifting it off the flatbed.

It went up slowly. For a hundred-ton crane to lift a thirty-ton column is not as easy as it sounds. When cranes fail, it is not usually a case of dropping too heavy a load; they tip over because they're reaching too far. This crane, whose centerpoint was out in the middle of the street, had to pick the column from the truck and swing it over the edge of the hole, and then extend its boom about another twelve feet to the spot where that particular column was supposed to be deposited. Imagine holding a heavy barbell up at your shoulders, with your elbows bent; then imagine straightening your arms to hold it out away from your body. The engineer in his cab couldn't see the bottom of the hole. He couldn't see the steel at all once it began descending, so he watched a man on the edge of the wall giving hand signals, who himself watched a man below guiding the piece with a rope. The piece, carried horizontally in a cradle of heavy chains, swung out over the edge of the hole and then began its descent, slowly, a foot or so a second. When it was just above the bottom the signalman waved for the engineer to boom out, simultaneously letting the piece down and extending it away from the wall. Delicately, the engineer shoved at a lever. The engine strained. The huge machine shuddered and roared and suddenly began tipping over toward the hole. The back outriggers lifted off the ground, six inches, eight inches. The whole machine was shaking. The engineer mashed a lever, and the clutch slipped. The cable went slack as thirty tons of steel dropped like … 60,000 pounds, and the crane, no longer being pulled into the hole by its load, righted itself with a crash.

The engineer killed the engine, spat his cigar into the street, and cursed. His face was gray. He reached around behind his seat and pulled out a thick book of specifications and began thumbing through it for the table that would tell him why he had almost fallen into a sixty-foot hole with his half-million-dollar machine.

A short, round man in a dark suit, perhaps the owner of one of the businesses on the block, stopped one of the ironworkers on his break and asked what they were building. This was a question that had been asked since the first hammer swung on this site more than a year earlier, and the different trades answered it each in their own way. "A parking lot," the wrecking crew replied, as they leveled the old building. "A swimming pool," the excavators answered, as they blasted and hauled the rock. Now the ironworker, who would spend the next year of his life crawling higher and higher on the steel beams of this building, looked piercingly at the man for a moment and then said meaningfully, "a building."

And as the man walked away, with a perplexed nod of thanks, the ironworker turned to his partner and asked, "What the hell is this damn building supposed to be, anyway?"

"I dunno," his partner replied, with no more interest than if he had been asked where the architect had gone to school; "another fuckin' hotel, I guess."

2

What impressed most passersby wasn't the steel, but the size of the hole itself. The hole had taken about eight months to dig. More than 50,000 cubic yards of rock had been honeycombed with drills, packed with dynamite, blasted into chunks, and hauled to the street, where it had filled dump trucks 5,000 times over. Except for one corner, where a four-story building sat atop a narrow wedge of real estate that had escaped as if by divine protection from being pulverized by progress, the hole was generally square in plan, around 200 feet on a side. This was large, although not unusually so, for the footprint of a midtown office building, but the hole was also exceptionally deep. The bottom sloped down slightly from west to east, and the site itself was on an almost imperceptible north-south grade, but at its deepest point along Broadway the hole was nearly sixty feet from its concrete bottom to the lip of the sidewalk. A four-story building could have been dropped into it and covered back up with dirt and no one would know it was there. On the Broadway side, less than a yard away through the rock, a subway tunnel carried tens of thousands of unsuspecting commuters a day. Before the foundation walls were poured, the outside of the tunnel wall was actually visible from the hole, and you could have knocked a hole in the wall to watch the trains go by. A man standing in the bottom of the hole would have had to look up to see the subway.

Only a few buildings in New York have foundations this deep. People passing by would glance into the hole and remark knowingly that it must be for a very, very tall building. That reflects a common misconception that a tall building is kept from toppling by the part of it that is stuck in the ground, like a fencepost. The building stands up because its columns are bolted into bedrock, and the soundness of the rock is what matters, not the depth. This hole was as deep as a four-story building because its basement would in effect be a four-story building, a plan that had nothing to do with engineering necessity and everything to do with the economics of New York City real estate. In Manhattan, as elsewhere, title to a piece of land extends out to space and down to the center of the Earth. You have no business being in real estate if you're not willing to go at least that far to make a profit.

It was almost exactly a century since man had commenced his trudge toward the heavens. The title of first skyscraper is a contested one, but most historians place the origins in the 1880s. There are pretenders in both Chicago and New York. The erection of habitable structures higher than approximately six stories had awaited a safe, reliable elevator, first demonstrated by Otis in 1857. A second barrier could only be crossed after engineers had learned to hang the building, as it were, on a framework of steel columns and beams. Before the steel frame (and its short-lived predecessor, the cast-iron façade), the upper floors of buildings were supported by the masonry walls below, which had to be made proportionately thick as the height of the building increased. This process reached a point of diminishing returns at around ten stories. Well into the nineteenth century, railroads were laid down, steamships dispatched across the globe, and telegraph messages transmitted at the speed of light, all from structures not fundamentally more advanced than a Romanesque church. From its first appearance, the skyscraper therefore was invested with a unique aura, as "the most distinctively American thing in the world," in the words of the great builder Colonel W. A. Starrett, writing in 1928, two years before he and his brother Paul built the Empire State Building.

> The skyscraper, to be a skyscraper, must be constructed on a skeleton frame, now almost universally of steel, but with the signal characteristic of having columns in the outside wall, thus rendering the exterior we see simply a contin-

uous curtain of masonry penetrated by windows; we call it a curtain wall. This seemingly continuous exterior is supported at each floor by the beams or girders of that floor, with the loads carried to the columns imbedded in that same masonry curtain, unseen but nevertheless absolutely essential to the towering heights upon which we gaze with such admiration and awe—and pride, our everlasting pride in our completely American creation.

This is all true, but it should not blind us to the fact (as Starrett himself was well aware) that what was most distinctively American about the skyscraper is its purpose, which is to make money. A building, if it is successful, takes on a kind of teleological necessity once it is built, as if no other possible building could have been contemplated in that particular location. We see the arrangement of shapes the architects refer to as the *massing*, the heart-stopping shimmer in the reflections of the clouds as the wind sucks at the black glass of the windows, the checkerboards of granite on the lobby floor, and to us that is the self-evident end and purpose of all that vast labor. But properly regarded, the physical building is merely the three-dimensional projection of a set of documents known as the pro-forma, the calculations that demonstrate how a given piece of real estate can make money. Thus architect, engineer, ironworker all dance to the tune called by the developer.

The developer of the project at 45th and Broadway was a partnership formed expressly for the purpose: Broadway State Partners. There were two principal partners in Broadway State, and some smaller interests parceled out here and there, but for practical purposes the property was being developed by a man who was spending that Saturday morning with his wife and two young daughters at his Stanford White country house in East Hampton, Long Island, a man whose name was becoming known to New Yorkers who took an interest in the face of their city, Ian Bruce Eichner.

Eichner's calculations for this property were complex. They included parking, because parking is cheap to build, relatively profitable, and a valuable amenity for the occupants of almost anything else that might go on the same lot. They included movie theaters, owing to a historical coincidence, that this land once housed the headquarters of one of the great theatrical chains, Loews Inc. In an unusual and daring move for midtown Manhattan, the pro-forma also envisioned four floors of shopping and restaurants, which accounted for the determination that the basement would go down sixty feet come hell or—what was much more likely in midtown—high water.

Above all that would be a tower of approximately forty floors. The pro-forma had gone through several versions. At first the structure was planned to be a hotel. The hotel was described in several drawers full of documents prepared for Eichner Properties, Inc., in the winter and spring of 1986. Described, that is, not in any of its particulars, but as a set of financial abstractions, a black box whose output was money. In these documents, the success of the project is a matter of Cartesian certitude. Assume a hotel on the corner; and from that simple, singular assertion derives a whole literature of budgets and cash-flow analyses, of thick spiral-bound brochures shimmering with optimism, of feasibility studies trailing elaborate origami constructions of pleat-folded spreadsheets. Busloads of phantom tourists are conjured up to pass through the presumed lobby, leaving behind mounds of the coin of this hypothetical realm, "constant dollars." On the subject of architecture, furnishings, appointments, and ambiance the documents are essentially silent. They describe very specifically, though, how every nickel a guest brought in the door with him would have been spent by the time he left, so that it is possible to say that if a 600-room first-class hotel had been built on that corner, in 1991 its various restaurants, cafés, and banquet rooms would have served an average of 376 lunches a day including eighteen to people (agoraphobics? stool pigeons hiding from the mob?) who unaccountably chose to have lunch brought to them in their rooms.

Invariably, though, the pro-forma is several steps behind reality; otherwise nothing would ever get done. Long before there were plans of any kind for this project, Eichner looked at the corner of Broadway and 45th Street one afternoon in 1985 and bought it for $48 million, knowing only that he would have to build something there or go broke trying. As the black box began to take shape, the hotel changed, first to a mixed-use tower of offices and condominium apartments, and then to its final form of (from the bottommost cellar up) parking, movie theaters, shopping, restaurants, and thirty-six floors of offices. But right up to that very day in 1988 when $20 million in steel columns, beams, spandrels, and purlins started going into the hole, it remained a matter of faith that those thirty-six floors of offices would someday be occupied, because not an inch of them had yet been rented.

In the abstract, there ought to be nothing very hard or complex about making money in real estate. One is providing a commodity for which there is proven demand, using time-tested materials and techniques. Over the long run, real estate almost invariably appreciates. The trick is to get into the long run. The budget for Eichner's building, on that June day in 1988, stood at approximately $320 million, roughly a quarter of which was already gone, and all of which would have to be spent before the building could hope to make any money. Borrowing rates that summer were running at around 9 percent, so interest costs alone were accruing at around $7 million a year, and headed up. If you were going to make $300 million worth of almost any other product, you would make a few of them first and see how they did. In fact, other kinds of real estate often are developed precisely in that fashion. Subdivide a potato farm, and you build on it a section at a time, selling off the houses and paying down the loan, refining the design as you see what sells. You can't build a high-rise office building that way, though. It goes up all at once, and if you made eight-and-a-half-foot ceilings to save money and it turns out that tenants all want nine, you can't go back and add six inches to every floor. The interest clock doesn't stop while you think it over. Guess wrong and you may wake up after four years and discover you've been working all that time for the banks. Luk Sun Wong, the director of development for Eichner Properties, once likened his job to running toward the North Pole with a bucket of water; as he goes along, things get frozen into place. But the game is lost if he ever stops running.

The site was on the northeast corner of Broadway and West 45th Street, which on a map or from the air you would instantly recognize as one of the most prominent intersections in the city of New York. It is in the geographic center of the area known as Times Square, which takes its name from the near-intersection of Seventh Avenue, which runs in a direction New Yorkers parochially refer to as north-south (the New York street grid is oriented toward the local geography of Manhattan rather than that of the planet); 42nd Street, one of the extra-wide east-west streets that occur at intervals of eight to fifteen blocks up and down the island; and Broadway, the lone exception to the rigid cartography of midtown Manhattan, slicing through the grid at a shallow northwest-southeast angle. In the narrow wedge bounded by these streets is the triangular building where *The New York Times* had its offices for most of the twentieth century. The Times has since moved around the corner to 43rd Street, but the building retains a certain distinction as the setting for one of the minor celebrations in the American calendar of secular observances, the lighted ball that descends at midnight on New Year's Eve.

But the map shows that 45th Street is where Broadway and Seventh Avenue actually cross, the chokepoint, the knot in what David Childs of Skidmore, Owings & Merrill would take to calling the "bowtie" of those two gently diverging avenues.

On the ground, however, the corner of 45th Street and Broadway was just another crowded, workaday intersection, wholly unconscious of its uniqueness. Eight lanes of traffic, all headed in the direction of the Equator, or "downtown," rush by on Broadway and Seventh Avenue. The avenues are separated by a narrow triangular island with a low iron fence intended to discourage jaywalkers, a couple of concrete planters holding the skeletons of shrubs, and no other artifacts of civilization save litter. On the four corners of the intersection were the following: on the southeast, what passed for a men's clothing store in the 1980s, its windows filled with running shoes and football jerseys, occupying one shrunken corner of what had once been the great Bond's, haberdasher to visiting drummers since the days of the Hoover collar. Across Broadway, a dark glass office building in the econobox-modern style of 1972, taking up the entire blockfront between 45th and 44th Streets. On the northwest corner, the narrow edge of one of the two monumentally bleak five-hundred-foot-high slabs that framed the Marriott Marquis, one of the architect John Portman's famous atrium hotels, which pays New York the left-handed homage of assuming that it has to have everything Atlanta and Dallas have. In a 1987 *New York* magazine article, "The Buildings New Yorkers Love to Hate," it was rated second, just behind the Pan Am building. This was a tribute both to its inherent ugliness and the dubious history of its site, on which two famous old theaters, the Helen Hayes and the Morosco, were demolished to make room for it. Its façade sported a gesture of elephantine playfulness, a huge Kodak blowup of monstrous toddlers romping with giant puppy dogs.

The site Eichner was buying was on the east side of Broadway, between 45th and 46th Streets. The corner of 45th was occupied by a steak restaurant, advertising "all the beer you can drink," a tourist trap of the most depressing obviousness, the walls filled with illustrations of improbably frothy cocktails and unrecognizable caricatures. Its neighbors were, in order, a novelty T-shirt store, a movie theater, the lobby of the office building at 1540 Broadway, and another novelty store, its grimy windows filled with souvenir junk of all kinds. A Howard Johnson's restaurant took up most of the rest of the block, except for a ramshackle building on the corner whose twenty-foot frontage had been divided into two storefronts at the margins of habitability. These were a hot-dog stand and a representative of the species of camera and electronics store that is to twentieth-century New York what relic-mongers were to eleventh-century Jerusalem. The first evidence of construction work on the block was a heaven-sent boon to this establishment, in just the way that the comet of 1066 must have been to the business in slivers of the

True Cross; it lent verisimilitude to the "Going Out of Business" sales.

Several other commercial enterprises might be under way on this block on any given morning. A man in a leather cap was often seen there, offering to sell *Jesus Christ's own wristwatch* for just forty dollars … no, he doesn't actually claim that, although if he did, it would be no more preposterous than his cardboard sign saying "Rolex." Two men would sometimes appear with folding chairs and an orchestra consisting of empty plastic buckets of joint compound and the trays and racks of an old refrigerator. And near a street sign displaying several different and increasingly emphatic ways of saying No Parking, there were a couple of coin telephones, which one day would lead Mario Tarrant, the superintendent of the wrecking crew, to remark that the neighborhood was so tough that the phone booths worked in pairs.

The movie theater was the Loews State, the flagship of the great chain when it opened in 1921. It was "an ornate 3,200-seat house in the nondescript style that was becoming oppressively characteristic of the architecture of the new temples of the movie age," wrote Bosley Crowther in his history of Loews and its glamorous offspring, Metro-Goldwyn-Mayer. "Marble vestibules and stairways, a foyer fountain and French furniture manifested its elegance." Above the theater, at the address of 1540 Broadway, Marcus Loew built an office building for his headquarters. The building was designed in 1918 by Hugh Tallant and Arland W. Johnson in the eclectic classical style of the age. Its seventeen stories were faced with tan limestone; it had an elaborate decorated cornice at the roofline and a dentilled frieze halfway up, and monumental columns framing the bays from the third floor to the sixth. Inside, though, the grandeur was all in the movie house. Squeezed by the theater lobby, the office lobby was barely more than a hallway. As far back as 1939—near the height of MGM's power and wealth—*Fortune* magazine described the headquarters as "modest to the point of dinginess. … Overshadowed by the Paramount Building [two blocks south] and many a flyspecked Times Square Hotel." The building's dignity was not enhanced by being used as a giant billboard for the theater below. It was there, during the run of *The Seven-Year Itch*, that the famous larger-than-lifesize illustration of Marilyn Monroe caught in the updraft from a subway grating smote bus drivers into hebephrenia until it was removed as a threat to the public safety.

Anyway, it was a famous building in its day. There was a screening room and executive club on the top floor, The Lion's Den. Ted Arnow, who started in Loews publicity department as an office boy in 1933, and was still with the company fifty-three years later, remembered being summoned there one evening and standing in the shadows when Joseph R. Vogel, the head of the theater division, rose and announced, "Gentlemen, I give you the president." "I thought, oh, my God, it's Roosevelt," Arnow recalled, but it was Loews' Nicholas Schenck; he walked into the room and greeted everyone, "Hello, boychiks!" This is a story that has been told about Schenck at least three times in as many different settings. Howard Dietz, the legendary MGM press agent and songwriter, had a large office on the third floor containing his collection of funny hats and, in an anteroom, the green upright piano to which he would dash between bouts of dictation to his four secretaries. It was there that he wrote "Dancing in the Dark" and "You and the Night and the Music." "During the war Kurt Weill rushed into Howard's office and said, 'Quick, Howard, I've got to have a song about Hitler in fifteen minutes,' and Howard went to his piano and wrote a song called 'Schicklgruber.' I'm still getting royalties on that," Dietz's widow, Lucinda Ballard, recalled, more than forty years later.

By the 1980s, whatever cachet the building once enjoyed was long gone. The theater itself had been renovated in 1968 into a twin, applied to whose style "nondescript" would have to be considered a compliment. Loews had been acquired by the Tisch brothers, Laurence and Preston, as the centerpiece of a huge hotel, insurance, and real estate conglomerate, and the headquarters moved to 666 Fifth Avenue. The office floors were divided into smaller and smaller parcels to operations on the margins of show business: an animal talent agency, a pornographic filmmaker, a guy with one small room whose business was not only unknown, but whose very name was secret—the building's last managing agent, Sidney Roberts, had to learn a secret knock to get past his door. An upper floor belonged to an outfit called the Cashier's Training Institute, apparently aboveboard but equally mysterious to Roberts: "I don't understand it. They take these Puerto Rican girls and they charge them hundreds of dollars for three weeks to learn how to operate a *cash register*?" In 1985, Loews astonished the entertainment industry when it sold off its 226 theaters to a group of Los Angeles investors, for a reported price of $165 million. Along with the deal went 1540 Broadway, and the new owners immediately began looking for a way to turn the property into useful cash. The head of real estate for Loews mentioned the building to a man he did business with, a parking-garage operator named Darryl Mallah, who had the parking concession at several Loews hotels, and Mallah immediately thought of the man he considers the smartest businessman he ever met, a real estate developer named Ian Bruce Eichner.

3

Darryl Mallah is one of the unsung geniuses of New York City. In 1949, when Mallah was a boy, his father, Joel, opened a parking garage in the borough of Queens. Years later, when he was just getting out of college, Mallah made one of the most brilliant decisions in the history of real estate: he decided to go into business with his father. By the mid-1980s, the family ran approximately seventy-five parking garages around the city, almost all underground, like ruby mines. New York City's policy of discouraging people from commuting in their cars has had the unintended effect of turning parking into one of its leading industries. The city limits the construction of new parking garages, on the sensible but unproven theory that people won't drive into midtown if they have no place to put their cars. But it places no limits on how much garages can charge. For a certain class of New Yorker, whose self-image did not extend to learning how to use the subway, the choice between living in a luxury high-rise on the East Side or a house in Connecticut came down to paying Mallah $300 a month to board his car near his apartment, or fifteen dollars a day to park near his office.

Mallah met Bruce Eichner in 1984 through a man named Seymour Lourd, who also operated a parking garage. Lourd's garage was on 87th Street near Broadway, in the fashionable residential neighborhood of the

Upper West Side. Bruce had an option to buy the building, for around $3 million. Obviously, if the site were to be worth anything to him as a developer, he would have to buy Lourd out of his lease, which had more than ten years to run. So he called Lourd and asked him what it would take to induce him to part with his lease.

Lourd replied that he would give up the garage business when people learned to fly.

Bruce decided to treat this as a negotiating ploy. "I'll be here," Bruce said. "You can talk to me now, or you can talk to me later. The longer you wait, the less you're worth to me."

Bruce waited a year before calling him back. Now Lourd agreed that he might be willing to sell his lease, but he would have to ask his friend, Darryl Mallah, to help him set a price.

This Mallah did in about five minutes. He calculated a fair-market value for Lourd's lease, discounted for present value, and came up with a figure of around $5 million—two-thirds more than the price of the building itself. As part of the deal, Lourd was given a twenty-year concession for a garage in Bruce's new building, which he turned over to Mallah. So it was natural for Mallah to think of Bruce when he heard about 1540 Broadway. Logical, except that Mallah also deals with many of the other top developers in the city, and he could have brought the deal to any of them. Bruce has a lot of strengths as a businessman, but perhaps his greatest is his ability to make people believe in him. Mallah received no finder's fee for helping Eichner make a deal on which he stood to make tens of millions of dollars. But, said Mallah, "I see a lot of success for Bruce. I think he's gonna be an even bigger player, ten years down the road, and if he remembers that I once helped him … well, I figure it can't hurt."

In late 1985, Eichner felt he was approaching a turning point in his career as a businessman. The career at that point was twelve years old, and Eichner himself was forty. A few years earlier, it would have been unimaginable for him to pay $50 million for a building, or for anything else. Manhattan's real estate treasure was for years the closely guarded property of a handful of families, which almost no outsiders dared penetrate. The great names were Tishman, Uris, Rudin, Durst. It was understood that what was passed down from father to son was not just portfolios, but reputations, contacts, and savvy: the password that got you inside the door of Chase Manhattan, the secret handshake to win the confidence of the union bosses, the right dialect of Yiddish to do business with the city government. Eichner lacked these early advantages.

His father was an English professor, later dean of men at the New School for Social Research, "the kind of guy," Bruce once told an interviewer, "who, if you gave him a substantial delegation of authority, would bankrupt IBM in six months." The values Eichner absorbed at home included disdain for the practice, ethics, and products of big business. In particular, his father disliked the oppressive scale of big new office buildings. It was natural for Eichner, graduating from college in 1966, to think of becoming a lawyer. The one early sign of greatness Eichner will lay claim to is that he finished at the bottom of his law school class.

He went to work as an assistant district attorney—a prosecutor—in the borough of Brooklyn. Here he fought crime—or, more precisely, he fought defense attorneys—with the energy, tenacity, and imagination that have played so big a part in his subsequent success, although at the time they just made him a nuisance around the courthouse. "I was a crazy guy," he admits. "I wanted to try everything. I would fight bail applications. I would stand up, I would pound the desk. Your Honor! This man is a danger to the community. And the judge would say, 'Sit down, you're a bigger danger to the community.'" The signal to leave, he said, came after he was transferred to the trial bureau, and was handed a case that was such a mess he didn't know where to begin to rescue it. "Who handled this piece of shit at the grand jury?" he demanded of his chief, and when his chief suggested he take a look in the file, the first thing he saw was his own initials. He left the district attorney's office, but he stayed in government, climbing the obscure career ladder of an expert in court administration and criminal justice. And then one day in the early 1970s he looked up the ladder, and saw above him an endless series of graduated sizes of backsides, of assistant commissioners waiting to become deputies, of deputies waiting to become commissioners, commissioners waiting to become judges, and he said to himself, *What makes me think I'm going to get to the top any faster than any of them?* And the realistic answer, from the man who graduated eighty-third in his class at the University of Cincinnati Law School, with no significant political connections or family money, was "Nothing."

Originally his idea was that real estate would be a sideline, a way to improve his standard of living without having to leave government for the private sector. A colleague introduced him to Park Slope, a Brooklyn neighborhood of impressive brownstone townhouses now far gone in decrepitude. The gentrification movement that would eventually spread its blight of brick-walled espresso bars to every city in the land was just gathering momentum there, and, in one of Eichner's favorite expressions of nonchalance, "you didn't have to have a Harvard M.B.A. to see the potential." With an investment consisting primarily of dozens of evenings spent buttering up the landlady in her cuckoo-clock-filled apartment next door, he bought a four-story rooming house on Montgomery Place.

It was true, you didn't have to be a genius to hit on the idea of buying a brownstone in the early 1970s for $30,000. Hundreds of people did just that, ripping out miles of antiquated plumbing and wiring, peeling back sedimentary layers of linoleum from oaken floors, hiring superannuated Italian craftsmen to duplicate the plaster moldings and coves. And those who still have their buildings could sell them now for half a million dollars or more. But very few of them got rich at it, the way Bruce got rich. The distinguishing characteristic of a successful entrepreneur is the ability to move on to the next opportunity, to evaluate the money-making potential of a given enterprise entirely apart from its psychic rewards. As soon as his first building could support a bigger mortgage, he refinanced and put $10,000 down on a building on Seventh Street. The first full year he owned it, the Seventh Street property returned a profit of $3,300, and Eichner assumed he was set for life.

Eichner's relationship to real estate is essentially utilitarian. When he goes back to look at his old buildings, it is not to see how they stand up against the changing skyline, but to critique the deal that the building represents. The romance of construction leaves him utterly cold. He cannot imagine why anyone would take an interest in such a subject. "The minute Bruce closes on a loan, a shovel turns over once—okay, for him the building's done, it's time to go on to something else," says one woman who worked closely with him. In terms of architecture, the late Victorian age isn't even his favorite period. In taste he is probably closest to Helmut Jahn, the flamboyant postmodernist whose skyscrapers stand out in the drab skyline of most American cities like a bottle of Chartreuse in a milk crate. This notwithstanding one of the most tumultuous architect-client relationships in the history of the profession. Jahn was once profiled by *GQ*, which said of him that "he dresses like he designs—to kill." It is an open question whether Jahn's purple loafers were of greater or lesser lethality than Bruce's bird-of-paradise neckties. Around 1980, when Bruce could have bought any brownstone in Brooklyn, he chose instead to build a new house on the Promenade, in the heart of the Ur-brownstone neighborhood of Brooklyn Heights. Bruce's house conformed, in its general scale and massing and color range, to the sacred canons of brownstonedom, but it had a radical open-plan interior. Taking into account advances in central heating and insulation over the preceding 110 years, it had large windows open to the magnificent harbor and skyline views. The guardians of brownstone authenticity in the Brooklyn Heights Association regarded it as a desecration second only to the appearance of a Burger King on Montague Street a few years earlier.

Inevitably, what started out as a way to enable him to stay in the public sector became an end in itself. The deals kept getting bigger and, as he put it, "more interesting." He bought the Franklin Arms, a decrepit welfare hotel, gutted it, and turned it into twenty apartments. He made $600,000 on that deal, and he made the acquaintance of Howard Hornstein, a shrewd, avuncular Brooklyn lawyer and member of the City Planning Commission who was to play a big role in Bruce's later projects. Eichner's last major project in Brooklyn was the Hotel Margaret. This was a magnificent copper-mansard building overlooking the Brooklyn Heights Promenade, commanding that incomparably cinematic vista of the Brooklyn Bridge and the Manhattan skyline.

In renovating its twelve stories, carpenters had to work around wooden beams two feet thick. Bruce built forty-eight condominium apartments in the Margaret, of which about thirty had already been sold by January 31, 1980, when he closed out his construction financing with Citibank. Around two o'clock on that bitterly cold night, he was awakened to be told that the Margaret was in flames. The wooden beams burned for two more days, and then what was left of the building was pulled down to the ground.

The result was devastating for Eichner. The building was insured, so he didn't actually lose any money, unless you count the $2 million he expected to net from the sale of the apartments. The insurance couldn't compensate him for the delay in getting the project started again. The delay stretched for years when the Brooklyn Heights Association challenged his right to put up another twelve-story building on the site. They contended that any new building would have to conform to the current zoning and landmarks laws, which would have limited Eichner to approximately a five-story structure.

Eichner regarded this act with the deepest imaginable scorn. He called it "irrational," the most damning condemnation he could deliver. He fought it for five years, in the bureaucracy and the courts, and when he won, Howard Hornstein had to tie him in his chair to keep him from calling the newspapers to gloat. On Howard's insistence, Bruce hired a public-relations consultant to put out a statesmanlike statement of victory. And then he sold the land. He had more interesting things to do.

Bruce was looking beyond Brooklyn. He had founded Eichner Properties, Inc., in 1978, with one employee and office space in his house; by 1985 there were around thirty people working in a cramped suite of offices at 625 Madison Avenue. He completed his first major Manhattan development in 1983—the Kingsley, a forty-story luxury condominium on First Avenue and 70th Street. As New York City rents began to climb from the merely outrageous to the insupportable in the late 1970s, Bruce had been in the forefront of the switch to building apartments for sale. From the point of view of an ambitious developer, a condominium has the great advantage of returning your money right away. The minimum goal, the fallback, is to break even on the sale of the apartments, which then leaves you owning free and clear whatever ancillary space you retained (parking, retail, health club). The upside is to get swept along by rising prices and sell the apartments for a third more than you projected, and that's what happened to the Kingsley, which opened in a market that wavered between booming and panic.

Bruce was lucky, but he was also smart. He analyzed the way a typical apartment house was built. Consider the lobby. Bruce regards the lobby as one of his most important selling tools. Traditionally it was the last thing to be built in an apartment house, because otherwise you'd have to build it twice, after the workmen on their way to finish the apartments upstairs stole everything they didn't break. In a rental building it didn't matter what order things were finished in; people moved in and started paying rent whenever the building was done. But Bruce was selling apartments, not leasing them. If customers had to walk through a muddy cavern filled with dangling light bulbs to get to the model apartments, it was going to be that much harder to convince them to part with $400,000. If he reversed the usual order and finished the lobby and model apartments first, he could start selling right away; then the apartments could be finished while waiting for the sales to close.

Another example: Most residential buildings in New York up to that time had been built in "lines"—that is, with the same apartment floor plans repeating all the way up the building, which is the least costly way to build them. Thus the top, and most desirable, floors would have the same mix of small and large apartments as those near the ground. It was apparent to Bruce that this did not accurately reflect the social and economic reality of New York real estate. Bruce was building forty-story corner towers, and views were one of his most important assets. The people who could afford to pay the most for a view, clearly, were the ones who were buying big apartments. People who came to buy a studio apartment might pay a small premium for a view, but if they had a lot more to spend, they would almost certainly rather have additional space instead. So Eichner built his buildings in tiers, with the big apartments clustered near the top. It was more expensive to build this way, but it was justified by the return. Eichner's philosophy was to make his buildings every bit as expensive as they needed to be. But not a penny more.

By late 1985, Eichner had three other condominium projects in varying stages of completeness. These were his Upper West Side project, the Boulevard (355 units); the Royale, with 205 units, at Third Avenue and 63rd Street; and the America, with 200 units, at Second Avenue and 85th Street. And the jewel in the portfolio, Cityspire, the slender, dome-capped skyscraper on West 56th Street around the corner from Carnegie Hall, for which Jahn was commissioned to design a building that was to house not just Bruce's offices, but eventually his home. This was the next generation of Eichner buildings, a mixed-use tower with 330,000 feet of office space at the bottom and 340 apartments above. "Sales of apartments subsidize the commercial rents," he reasoned; "you start the apartments at the twenty-fifth floor, and all of a sudden everyone's got views." The total value of these developments, once they were completed, was projected to be over $500 million. Early in 1986, Eichner was profiled in a *New York* magazine story on "the brash new builders," where he was described as "builder-iconoclast." Said Eichner to the writer, Joe Klein: "I have more money than I ever thought existed in the world." But he was learning fast: around the same time he remarked to Howard his discovery that "if you have only $5 million, you're not rich anymore."

Bruce continued to make money, although the astonishing success of the Kingsley proved difficult to duplicate. The market grew more competitive in the second half of the 1980s. A tax incentive for builders expired in the fall of 1985, and a number of projects were rushed into the ground to take advantage of it, leading to warnings of a condominium glut ahead. The formulas for making money in a competitive market are no secret. One is simply to start out with more money in the first place, so you have a cushion if things go wrong. "I sometimes wonder," Bruce reflected, after a day spent beating his head against the stone wall of a major commercial bank, "if life wouldn't be easier if I had a billion-dollar portfolio and could just ask the bank for $20 million anytime I needed it. And then I think, no, if I had that kind of money, I wouldn't be half as good as I am." (To which Luk Sun responded, with characteristic bluntness, "That's bullshit. If Bruce had that much money, he'd be going to the bank for $2 billion.")

The other technique is to somehow imbue your projects with extra-economic value, or hot air. The best example of this was Donald Trump, who until his own timely collapse managed to extract an incalculable, but real, premium for his apartments based on the glamorous associations of the Trump name. Bruce was an early Trump skeptic. He was baffled by Trump's handling the rebuilding of the ice-skating rink in Central Park, a project Trump took on after the city's engineers were defeated by the job of making water freeze in the winter. Every week, Trump held another press conference at the rink to describe how brilliant he was, and every week the city looked worse and worse by contrast. Bruce considered this a public-relations triumph at the cost of a potential long-range political disaster. Trump at the time was seeking approval for a monumental scheme to redevelop a large tract of land on the Hudson River, including his latest version of plans for the world's tallest building. Within months of the skating-rink opening, he was engaged in a noisy public feud with New York's mayor, Ed Koch, a politician who had made vindictiveness his public trademark. "You know what I would have done?" Bruce said one morning, looking at a *New York Times* article about an exchange of insults between the mayor and the developer. "I would have gone to the mayor in the dead of night. I would have whispered in his ear. I would have said, 'Mr. Mayor, I will fix your skating rink for you. But on one condition: that you must never breathe a word of it to anyone else!'"

Eichner's first dealings with Trump came in 1988. They met to talk over a deal in Trump's conference room, filled with pictures of the great man with the famous people who have been privileged to meet him. In a preliminary exchange of pleasantries, Trump brought up a property both men had bid on. Trump won it with an offer $20 million higher than Bruce had been willing to pay. Bruce complimented him on winning fair and square. Trump discussed his plans for the property. Bruce told him that never in his career as a developer had he heard such a brilliant concept. Trump pulled out some drawings, and Bruce assured him that it would be a worthy addition to his magnificent portfolio of first-class buildings. Finally they got down to business.

A week later, Bruce got a phone call from Trump's lawyer. Donald is pretty busy in Atlantic City, the lawyer said. But he remembered how impressed Bruce was with this property they talked about. Maybe he'd like to make an offer for it?

4/4

Without a personal fortune behind him Eichner had no choice but to work harder. He had to extract every last penny of value from a given site. He pursued this with an obsessiveness that would be considered pathological in almost any other sphere of human endeavor. Every choice had to be examined from every possible angle, every alternative explored. Take the question of nine-foot versus eight-foot-six ceilings. That simple dichotomy unfolds, under Luk Sun's relentless probing, into a manifold of potentialities, each with its unique advantages and problems. You could split the difference and go with eight-foot-nine. You could go with eight-foot-six and seek an architectural treatment that would make it look like nine feet. You could, as a frustrated architect suggested after one interminable afternoon devoted to this topic, make it eight feet and rent only to midgets. Or you could go with nine feet and try to browbeat your contractor into building it for the same cost as eight-foot-six. Different issues call forth different solutions, and Bruce's only unwavering principle is that all the alternatives be explored. "My god is process," he is fond of saying. It is only to the uninitiated that he appears to worship chaos instead.

In particular, Bruce became expert at the game of maximizing his Floor Area Ratio, or FAR, also known as "bulk." FAR is a zoning tool to regulate density. It is the ratio of the total usable floor area in a building to the size of the lot on which the building stands. Thus, in an area zoned for 15 FAR, a site of 30,000 square feet could support 450,000 square feet of usable space.

Overlaid on this restriction were the height and setback regulations, which govern the overall shape, or massing, of the building. These were intended to assure enough light and air at street level to permit pedestrians to see and breathe, and to achieve certain officially sanctioned esthetic objectives. In the Times Square area, for example, buildings along Broadway were required to rise straight up from the sidewalk to a height of no more than sixty feet, and then step back at least fifty feet, because sixty feet approximates the height of the old four- and five-story buildings that predominated there until recently. Whether or not someone walking along the street would be fooled by this is academic. The point is that filling that hypothetical site with fifteen floors of 30,000 square feet each would not be acceptable. Nor would a ninety-story tower with 5,000 square feet on each floor. But the FAR is the key determinant of the economic value of a given site, and it is taken for granted that a given building will approach its maximum FAR so closely that if a tenant builds a birdhouse on the thirty-eighth floor, the building will be out of compliance by just that amount.

Eichner, like many other developers only more so, regarded the nominal (or "as-of-right") FAR of a site as a starting point for negotiation, rather than a ceiling. The city treated FAR as a form of property, which could be sold or leased to owners of adjacent lots. In these transactions it was sometimes referred to as "air rights." The 30,000-square-foot lot above might have a 10,000-square-foot lot next door. The owner of the bigger site could buy the smaller one, tear down what was on it, and merge them to build a 600,000 square-foot building (40,000 square feet × 15 FAR). Or he could just buy the air rights, the difference between the maximum allowable bulk on the smaller site and the size of whatever building happened to be there. The smaller lot might have a five-story loft building, say, comprising 50,000 square feet. Then up to 100,000 square feet of air rights could be sold to the site next door. Thus the owner of a 30,000-square-foot site could build a 550,000-square-foot structure. The loft would remain, but the owner would surrender forever the right to build something bigger in its place.

As the traffic in FAR grew, the city government saw no reason to be excluded from the trade in this valuable commodity. The city, after all, created FAR by fiat and could dispense it as it chose. It was a short leap to the idea of giving FAR bonuses to encourage developers to provide public amenities that the city considered desirable, such as plazas or arcades. Better yet, developers could be induced to pay for improvements that were in theory the city's own responsibility, such as fixing up subway stations. Almost invariably, developers found these air-rights bonuses cheaper per square foot than the FAR that came with the land in the first place. In some cases—such as the 1 FAR bonus for a pedestrian "galleria" running through the middle of a block—the cost could be buried in the design of the building and the additional space was essentially free. Getting something for free that you could then turn around and rent for hundreds of thousands of dollars a year was an example of what Bruce thought you didn't need a Harvard M.B.A. to recognize as a good deal.

Few air-rights deals were as elaborate as those that went into Eichner's flagship building, Cityspire. Cityspire ended up with more than twice the FAR with which the site had started. Other developers had looked at the site—a garage on West 56th Street, between Sixth and Seventh avenues—but none had Eichner's persistence and imagination in pursuit of something for nothing, or almost nothing. And none had Howard Hornstein, who joined Bruce in the mid-1980s directly after leaving the City Planning Commission, where he had spent the preceding eight years. Together they negotiated a deal in which Eichner obtained nearly 300,000 square feet of air rights from the City Center Theater next door, in exchange for $6 million in contributions to the New York City Opera and the New York City Ballet. That works out to twenty dollars a foot for space that would be sold later as apartments at prices of over $400 a square foot. Of course Eichner had to build the apartments first, but it was still a very good deal. Then they obtained a bonus of around 130,000 feet in exchange for renovating the theater itself. As of March 1987—approximately five years after a new midtown zoning ordinance took effect—the City Planning Commission listed thirty-five major new buildings that had won approval under its provisions. Only two had more space than Cityspire's 733,000 square feet, and none matched its 812 feet of height. It was the second tallest reinforced-concrete building in North America and the tallest residential building in New York City. And guess who was going to live at the top?

But what kind of Manhattan would he see from those windows? In his darker moments, he imagined a city in which all the big deals were already done, all the big sites developed, all the fortunes made and moldering away in damp Southampton mansions; in short, the Tokyoization of New York City, defined as a situation in which all the land is built out to its theoretical potential and real estate development has to await the next earthquake. He had built his career and reputation as a businessman on his knack for spotting value, and he no longer saw very much value in the sites he was being offered. Instead, people no smarter than he were doing leveraged buy-outs on Wall Street and making money not in increments of five or ten million dollars after three years of toil and anxiety but hundreds of millions at a time. There was risk in the mergers and acquisitions game, certainly, but what was the risk in buying a running corporation, with assets and a cash flow, compared to trying to build a building, where you started not even from the ground, but thirty or fifty feet below? He had begun to wonder if he was in the wrong business.

With that in mind, when he examined 1540 Broadway, this is what he saw. He saw, first of all, that the site would be big, the biggest he had ever developed. The Loews parcel, comprising the movie theater, the office building above it, and a couple of adjacent four- and five-story buildings, occupied about 35,000 square feet, or about four-fifths of an acre. There were, in addition, two outparcels that logically belonged with the assemblage but that Loews didn't own. These were 1544 Broadway, a building near the middle of the block housing the souvenir shop, and 1550 Broadway, the corner building that housed the camera store and the hot-dog stand. Each of these had about twenty feet of frontage on Broadway and ran a hundred feet back to the east, so the two together would add 4,000 square feet to the entire site. The price Loews was seeking for its parcel was around $50 million. This works out to a little over $1,400 a square foot (or ten dollars a square inch). But what mattered was that virtually the entire parcel was in an 18 FAR zone, the densest as-of-right zoning in the city at that time. This would lend itself to a building of 630,000 square feet, making the price just under eighty dollars per square foot of FAR, which was about what prime midtown sites were commanding at that time.

Naturally, Eichner looked for ways to increase his FAR, and the first thing he saw was the Lyceum theater, just east of the site on 45th Street. The city encouraged the sale of FAR from legitimate theaters and from designated landmarks, as an alternative to tearing them down. The Lyceum, built in 1903, with an elaborate Beaux Arts façade by the architects Herts & Tallant, was also a landmark. This happy coincidence of cultural and economic purposes would yield approximately another 100,000 square feet of bulk for the Loews site.

The site was attractive for another reason. The city was encouraging development in this part of the city by partially abating real estate taxes on new developments. The abatements ran on a declining scale for the first ten years after construction began. Over the second ten years, the city would recapture the money, but in the meantime the developer would get the benefit of an interest-free loan of several million dollars. The assumption was that this benefit would be passed along in the rent, giving the new West Side buildings a competitive edge.

But if there were opportunities to be exploited here, there were also dangers. The most obvious was that Eichner wouldn't get the outparcels, for whatever reason. "We can live without the corner piece," Bruce told Howard early on, "but it is clear that if we don't get 1544, we will have an unbuildable parcel. What is the likelihood we will get it at a rational price?"

"The likelihood is that if you throw enough money at it, you will get it," Howard said. "That's always the case, except when it's not." The landscape of New York in fact is filled with monuments to the stubbornness, or greed, of property owners who insisted on planting their shabby little tenements squarely in the path of progress. In 1984, the real estate developer Seymour Durst and architect Andrew Alpern had published a book dedicated to exposing "the malevolent impact of holdouts on the face of the city"—namely, the millions of dollars in potential profits lost by developers who couldn't build the buildings they wanted. They also deplored the esthetic effect of crummy old walkups juxtaposed with magnificent new glass office towers, looking like old uncles passed out on the table in someone's wedding pictures. An inordinate number of these establishments seem to be restaurants and bars, whose owners often develop irrational attachments to their business that the proprietors of, say, overnight photo-processing labs seem immune to. A check of the property at 1544 showed that it was owned by an out-of-town estate. Bruce took this as a good sign, since trustees are bound to follow the most prudent course, which could be construed as selling out at the market price. But you couldn't ever tell.

There was another risk as well. That the site was zoned for 18 FAR was the effect of a deliberate policy decision by the city, in its 1982 revision of the midtown zoning code, to encourage development in the western part of midtown. It would seem that it had no choice. In the five years leading up to the change, twenty-eight new buildings with over 14 million square feet of space had been built in east midtown, roughly the blocks in the Forties and Fifties from Sixth Avenue to Third. There had been, of course, virtually no compensating increase in the capacity of the streets, subways, or sidewalks serving that area. Huge new buildings had gone up on midblock sites with only narrow side-street frontage, a departure from the convention that major buildings needed the convenience, sight lines, and prestige of an avenue entrance. Over that period, the land prices in these blocks had increased at an average annual rate of 57 percent. This area was now designated the "stabilization area"; its maximum FAR was set at 15 on the avenues and 12 on midblock sites. Sites in the "growth area" between Sixth and Eighth avenues were fertilized with a bonus of 3 FAR, for a total of 18 on the avenues and 15 on the side streets. But this growth was not to be permitted to run unchecked. At midnight on Friday, May 13, 1988, the bonus would lapse. A development had to meet three conditions by that date: plans approved by the Department of Buildings; a finished excavation; and "substantial" completion of its foundation. If this test was not met, the site in question would lose its bonus, which on the Loews site would amount to a little more than 100,000 square feet of floor area.

This had two effects, from Bruce's point of view. It meant that if he missed the deadline, he would have a disaster on his hands. But the number of potential disasters in real estate is so great anyway that one more was not in itself a deterrent. Practically speaking, the sunset clause meant forgoing the exotic air-rights bonuses Bruce specialized in, because they added months to the time it would take to get the building approved. He would have to confine his appetite to the FAR that came with the site, plus whatever he could buy or lease from the adjoining properties, and build his building "as of right."

It was of more concern that this sunset provision in effect placed a lid on the future potential of the area. It was widely expected that development would move to the West Side, because of the FAR bonus, and because it had nowhere else to go. But at this date, halfway through the six-year life of the bonus, there was not yet much evidence of it. The area still awaited the critical mass of new projects that would drive values to the insane levels everyone hoped to see there. Under the auspices of the state, several large office buildings were planned for 42nd Street between Broadway and Eighth Avenue, the most vividly anarchic of the blocks in the neighborhood, filled with peep shows and kung fu movie houses. In early 1986, the developer chosen to bring this vision to fruition predicted that ground would be broken the following year. Bruce, with his years of experience in the public sector, discounted that prediction by at least twenty-four months. Even that turned out to be optimistic; in the summer of 1992 the project, still not begun, was postponed indefinitely. But Bruce was very interested in what was happening on the other privately owned potential development sites. As a subsequent appraisal of the Loews site by the brokers, Cushman & Wakefield, phrased it, "Despite the existing and proposed developments, the many theaters and hotels in the area and the proximity to local transportation, [the neighborhood], especially to the south at 42nd Street, still contains sex shops, violent movie houses, hustlers, drug dealers, prostitutes and extremely high crime levels reflective of the overall street environment. It is our opinion, however, that as development continues … office, hotel and theater uses will displace most of the threatening and undesirable street conditions." To someone about to spend $50 million on a dilapidated office building, that couldn't happen soon enough.

5

Before he could take the next step, though, Bruce needed a partner, because he certainly didn't have $50 million of his own, and if he did, he wouldn't use it to buy the Loews building. Bruce leveraged his ability, experience, and reputation and let other people put up the money. The man he called was Stephen J. Berini, a vice president of VMS Realty Partners, in Chicago. Berini was a deeply tanned, sleekly handsome man then in his mid-thirties who had had the benefit of the greatest mentoring in the history of real estate. He had sat by the side of Ernest W. Hahn, the California shopping center developer of legendary canniness; and then, after the Hahn company was acquired by a subsidiary of Olympia & York, he became a protégé of O&Y's Paul Reichmann of the Canadian family that owned what might have been the largest private real estate empire in the world. From Reichmann he absorbed patience, a sense of proportion, and a longer-term perspective on the world; from Hahn he learned how to get along with people like Bruce, who negotiated every point in a deal as if he were trying to get his mother on the last train out of Berlin.

VMS Realty Partners, only five years old at that time, was already a giant in the field of packaging and syndicating real estate investments. Its founder, chief executive, and guiding genius was a portly lawyer in his mid-thirties named Peter Morris, whose corporate biographies never failed to mention that he graduated summa cum laude from Princeton. With backing from his partner Robert Van Kampen, a multimillionaire bond broker, Morris bought properties all over the country and sold them off piecemeal as limited partnerships. What he sold was, essentially, depreciation: a chance for ordinary Americans with ordinary six-figure incomes to save on their taxes by engaging in the fiction that they owned property that grew progressively less valuable. Deals like this had been around for a long time, but tax changes in 1981 made them vastly more attractive to private investors by speeding up the depreciation schedule for real estate. Originally only thirty-five limited partners were allowed into a given deal, but then that ceiling was lifted, and within a few years there were more than a thousand brokers selling the hundred-odd VMS limited partnerships. By the mid-1980s VMS had a portfolio valued (by itself) at over $5 billion, heavily weighted toward developments whose modest size was offset by pretentious double adjectives in their names: "Executive Center Southgate, Denver"; "Waterview Colonial Manor, Portsmouth, Virginia"; "Spring Brook Village, Houston."

On the horizon, though, was the threat that Congress would change the rules again, out of fear that if this game continued to grow exponentially soon no one in America would owe any income taxes at all. The 1986 tax reform act essentially killed syndication by requiring people who deducted real estate depreciation to actually take some role in managing the properties they "owned." But VMS was already gearing up another source of capital, the "real estate investment trust." This was a publicly traded security sold in units of only $1,000, to investors lured by the dream of sitting back and letting the Bruce Eichners of the world make them rich. The trusts wouldn't actually own any real estate; they would loan money to VMS and its partnerships, creating an almost limitless source of captive capital for Morris to play with. Over the next few years investors would put over $1 billion at his disposal in this way.

In 1984, VMS broke new ground in another fashion: it became the first major syndicator to develop its own projects from scratch, rather than buying existing properties. The partners established VMS Development Corp. as a subsidiary for this purpose, and hired Berini to run it. Berini, moving to New York, joined a tennis club in Queens, and one day he met Bruce there. "We liked how we worked together; we thought we both had our feet on the ground," says Berini. "When Bruce said the Loews site was going to come up, I said I was interested, and in five or ten days we had a handshake on the deal." Eichner and VMS Development Corp. formed a partnership: Broadway State Partners.

VMS was a logical choice for Bruce. It had access to money from the trusts; it had experience in running hotels, and Berini had experience and contacts in retail development. The Berini-Eichner partnership was to prove a good, although not entirely untroubled, one. A certain amount of macho posturing goes on in these relationships. The party who brings the money to the table demands respect, even if the money isn't, strictly speaking, his own; this runs up against the arrogance of the side that believes it's doing all the work. "The way the joint venture was done, we're fifty-fifty partners," Berini observed pointedly one day. "But all along in Bruce's mind he was the development partner and VMS was the money partner. I'm just glad I didn't have to find out whether he could come up with his half of the dollars." Bruce's attitude was that he needed VMS's money, but someone else's money would have done as well, while there was no project without Eichner. "The difference between Bruce and me," says Berini, "is he puts himself under pressure every day; I'll work to close a deal and then I like to check the water for a while." Around this time, VMS invested in the Westin Maui and Kauai hotels in Hawaii, and not long after Berini moved to Santa Barbara so he could keep a closer eye on the Pacific Ocean. He would fly back to New York occasionally for meetings, and after a while even those trips became infrequent.

From the beginning it appeared that Eichner and Loews were destined to do a deal. Loews wanted to remain on the site with a multiscreen theater in the new building, and that was fine with Bruce; a theater would fit well with the hotel he was planning. In his mind, he had topped off the hotel with twenty floors or so of hotel apartments, which by themselves might bring in close to $100 million when sold. Forty-fifth Street and Broadway was, on the face of it, an unlikely place to call home. The only recorded inhabitant of the area in living memory was an ancient prizefighter named Izzy Grove, who for seventeen years had slept on a cot in his sixty-dollar-a-month "office" in the 46th Street annex to 1540 Broadway. Someone interested in living in Times Square presumably wouldn't be bothered by the absence of such conventional amenities as supermarkets and schools. He would be, say, a West Coast talent agent who wanted a pied-à-terre in New York within walking distance of Sardi's; a divorced partner in a Sixth Avenue law firm who could bill an extra $400 a day by cutting down his commute; or a Japanese businessman who didn't know any better. Not long before, the Taft Hotel a few blocks up Seventh Avenue had been converted to condominiums and sold out at $350 a square foot. The apartments at the top of the Broadway State building would have great views and services from the transient hotel below. New Yorkers, God knew, had colonized even less promising areas.

At the bottom of the building Bruce envisioned retail. Hotels, of course, typically had shops on the ground floor for the convenience of guests. The new zoning code required retail shops at street level, even for office buildings. This was a big change from the pre-1982 era, when a first-class building might tolerate, say, The Four Seasons in its ground floor, but any establishment less decorous would have been regarded as compromising the dignity of the commerce taking place above. In those days, of course, office buildings were set fifty feet back from the street in marble plazas, and shops in their ground floors would have been invisible to passersby anyhow. Bruce intended to take advantage of the most salient characteristic of his location—the twenty-four-hour-a-day thronging, surging, clamoring crowds—and turn it to his advantage. He would not have a banal restaurant, a dreary newsstand, a stuffy haberdasher; he would have a multilevel urban mall, an atrium filled with young bankers spending money as fast as they could make it upstairs. You didn't have to go to Harvard Business School to see the potential; and besides, shopping malls don't need windows; therefore, they could go below grade, *and basement floors don't count as FAR.* You don't have to be a rocket scientist to recognize the potential there.

One of Berini's contributions to the Broadway State project was to bring aboard an experienced real estate lawyer, Martin D. Polevoy of the firm of Bachner, Tally, Polevoy, Misher & Brinberg. One night in late 1985, Polevoy was up past midnight reading the leases for all the dozens of tenants in the Loews property. By and large he saw no problems, but one of the leases, for an establishment known as "Eighth Restaurant Corp.," had an unusual phrase in its demolition clause. The standard demolition clause in a commercial lease provides that if the building is to be torn down, the landlord advises the tenant that his lease is being terminated, and after a fixed interval, typically around ninety days, the tenant vacates the premises without recourse to racial or ethnic slurs against the landlord. In practice, to set the process in motion it is customary for the landlord to send around three guys in size 46-Long overcoats, one to knock on the door, one to serve the tenant with the notice of termination, and one to take a picture of the tenant receiving the notice. Often a small amount of money changes hands as well, to secure the tenant's cooperation and keep him from tasting the iniquitous pleasures of Landlord-Tenant Court. Sometimes the payment isn't all that small, if the landlord is in a big-enough hurry or the tenant thinks he has some claim on the sympathy of a judge.

But the lease for Eighth Restaurant Corp. had one difference, which on the face of it was innocuous. It provided that the landlord had the right to terminate the lease upon issuance by the Department of Buildings of a demolition permit. The problem was that the Department of Buildings will not issue a demolition permit for a building unless the electric and gas services have been disconnected; and Consolidated Edison will not disconnect the utilities unless the building is already vacant. In short, Eighth Restaurant Corp. didn't have to leave the building at all until its lease was up on May 31, 1991 … unless, of course, Bruce chose to buy them out.

How big a problem this posed would obviously depend on whether Eighth Restaurant Corp., whoever they were, knew the significance of this clause. Possibly they didn't; the lease dated back a number of years, and it might have just been a case of sloppy draftsmanship. The next morning Polevoy placed a call to Bruce.

"You've got a problem that may not be a problem," he said. "Do you know who this Eighth Restaurant Corp. is?"

"It's a guy named Murray Riese," Bruce replied. "Is that a problem?"

"That is a big problem," Polevoy said.

Polevoy knew the Riese organization well, as did anyone else familiar with Manhattan real estate in the 1980s. Murray Riese and his brother Irving had begun business together in 1940 with a single midtown coffee shop. By the mid-1980s they controlled an empire of 300 restaurants in Manhattan and on Long Island, with sales estimated at $250 million a year. The restaurants operated under more than thirty different names. The majority were national or regional franchises. Most of the rest were local variations on the Irish pub/steakhouse/Broadway hangout theme—the poor man's Palm, the tour-bus "21." Somewhere along the way, the Rieses made the discovery, so common in New York, that almost nothing you do inside a building is as profitable as owning the building itself. It is not even necessary to own it, for that matter; it can be cheaper and just as effective to control it with a lease. Their restaurants sat on key corners in Times Square and elsewhere, giving the tourists all the beer they could drink while awaiting a real estate developer to walk in the door and order champagne for the house.

The Rieses had controlled the corner of Broadway and 45th Street since 1957, when they bought up the lease of a place called the Mayflower Doughnut Shop. It had changed names several times since then as leases expired and were renewed. In 1976, they entered into a lease for a restaurant subsequently known as Steak & Brew Burger, and the demolition clause was planted among Loews' unsuspecting lawyers, as Polevoy put it, "like a time bomb." Now it was about to go off. Polevoy told Eichner he thought the impact on the deal would be to cost him "a fair amount of money, namely millions."

The problem was that this discovery came after Eichner and Berini had already reached an agreement with Loews president Bernie Myerson to buy the property for $48 million, on the assumption that all the leases had valid demolition clauses. One day in the fall of 1985 the partners met in Bruce's office at 625 Madison. Berini was sprawled on a sofa; Bruce sat at his desk with his back to the windows that looked across 59th Street to an office building that had been finished a year earlier and remained almost entirely vacant: a memento mori for a developer, like giving a city councilman a view of the Federal House of Detention. His quarters had not yet caught up with his rising fortunes as a developer.

Bruce is a man of medium height, lithe and quick on his feet. Photographs rarely do him justice. He is best appreciated just as the first notes of a full-blown monologue are sounded, when his eyes come alive with a faintly predatory intelligence and he leaps exuberantly, effortlessly to a level of abstraction far above the power of mere note-taking to follow. You can always tell when someone in the office is on the phone with Eichner; he or she sits in unbroken silence for as long as five minutes at a stretch. Architects who have to make presentations to him find themselves speaking faster and faster as the meeting wears on. The problem is that language cannot adequately convey the holistic workings of Eichner's mind. His speech is littered with lists of "three important points" or "four key issues," continually subdivided and reshuffled in a doomed effort to impose some sort of Cartesian order on the multiplex processes of his thoughts. It is only afterwards, reviewing one's notes of a conversation that at the time seemed to consist mostly of unparsable ellipses and footnotes, that one realizes he has outlined a scheme of such pellucid brilliance that a kindergarten teacher, armed with it, ought to be able to go out and make a fortune.

Bruce took a large bite of one of the two glazed doughnuts with which he fuels his morning harangues. "Well, partner, what do you want to do?" he asked Berini pleasantly.

"What do I want to do? I want to jump up and down and scream."

"I know, but at the end of the screaming, where do you want to be? You want the price to come down?"

"That would seem to be fair."

"Maybe so," Bruce agreed. "We make the argument, we made a deal to buy a suit, it turns out we can have the jacket now but the pants won't be finished for three years, we're entitled to a reduction."

"It's worse than not finished, someone else is wearing them."

"Whatever. Here's what we've got to weigh, though. We made a good deal on price. At the end of the day we're going to pay X for the land and Y for the relocation. Y is going to be a little more than we thought it was going to be, but it's still going to be a number. It's three million instead of two million, or it's three-five or four. It is what it is. The real question is, is X plus Y a rational price for that property, vacant and ready to go, or isn't it?

"Because there's another player out there, and I think his X is a bigger number than our X. If we go back to Bernie and say we're making this lease problem his problem, and he has another offer in his hip pocket, does he tell us to take a walk?"

"But," Berini objected, "the other guy will find out about this problem. They'll want to take something back, too."

"Sure. So if Bernie tells us to walk, that's Bernie's risk. Our risk is, do we want to lose?"

"And break up this beautiful friendship, Bruce? I'm just getting to like you."

In the end, Eichner and Berini stuck by their offer. They used the leverage the Riese problem had given them to put off the closing for nearly six months, instead of the thirty days Loews had been seeking. Bruce called this "trading a real exposure for the perception of an exposure." They could use the extra time to work on their financing. Had they realized how complicated the financing would turn out to be, weaker men would have turned back right then.

Citibank had been Bruce's lender on his residential projects, and he talked first to the officer he'd been dealing with there, a vice president named Alan Rosenstein. What he sought was to borrow the entire $48 million purchase price. He needed to borrow more than that, in fact, because the loan also had to cover the costs of relocating the tenants and the preliminary development work on the project. In order to borrow more than the property was worth, the partners would have to provide additional security. VMS would come up with property worth $15 million from its own portfolio and offer it as collateral. Citibank wouldn't even have to take the collateral directly. VMS's corporate banker, European-American Bank (owned by a British, French, and Italian consortium) would take the collateral and issue Citibank a $15 million letter of credit. A letter of credit is a bank's solemn promise to pay a specified sum if certain conditions are met—in this instance, a default on the land loan. If Broadway State couldn't repay the loan, Citibank could call the letter of credit and collect the $15 million. European-American in theory then would turn and seize the collateral pledged by VMS. This deal, which sounds complicated, was actually a model of simplicity and straightforwardness. It also would seem to offer Citibank plenty of protection. But as the deal made its way up the signatory chain at Citibank, someone balked. The bank did not care for the idea that the Riese Brothers might have to be driven out of the building by pelting them with hundred-dollar bills. They weren't comfortable with the neighborhood. One morning less than a week before the sale was supposed to close, Bruce showed up at Citibank for what was to be a straighten-out-the-details session and was told the deal was off.

Bruce didn't get mad, or in any case he didn't get visibly mad; he asked to borrow the phone, and invited himself to lunch with the chairman of European-American, Ray Dempsey. Dempsey ordered in sandwiches. In one of his most impassioned and brilliant performances in a career that has not lacked drama, Bruce sold Dempsey on the idea of stepping in where Citibank—a bank twelve times the size—had feared to tread. "The value is there, Ray," Bruce told him. He also told him EAB would get its money back in six months, at which time the loan would be replaced by a larger loan to pay for the construction of a new building. And undoubtedly that's what Eichner believed, that he would have his construction financing in six months, except if he didn't.

6

While all these things were going on, the team that would build the Broadway State Project was gradually being assembled, by a seemingly random process of agglomeration that reflected Bruce's beliefs in creative tension and the ceaseless questioning he calls "process." Far from surrounding himself with yes-men, Bruce seemed bent on hiring people who didn't know the meaning of the word.

Of course, the process was not random at all. Howard, for example, came to Bruce at the end of a four-year courtship. Howard's expertise was in big-picture political and governmental contacts. It was he who brought Bruce around to get to know the mayor, he who guided Cityspire through the bureaucratic torment known as Uniform Land-Use Review Process, or ULURP. Howard had an associate, Andrea Kremen, a former lawyer for the City Planning Department. She was in her late thirties, auburn-haired, with large dark soulful eyes and a manner that varied over the day from pointed to sardonic.

There was Luk Sun Wong, who had been development officer for the Royale, which was by this time well-launched on construction. Wong was in many ways a brilliant guy: a preternaturally shrewd businessman, an architect who was probably the only person in the office who could win an argument on a design point with Bruce. Handsome, barrel-chested, with blunt, emphatic, regular features, he was a man of great physical presence, especially when he was angry and jabbing the tabletop with his thick, powerful fingers. Then his voice would shift into a menacing growl and he would start to slur his participles like a gangster and disdainfully lift an offending invoice and say: "I'm not gonna pay for this, okay? Okay, I'm NOT PAYIN', OKAY?" He was also capable of great charm, but he dispensed it only on a need-to-know basis, because secrecy, like economy, was one of his great passions. There was an air of almost savage privacy about him at times, emphasized by the three opaque monosyllables of his name, which he had chosen to keep at his naturalization, despite a friendly suggestion from the immigration officer that life in America might be more convenient as Larry Wong.

Henry Miller, Bruce's captive banker, came to Eichner in 1986. Miller was in his early forties, soft-spoken, cultivated, with a mordant whiff of pessimism about him. On the face of it, he was an astonishing person for Bruce to hire. Henry was a managing director of Shearson-Lehman, a position whose annual salary and bonus were in the range of half a million dollars. In coming to work for Bruce he gave up most of his income—not, of course, out of altruism, but for the chance to obtain a sum that could be regarded as capital. They had met on the beach in Sardinia in 1984, when Henry's wife was loudly complaining about the price of apartments in New York. Bruce had stalked over to say she didn't know what she was talking about. When Bruce called Henry in the summer of 1986 to tell him he was buying a company, Henry was interested. He was discontented in his old job; he had come up on the Lehman Brothers side, and after the acquisition by Shearson found that working for a 26,000-person firm that was primarily a brokerage was not as much fun as being a ranking executive of a small, elite investment bank. Still, he walked away from all the perks that go with being a successful Wall Street banker to plunge into the succession of eighteen-hour days that are familiar to experts in mergers and acquisitions. "I had," he said, "a lot of explaining to do to my wife."

The company was Alexander's, a retail chain of fourteen stores sunk deep into senescence, sustained by ancient leases for as little as two dollars a square foot. As soon as that game ended it was headed straight into the toilet. But Alexander's had one brilliant asset, its store on an 80,000-square-foot lot across the street from Bloomingdale's, the Golconda of development sites. Bruce's plan was to sell off all the inventory, close all but one or two of the stores, and be left with the empty site across from Bloomingdale's. Bruce and Henry have very different recollections of what their net cost for the site would have been at that point. Obviously there was a range of possibilities. Henry says they could have been out of pocket as much as $150 million, which is roughly the fair-market value of the site. They would have gone through the whole incredible exercise just to get something for what it should have cost in the first place, except that was the only way to get it. Bruce prefers to talk about the outcome if everything had gone exactly as they hoped, in which case they would have ended up owning a block in the very heart and stronghold of New York's real estate treasure for more or less nothing.

In the end, the deal fell through. But The Everest Group, which was the name of the M&A partnership Bruce and Henry had formed, lived on, and so did Henry. All through the following year and beyond, a flurry of meetings and conference calls and mysterious overnight trips would signal that Bruce and Henry were on the verge of another deal. Betweentimes, Henry worked on Bruce's real estate financing, alongside a young woman named Lydia Robinson, who had come from the real estate division of Continental Illinois Bank. Lydia would shake her head in amusement when she saw Henry standing at the Xerox machine or digging into his pocket for quarters for the soda machine—Henry, who had given up the partners' dining room at one of Wall Street's richest firms.

And there was Mitchell E. Mailman, director of construction. He was a tall, rangy man with the lush, curly beard of a zaddik and long and violently unkempt black hair, but always immaculately turned out in a dark suit and white shirt with a bow tie chosen to complement one of his many pairs of colorful braces. Mitch was a fascinating man, an ocean sailor, a connoisseur of California wines, a gourmet chef who once prepared an eight-course meal—kosher, no less—for a *New York* magazine writer who was doing an article on "Men Who Cook." While still an undergraduate at Columbia, where he took degrees in both architecture and engineering, he founded a company that did specialized construction and repair work for electric utilities. Mitchell met Bruce in 1982, when he was a construction manager for Tishman Construction Co., the biggest builder of high-rises in New York City. Tishman was going to build the Kingsley for Eichner, and Mitchell's services had been requested as project manager. Mitchell, whose nickname at Tishman was "Karastan" for the number of times he was called on the carpet, refused. He considered an apartment house a genre of building utterly lacking in subtlety and challenge. "I said, 'I want to be proud of what I do.' To me, an apartment house meant Section 8 housing. I didn't go all the way through high school just to build apartment houses. Then I left for a sailboat race to Bermuda, and when I got back, John Tishman called me into this meeting. The meeting was already going on, and there was Eichner when I walked in, and Tishman said, 'Mr. Eichner, this is Mitchell Mailman. He's going to build your building.' So what was I going to say then?"

"My first impression of Bruce," Mitchell added, "was that he was a rich kid playing with his daddy's money. We all know now that is not true, but back then that's what I thought."

There was a special bond between Mitchell and Bruce that no one else in the office quite understood. In office debate, Bruce might defer to Howard's wisdom and experience, and Luk Sun or Henry could sometimes sway him with logic, but Mitchell was the only one who could shout Bruce down, or would even try. Mitchell's full-throat roar, which would carry well in a North Atlantic squall, was as effective as a bludgeon in the tight quarters of 625 Madison Avenue. Late in 1986 a decorous blond young woman named Alice Hoffman was hired for the project. She had a degree from MIT, where she was one of a handful of women to study construction management. One of her first acts in her new job was to write a long memo on applying "value engineering" to the choice of a structural system (concrete, steel, or a combination of the two) for the Broadway State building. "Value engineering," of which Alice was a devotée, is a systematic approach to decision-making in construction, providing a way to compare directly the costs and benefits of various alternatives.

To Mitchell, her suggestion of hiring an outside engineer to study this question represented an expensive way rediscover the obvious. His reply came seventy-two hours later in a six-page, single-spaced memo discussing every conceivable ramification of the concrete/steel issue as he saw it. Clearly the proper thing for Alice to have done at that point would have been to march into Mitchell's office, throw the memo down on his desk, and engage him in a shouting match that would have stopped traffic on Grand Army Plaza. Instead, she apologized for any unintended breach of Mitchell's prerogatives and said that she was looking forward to working with someone who obviously had so much to teach her. Mitchell snapped back that he had no time to teach her what she was supposed to have learned at MIT. From that time on Mitch made it his business to keep Alice from so much as saying good morning to any of the contractors on the job. He was certain that they would walk away from the meeting spitting mother-of-pearl buttons and picking long blond hairs from between their teeth.

This was a grave injustice to Alice. But it passed almost unnoticed in the great hurly-burly rush of the project. One day in the early spring of 1987, a woman named Cynthia Thompson sat at her desk at 625 and talked about her two and a half years with Eichner Properties. She had managed Bruce's 85th Street project, and just begun work on 1540 Broadway, when she looked down the road and decided she didn't want to continue. "You have to make so much money in New York just to stay alive, you have to work fourteen-hour days just like all the lawyers and you never get ahead. New York is the most incestuous town of all. I couldn't carve out one night a week to have dinner with friends, or read a book, or cook a meal. I finally gave up my ballet tickets this year, because I couldn't say at seven o'clock, 'Sorry, guys, you finish designing the lobby.'" In two weeks she was moving with her boyfriend to Honolulu, where they hoped to open a small architectural practice, designing and building three or four houses a year. "Construction is the ultimate boys' club," she said. "A very aggressive climate, a man's world, and they steamroll over anyone who pauses to check his watch."

7

The architect would be Helmut Jahn, of Murphy/Jahn, he of the immense ego, the hundred-dollar fedoras, the soaring crested and domed towers. Jahn was then at the peak of his vogue, an architect who defined his era much as Mies van der Rohe had defined his, whose buildings erupted from the ground like a champagne fountain at a Beverly Hills wedding. Bruce was very pleased with Jahn's controversial design for Cityspire, whose top echoes the Moorish dome of the neighboring theater far below, and whose lobby displayed a striking, if faintly authoritarian, elegance. "Times Square seemed the ideal spot for a hotel with a certain design flair," Bruce said, and Jahn seemed to agree. "Ever since I came to New York in 1966," Jahn wrote Bruce in August 1985, "I found the exuberance and the excitement of Times Square and Broadway one of the most exciting experiences anywhere. To continue this tradition with a new building that incorporates this urban drama is a 'dream assignment.'" He sent a copy of his first sketch, which was pretty hard to read, being filled with dramatic slashes and thickly crosshatched shadows, but it appeared to depict two arms of a cruciform tower rising out of a low glass base and capped with a monumental central pyramid.

As time went by and the iron fist of Zoning clamped down on the fragile conceits of Art, the massing became less extreme, less idiosyncratically Jahnian. A second architect, Alan Lapidus, was brought onto the job as an expert on hotels. Lapidus was the son of Morris Lapidus, who designed what was in its day the most famous hotel in America, the Fontainebleau in Miami Beach. Alan Lapidus had been the architect for the Trump Plaza hotel in Atlantic City. For 1540 Broadway, he envisioned a "sky lobby" overlooking a retail atrium. Guests would ascend to this floor in glass-walled elevators, from which they could look out on the crowds shopping while the shoppers watched the elevators—a synergistic approach to creating visual interest that did away with expensive waterfalls, and simultaneously gave guests the reassuring sensation that whatever happened to them in the elevator, there would at least be witnesses. A version of the building incorporating Lapidus's ideas was bound into a prospectus for potential lenders in late 1986. It showed the building heroically outlined against the sky and bathed in a nimbus of light as if by the sun rising mysteriously out of Sixth Avenue. In this rendering, a slender slab, almost a knife edge running east and west, rises to a height of sixty stories out of a blocky base; another slab intersects this tower at a right angle and runs to about two-thirds of its height. The former was clad in slick gray glass; the latter was checkered by a two-story grid of alternating wide and narrow mullions, a contrast that emphasized the sleek proportions of the tower. It was never built, except out of plastic, one of four or five small white models that sat on the windowsill of Bruce's office until the move to Cityspire, after which they disappeared. But by then a lot of things had changed.

One of the changes was in Eichner and Berini's attitude toward a hotel on the site. They had in mind a medium-sized hotel of around 600 rooms, oriented not toward convention-goers but toward the upscale business and tourist trade. To gain access to a nationwide reservations network, they looked into a joint venture with Ramada Inns. Ramada drew up a program for a "Ramada Renaissance" hotel, described as "a first-class lodging experience in the upper mid-price tier." Bruce studied it curiously. The first thing he saw was that hotels are ridiculously prodigal of FAR. They have huge laundries, maids' rooms, and offices of all kinds, plus ballrooms and meeting rooms and acres of corridors and lobbies. Hotels also have an insatiable appetite for expensive vertical transportation. The 600-room hotel, occupying 472,000 square feet, was going to need as many elevators as an office building of twice the size. In the core alongside these elevators would run the express cars to the residential floors above. The core was threatening to swallow the building. A budget summary in March 1986 projected the hotel portion of the building (including a pro-rata share of common expenses such as excavation) to cost just over $160 a square foot, at a time when the rule-of-thumb cost for first-class office space was around $100 a foot. Looking ahead to 1993, when an "upper mid-price tier" room was priced at $242.60, gross operating profit was estimated to be $18,482,000.

On the face of it, that is a fascinating number. And what's fascinating about it is this: that after all the intricate calculations that went into deriving it, taking into account everything from busboys' wages to the price of a drink at the bar, it was almost exactly what that same amount of space would return if it were built and rented as offices instead. An appraisal of the site by the brokers Cushman & Wakefield applied a simple inflation factor to current office rents, and projected that in 1993 a first-class building at 1540 Broadway would command an annual rent, net after operating expenses, of thirty-nine dollars a square foot; 472,000 feet of space at thirty-nine dollars a foot works out to $18,408,000 a year. Some deep organic principle of real estate appears to be at work here. Bruce simply observed that if the hotel didn't make materially more money than the office, and the hotel space was going to cost 60 percent more to build, you didn't have to have three degrees from Oxford to know which was a more rational approach.

The question all along had been whether the Times Square area would emerge as a first-class office address, to compete with the avenues east of Fifth for the finite number of law firms, banks, publishing houses, certified public accountants, insurance companies, brokers, advertising agencies, and public relations consultants that even New York City's booming economy could support. These were the prime tenants who took space five, ten, or twenty floors at a time, whose names looked impressive on a building's directory, and whose employees lent an air of prosperity and purposefulness to the very corridors of the buildings they inhabited. Increasingly it began to seem as if the answer would be yes. "Five years ago if you said to somebody, 'I've got a great building for you at Seventh Avenue and 46th Street, or 42nd Street and Broadway,' they would have thrown you out of the office," a prominent broker was quoted as saying in the *Times.* "Now all the major builders are active on the West Side." The government-sponsored redevelopment of Times Square itself—the 42nd Street corners—was still bogged down in lawsuits and controversy. But other projects were moving ahead. The silver shoeboxes of Sixth Avenue were moving closer. Between 44th and 47th streets alone, three office buildings and a hotel were preparing to go into the ground on the blocks between Sixth and Seventh avenues. Just across West 45th Street from the Loews site, Tishman-Speyer, a major developer, had optioned the old Bond's store. Across Broadway and up three blocks, on the site of that monument to the First Amendment the Pussycat Theater, Zeckendorf was planting a Holiday Inn Crowne Plaza hotel with 200,000 square feet of offices. David and Jean Solomon, a young and ambitious husband-and-wife development team from Chicago, had two projects under way within a couple of blocks of each other, on the west side of Broadway between 47th and 48th streets (site of the Strand Theater), and across Broadway at 49th (where the Rivoli Theater stood), with a total of almost two million square feet. And—most impressive of all—the larger of the two sites had reportedly been leased in part to the investment bankers Morgan Stanley & Company, than which there could hardly be a better indication of a neighborhood's prospects.

There was, however, a substantial sentiment that this would be a desecration. This was the position of the Municipal Art Society, a civic group that boasted a long history of fighting skyscrapers. The society commissioned a rendering of the Times Square of the future, a wide place in the road lost at the bottom of a seventy-story canyon. It warned New Yorkers that "New Year's Eve would move to another city" if skyscrapers displaced the bars and nightclubs that were the natural temples to this holy municipal celebration. The problem was not just the buildings, it was the very people who were going to work in the buildings. The thousands of "squashed-plain yuppies," in the words of the society's president Kent Barwick, descending in their brass-trimmed elevators at six o'clock, blinking uncomfortably in the vulgar glare of the neon, a great anxious, shuffling, briefcase-swinging horde filling the sidewalks, sweeping before them all evidence of the vivid, raffish life of Broadway. Broadway was more than just a theater district; it was pinball arcades, garish cheap restaurants for ghetto kids trying to impress their dates, strip joints and peep shows (although that industry had been in decline since the invention of the home video recorder)—a whole infrastructure of tawdry glamour that was fundamentally incompatible with the favored haunts of young stockbrokers, namely Nautilus rooms, sushi bars, and storefront cash machines. Around this time, the American Institute of Architects held its annual convention in New York and invited Brendan Gill, the all-purpose esthete (a former theater critic who had gone on to write on architecture for *The New Yorker*), to address a seminar on the future of Times Square. The situation, Gill intoned, is more desperately tragic than it has ever been. We are facing the almost total disappearance of the psychological life of Times Square as we have known it. It is perfectly obvious that we will end up re-creating Times Square at the bottom of a well. We are going to be down in a pit. There is no possible way you could fill that whole area with office buildings fifty stories high and not fill it with deadening inhibitions. ... There is a subtext to this. Much of this effort has been to drive the blacks and Hispanics out of Times Square. This has been their village green. Of course it's true that for eight hundred feet of West 42nd Street there is crime and drug dealing ... but crime won't disappear by moving it off Times Square.

When the Manhattan street grid plan was established in 1811, Broadway was allowed to become the exception. At every point, where Broadway hits one of the wide cross streets, the entertainment district has alighted there, at 14th Street, then at 23rd, 34th, now at 42nd. The planning commission lay down like a doormat—a doormat!—on the pretext of luring developers from the East Side to the West Side, when they needed no luring; they upzoned the West Side when it should have been downzoned. None of this was necessary; it was the product of people eager to become multimillionaires in a few years ... and that is what we all must bow our heads to.

It is, of course, a matter of opinion whether the Planning Commission lay down like doormats before the developers. The commissioners didn't think so. They had enacted stiff setback requirements for buildings to preserve some of the open feeling of Times Square's traditional architecture, although of necessity this meant that the buildings would have to go higher to achieve their full FAR. The Planning Commission, together with the New York City Landmarks Preservation Commission, had erected an almost invulnerable wall of bureaucracy around the forty-odd legitimate theaters in the area. Of course, a thriving theatrical community depends on more than just theaters. Whole subdistricts of related businesses had sprung up on the fringes of Times Square. West 48th Street east of Seventh Avenue was its own little Vienna of music shops, their windows full of electric guitars hanging by their necks like hams. On this sacred soil the very Beatles bought their guitars, but a developer could wipe it out as casually as he would fill in Walden Pond. When this was pointed out to the Commission, they proposed a rule requiring new developments to set aside 5 percent of their space for "theater-related uses," which could include theaters themselves, movie houses, or ancillary businesses such as costume or music shops. The developer Seymour Durst promptly announced that this outrage might cause him to abandon plans for an office building on West 47th Street.

For his part, Barwick thought the regulation was little better than meaningless, in the face of the demolition of the great movie houses. "There will be duplexes, triplexes, quadraplexes, and octoplexes," he wailed to the *Times.* "There will be no end of darkened closets in the basements of new buildings. But the excitement of premieres, the magic of Hollywood on the East Coast will be lost."

The larger problem, clearly, was that the zoning and landmarks laws were a blunt tool to safeguard what people cherished about Times Square, which was a factor not just of architecture but intangible qualities of light, sound, and psychic energy. A theater can be preserved, but not, with any plausibility, a pinball parlor, much less the sailor who comes to play in it. In particular, the redevelopment of Times Square seemed to threaten the great electric signs that still beckoned to romantics from around the world. These were among the most cherished icons of a mostly bygone New York—the Camel sign, with its cheerful smoker continuously exhaling great rings of steam; the immense block-long waterfall, flanked by huge and unaccountably naked figures of a man and woman, that gushed on the roof of Bond's. True, the new generation of signs substituted a cool, silent electronic flicker for these naïve mechanical gimcracks; and they now mostly glowed with the logos of Japanese camera and stereo companies. Nevertheless the prospect of their loss galvanized New Yorkers who cared about their city's heritage, none more than Tama Starr, a young woman with a pleasantly forthright manner who represented the third generation of her family to build and operate electric signs in Times Square. Tama Starr's business, the Artkraft Strauss Sign Corporation, had built virtually all the famous Times Square signs in a factory on Twelfth Avenue. Tama herself dropped the lighted ball that at midnight each December 31 signified that New York had survived into another year. On 1540 Broadway itself, an Artkraft Strauss employee periodically ascended a scaffold to hand-paint a movie advertisement directly onto the bricks of the north wall. As the redevelopment of Times Square appeared imminent, at seven-thirty on a March evening in 1984 Tama Starr organized a protest. This turned out to be among the most attention-getting demonstrations in the history of political action in New York City. She turned off the signs—all thirty-one of them, at two-second intervals, so that the television cameras could record the darkness as it spread over the square from south to north. The blackout that followed lasted half an hour. A few months later, the City Planning Commission began studying regulations to require signs on new buildings in Times Square.

Paul Marantz, a well-known lighting designer, helped the city draft the new regulations. In part, this meant drawing up the standards for size, placement, illumination, and animation to be written into the city's zoning code. He considered this a necessary, but ultimately pointless, task. Architects had to know what was required of them, of course. But the very act of writing regulations interfered with the desired effect of "rambunctious diversity." The Great White Way had evolved by fortuitous, random processes of free enterprise at its most basic level, an attempt to outshine the competition. "What we want," Marantz explained, "is for one guy to rent a sign and the guy next door to try to put up a sign that will kick the hell out of him. That's why we discourage people from doing this as art, which is the first question everyone asks. This is not about art. If you want to see a light show, go to Dallas."

Marantz's real agenda was to conduct an exercise in cultural subversion. Rather than allow the broadcloth-backed yuppies to transform the neighborhood into their own bloodless image, he sought to create an environment that would transform *them,* once they stepped outside their cold marble lobbies at close of business. He was inspired by the example of the South Street Seaport, a collection of restaurants and high-class knickknack stores in the financial district where young stockbrokers head after work to reel through the streets like sailors on leave. Marantz imagined the buildings of Times Square as sober towers of commerce and professionalism all day long, suddenly erupting into million-watt roadhouses at night, great glassy strumpets of buildings shouting BEER and FAST CARS and SEXY MUSIC at the sky. As an example of the kind of thinking he hoped to encourage, he suggested a sign advertising orange juice, in the form of an eighty-foot-diameter orange balloon that spent the day packed in a closet and then, as night fell on the city, inflated with a whoosh, tethered to the roof of a building and hit with a battery of spotlights. "If we have just neat little banker-approved signs, it will be a travesty," he warned. "Unless the culture changes to something like what you have in Tokyo, where it is perfectly acceptable for a lawyer to have his office behind a hot-pink neon lingerie sign, it's all meaningless."

This was not instinctively obvious to everyone at first. It took the city more than two years to adopt the regulations, after prompting by editorials in both the *Times* ("Signs of Life in Times Square") and the *Daily News* ("Times Square Ain't Vanilla Ice Cream"). Marantz and the rest of the consultants had done their work well, given that no one had ever attempted anything quite like this before. For more than a year afterward, even experts in the city's zoning code were baffled by some of the wording in the text. One thing, however, was clear: that whatever else the signs would be, they would have to be big. It is possible no one really understood how big until someone sat down and applied the formula to some actual buildings. When that was done for the building Bruce was planning, it came to the eye-popping figure of around 15,000 square feet, more than a third of an acre.

Developers, for their part, regarded signs as part of a plot to so blight their beautiful new buildings that they would never be built. The notion of plastering office buildings with electric signs ran against the prevailing fashion for marble and granite evocations of a generic pastness, confusingly designated "Postmodernism." David Solomon was particularly eloquent on the topic. "What visitors want to see is the Champs-Élysées," he told a reporter from the *Times.* "They want trees and clean streets … museums and sidewalk cafés. Investment bankers and lawyers don't want to work in an environment surrounded by flashing lights." Eichner was publicly silent. His preferred method for communicating with City Hall was not through *The New York Times,* but with a phone call to a well-placed official in the bureaucracy. Getting caught up in these battles—the *Times* described Solomon as "waving his arms" in agitation—distracted one from the more important question: how to take advantage of the givens of the situation. His interests, in any case, were not necessarily identical with those of Solomon, who was planning to lease his building to Morgan Stanley. Eichner was, of course, concerned about how the signs would affect his chances of leasing his office floors. But he was also planning theaters and five stories of retail, intended to appeal to tourists and theatergoers, so he had a certain stake in razzle-dazzle as well. And somewhere along the line he asked Luk Sun, who in turn asked Alice, to find out what 15,000 square feet of signs might bring in the way of rental. The answer was "over a million dollars a year."

8

Meanwhile, there was a building to run, at least while the tenants remained. A seventeen-story building, even one as unpretentious as 1540 Broadway, still needs cleaning, and a variety of other services ranging down to a $44.96 monthly tab for extermination. There are other developers, who if they saw a $45 item to get rid of mice in a building that was going to be torn down anyway, would be able to think of nothing but "Hey, that's the equivalent of ninety cigars!" And there are many who would regard mice as allies in the effort to empty the building of tenants. Bruce had a more enlightened attitude, which is that the deck is stacked in favor of tenants anyway, so you might as well save yourself the trouble of fighting them. They'll get themselves a lawyer who wants to run for Congress, and the first thing he'll do is call up the *Village Voice.* Then you'll have a meeting at City Hall and as soon as you walk in the door everybody in sight dives under his desk. Bruce's approach also reflects the influence of Howard. Howard is no pushover, but he has an unusual condition for someone who was profiled in the magazine *Manhattan, Inc.* as one of "The New Fixers": He likes to sleep nights.

Most of the relocations at 1540 went smoothly. The typical deal gave the tenant a couple of months' free rent in exchange for a signed agreement to leave. The Rieses, of course, were the major exception. In dealing with Murray Riese, the Broadway State team had one small advantage, and one big disadvantage. The advantage was that Riese was immune to any kind of sentimental attachment to his business. At one meeting that ran well into the afternoon, Polevoy suggested ordering some hamburgers. Murray Riese said he wasn't hungry. "We'll send to one of your restaurants, Murray," he said grandly. "You eat that stuff?" Riese asked incredulously, pulling from his briefcase a small bag of dried fruit, seeds, and nuts. So there was no chance that Eighth Restaurant Corp. would turn into the sort of irrational holdout that developers fear most. The corresponding disadvantage was that, unlike a typical holdout, the Rieses could wait for Eichner to come to them. If you offer a hundred thousand dollars to a dry cleaner to move to the next block, that is a windfall that is not likely to be repeated in the owner's lifetime. You hold the ultimate threat of walking away; a deal will be struck at the precise point where his greed and fear intersect. "The Rieses, on the other hand, are very successful and I assume wealthy people," Polevoy observed. "If they miscalculate and you walk away from the deal, then okay, they lost one. It doesn't affect their lives any."

They met mainly at Polevoy's office at 380 Madison Ave., and once or twice at Riese headquarters above a Roy Rogers near Madison Square Garden. Murray Riese was cordial through the whole months-long ordeal. A writer for *Crain's New York Business* once described him as "looking like an overindulgent grandfather ... [bearing] no resemblance to the piranha many real estate brokers depict him to be." The Broadway State team had the same reaction when Riese would put his arm around their shoulders in a paternal way and tell them that they might as well give him what he wanted, or he'd ask for more. It's amazing the things people think of in situations like this. The Riese lease covered not just the corner occupied by their restaurant, but additional space on the ground floor and basement that they sublet to others. These subtenants would have to be vacated as well, but Riese refused to let Bruce or Berini talk to them until he himself had come to terms. The effect of this was to put additional pressure on BSP to settle with Riese, because they would face further delays of uncertain length even after the main deal was made. It would have been bad enough if the subtenants were just another T-shirt or camera store trying to convince a judge that no other venue on the globe was as suitable for fleecing Japanese tourists. But among the subleases held by the Rieses was one for a few thousand feet of basement space that was home to the General Douglas MacArthur center of the USO, the place homesick GIs and sailors all over the world knew they could count on for a milkshake, a kind word, and discount tickets to *O Calcutta!* The thought of searching Landlord-Tenant Court for a judge willing to throw the USO into the street was almost enough to make Howard wish he had never left the public sector.

After weeks of meetings, an agreement was more or less on the table. The Rieses would be bought out of their lease for a large sum, payable over several years. They were given a lease on a restaurant to occupy the same corner in the new building, which for tax reasons was treated as an amendment and extension of the existing lease. And they negotiated a substantial monthly compensation for all the beer they didn't give away while waiting for the new building to be finished. "I'm very excited about this," Riese said genially. "This is going to be the most valuable real estate in the United States in a few years. It'll be more valuable than Fifth Avenue. It will be more valuable than the Ginza. I'm proud to be part of it." To underscore his pride, he submitted a list of requirements for the restaurant in the new building that implied he was planning on catering the 1992 conventions.

"It could have been worse," Mitchell said, after Riese had ambled off with his lawyers. "He didn't ask for a revolving dance floor."

"I hate to tell you this," Polevoy said, "but he isn't finished with you yet. He hasn't bargained enough. Drawing up the papers is just the start of negotiations."

The next day they were back in Polevoy's office, going over the papers, when Murray Riese looked up pleasantly and said, "My brother is mad at me."

"Why is that, Murray?" Luk Sun asked cautiously.

"Because he feels I gave up too much to you guys. He said to me, 'Murray, we can't get paid out over all that time. I won't live to see the money.'" Irving Riese was two years older than Murray, who was sixty-one at the time. "I've got another suggestion for how to structure this ..."

Luk Sun stood up.

"In that case, Murray, I'm leaving," he announced.

"What's wrong?"

"I don't have to put up with this, that's what wrong!" Luk Sun erupted. "We negotiated every point in this deal thirty-five times, and you want to put it all back on the table, I've got better things to do than sit through it for a thirty-sixth time, okay? You guys make the deal and call me when it's ready to sign."

Berini looked panic-struck. "How can you do this to me?"

"Just watch," Luk Sun answered. And he walked out of the room.

"Gee," Murray Riese said, with a sigh, "I had no idea he was so sensitive."

Berini managed to patch things up, but a few days later he called Wong in panic, because the negotiations had reached the stage of specifying the requirements for Riese's space in the new building. Riese's requirements for plumbing, electricity, and especially for kitchen exhaust made Luk Sun gasp. "Is he going to cook food in there, or electrocute it?" he grumbled to Mitchell one day.

"I don't know," Mitchell replied, "but with this amount of kitchen exhaust, he won't need any signs outside, he can just open his doors and suck people in off the street."

Bruce and Howard themselves handled the negotiations to buy the Lyceum's air rights. The man they had to deal with was Gerald Schoenfeld, the chairman of the board of both the Shubert Organization, which owned and ran sixteen Broadway theaters, and the Shubert Foundation, which received all the income from the theaters. Schoenfeld was a portly man with a large, bald head, a booming voice, and a piercing gaze behind gold-rimmed glasses. He was often considered the most powerful man in American theater, a post he inherited as the lawyer for the Shubert family; and, to the outrage of the Brendan Gills of the world, he seemed to approach the theater as a subspecialty of the real estate business in which you happened to rent space one seat at a time. The problem Bruce and Howard had in dealing with Schoenfeld was that they were trying to make a deal to save a theater that Schoenfeld didn't want to be saved. It would have been fine with him, in fact, if it could be torn down. Of course, he couldn't tear it down, because it was a landmark, unless he could prove that keeping the building entailed grave economic hardship. But as part of the deal to sell the Lyceum air rights across the zoning boundary to the Loews site, Schoenfeld would have to give up even that problematic escape clause. He would have to enter into a binding covenant with the city to maintain the building and operate it as a theater for as long as the Broadway State Building lasted—in practical terms, forever. In Schoenfeld's opinion, if you stood this proposition up next to Communism, you couldn't tell them apart. "The Lyceum," he magisterially informed Bruce, "is not an asset. It is a liability. It doesn't make any money, it loses money. It is the oldest theater extant, a two-balcony house [second-balcony seats are hard to sell] on the wrong side of Broadway. Nevertheless, the city has seen fit to mandate its continued existence, without any thought to the consequences, in an appalling demonstration of ignorance and lack of sensitivity, which I might add is just the opposite of that which is manifested by the city fathers where sports teams, stadiums, and arenas are concerned!"

That was one of Schoenfeld's great disappointments in life—that the city spent $100 million to fix up Yankee Stadium, but wouldn't give a nickel toward keeping *A Chorus Line* operating. Stripped to its essentials, Schoenfeld's case was this. All through the 1970s, a dark time in the history of both Broadway and New York City, when you couldn't have given away a theater, Shubert had kept the buildings open. Even the Lyceum was maintained to Shubert's legendarily high standards. Now that they were finally worth something as real estate, the city refused to let him cash them in.

Schoenfeld was seeking the one thing the city had never permitted: the right to sell air rights to the highest bidder, even if that bidder didn't happen to have a lot adjacent to the theater. It is hard to say how much more money this would have generated for the Shubert Organization, but it could easily have been tens of millions of dollars. And it would have turned loose something like three million square feet of FAR from all Broadway theaters put together. In the absence of that, Schoenfeld conceded with a shrug, he was obligated by his sacred fiduciary trust to consider whatever pittance Bruce might be willing to offer. If he didn't make a deal with Bruce, he probably wouldn't make a deal at all. That would be okay with him.

For someone with his back to the wall, Schoenfeld did a remarkably good job of negotiating for himself. He invoked the horrors of inflation as they might affect the Shubert organization far into the next century, committed to the upkeep of a hundred-year-old theater. He pointed out that any amount he received in a sale would be diluted by taxes anyway. This gave Bruce his opening. Bruce proposed that the air rights could be leased instead of sold, providing a steady flow of money to maintain the theater. For Bruce, it had the corresponding advantage of less cash to come up with right away. Schoenfeld quickly agreed that this was a splendid idea. Naturally, he added, the lease payments would be adjusted to take inflation into account. For approximately 120,000 square feet of air rights, they struck a deal at an initial rent of around a half million dollars a year, frozen for eight years and thereafter escalating with the cost of living.

There were a few other matters to clear up before building could start. One was acquiring the property at 1544 Broadway, a shabby four-story building with twenty feet of frontage smack in the middle of the blockfront. The property was owned by several members of a New Jersey family, either outright or as the beneficiaries of a trust that was run by a New Jersey bank. That is, they owned it as far as they were concerned. They paid taxes on it, received rent from it, and when Bruce asked if they were interested in selling, a price was mentioned and they struck a deal. The price was $5.6 million, which by coincidence works out to $2,800 a square foot, exactly twice what Bruce paid for the surrounding Loews parcel.

Owning a property is not necessarily the same thing as being able to sell it, however. To state the obvious, when a piece of real estate is sold, it stays in the same place, and what actually changes hands are pieces of paper signifying its ownership. An extensive body of law has grown up around the procedures to verify the actual unambiguous ownership of a specific piece of property. Banks in particular are sticklers for this stuff. Invariably, before they will issue a mortgage, they require the buyer to hire a title company to investigate the seller's claims to own what he purports to be selling. If it subsequently turns out that the land under a new skyscraper actually belongs to a retired merchant seaman who is the missing heir to a nineteenth-century patent-medicine fortune, the title company is on the line. This makes them among the most gimlet-eyed and implacable practitioners in the entire legal profession. Of course, in a place like midtown Manhattan, most transactions are pretty well documented, and the title company can just work forward from the most recent sale or mortgage. But when the lawyers went to look at the records of 1544 Broadway, they discovered that the property, incredibly, had been in the same family for over 100 years. As it passed down by inheritance through the generations, nobody bothered to dot the *i*'s on the paperwork that otherwise would have accompanied a change in ownership. In other words, contrary to every dictate of common sense, it turned out that for legal purposes, the longer the property stayed in one family, the *less* secure their title to it actually became.

Bachner, Tally, put Donald P. Perry, their trusts and estates partner, on the case. Perry traced the ownership as far back as 1870, when it belonged to a couple more or less lost to history except for their names, Leonard and Ann Amanda Appleby. Exactly what the property consisted of Perry is unable to say, but the neighborhood was an obscure and unfashionable part of the city in those years, and the two- and three-story buildings that appear in contemporary photographs housed stables, mason's yards, and other establishments found where land is cheap. A few years later the area where Broadway and Seventh Avenue cross would become the home of the city's finest carriage-builders, and, taking its name from the corresponding district in London, be known as Longacre Square.

In 1870, the Applebys put 1544 Broadway into a trust for their grandchildren, Leonard A. Bampton, Sr., and Julia Bampton Robinson. Records showed that Julia's share had been passed to her two children, who apparently died without leaving descendants, and thence to their father, Julia's husband. On his death in 1926 it reverted to Julia's brother Leonard, who thereupon owned the entire property. Perry's problem was that no will had ever been filed for Julia, and the title company therefore regarded it as mere speculation that she was indeed dead, and not liable to turn up any day with Edward Bennet Williams in tow, demanding that someone get that damned skyscraper off her property. People can be very unreasonable at her age, which would have been at least 116. Or—worse yet—suppose she had run off with a circus strongman and had seven more children, with by now scores of descendants scattered all over the country? What title company in its right mind would take that chance?

To resolve this question, and a few others relating to the ownership of 1544 Broadway, took approximately fifteen months.

"That's an impressive amount of time," someone later said to Perry.

"Well," he said modestly, "we got some lucky breaks along the way."

Fifteen forty-four posed another problem as well. The building was netleased to a Chicago company, Victory Square Corp. That is, Victory Square paid a fixed rent for the building, paid taxes and operating expenses, and subleased it to the store on the ground floor, pocketing the difference as its profit. Unlike an ordinary commercial lease, the net lease had no escape hatch for demolition. "Only in New York does this happen," Bruce observed, not without relish. "You've got deeds dating back to practically the Civil War, you've got three layers of people to be bought off every step of the way. I'm just sitting here waiting to find out that the guy in Chicago died and the lease is now part of the estate, which he left to the Salvation Army.

"That's what makes the game fun."

"Forget the fun. Are we going to get this guy out?" Berini asked anxiously.

"Trust me," Bruce said. Victory Square was a company that used to operate a haberdashery shop in 1544 Broadway. Long ago it had been absorbed by another Chicago company, which apparently was in the business of leasing coin-operated kiddie rides in shopping centers. "I don't think we're exactly in over our heads here," Bruce said. He put in a call to the head of the parent company. "A nice guy, a smart guy, but he couldn't find Times Square with a map," Bruce reported to Howard. "We'll give him what his lease is worth." Meaning: what it was worth to Victory Square as the seller, the amount they would otherwise have realized from the lease over the remainder of its term, discounted for present value, inflated just enough to give them an incentive to sell. The Riese lease was also bought for "what it was worth," but what it was worth to Bruce as the buyer. The difference is the difference between the several million dollars that the Rieses got, and $400,000, which is what Victory Square was paid.

That left the corner parcel, 1550 Broadway. This was owned by a family named Rubinstein, headed by two elderly brothers, Morris and Jack. The Rubinsteins were also in the restaurant business. They ran a Howard Johnson's in the Loews building, and another one across the street. Everyone agreed that Morris Rubinstein was a gentleman. He surrendered his lease on the restaurant in the Loews building without a murmur when the building was sold. But while the Rieses eventually were brought to the table, biting and gouging, because it made economic sense for both parties, all the gentlemanliness in the world couldn't bridge the distance between bid and asked on 1550 Broadway. Bruce had paid $5.6 million for 1544 Broadway, which was the same size. He made a first offer of $5 million for the corner. The Rubinsteins asked $10 million. Morris's son, who handled most of the negotiations, claimed the building was worth that much. It had stores: the camera store, the hot-dog stand, and a tour-bus office on the 46th Street side. It also had signs—two huge neon signs, one covering three floors of the building itself, the other on the roof, angled for maximum visibility to the eight lanes of downtown traffic. Together, those signs could bring in as much as as $40,000 a month, or $480,000 a year; capitalized at 10 percent, that was almost worth $5 million in the bank right there.

From Bruce's point of view, though, if $1,400 a square foot was a rational price for the bulk of the site, and if $2,800 a square foot was rational for the essential middle piece, $5,000 a square foot was crazy for a corner that he did not absolutely have to have. The premium could only be justified by 1550's nuisance value. But Bruce doesn't pay for nuisance value. Dealing with nuisances is part of his job. "I think they thought Bruce would cave in and say he had to have their building," mused Sidney Roberts, who worked with Eichner on the negotiations. "But Bruce is a funny guy. He doesn't cave. The son tried to show me how the building could be worth $10 million, but I personally don't see why you'd want to own that crummy little corner when you could take $5 million and put it in a nice shopping center somewhere."

And that was that.

Or not quite entirely that, however; for there was one small matter outstanding. A very small matter: an inch. The inch was the width of a strip, seventeen feet long, in the middle of the block between the Lyceum theater and the Loews parcel and belonging to neither. This apparently was the result of some faulty surveying back in the nineteenth century that gave the north-south dimension of the block as 200 feet, eight inches when in fact it is 200 feet, ten inches. Accordingly, when the block was divided into lots, the deeds gave the incorrect half-block distance of 100 feet, four inches. In 1902, when the land for the Lyceum was being assembled, the mistake was caught and that parcel was correctly described as 100 feet, five inches deep. But the deeds on the 46th Street side were never amended. Naturally no one observed this discrepancy in building on the site. The walls of the existing structures adjoined; to leave an inch unexcavated and vacant between the Lyceum and Eichner's new building would have been absurd. Tracking down the actual owners of the strip—the heirs of nineteenth-century landowners who sold off the original plots—was obviously not going to be practical, either. It turns out the law has certain escape clauses for situations like this. One could argue "adverse possession," i.e., that the preceding owner, Loews, had been in "open and notorious possession" of the strip for at least ten years. Or one could claim title by virtue of an improvement to the land, the improvement in this case being the new building. Meanwhile, though, the law—or, more exactly, the lawyers in the title company—demanded a cosmetic solution to give at least the appearance of clean title to the entire parcel. The answer was to set up a dummy corporation to claim title to the missing inch, and then transfer it to Broadway State Partners. The name of this dummy corporation was Bego Corp., suggested by Mitchell in honor of Ben Goldberg, the surveyor who uncovered the mistake in the deeds. Thus Broadway State could point to an actual bill of sale (for a dollar) and deed for the land; anyone doubting it could take the matter up with Bego Corp., and good luck to them.

The documents concerning this procedure made a stack considerably thicker than the missing inch. But only then could Bruce be said to own:

ALL that certain plot, piece or parcel of land, situate, lying and being in the Borough of Manhattan, City, County and State of New York, bounded and described as follows: BEGINNING at a point on the easterly side of Broadway or 7th Avenue distant 20 feet 9 inches southerly from the intersection of the easterly side of Broadway or 7th Avenue and southerly side of 46th Street; RUNNING THENCE Easterly parallel with 46th Street and part of the distance through a party wall, 100 feet; THENCE Northerly parallel with the easterly side of Broadway or 7th Avenue 20 feet 9 inches more or less partly through a party wall to the southerly side of 46th Street …

[and thus along six more right-angled jogs and detours through the schist of Manhattan, the land of the Algonquins, the blocks and lots of nineteenth-century stablekeepers and fishmongers, the brick walls erected by hundreds of sweating immigrants in the dawning years of the century, ending up …]

Northerly along the easterly side of Broadway or 7th Avenue 180 feet 7 inches to the point or place of BEGINNING.

9

One thing that was supposed to happen during this time didn't, though. The construction financing that was supposed to repay European-American Bank's land loan within six months didn't materialize. Maybe this shouldn't have surprised anyone. This wasn't a $30 million deal, it wasn't even a $100 million deal, it was a $300 million deal. More expensive buildings have been built in New York, but most of them were developed as corporate headquarters, internally financed, and without the risk of opening up one fine day to discover that all the potential tenants had moved to New Jersey. As a purely speculative venture, the Broadway State project was in a class halfway between real estate and leveraged buy-out, and it tickled Bruce to be doing a deal this big, but it didn't make it any easier to raise money.

There were approximately four banks in New York at that time in a position to make a construction loan of that size, and even they would probably try to spread the risk by farming out, or syndicating, the greater part of it to other banks. The four were Manufacturers Hanover, Chase Manhattan, Bankers Trust, and Citibank, and of these, Bruce had a substantial relationship only with Citibank. That Citibank had already passed on the project once, leaving Bruce with a week to come up with $50 million to buy the site, did not prejudice the possibility of their making the construction loan. The real estate business was built on personal relationships and trust; you did not, if you could help it, ask for a loan of close to $300 million by picking up the phone and introducing yourself to a bank.

And Citicorp was rapidly expanding its commercial real estate lending. The banking industry was being essentially reinvented in the 1980s. Two areas of business that had been crucial to the growth of big money-center banks, overseas development loans and general corporate lending, were diminishing in importance—the former because it turned out the loans didn't get repaid, and the latter because corporations preferred to borrow in the debt market. The new growth areas were in leveraged buy-out loans and in commercial real estate. The 1982 Garn–St. Germain Act, which did for banking what the invention of the handgun did for bank robbery, lifted the ceilings on how much of a bank's portfolio could be in real estate loans, and greatly eased the equity requirements for borrowers. Citibank, as the largest American bank, led the way in these new areas. By the end of the decade it had over $8 billion in outstanding loans for leveraged buy-outs, and more than $13 billion in commercial real estate—a doubling in just five years.

Leaving the construction loan aside, Bruce's bigger problem in early 1987 was with the other part of the deal, the equity. In an analogy to a home mortgage, equity would be the down payment—that is, a sum pledged by the developer to assure the bank that if it had to foreclose, the project would retain enough residual value so that the vice president who made the loan wouldn't be transferred to a branch office in Ozone Park. In the event of foreclosure, the equity partners would stand to lose part or all of their investment; on the other hand, if the building made money, they got the profits.

How much equity would a $300 million project require? Hard to say, because each deal is unique. Bruce could not simply ask Citibank, because the response would be, in effect, "Bring us the deal, and we'll tell you if it's enough." But Bruce and Henry were working on the assumption they would need somewhere in the vicinity of $50 million. Naturally you don't just write out a check for $50 million at the start of the process and take it to the bank. The entire history of real estate financing can be seen as an endless struggle to substitute other things for cash: guarantees or pledges or letters of credit; variously collateralized, cross-guaranteed, and underwritten; ingeniously hedged with conditions and contingencies intended to limit, subdivide, redistribute, and disguise the awful risk that any one party might at some future date be required to actually produce legal United States currency. The bank casts a cold eye over these proceedings and then in the last five minutes imperiously signals either thumbs up or down. This is the process that Bruce sometimes wishes he could cut short by transforming himself into a Rudin or a Durst.

At various points in the history of the Broadway State Project, Bruce personally had issued guarantees totaling over $30 million, which was impressively more money than he had in cash at the time. That was okay with the bank, which by its very nature likes to have you on the hook even if it can't eat you. But Bruce considers the danger of losing a substantial fraction of one's own net worth in a deal gone sour one of the least attractive features of capitalism. Which led him, in early 1987, to reassess the partnership. Eichner and VMS were essentially fifty-fifty partners. Eichner's original plan was for VMS to come up with the liquid equity, the cash and letters of credit. But VMS's money had to be borrowed from the Real Estate Investment Trusts at four or more points over prime; it was essentially short-term financing suitable for buying land but not for a three- or four-year construction process.

By the spring of 1987, much of the risk in the project had been mitigated. The land had been assembled and the tenants were being relocated; the concerns about the neighborhood were subsiding. But there was still no equity. One day in March, Eichner put his feet up on his desk to see if there was a way to turn this problem into an opportunity.

"I have a feeling," he said; "the kind of thing you feel in your fingers. It's what kingdoms are built on. Charlemagne must have had this feeling. When I started this thing with VMS, we were going to do a hotel and residential building. VMS was picked because they had hotel experience. They own and operate them all over the country. But as the world unfolds, the hotel turns out not to be viable, and VMS is unable to make a material contribution to the construction financing, either equity or debt, leaving Eichner to produce both. Now it seems VMS has a choice: either they can be the equity, or logic would dictate that they step out."

There were several possible advantages to finding a substitute for VMS, in Eichner's viewpoint. First, a strong equity partner would impress the bank. VMS was successful at what it did, but it was a syndicator, cash-poor and highly leveraged. If Bruce could produce a partner who put up actual cash, the bank might be sufficiently dazzled that it would forgo personal guarantees from Bruce as part of the equity. Furthermore, a new equity partner would be buying into an assembled, vacant site, and would thus face much less risk than the original partners did when they first bought 1540 Broadway. Accordingly, the partner might be willing to accept a smaller share of the equity than VMS's 50 percent. Even if VMS retained a share, the total might still be less than half. You didn't need three degrees from Oxford to see that this would leave *more* than 50 percent for Eichner.

Who might this other partner be? A Japanese construction company would be a logical candidate. By Japanese standards, American real estate was a bargain. In the previous six months, investors from Tokyo had paid $610 million for the Exxon Building a few blocks away on Sixth Avenue, the highest price ever for a Manhattan office building; they had picked up ABC headquarters (also on Sixth Avenue) for $175 million and as a kind of lagniappe snatched up Tiffany's Fifth Avenue store for $94 million. And the Japanese were not confining their interest to occupied buildings. Japanese construction companies were eager to break into the North American market. At the opposite end of the very same block as the Loews site, on the west side of Sixth Avenue between 45th and 46th streets, the New York Land Company had gone into partnership with the Japanese giant Kumagai Gumi to build a forty-eight-story office tower. But the Japanese were notoriously conservative investors, slow to commit themselves, and a series of polite meetings in Tokyo and New York had netted Bruce little more than an impressive collection of business cards.

So in the second week of March, 1987, Bruce and Henry were basically looking at two potential deals, one with Westinghouse Credit Corp., the finance subsidiary of the Pittsburgh-based industrial company, and one with Salomon Brothers, the investment bank. There was nothing inherently logical about the process by which these two particular concerns emerged as the two finalists. They happened to be two companies with which Henry had done business while at Shearson Lehman, at which some of his old contacts were still in place. The latest extension of the land loan was due to expire at the end of the month, and Bruce was waiting for a deal to be put on the table, with the patience and serenity that were his trademarks.

Henry: "I come from an environment, investment banking, where patience is critical. You can't push string. Things have to run their course. All you can do is, with a certain amount of persuasiveness, bordering on mild aggression, try to get them to look at your deal before the ninety-five others they have in front of them. If you push too hard, you tend to force the conclusion opposite to that which is desired. You can always get a quick no.

"Is this alien to Bruce's makeup? Sure. I will say that I was more than moderately surprised at how patient he was with the Japanese. But his patience is at an end. I have the same argument with my wife, who is at Merrill Lynch, and more impatient than Bruce: you have to put yourself in the other person's shoes and understand what he wants."

The two deals emerged in very different form over the succeeding weeks, as they were fleshed out in an interminable series of meetings, phone calls, and letters (invariably sent by fax or overnight courier). Salomon was offering to put up cash. Not the full $50 million, only $27.5 million, and they wanted a 50 percent share of the project. Salomon also offered to help negotiate the bank loan. Not just offered; they insisted, and demanded a fee of several million dollars for their assistance. Since Bruce didn't think they would get a better deal than he could himself, he considered this gouging pure and simple. There were, however, extra-economic implications to the Salomon deal. On the plus side, there was the prestige of becoming a partner of Salomon Brothers, which was then at the peak of its cachet as one of Wall Street's most fashionably vehement firms. On the other hand, Salomon would be a much more active partner than Westinghouse. Their approach Henry described as "brute force." Lydia Robinson came back trembling from an early meeting describing how one Salomon vice president had outlined a plan for the ruination of a colleague with whom he had some disagreement, and said to Bruce, "We don't want to be partners with THOSE guys, do we?"

Bruce's real problem with the Salomon deal was that they wanted him to bear the entire construction risk. If the project went over budget, he would have to come up with the additional money himself. Which he might do, if he could treat that money as a loan and get it back at the end, but under Salomon's proposal there was no provision for him to be repaid. "You would have to be fairly desperate to take a deal like that," Bruce mused. "It puts all the risk on me. The effect is to make you want to not spend money, however justified it might be in terms of the project. And I don't think that's a rational course. The entire psychology it creates is negative. You don't always get what you pay for in life, but you almost never get what you don't pay for."

Westinghouse had a very different deal in mind. They wanted to sell, or more accurately rent, their name. That is, they would guarantee a sum, not to exceed $45 million, which Eichner could use at his discretion, subject to 140 pages or so of conditions. He could use this guarantee as collateral for a bank loan. He could cash it in directly from Westinghouse, although only after four years had gone by—in other words, after the project was already built. Or he could take the guarantee and wave it in front of the bank's face to make them feel better and hope that it never had to be used. In exchange for this service, Westinghouse wanted an immediate fee of $4 million and a 40 percent share of the equity. That is, those were the conditions just for issuing the guarantee. If Westinghouse ever actually had to produce any of this money, even a dollar, it was a whole other ballgame. In that case, Westinghouse's equity share would increase to 50 percent, and whatever they put up would be considered a loan at 2 percent over prime, with a floor of 11 percent. And, just to make sure he didn't trifle with his partner's money, Bruce was expected to personally guarantee up to $25 million of that loan.

On the face of it, this was a scheme for Westinghouse to coin money. Provided, that is, that the development went more or less as planned. The significance of the Westinghouse offer was this: Bruce would have to navigate the dangerous storms of construction, and the treacherous calms of leasing, and then, after four years, if he was still afloat, his partner would get into the boat with him, provided Bruce would personally guarantee his safety.

If one could get past brooding about this, there was Citibank's reaction to consider. Citibank didn't like the idea of giving away equity to a party who didn't put up cash. "That's a philosophical issue," Henry said. "My feeling is, if the deal works, philosophy is something you discuss after work. But I don't know if the bank will see it that way. The bottom line is, we've still got a long way to go on this one."

One chilly morning in late April, with the sky over Manhattan the color of wet concrete, Bruce took stock of the situation. His office was always especially dreary in wet weather, because the rain made huge ugly drips down the precast concrete panels of the building across the street. And this was a dreary day to be thinking about financing a $300 million office building in Manhattan. The morning newspapers had reported that J.C. Penney was moving its headquarters with 4,000 employees to Plano, Texas, vacating over a million square feet of space in its building on Sixth Avenue. This followed by two days a similar announcement by Mobil, which was relocating to Fairfax, Virginia. The dollar was down to around 138 yen, and the stock market, while still up around 2,200, was acting very nervous. The Business section of the *New York Times* carried a story on investment bankers who managed to go into personal debt on incomes of over $1 million a year. Henry was quoted at some length on the attitudes of a few of his peers: "There is the desire to possess quality things, the desire to show off. … There is a lot more spending on apartments than elsewhere and a tendency to hire name decorators and then spend an imprudently high percentage of net worth with them."

"When you start a project like this," Bruce mused, "you send a bunch of balls down the hill and hope they arrive at the bottom more or less at the same time. The balls are now congregating dangerously close to the bottom. Everything hinges on Westinghouse's ability to present a deal in the next few days that Citibank finds acceptable. Otherwise everyone's going to go back to square one, and probably unhappily, because the game clock will have wound down. EAB has been in there for much longer than they wanted, with no immediate promise of release. VMS in its mind will have made an agreement in principle to step out only to find that it can't get out now because there is no one to replace them with.

"Now the fact is, even if we make a deal with Westinghouse tomorrow, at best we're gonna get a series of agreements in principle, which will take probably a couple of months to reduce to paper. VMS may not want to stick around that long, if they're not in the game any longer, but meanwhile, remember, they're providing $15 million in collateral for the land loan. If VMS pulls out, then EAB is somewhat naked on the horizon. They will want me to collateralize that position with all sorts of personal guarantees."

"Are you in a position to do that?" he was asked.

"You mean literally, emotionally, spiritually? Literally, yes. Emotionally, perhaps less so. I'm troubled by that."

"You have to talk to Mrs. Eichner about it?"

"No. It's worse having to talk to yourself because if someone else says no, maybe you listen to them."

He turned to look out the window; the rain had now soaked the whole side of the building across the street to a uniform coffee dregs gray-brown. "You don't see, from the outside, the incredible emotion expended at each step, at each breakpoint in doing a deal. Between the time you took title and today, three issues have been settled. One: what you thought was the great issue the day you bought the property, getting possession.

"Two: what were the possibilities you would be able to empty the main site for a reasonable amount of money in a timely fashion?

"Three: what were the possibilities of making an air rights deal? The sum and substance of all three being to give you a site that has value.

Here we are fourteen months later, you've done everything you set out to do, by dint of tremendous effort … and all you've done is gone to the beginning.

"However, like a great symphony, in the background, heard by me the conductor, there are two strains that will build to a crescendo. One has already. This is a nonproject as of this moment. There is no equity, there is no debt. While the masses of people that represent the Loews project are playing furiously away, the stage is going out over the precipice. To keep that from happening, there's an enormous amount of energy that Eichner is spending personally, negotiating, pushing, prodding, because we are talking about a $300 million project.

"Now, it gets to be June, July, the Lord's will is done, and there either is or isn't financing, and you say to yourself, Good, it's now empty, it's now financed. Now the real game will begin, you've gone through this monumental effort to get to the beginning: to build the building, to find out what Western civilization will say.

"If I could teach my kid anything in the whole world, it would be that the real good feelings come not from success but from your level of effort. It's the only thing you have any control over. You could put out your heart on something, and the fucking hotel burns down."

10

It was around this time that Bruce began to think about looking for another architect. Jahn seemed, in Bruce's opinion, a little stale on the building. This, he acknowledged, was not entirely the architect's fault. Jahn had been commissioned to design a hotel, and after a year of work it had turned into an office building. Moreover, as the hotel disappeared the retail began to loom larger in Bruce's plans. But he wasn't sure that Jahn was the right person to design the retail atrium. Shopping centers were a separate world within architecture, a fantastic world of hanging tropical ferns and turn-of-the-century gas lamps, of tiled Roman fountains surrounded by rustic redwood benches, of cozy Victorian illusions of stained glass and preweathered brick. It was a little hard to see what Jahn's genius, his flair for the dramatic gesture flung against the skyline, had to do with any of this.

At the same time, Bruce was growing unhappy with the way Jahn was handling the commission for Cityspire, whose concrete skeleton was already emerging from its wooden sheathing at the rate of two floors a week. Bruce had wanted an impressive, elegant building, and Cityspire was all of that. But he had reluctantly come to the conclusion that Jahn had no conscience about money. Not that he was dishonest, just oblivious to the screams of agony from those who had to foot the bill for his perfectionism. Jahn's attention to details such as the arrangement of buttons on the elevator control panels was legendary, all the more so after the Cityspire cabs had to be redesigned to accommodate the more pleasing three-across panels instead of narrow stacks of two-across buttons. From its rosy granite base to its glittering dome, every facet of the many-sided building had a little grace note, a reveal or a chamfer that elevated both its beauty and cost beyond the ordinary. "If God is in the details," Luk Sun muttered one day, "then Jahn is practicing to be a saint." And if God wasn't in the details, he thought to himself, it was too bad, because nobody else was going to see this stuff 700 feet off the ground.

On issues of architectural integrity Jahn was unyielding. A long struggle over the choice of color for the glass and metal parts of the Cityspire curtain wall ended in a victory for Jahn's choice, green, a color Bruce dislikes. There is a seeming paradox here. Bruce takes design seriously. He is meticulous about his wardrobe and surroundings. His office shows a partiality to modern furniture in rich, dramatically grained woods and polished black marble. But Bruce is scrupulous about not letting his personal taste interfere with his business judgment. Jahn correctly foresaw—indeed, helped bring about—the emergence of green in the late 1980s as the color of choice in the Manhattan skyline. Once he was convinced of the rightness of Helmut's position, Eichner was able to put aside his own feelings about the color. But he doesn't see why his architects shouldn't be able to make the same sacrifice. "Go up to the forty-sixth floor of this building where it sets back and look out the window," Bruce said bitterly. "You'll see a wall. A parapet. The wall is there for the *design intent.* It's there to *carry a line.* Helmut Jahn ought to be buried in that wall, and there should be a plaque there, so that everyone who buys an apartment on that floor can look out at it and know that they're looking at a wall instead of Central Park so that Helmut Jahn can rest easy knowing that his *artistic integrity* is intact."

Two firms were under consideration to replace Murphy/Jahn. One was Clark Tribble Harris & Li, a firm that was new to New York but since its founding in 1973 had done some notable work in the South; its most significant credit was the Georgetown Park development in Washington, with 210,000 prosperously bustling square feet of retail space. The other was the largest and best-known architectural partnership in America—Skidmore, Owings & Merrill.

On Christmas Eve, 1986, Gerald Li, the design partner for Clark, Tribble, came with several associates to a meeting at Eichner's offices on Madison Avenue. More than a dozen people in all crowded around the table in the conference room, which was windowless, stuffy, cluttered with the detritus that collects in developers' offices: fraying rolls of drawings and lost pieces of models, slabs of wood veneer and samples of marble, granite, terrazzo, and ceramic in variously colored squares. Clark, Tribble's drawings for a "Mixed-Use Tower for Times Square" covered the walls. They showed an irregular, roughly **L**-shaped building rising fifty-three stories in 616 feet, with a semicylindrical crown like a Quonset hut on a flat roof. The floor plans were elaborately color-coded by use: residential in yellow, office space gray, theaters orange. Retail was a lovely dusky rose.

It was apparent that a lot of time and effort had gone into the presentation, all of which would be wasted if Clark, Tribble didn't get the job. But this was the norm for architects, who can be frantically busy for months at a time doing work that not only never gets built, it never gets paid for. After just a few minutes of Li's well-rehearsed presentation, Bruce interrupted.

"I want to see if we can frame some issues here," Bruce said, leaning back in his chair and raising a pencil. "This is a retail atrium in a city where retail atriums have tended to die an early and horrible death. You have one big advantage: you don't have to go far for your population. They're wandering back and forth in the street. But Herald Center [a struggling multistory shopping center at 34th Street and Broadway] also has a population. Their problem is, they don't have an identity. You don't know what you're going in there to buy. Trump Tower has a clear upscale image; you don't go in there to buy a T-shirt. And it has Trump himself. But I suspect that three-quarters of the people who walk into it don't buy anything. We want people to come into this mall to buy, not to shop."

"What is wrong with Trump Tower," Li said, "is he didn't make it a public, urban space, but the living room of a king. It's intimidating. There's a lack of visibility. I still don't know what shops are in that building. We've got to make this one like a New York street. We believe in the Arquitectonica approach, bringing the outdoors inside."

Bruce: "The question is, did Trump put his feet up and say, 'I want a king's living room'—or did people look at it afterwards and say that's what you've got? It's amazing to me that you have hundreds of projects going on at any one time in New York, and I'll bet that 80 percent of them are substantially completed without market research."

"We work in sixteen states, and New York is not like anywhere else in the country. New York believes it knows everything," Li said.

"See, that's the difference with this organization," Bruce said. "We don't have all the answers, I just think we're a little better at asking the right questions."

Li returned to his presentation. Bruce listened for a while longer. He asked some questions. Soon he had heard enough. "Thank you very much, Gerry," he said heartily, "a very interesting presentation."

Li appeared surprised. "I think, ummm, just to sum up, that this firm has a unique philosophy and approach that is especially well suited to a project that is as sensitive and demanding as this ..." he said hastily, as his associates began unpinning the drawings and rolling them up. Bruce was standing, a picture of cordial attention. Handshakes. Goodbyes. Bruce sat down again.

"Let's talk about what's important," he said briskly, as soon as the architects were out of the room. "Do we choose one architect for the whole building, or is this special enough to choose one for retail? Have we decided that?"

"What are the integration problems with two architects?" Howard asked.

Alice: "You have to put one in a subordinate position and make the other one in charge."

Bruce: "No, you can be in charge. Look, these guys don't know anything about offices. Let's get a first-class office architect for that and if we use these guys, we'll let them do what they know."

Skidmore, Owings & Merrill, founded in Chicago in 1936, is the most distinguished firm of architects in the world. It is distinguished not only for the number and significance of the buildings it has built, but also for its dedication to an idea, the idea of Modernism. So strong was SOM's commitment to the philosophy enunciated in post–World War I Germany by Ludwig Mies van der Rohe, Walter Gropius, and others that the firm was once nicknamed the Three Blind Mies. The philosophy was of an architecture that expresses the highest intellectual ideals of the twentieth century, an architecture as pure as a prime number, as beautiful as an I-beam in its perfect fit of form and function. It was an architecture for an era that had looked inside the atom, in light of which it seemed absurdly petty and even dishonest for architects to be fooling around with dentillations and flutes and fillets on columns whose original function—to support the roof—could now be done so much more efficiently and forthrightly with modern materials. In their lack of superficial ornamentation and the crisp angles of their sheer glass walls, Skidmore's buildings expressed confidence, honesty, and unity of purpose. In their rejection of the hierarchy of base, shaft, and spire that marked an earlier generation of skyscrapers, in the monotony of their window modules, whose shimmering surfaces might conceal the chairman of the board or a blank column enclosure, they expressed a clear vision of modern social organization: each functionary bounded by the mullions of his designated square, like boxes in a life-sized Table of Organization.

In 1952, SOM's New York design partner Gordon Bunshaft electrified the world of commercial real estate with his first important office tower, Lever House, a twenty-one-story-high slab of glass and metal on the west side of Park Avenue between East 53rd and East 54th streets. Set in a blockwide plaza, the building represented a radical and welcome break with the Park Avenue streetscape of shoulder-to-shoulder masonry apartment houses. Lever House also was influential in establishing what came to be known as the International Style as the preferred—indeed, for a long time virtually the only—choice for important new corporate office buildings not just in New York but across the country. That the style degenerated into the cheap and banal glass boxes that littered the American corporate landscape in the 1960s was not really SOM's fault. The firm of Emery Roth & Sons, which designed seventy-seven midtown Manhattan office buildings in the forty years after World War II—roughly five times as many as Skidmore and perhaps half the total—undoubtedly deserves most of the responsibility. But that was a distinction sometimes lost on the public, which viewed Skidmore as synonymous with glass-and-metal buildings.

The reaction to Modernism that set in around 1980 caught Skidmore's New York practice unprepared. The re-emergence of stone on office building façades was a disturbing development in its own right. The uses to which it was put—the odd blend of historical allusion and fantasy that came to be called Postmodernism—was downright shocking. "You've got to understand, modern architecture is not just a style but a belief," one SOM partner explained. "A belief about the kinds of materials appropriate to twentieth-century buildings, a commitment to honesty of expression. For those who really believed, they could not conceive of any other way of doing architecture." One of those who really believed was the great Bunshaft, who held sway in New York until his retirement in 1979. It was only after Bunshaft was gone that the Skidmore partners attempted to make peace with Postmodernism. A panel of four mostly academic architects assembled by the editors of the Harvard Architecture Review confronted a team of SOM architects at the Harvard Club. As recounted in the official company history of that period (a sober, silver-jacketed 400-page volume with text in English and German), "SOM's recent buildings were neither abstractions nor uncaring about urban and historic context, but SOM's critics wanted more. Many rejected early modern architecture's measures of efficiency, economy and mechanism. ... What the Postmodernists wanted was never clear. Sometimes they fashioned shiny worlds of exposed machinery, [they] ornamented façades with whimsical stylistic quotations, and manipulated masses and voids to butt contrasted scales. ...

"However entertaining, those discussions did not deflect SOM from its aesthetic heritage."

Tom Wolfe gives another account of this meeting in his popular history of modern architecture, *From Bauhaus to Our House.* "At no time," he writes, "did it seem to strike anyone present as funny that here were the leading architects—commercially—in the field of large public building in America, and they were willingly ... sitting still for a dressing-down by four architects who, between them, could claim few buildings larger than a private house."

At the same time, SOM faced another challenge from the changing nature of its practice. Its great office buildings had been built as showcases for large corporations—clients who made money in some other business and didn't necessarily expect to turn a profit on their headquarters as well. Lever House, for example, had its plaza at the expense of literally acres of floor space; it got less than 220,000 square feet of offices on a site almost as big as the one Bruce was building on. This was a factor of zoning, which at that time encouraged skyscrapers to be built out to the sidewalk, but to occupy smaller and smaller fractions of their site the higher they went. This typically resulted in the successively smaller tiers of floors called the "wedding-cake" look. A tall, straight-sided building, therefore, which of necessity would use just a fraction of the site available at its base, would also necessarily sacrifice much of its FAR. The zoning code was changed in 1961 to make this tower-in-a-plaza design less uneconomical. But until then only a very rich and self-assured corporation would have given away all that rentable floor space just to make an esthetic statement. It was only in the mid-1960s that, after much soul-searching, SOM's New York office designed its first speculative building. By the 1980s, though, these had become the bulk of the practice. As the company history observed unhappily, "even SOM was limited in how far it might lead a developer towards artistic patronage, or press his office tower to benefit an urban neighborhood. Artistic integrity as a way to profit had to be demonstrated every day."

The man SOM chose to lead its New York practice through these difficult times was David M. Childs, who came to New York in 1985 after fourteen years in Skidmore's Washington office, the last ten of them as senior design partner. That is a descriptive title, not a formal one; in theory all partners of Skidmore were equal, but Childs took the high-profile job in New York with a mandate to save its endangered skyscraper franchise. Childs—a graduate of Yale and the Yale School of Architecture—was in many ways the total opposite of Helmut Jahn. Jahn was magnificently dapper, temperamental, scintillating, Germanic in manner and accent; Childs was taller, tweedier, with a charm that a few years earlier (he was in his mid-forties at the time) must have been boyish and now was ripening to urbanity. Like many successful architects, Childs was a spellbinding speaker. Architecture is the only plastic art that is not practiced in its finished medium. Between even the greatest architect and immortality stands the inescapable figure of the owner, who must be placated before the effusions of genius can be rendered in steel and glass and stone. In the Eichner-Childs relationship, Childs held an edge in delicacy and elegance of expression, while Eichner overmatched him in strategizing and in sheer forensic bloodlust; in their own ways, though, they were equal in tenaciousness.

As a designer, Childs had been influenced at Yale by Robert Venturi, whose 1966 book, *Complexity and Contradiction in Modern Architecture,* was a seminal work in the Postmodern movement. Washington is a low-rise city with a lot of classically inspired nineteenth-century architecture, and Childs found it a congenial place to work. He was popular in official circles and got some of the most prestigious commissions the federal government had to offer, including the renovation of the Washington Mall; Constitution Gardens, a new park adjoining the Lincoln Memorial; and improvements to the historic railroad stations on the Washington-Boston Amtrak line.

To no one's surprise, Childs quickly established himself in New York City. He joined the board of the Municipal Art Society, and within a short time Skidmore had landed some major New York commissions, including the plum of William Zeckendorf's Worldwide Plaza, a huge office and residential complex occupying the entire block between Eighth and Ninth Avenues at 51st Street where the old Madison Square Garden had stood. Not long afterward, *Fortune* magazine featured

Childs as one of seven corporate "Architects for the 1990s." (Jahn was another.) Childs—dubbed "The Classicist"—was photographed looking pensive, sitting on the highly patterned marble floor of an office building that seemed to have been inspired by a Renaissance palazzo. "Childs loves columns, arches, and wedding-cake skyscrapers," the text noted approvingly. Cynthia Thompson, who had worked for Skidmore before coming to Eichner Properties, suggested his name, and Luk Sun brought him around to meet Bruce. Bruce took advantage of the meeting to deliver a full-blown monologue on his conception of the proper role of the architect vis-à-vis the developer, based on his educational experience with Jahn.

"I don't want a designer who's going to think of this building as a monument to himself," Bruce warned Childs.

And Childs, pragmatic as always, quickly responded: "That's fine with me. What's important is not to have a lot of nice drawings, but to get it built."

11

Before a new building could rise on the block, though, what was there would have to come down. This is the first step in the great cycle of demolition, excavation, and construction by which the city renews itself in an endless churning of dirt. Each step along the way is accompanied by paperwork. All the building code violations on the existing building had to be discharged. A clean slate with the Buildings Department would be a prerequisite for eventually occupying the new building on the site. One might imagine that a building that was scheduled to be torn down would merit less attention from the Department of Buildings, but this seemed not to be the case; as the building emptied, the zeal of inspectors for finding obstructions on fire stairs and missing bulbs in exit signs was redoubled. Luk Sun was fanatical about these. He instructed Alice that each fine had to be paid, and not just paid but the payment certified and the discharge of the violation verified, as if driven by fear that the project might be stopped forever by a violation that could not be cleared because the building in which it occurred no longer existed. In truth, this has never actually happened, but if there is one principle that guides people who do business with the city government, it is to assume that there is no act too irrational to be perpetrated by the bureaucracy.

The buildings that had to come down were the following: the office building, with the theater lobby on its ground floor; the theater itself, behind the office building to the east; a six-story brick annex on 46th Street; the Howard Johnson's restaurant at 1546 Broadway; and 1544 Broadway, the outparcel in the middle of the block—except that by the time demolition was supposed to begin, in March 1987, the sale of 1544 was still not final, and the store on the ground floor was still in possession. The store's owner had signed an agreement to get out by the end of April, but apparently had a change of heart when he realized he had given away cooperation that he could have sold instead. So he had filed suit in Landlord-Tenant Court, seeking to stay an additional sixty days. His lawyer implied he could change his mind for "serious money," which is another way of saying "$100,000."

Luk Sun wanted to offer $50,000.

"Screw him," Bruce retorted. "Go the court route. I can't see paying him $50,000, as a matter of principle and a matter of tactics. You can get this guy out whenever you want, for dollars. He doesn't want to stay, he doesn't have a lucrative business to protect."

"And I'm concerned," persisted Luk Sun, "that we'll be sitting here April 30 and we'll be saying, now what's our strategy?"

Bruce considered this for a moment. "If you want to do it now," he said, "then let's look for the bottom. Let's offer him $10,000. If the number gets too high, we'll take our chances in court."

All of the other buildings were, of course, empty. The directory in the lobby of 1540 was blank, the nut-brown marble looking gloomier than ever. The elevators still ran when someone pushed one of the Art Deco call buttons, a small round brass plaque mounted to rock up and down on a larger one. The banks of relays in the roof shed would begin a desultory exchange of clicks, and then one of the cabs would lurch into motion, drowsily hunting the source of the disturbance. On an upper floor, the elevator opened onto a warren of small offices, linked by an elaborate network of corridors, doorways, and sliding-panel windows leading to a rear room that had been the home of something called the Universal Costume Company. The floor was covered with discarded theatrical garments: a black-and-silver feather boa; several elaborately embroidered sombreros; a dingy tangle of lace petticoats. Through the long-unwashed windows, one could see over a jumble of grimy rooftops to the gleaming towers of Sixth Avenue.

The building had served for almost seventy years, and now it awaited only someone to pull the plug. That's not just a figure of speech. The city sensibly required shutting off the gas and electricity before tearing down a building. Or, more precisely, it required a letter from Con Edison certifying that gas and electric service had been terminated before it would issue a demolition permit. This task Con Ed would entrust to none other than its own technicians, whom it dispatched according to its own rules and in its own good time. Thus in early March, 1987 work on the entire multi-hundred-million-dollar Broadway State project was stalled before it could begin, awaiting Con Ed to send a man with a wrench. Other developers, it is rumored, have been driven literally crazy by delays of this kind. Just two years earlier and a block away on West 44th Street, the developer Harry Macklowe had held an option to buy two of the cheap residential hotels known as SRO's (for single-room-occupancy), whose rapid conversion to more lucrative uses was said to be exacerbating New York's housing shortage. With just days to go before a city moratorium on razing SRO's took effect, there was still no utility shutoff. The demolition company hired by Macklowe therefore began tearing down the buildings without a permit. The hue and cry from an outraged public was intense, especially on the part of *The New York Times,* whose editors would have walked right down the fatal block on their way to drinks at the Algonquin. Macklowe, who claimed he had no knowledge of the illegal demolition, was not charged with a crime. But the city sued him for $10 million, and he ended up making a $2 million contribution toward housing for the homeless, a sum only slightly offset by the thousands of dollars in campaign contributions self-righteously returned to Macklowe by the mayor and comptroller. But he got to build his building, and just to show he wasn't embarrassed by any of this, he named it after himself, the Hotel Macklowe.

Meanwhile, 1540 Broadway was being laid out for dismemberment. Already the walls had been sliced open, the asbestos insulation carefully removed from the pipe chases and sealed in plastic bags. A lattice of steel rods was rising up the sides of the building; when it reached the roofline, a thick course of wooden planks would be laid for the men to stand on when they knocked the walls down. Since the city did not recognize this as a building under demolition, Mitchell had obtained the permit for this scaffold under the subterfuge of repairing the building's cornice. A wooden fence around the site kept pedestrians at bay, and provided an ideal medium for posters promoting movies, record albums, rock concerts, and lectures by Indian swamis. The surge in midtown construction had as one of its spinoffs a boom in this minor branch of the advertising industry. Starting around midnight, a poster company could slap up 2,000 posters before dawn, and get paid one dollar for each. Occasionally noncommercial messages would appear as well. For a while the fence was stenciled every few yards with the unexplained message "Overeating Causes Death." If this was directed at the construction workers, it seemed not to make much of an impression.

The demolition contract was awarded to Associated Wrecking, Inc., of New Jersey. Associated was run by Artie Baris and Ira Pollack, second-generation partners in a business founded at the end of World War II by their fathers. Many of Baris's relatives also ran demolition companies in New Jersey whose names started with the letter "A," including the suggestively named Avalanche Wrecking Corp. Baris was perpetually tanned, with a full head of curly dark hair and a collection of impressive gold jewelry. He had mastered the remarkable trick of walking across a field of smashed bricks and chunks of concrete studded with rusty prongs of steel reinforcing without leaving so much as a damp spot on his suit pants. Ira was the inside man, dressed most days in a windbreaker and chino slacks.

It should come as no surprise that the members of Local 95 of the International Brotherhood of Housewreckers are as a rule the biggest men in construction. Demolition is one of the few jobs left in New York City in which a man's worth is still measured by how much he can lift and how hard he can hit. The wrecking ball that New York City buildings are said to face is usually a metaphorical one. You demolish a building in midtown Manhattan by hitting it with a hammer, by prying it apart with iron bars, and by cutting the steel skeleton with torches. In other cities wreckers may let gravity do most of the work, cutting or dynamiting the columns at the base and letting the building fall into a heap. Those places usually don't have subways running within a yard of the site, though. And in any case, if you took down 1540 Broadway all at once like that, where would it go, except right out onto Broadway? The limiting factor in clearing a site in New York City is not usually demolition as such, but storing and disposing of the steel, the scrap iron, and the rubble of concrete, brick, plaster, and wood fibers known to the trade as "dirt."

The other remarkable thing about demolition is how utterly empirical it is. Associated does not even employ an engineer. "If you asked an engineer to tear down a building," says Ellis, "he'd spend six months studying the plans for the building, and you'd never start." That is, if he could find the plans; Ira has had so little success searching for records of prewar construction in New York that he has given up looking. Even if he had them there would be no guarantee that what was shown in the drawings corresponded to what was physically in place in 1987. One goes by accumulated experience and the evidence of his own eyes. Even so, death lurks in every corner of these rotten old buildings. In that same spring of 1987 three of Associated's men were injured at another job just a few blocks away, when the beam they were standing on collapsed onto a pile of rubble twenty feet below. The building was bearing-wall construction, meaning that the beam was not tied to a supporting column, but held up by the masonry of the wall itself. "It just pulled out of the wall," a shaken and sober Artie Baris explained the next day. "It's supposed to be sitting on at least three courses of brick. It was sitting on one."

Wrecking is always dangerous. Ironworkers go higher above the street, but as Ira observed, "they're ironworkers because they'd rather walk on a clean three-foot beam than a dirty eight-inch one." Perhaps not coincidentally, of all the trades that were to work on the Broadway State Project, demolition had the highest proportion of blacks, except for security guards. Not only were blacks a majority of the demolition work force, but within it they held the most prestigious jobs. The "barmen" swinging hammers and the "pickers" sorting the debris into piles on the ground were mostly recent Polish immigrants. Union wages were seventeen dollars an hour with double time after seven hours. The men worked from seven in the morning until six at night. Some weeks Ira's bookkeeper drew up checks for over fifteen hundred dollars to each of the men on the Broadway State job.

This was a large building to be demolished, but its height posed no unusual difficulties. The hard part of the Broadway State job would be the movie theater. The theater was a box eighty feet high, 100 feet wide, and around 150 feet long, with no intermediate columns to support the roof. Modern engineers have a variety of ingenious techniques to suspend roofs across such long spans. But the solution in 1918 would have been to treat it like a big steel bridge and span it with truss girders—two parallel steel beams, one above the other, with diagonal bracing triangulating the space between them. One morning Ira and John Ellis climbed to the top balcony of the theater, and went through an unmarked door and up a ladder to emerge in a vast, dim space crossed by enormous trusses extending far into the gloom. There were three each running transverse and longitudinally; they were covered with a thick fireproof coating of lathe and plaster, and they were among the biggest girders Ira had ever seen in a building, ranging in depth from eight to nearly twenty feet.

"I'll bet there's fifty tons of steel in that big one," Ira muttered.

"Bloody big trusses," agreed Ellis.

"How the hell am I going to get those things out of here?"

"Very carefully, I should think," said Ellis.

Eventually, after several weeks of frustration, a crew came to cast 1540 adrift from the Northeast power grid, and—with the letter from Con Ed, certifications of asbestos removal, rodent extermination, insurance, workmen's compensation, and several other essential documents—the demolition permit followed. Around the same time, the third week of April, there was good news about 1544. Lydia had offered the subtenant $10,000. A few days later she reported that he had dropped his demand to $37,000. "I can't believe it," she said delightedly. "Nobody goes from $100,000 to $37,000. I think he sees he's on poor legal ground and just wants to pay his lawyer and maybe have $10,000 left over in his pocket." But Luk Sun, who at one point had urged settling for $50,000, did not jump at the chance to make a deal for $37,000. Lydia agreed. "You can never just meet their price," she said. "Then they think they didn't ask enough and they'll come back and hit you for whatever they can carry away. We'll go up to $20,000 and see what they do."

The demolition was mapped out carefully ahead of time by John and Ira. A large building is demolished from the top down and the inside out. The first step was for men to chop a twelve-by-twelve-foot hole in each floor of 1540. Debris pitched down this open chute would land in a heap in what had been the theater lobby. One Sunday in late May Ira closed 45th Street for the day and brought in a 200-ton crane with a 300-foot boom, and put six machines on the top of 1540 Broadway. The machines were two John Deere frontloaders; a Bobcat, which is a small wheeled vehicle with a pair of strong pincerlike jaws; and three hoe rams. The hoe rams look like small, self-propelled artillery pieces. They are mounted on tracks, and a man stands behind them and drives them with an array of levers and valves; the business end is a kind of horizontal turret that carries a thick steel hammer. The whole thing is run by high-pressure air brought from a compressor in the street in thick yellow hoses that festoon the wreckage of the building and occasionally break loose from their couplings, hissing like banshees and writhing violently across the floor like large, dangerous snakes.

A hoe ram is really just a big jackhammer. Its name suggests something that pulls back and smashes down like a pile driver, but that is misleading; rather, it seems to bury itself in a concrete floor with a rapid burrowing motion. At such times it resembles less a piece of military equipment than a giant bloodsucking insect.

One day early in June Mario Tarrant, Associated's foreman, climbed fourteen flights, as he did half a dozen times a day, to where the building now ended. The original office entry was boarded up, the lobby a shambles; to enter the building Mario went up a makeshift set of stairs on Broadway and climbed in through a second-floor window. Crossing to the stairwell, he caught glimpses of the chute, where chunks of debris rained constantly, amid showers of sparks from the cutting torches and a gray drizzle of dust mixed with the water intended to keep the dust down. It might have been the back office of hell. The sixteenth floor was now open to the sky, all interior partitions demolished, hoe rams beating out what remained of the concrete slab. One level below, the John Deere was charging across the floor, sweeping the fallen chunks of concrete down the chute. Mario emerged onto the fifteenth floor with a tremendous bellow intended to warn the John Deere operator not to grind him to mush or shove him down the chute. To reach the topmost floor he climbed a steep, makeshift ramp of I-beams. He bent over to grab the outer flanges of the beams with his thick gauntlets and scrabbled up the broad middle part of the beam, the web. Later, when the floor was almost gone, the machines would ride these beams down to the fifteenth floor to begin again the cycle of destruction.

The working floor of a building under demolition has a harsh beauty, like a desert. The Bobcat picked up a steel beam in its jaws, shook it a few times like a terrier with prey, and then, twirling gracefully on its close-set wheels, dropped it delicately down the chute, where in a few seconds it would smash to the ground with a hideous clang. Bare steel columns stood silhouetted against the sky. Chunks of concrete clung to webs of steel bars, which in turn were draped mosslike over the surviving beams. In among this a length of plumbing pipe, bent and crushed in several places, had jammed; from it depended a six-foot stretch of electrical cable, whose outer sheathing had begun to unwind spiralwise, while a fixture still miraculously connected provided just enough weight to keep the whole coincidental contraption in precarious balance. Someone pointed this out to Ira, who was stalking the floor, muttering into a hand-held radio.

"What are you pointing to?" he asked suspiciously.

"That over there. It's a mobile. Calder must have worked in demolition."

Ira squinted, then shrugged. "It's in the eye of the beholder, I guess," he said.

The outside walls on this level had mostly been pulled down, but a section on the north face of the building still stood. Men with hammers broke through the plaster and masonry to expose the columns and beams running through the wall. The steel was covered with a thick furry coat of cement fireproofing, intended to keep it from softening in the heat of a fire. In the same way the coating would keep the steel from being cut by a torch. A hoe ram trundled up and, raising its turret, laid bare the steel with a few quick strokes. Men with torches cut the beams, isolating a thirty-foot section of wall; then they cut almost through the columns at a forty-five-degree angle, leaving them attached by a small flap of steel on the inside flange. A length of steel cable was looped around the upper beam. Its ends were shackled to a Deere and to one of the hoe rams. Mario climbed in the seat of the Deere and, with a whoop, drove backwards across the floor at the same time that the man behind the hoe ram shoved his machine into reverse. The cables went taut; the wall buckled in the center and then fell down onto the slab with a crash. Men rushed forward with hoses, as if at the scene of a disaster, to quell the cloud of gray dust.

"I'm proud of what I do," Mario exclaimed, climbing off the seat of the Deere. "I don't like to say it 'cause it doesn't always work out that way, but I'm really pretty good."

Not long afterwards, the Housing Court judge, having weighed the plea of the tenant in 1544, ordered him out by the end of May. Having gambled and lost, he forfeited the right to get anything. "I can't believe it," said Lydia. "The last tenant is finally going to be out."

"Get a sheriff there to make sure it happens," Howard advised. "It's worth the $600. See, sometimes the law does what it says it's supposed to. He cost himself $20,000."

Lydia: "Yeah, that's why I think he'll come back at us again ..."

"Forget it, he's dead. The train left the station."

And just as well, because a few days after he finally packed his remaining T-shirts and souvenir teaspoons off to more hospitable surroundings, two men walked out onto the scaffolding on the north side of 1540. They were carrying a crowbar with which they tried to reach a large vertical shaft or duct that ran up the building wall. The bar they had wouldn't quite reach, so they went back for a longer one, longer than a man is tall, and with this they poked and pried for a few minutes until a layer of bricks about ten feet by six came loose and fell as one piece. The chunk, after falling more than 100 feet, hit the roof of 1544, and the impact collapsed the roof and the next two floors below and blew the back wall off like a bomb. The men looked down at it for a moment, shrugged, and went back to their job.

12

For the architects, the Broadway State Project represented one of the most sought-after opportunities of the 1980s, a "contextual" building. Elsewhere—in Houston, for example—architects could design "object" buildings in the isolation of their traffic-bound islands, pure forms rising into the sky from a regular, flat, neutral, empty square. Many architects, it is true, confronting the limitless possibilities of unbounded Euclidean space, chose as their preferred form a rectangular solid of the approximate proportions of a shoebox stood on end. But that would clearly not be possible in Times Square, even if someone wanted to do it. This site called for a more sophisticated idea, or theme, that which architects refer to in school as the "parti." Whatever was built here, on this misshapen plot Bruce had cleaved and hacked from its encumbering tangle of trusts and heirs and leaseholders, would have to look as if it belonged exactly on the corner of Broadway and West 45th Street, and nowhere else on the globe.

Certain things were obvious as soon as the architects began their consideration of the site. They faced, in addition to Bruce's complex and rigorous program, the stringent midtown zoning, overlaid with a whole other set of specific regulations for Times Square. The overall massing would take the form of a tower rising out of a sixty-foot-high base, because that was what was required by zoning. In general, the tower would have to be set back from the building line fifteen feet on the side streets, and fifty feet on the western, or Broadway, face (although, if its outline were irregular, a portion of it could come as close as thirty-five feet). The base would have to fill the site entirely. That was a radical change from even five years earlier. For two decades after the 1961 zoning revision, the city had promoted the construction of office towers modeled on the pattern of Lever House and its even more honored successor, the Seagram Building. The results were visible all up and down Park, Third, and Sixth avenues. The slab-sided towers, once so liberating, were now regarded as banal and dull; the plazas, conceived of as a welcome refuge from the bustle of the streets, were derided as ugly, sterile, and alienating, parking lots for pedestrians. Now along the great avenues the city required architects to maintain the "street wall" of building façades. This regulation was particularly stringent in the Times Square area. The phenomenological character the city sought was not just crowds as such, but crowds in motion, thronging the sidewalks on their urgent missions of business or pleasure, like the flickering bulbs of the great signs, chasing themselves endlessly around the block. If you wanted to sit on a bench and read a book, you could go to Central Park.

In another provision, diabolically calculated to make it impossible to line Broadway with boring office lobbies, no single-use—a lobby, a restaurant, a shop—could occupy more than 20 percent of the building's total avenue frontage. In the case of the Broadway State building, with 180 feet on Broadway, that amounted to thirty-six feet. The effect of these regulations—narrow frontage permitted on Broadway, the tower set back toward the east—was to move the office entrance off Broadway altogether, around the corner onto West 45th Street. The city also required a "through-block connection" for new midtown projects with frontage on two side streets. This was a covered pedestrian corridor at ground level intended to relieve the congestion on the avenue sidewalks. In some areas, such as the blocks between Fifth Avenue and Park in the East Fifties, it was possible to travel a considerable distance through arcades, gallerias, and lobbies, emerging into public thoroughfares only for an eighty-foot dash through the fleets of bicycle messengers hurtling by at forty miles an hour. New York had striped pedestrian walks at the corners and "Don't Walk" signs, like any other city. But city planners had finally acknowledged that the population was so accustomed to seeing motor vehicles in gridlocked impotence that it had ceased to regard them as dangerous. Thus in Times Square, while the tourists stood like sheep at the corners, the natives could go bustling about their business on their own parallel network of unmarked crosswalks.

The through-block connection had to be at least 100 feet east of Broadway. So, logically, it would divide the ground floor in half. On the west (Broadway) side would be the retail atrium. The eastern half would have the office lobby on 45th Street, and behind that on the 46th Street side would be the loading docks and the entrance to the parking garage.

Regarding the tower, it would, of course, be tall—or, more precisely, it would have the quality of appearing to be tall, known as "verticality." That's the first thing every developer asks for, and Bruce was no exception. Bruce was accustomed to building apartment towers, whose slender profiles were the natural consequence of requiring a window in every room. Looking at the big square chunk of Manhattan real estate he had bought, he worried about erecting something that would look somehow squat. A developer's personal, emotional satisfaction from a building often seems to derive mostly from its height. Bruce himself, in an interview in *New York* magazine, referred to this trait as "weenie-waving." Tenants, too, invariably equate height above ground level with prestige.

But the actual height of a building is constrained by several factors. Cost, naturally: a taller building is more expensive in a thousand different ways, including a need for faster elevators and a stronger structural frame to resist the increased wind load. Height also must be balanced against floor-plate size. With the FAR fixed, increasing the number of stories in a building necessarily made each floor smaller. But prime tenants—those who take, say, 200,000 square feet or more—don't want to distribute themselves over too many floors. So, the *second* thing every developer asks for is a big floor plate. The golden mean for most office uses seemed to lie in a range of roughly 25,000 to 40,000 square feet per floor. If the floors were bigger, corner offices would be inconveniently far from the elevators. The advantage of "verticality" is that it doesn't cost anything, and it is limited only by the imagination of the architect and the gall of the developer in applying tricks such as inflating the floor numbers by skipping a bunch of them at the bottom of the building. Trump Tower has a five-level atrium, not counting the basement, but the office floors above it miraculously begin at fourteen.

Bruce's other requirement was that the building have some pizzazz. "You don't stand on the corner of Broadway and 45th Street in a gray flannel suit," he advised David. "You have to have an architectural solution appropriate to the area." But not, Bruce hastened to add, at the cost of alienating even the most conservative of potential tenants. It was impossible to stress this point too much. The building should be elegant, corporate, correct, uncontroversial. Service businesses such as law firms don't want to make a statement with their architecture; it sends the wrong message to their clients. That's why you almost never see a building named for a law firm. David should keep in mind that, in a sense, this building was competing for tenants with Park Avenue, and would have to overcome the perception that it was in a less-desirable part of the city, a perception that would be reinforced by a design that could by any stretch of the imagination be considered flashy or cheap. A design that might be architecturally appropriate for Times Square might be unacceptably radical for the potential clients of the building. David should get used to that idea right away. "Oh," said David cheerfully, "I absolutely agree. The ugliest building in the world to me is one that's empty."

Skidmore's own office was in the *Daily News* building, on East 42nd Street. The architects, on the eleventh floor, shared an elevator bank with the seventh-floor city room, and the two professions sometimes crossed paths in the late-night hours that are common to both—for, although a finished building was still three years distant, the calendar was already studded with benchmarks and deadlines that would have to be met along the way. Only full-fledged partners had private offices at SOM. David, in coming to New York, determined to have what he called "a very non-SOM office." There was no desk or drawing table, but a billowy sofa, an Oriental screen, a large glass coffee table with, he pointed out, a yellow metal base, not chrome.

The studio, where the designers worked, was in contrast very SOM: a spare open room two hundred feet long, filled with light from a bank of south-facing windows. The desks were arranged in a series of **U**'s. The theory was that each **U** would be occupied by a project team of five or six people, headed by a senior designer who sat at the base of the **U**. In practice, each team was assembled ad hoc for a given project, and people grew attached to their desks and resisted moving. But that was only in practice. The official SOM decorative touch was a series of grape ivy plants in highly polished steel planters at regular intervals along the tops of file cabinets. Models, drawings, and elaborate colored computer renderings were also scattered about. A pleasant, subdued bustle filled the room all day and into the evening, when it gradually gave way to a bitter, desperate frenzy. Architects who work all night on a project are said to be doing a "charrette." The term, David explained, comes from the Beaux Arts, where periodically a bell would ring and a cart ("charrette") would pass down the aisles, collecting designs to be graded; a student who ran alongside the wagon putting the final wash on his drawing was said to be working *"en charrette."*

As senior designer for the Broadway State Project, David chose a promising associate named Audrey Matlock, and installed over her an associate partner, Bill Hellmuth, who was regarded as something of a protégé of Childs's. One evening in early 1987, not yet late or frantic enough to be considered a charrette, Audrey sat down with a soft pencil and a piece of yellow trace paper and began to sketch. The finished products of architecture are plans (diagrams showing the horizontal arrangement of grounds or floors), sections, and elevations (or façades). But at this very early stage Audrey liked to sketch in three dimensions, to get a better feel for how the building would actually look. To guide her, she had a series of massing diagrams that showed different ways in which the building's bulk, including the FAR transferred from the Lyceum, could fit within the height and setback limits. There are zoning consultants who specialize in these calculations. Bruce had a whole set of these studies done even before he bought the site. But it was Audrey's habit to do the zoning study over herself, the better to understand the particularities of the site, so she could torture herself with the thought of what the city wouldn't let her build there.

In the Modern tradition, the architects of Skidmore, Owings & Merrill do not acknowledge the existence of distinctive individual styles. Modernism was not a "style" of architecture, nor did it contain "styles" within it. It was revealed truth, and therefore the end of style; its disciples were anonymous laborers among the pure planes and angles of God's parti. Accordingly, in theory at least, work emerged as the product of the office, not any individual within it. Doing business this way also had some practical advantages for the partners and employees of Skidmore, Owings & Merrill. While architectural practices often don't outlive their name partners, SOM continued to prosper long after the retirements of Skidmore, Owings, and Merrill. But by the 1980s that tradition had begun to break down. "The people I interview out of architectural school today don't want to spend the rest of their lives as acolytes at the shrine of SOM," Audrey said, "—at least, not any of the ones you'd be interested in hiring."

Certainly, that was never Audrey's intention. She had come to Skidmore from the very avant-garde firm of Eisenman, Robertson, astonishing her classmates at Yale. With Eisenman she had worked on a lot of competitions, and two projects that actually got built, a housing project in West Berlin and a factory to make diesel engines in Columbus, Indiana. The plant was intended to be the setting for an experiment in

Japanese-style worker-management cooperation. The workers, however, weren't sure they cared for cooperating with management. Somehow Audrey drew the assignment of trying to win them over. She got just friendly enough that when one of the workers shot and cooked a squirrel, she was invited to the feast.

"That's it," she told Eisenman when she got back to the hotel. "I've eaten my last squirrel for architecture. I'm going back to New York." She had decided that the problem with working with a genius like Eisenman was that her role would always be to help him put his ideas on paper. If you didn't want to be surrounded by geniuses, Audrey thought, SOM was as good a place as any. Anyway, she didn't want to spend her career working on drawings destined for the pages of architecture magazines. Eisenman would eventually design some important buildings, but commercial success eluded him until almost the end of the decade. Audrey wanted to build big buildings. Big buildings would be built in New York; someone would have to design them, and it might as well be her.

At Skidmore, Audrey was regarded as talented, clever, and charming, but somehow indefinably non-SOM. Audrey called attention to herself. She was outspoken rather than deferential. And although SOM would hardly be so petty as to hold an employee accountable for her outside interests, it could not have escaped notice that she rode a motorcycle rather than sailed, and would sometimes dance until dawn after working until midnight.

But, oddly enough, Audrey's architectural beliefs ran to a fairly rigorous Modernism, compared to those of most of her contemporaries at Skidmore. After fighting it for years, she had finally begun to make peace with the fact that she actually liked Sixth Avenue. Not every one of the buildings on it, maybe, but the much-maligned streetscape of mighty slabs in a row, majestic in their uncompromising conformity. You wouldn't want the whole city to look like that, but it was astonishing and awe-inspiring to come upon a half mile of it, developed not in response to some arbitrary plan but by the convergence of the esthetic and practical ideals of a dozen different corporations. Anyway she'd rather have that than a city filled with the despised baubles of the last century. She loathed office buildings with colonnades, turrets and gables and finials, the whole fussy vocabulary of Postmodernism. She liked polished steel, translucent glass, and cool, textured stone in slabs.

Unfortunately, the associate partner on the project, Bill Hellmuth, was a thoroughgoing Postmodern romantic reactionary. Hellmuth was a lanky young Princeton graduate, cut from the same cloth as Childs, pleasant-looking and charming with no distracting air of glamour. He doted on the quaint touches you find in the old apartment houses on Central Park West. Hellmuth's dream office building had turrets and finials and a giant globe topping off the roof. He did some sketches for the Broadway State site like this and proudly showed them around the office. Audrey tried to think of something to say about them. "Gee," she said. That night she stayed late and drew.

Audrey sketched in the base, which filled the whole site. Rising from it she drew two rectangular solids, two masses intersecting and overlapping. The dominant one was approximately square in plan, a strong slender tower, off-centered at the base to bring it as close to Broadway and 45th Street as the law allowed. At the scale Audrey was working in—one inch to fifty feet—it ran to almost a foot on her paper. The subordinate mass was a rectangle, and it was pulled to the opposite, northeast corner of the site. This accomplished two things. It achieved a strong vertical expression without sacrificing the valuable large floors, and it moved the building's visual center of gravity away from 1550 Broadway. To emphasize the second point, she lightly sketched in different wall treatments for the two masses. The side piece, the "bustle," got a relatively flat treatment that did not call attention to itself, while the central tower got a more articulated, assertive look, with strong horizontal bands at intervals up the building. Exactly what those bands should be in life she couldn't say. That is the great thing about drawing at this stage—everything is the same, a pencil line. Then she added one more piece to the building: a rectangular bulge on the west face of the tower, invading the setback to within thirty-five feet of Broadway. It looked like a nose, she thought, and, fulfilling one of the functions of the human nose, it gave the building a clear hierarchy of front and side. She had a sudden vision of someone walking into that space on a late winter afternoon as the signs flared into lurid, pulsing life and the herds of yellow taxis thundered by at six miles an hour far below, and saying to himself, *I have got to have this office.* That ought to make Bruce happy, she thought.

The next day Audrey showed her drawings to some of the junior associates. They drew some elevations, of the Broadway and 45th Street façades, and a couple of floor plans, just to see what they looked like and how a core might fit in them. The floors were of two different sizes, around 25,000 square feet on the lower floors and 15,000 square feet on the upper floors, where the bustle dropped away.

She also gave her sketch to an associate to make a model. SOM has a very state-of-the-art model shop with a computer-controlled laser cutting table. Audrey's previous project, an office building at Fifth Avenue and East 40th Street, had dramatic external trusses in the shape of a circle within a hyperbole. She had earrings made from the plastic models of these trusses and wore them on the day SOM presented the design to the client. But just to study the massing, stiff white paper, cut and scored by hand, was sufficient. Then over the next few days David, Bill, and Audrey looked at all the variations on this scheme. They moved the tower around, and moved the nose back and forth on the face of the tower; they made the bustle higher and lower; they tried the tower with cornices, spires, and penthouses of different sizes and shapes.

"What this building really wants to be," Audrey decided, "is a corner building. That's what we have, a corner site, only the corner happens to take up nine-tenths of the block. What I really would like to do is pull everything right out to Broadway, only the city won't let me."

But something could go right out on Broadway: a sign. Signs were not merely permitted but encouraged on the setbacks. The building had to have signs in any case, and one of the questions in the back of everyone's mind was where to put them without hopelessly blocking the views from the future office tenants' windows. Now a solution presented itself: a flat-sided vertical sign, a long narrow blade perpendicular to the street, running ten stories or so up the front of the tower, visually "pulling" the mass out toward Broadway. Such a sign would have excellent visibility up and down Broadway, with only minimal impact on the views from inside the building. By a curious coincidence, the old 1540 building had once had one as well, a giant vertical billboard that said "Loews State." The architects liked this idea so much that the sign quickly began to grow, until it ran up the entire length of the tower. As it grew it evolved from a flat blade to a three-dimensional truss, a great Tinkertoy concoction of metal struts. In plan, the struts formed an isosceles triangle whose base was the wall of the "nose." Its sides were open trusswork that could be lit, covered with glass, wrapped in fabric, outlined in neon, or hung with advertisements for Pepsi or Toshiba. Its apex was a metal pole as high as the building. Higher, in fact: it ran up beyond the roofline, culminating in an exuberant spire, a giant's spear thrust into the very quivering heart of Manhattan.

"We've pinned the bowtie!" David exclaimed.

There were meetings every week at Eichner's office, and in the third week of March Skidmore came to present this scheme. Audrey, Bill, and David were there, along with an SOM partner named Tom Fridstein. Fridstein practiced executive architecture. He dealt with the client and supervised the staff who produced all the thousands of drawings that would be required to actually build the building, and he sent the bills. This latter function did not endear him to Luk Sun. The associate under him, with the title of project manager, was a tall and soft-spoken young woman named Susanne Churchill. The five architects arrived in two cars, toting their rolls of plans and elevations, and swarmed over the conference room until they had covered every inch of wall space with architecture. "We've got something here that we think you're going to like," Fridstein said genially, "... so we'd like you to sign off on it today so we can get going." He said something like that almost every week, and as usual, everyone laughed.

The architects had also brought a site model, a box showing the surrounding buildings outlined in blank gray plastic. David placed the model of the new building on its base at the corner of 45th Street. "We have done something quite extraordinary on the west elevation here," he said, running a forefinger up the point of the triangle. "This line holds the building line, as you can see when you look down Seventh Avenue from the uptown side, yet the bulk of the building steps back from it. This isn't a point tower, like the Chrysler Building, or the Empire State. This is like a boat. It moves. And right at the bowtie, a very special, very emphatic spike. An exclamation point marking this unique spot in the city. At night it creates a cascade of light into the atrium, which is something you will have that is unique, instead of another crummy waterfall. This will be a great, flashing, exciting, living thing."

Bruce studied the design for a moment. "I'm a little worried about what it will look like during the day, when it's not a great flashing, exciting living thing, which is also when people will probably come to rent office space," he said. "My reaction is not a terrific one to that piece that sticks out in front. It looks like someone stuck something on that building. I don't see the integration there with the rest of the architecture that I would like to see."

"I think we can make that feature really special," David said, "and I don't know what else I can do besides that sign to make the building special."

"I don't know, either," Bruce said. "Can you have that piece as a design element of the building and have it not be a sign?"

"If it invades the setback," Howard pointed out, "it's got to be a sign."

This opened one of the great semantic questions the Broadway State Project would have to resolve: what was a sign? Could you, Bruce inquired, put decorative lights on the building, and call it a sign?

"No," Howard said, "it's got to say something."

"But does it have to say 'Eat at Joe's'?" Audrey asked. "What if you put up a giant Mercedes-Benz logo? The city couldn't object to that."

"Why does it have to advertise something at all?" Hellmuth asked. "What if you spelled out 1540 Broadway in twenty-foot letters?"

Andrea went to her office and returned with a copy of the zoning text. "Sign," she read in the section of definitions. "... is used to announce, direct attention to, or advertise ..."

"*Or!*" Howard exclaimed. "That's a great word, 'or.' Okay, we're directing attention to our building."

"That doesn't bring in any revenue," Luk Sun observed dourly. Over the next year, whenever anyone suggested a tasteful, noncommercial solution to the signage problem, Luk Sun would remind them that they were talking about throwing away a million dollars a year. Then whenever they proposed selling the space to the highest bidder, he would tell them they were jeopardizing $30 million in office rents from people who might not want to work in a building with a can of dog food on the side. This appeared to represent a perfect example of what psychologists call an "approach-avoidance conflict." But to Luk Sun this was simply how you did business. You asked for everything and let the consultants figure out how to give it to you; that was their job. Bruce understood this, of course, and that's why he trusted Luk Sun above almost anyone else, because Luk Sun wasn't embarrassed to ask for everything.

"The problem I'm having," Bruce said, returning to the model, "is I've never seen an exterior metal design I really liked. They look cheap. They make me think of the Beaubourg. That really ruined that part of Paris for me."

"Well," said David, "I think it's possible to have an elegance in metal that's not cheap."

"My second concern is the perception from inside the building. I'm not sure a corporate tenant would want a sign going down the front of the building 500 feet high. I think you might have designed the sign of the century here, but it would take the sign of the next century to get them in."

"Then why are they moving here?" David asked.

"Because they don't want to pay Park Avenue rents."

"Well, you've got an inherent contradiction, if they want Park Avenue here. The city won't let them have it."

Bruce asked Luk Sun for his thoughts. "I don't object at all to the vertical piece as a major design element," Luk Sun said. "But I would not want a sign on that piece. I agree with what Bruce said about the integration of the two elements. If you took that piece off, you wouldn't miss it, and you should. I wonder if you could do something to bring the building out into it. Maybe you could have balconies."

"An office building with balconies!" David exclaimed. "What a great idea!"

"An occupiable sign!" Bill echoed. "I can't wait for the New Year's Eve parties."

"King Kong will climb here next time!"

"So you'll work on that for next time," Bruce said briskly. "I think that's the direction we ought to be going in. Other than that, I'm moderately pleased up to this point. It looks like a nice, buildable building."

"You gave me a twenty-minute speech at the beginning of this project, and I took it to heart," David said. "This is a very rational, reasonable, waterproof building that's buildable."

When Skidmore returned a week later, they had no new drawings to show, but they reported making progress on the problem of visually integrating the prow with the building. The Skidmore approach was to integrate it structurally, in the expectation that the visual integration would necessarily follow. David reported that it appeared the result would be to give the prow a much denser texture of steel structure, more like the Eiffel Tower than an oil-drilling rig. He added that he was glad Bruce had made the suggestion about tying the prow into the building, because it would make it much harder to take the prow *off* the building when the cost-cutting occurred.

In the first week of April, David, Bill, and Audrey returned with new drawings and a model incorporating Luk Sun's suggestion for balconies. The intent was to have the balconies on every floor, but the model shop, having worked all night until 7:00 A.M., was able only to suggest that effect by locating them every four floors.

"I've never been rushed on a job like this," David said, while waiting for Bruce to arrive from another meeting. "Usually you're supposed to take a break after each charrette. Here we just go on to the next floor. I hope all this effort shows. I think it does. The drawings get better each time we work on them. If we worked on these for a hundred years, they would get incrementally better the last day."

"I hope that's not your plan, David," said Luk Sun, who had just come quietly into the conference room. He took a sip of his morning coffee, lit a cigarette. "The thing that troubles me, David, is that in every building I've ever done, the lobbies and public spaces are all done last, and as a result, when the money gets tight, okay, they're the things that get cut. Can we figure out a way to avoid that in this building?"

David (pleasantly as always): "Well, why did you pick the fastest building we've ever done to suggest that?"

"Also," Luk Sun went on, "I'd like to get started on picking some materials for the office lobby. If we get it done early it would be terrific in terms of marketing. People come in and see a finished lobby, they get a much better sense of what it's going to be like."

"Okay, we'll get our interiors people working on it." David sighed. "Just as we see the light at the end of the tunnel, there's another section of tunnel added."

Bruce bustled in, greeting everyone warmly; he appeared to be in a very good mood. He nodded approvingly at the drawings on the walls and settled back to listen to David's presentation. "I really like this," David began expansively, "because you get a kind of toothing effect, marking the transition from the open area defined by trusses, to the solid area defined only by the horizontal balconies, to the whole mass of the building, so we tie it all together, along the lines you suggested, Luk Sun."

"I like the prow idea," Luk Sun said. "I think it makes a distinctive, outstanding building. But I'm still not sure how you've brought it into the building. You could take it off and you'd still have a handsome building."

"Yes," David agreed, "but now it would fall down."

"It's a gutsy building," Bruce said. "And I'm not opposed to guts but I wonder if this is the right time and place in the market to be exhibiting it. My biggest concern is that you've got a program and a site that give you two radically different buildings, one that wants to make a dramatic statement on Times Square, and the other that wants to stand there in a pin-striped suit trying to look like he doesn't know the first guy. The implementation of that is really tough. I think we ought to discuss the audience for failure. If major corporations and law firms don't like what we're doing here, we're in trouble. My biggest fear as a developer is, we're in uncharted waters. I would like to suggest that we do something that's not been done before. Suppose we took this model around to potential tenants. I'm thinking of, first, a major real estate broker with experience in commercial leasing, and then a law firm, a bank, or a brokerage house."

Architecture! David had wanted to be a doctor, once, when he started Yale, and he would have been a doctor among doctors, wise, gentle, inspiring. An obstetrician, perhaps, bringing into the world a creature whose complexity it would take the designers and engineers of Skidmore, Owings & Merrill a frenzy of activity over the next thousand years to achieve … and when he held up a new baby and told the father, "Congratulations, you have a beautiful daughter," no one would have said, "Gee, let's get a second opinion on that!" No one would have said, "Well, let's show her to the marriage broker and get an idea of what she'll bring!" None of this *process,* this eternal questioning and second-guessing.

David, being David, didn't even blink.

"I think that's a great idea!" he said. "… I'd just like to raise a couple of problems I can foresee with this scheme, which by the way I think is absolutely the right way to go, namely that everyone is going to have his own personal reaction, and you've got to be careful not to get involved with their suggestions for the elevator cabs."

"Absolutely," Bruce assured him. "My concern is only that they not look at this model and say 'It's cheap, it's not corporate, it's not for us.' Once you're discussing details with them, fine, we're home free."

"Well," David said smoothly, "we always believe that the more input you have the better."

The meeting Bruce had in mind took place on a morning in mid-April. Bruce had corralled one of the leading commercial real estate brokers in New York, a small man with long gray hair and the baritone rasp of a lifetime smoker. He wore an expensive dark suit, a white shirt, and a heavy gold chain on his right wrist. He exchanged wary greetings with David. In the struggle for the developer's soul, the leasing agent and the architect are more often adversaries than allies. The model was brought into the room. "Take a good look," Bruce urged. "I'm curious to know what your reaction is to the prow."

The broker peered intensely at the model from several angles. He crouched down low to the table to get his eyes down to pedestrian level, then backed up for distance. "I think it's adventurous," he said judiciously. He turned to David. "Do you like the top?" he asked sharply.

"I wouldn't have done it otherwise," David replied with a weary smile.

"The question is," Bruce prompted, "how would Morgan Stanley react to this prow? Will they have a heart attack?"

"I'm just not sure," the broker answered. "It may be the most beautiful thing, it may be the most objectionable thing. I'm just not good enough to tell you. You can give someone a heart attack with the most innocent thing. I'll never forget walking George Lois through the Time-Life building, and he took one look at the lobby floor, marble terrazzo in swirls, and he said, 'I could vomit from that,' and he walked out. The space was perfect for him. And he didn't even get up in the building to see it. Bruce, the one thing I have to say to you is, you should listen to your stomach on this one. Do what you feel is right."

"You're right!" Bruce said, seemingly galvanized by this speech. "I've got a sense now of what I've got to do."

David tensed.

"Great," the broker said, dismissing the subject with a wave, "but first let me tell you about my new apartment." Business being concluded, he was off and running on a favorite topic, his latest apartment. "Princess Pahlavi bought it in 1978 for $1.8 million, which I know sounds like chicken feed now but back then was a lot of money," he began. "It's 13,300 square feet. It's $13.5 million. The most expensive apartment ever sold in New York. I need it like a hole in the head. But so what." He went on to describe the apartment in lurid, luscious detail. It had a fourteen-foot-wide staircase, a sixty-eight-foot-long gallery, six master bedrooms, three sets of French doors opening on the wraparound terrace.

David listened as politely as he could. Bruce affected tremendous awe. "Oh, you're in for it now," he gushed. "UJA is going to double your allocation next year." The man beamed. "Thanks for your time, I mean it," Bruce added.

"You know, Bruce," the broker said, as he stood to go, "you're the first guy who sought to pick my brains on this stuff ahead of time."

"Why would I do it afterwards?" Bruce asked. "If you don't like it then, what am I going to do about it?"

David and Bruce were left in the conference room. "Let's talk in my office," Bruce said.

Inside, neither man sat. "I'd like to say something about process here," David began. "That guy may have a lot of money and a great apartment, but I don't think he knows anything about how to get you a better building. And I don't know how he sleeps at night in his eighty-foot bedroom, stepping over the homeless people in the street."

"David, I don't care about his taste in architecture. I brought him in to tell us whether the building can be marketed ..."

"Look, SOM has designed office buildings all over the world," Childs interrupted. "We're not amateurs at this. This isn't the first time we've heard the word 'marketing.' You hired us because we know what we're doing."

"David, I don't like the building! I don't like the prow!"

"Okay," Childs said, seeming relieved to have it out in the open; "that's a different opinion than you had last week."

"It's not a different opinion!" Bruce said sharply. "Okay, it is. It's evolved. I didn't like it at the beginning but I wanted to see if we could tease it out into something that would work. I kept waiting for something else to happen. You've brought this to the highest possible point, and you've done a terrific job of it, and I still don't like it."

"Okay, I accept that. But we're back six weeks."

"Let me worry about that," Bruce replied. "David, I don't want you to misunderstand me. I'm not saying I don't like what you've done. It's not my job to like it or not to like it; what's driving this is the marketing."

"If they're what's driving it, we should have those guys in the meetings," Childs snapped.

"David, don't show your ego to me!" Bruce snapped back.

"I'm happy to do a new design," David said. "I don't mind throwing it out because I've got a whole lot more designs inside. But I think we're missing a big opportunity here. And we've just lost six weeks."

"I think we ought to take the prow off and try the building as it looks without it," Bruce said, less heatedly. "I think you've got a terrific building here that way."

"You can't just take it off the building, it's like taking strings off a tennis racket. We did that in response to a direction from you. We're being pulled in a lot of directions. I've got teams of people working nights and weekends, and they're burned out."

"David, I understand. You've done a terrific job and I don't know who else could have done it better."

"And we'll keep doing it, but I've got to know that we're going in the right direction. I understand what you want now, and we'll try to give it to you. But we're starting over. Not from scratch, but from farther back, probably, than even you realize." Mollified—or, in any case, his anger spent—Childs watched as Bruce shrugged on a floor-length navy blue epauleted overcoat and hurried down the hall to the elevator and out the building to where his driver waited to take him to another meeting. Then Childs walked wearily back to the conference room, unpinned his drawings and tucked them under his arm, and set off for the street, where his driver would take him back to Skidmore.

13

Architecture, of course, is only one of the arts necessary to construct a modern office building. Members of at least two other professional disciplines must be involved: the structural engineer, who takes the architect's floor plans and packs them with as many columns as a salt mine; and the mechanical engineer, who fills whatever space is left with pipes, ducts, cables, fans, pumps, switches, and the other miscellaneous hardware necessary to render the building habitable. Architects agree in principle that a building should stand up and have running water, lights, and air-conditioning. But it invariably amazes them that people would actually choose those things over a really great design. Hence the choice of engineering consultants is critical, because of the need for a good working relationship among men and women who would spend a year fighting over fractions of an inch.

The battle was waged at the perimeters of the building and especially in the core. Without strong control by the architect and developer, the core has a tendency to grow until it swallows the leasable space. Mitchell made this one of his causes. Early on, he noticed that the plan called for men's and women's toilet rooms on opposite sides of the elevator bank.

"David," he barked, "your father is a plumber? Is this why we have to have two separate sets of risers for this building?"

"Well," Childs replied mildly, "it seemed to work well structurally this way."

Mitchell assumed an expression of incredulity. "What kind of architect worries about how things work structurally? Next you'll be telling us you're doing something because it's cheaper."

"Oh, no," David assured him, "we get rid of those guys right away."

The logical choice for the structural design was Skidmore's own engineering department, which was undergoing a major expansion in New York. For many years SOM had only a handful of engineers on the East Coast; Skidmore buildings designed in New York either used outside engineers or borrowed them from SOM's Chicago office. An associate partner, Richard Rowe, was the ranking Skidmore engineer in New York in the mid-1980s. As a project manager for Tishman Construction Company, Mailman had built a building Rowe had helped engineer, with a reinforced concrete core and a steel perimeter frame. Mitchell—whose enthusiasms ran as deep as his dislikes—proclaimed this one of the great engineering feats of modern civilization. He considered himself fortunate to be living in the same century and city as an engineer of Rowe's gifts. He raged against the injustice that a real estate broker whose only requirement was that he look good in an off-the-rack suit could earn more money from leasing one building like this than Rowe might make in a lifetime. In early 1987, SOM closed its office in Houston, and the head engineer there, Bob Halvorson, came to New York as a full partner, outranking Rowe. Halvorson was a burly, soft-spoken man with thinning blond hair, but his diffident manner belied very strong convictions. Mitchell disliked Halvorson but he consoled himself with the thought that Rowe could still work on the project. In any case, the advantages of having engineers and architects share an office would still be there; they could fight in person instead of by fax. Bruce agreed that would probably save time.

The choice of a firm to design the building's mechanical systems was, if anything, even more important. When prospective tenants came to look at the building, they would have zero interest in how the building stood up, but the adequacy of the air-conditioning would be high on their list of questions. The mechanical engineer would have to design plumbing; electrical wiring; HVAC (heating, ventilating, and air-conditioning) machinery; and fire alarms, sprinklers, and smoke-exhaust fans, collectively known as life-safety systems. Bruce chose the firm of

Jaros, Baum & Bolles for this crucial role. JB&B designed high-quality installations and had a reputation for making sure the contractors performed. Mitchell's cynicism about human nature proceeded directly from his experience in high-rise construction in New York and the nearby suburbs. A mechanical engineer would specify, say, a four-inch pipe on his drawings, and the plumbing contractor would make his bid on that basis. Then the plumber would do the shop drawings, which his men would use to actually build the building, and draw three-inch pipe. The engineer would get the shop drawings for review. If he noticed the substitution, the plumber would be ready with an impassioned justification for three-inch pipe, based on his many years of experience in the trade, in which he had never yet seen an engineer so prodigal as to specify four-inch pipe when three-inch pipe was obviously adequate, and it so happened that three-inch pipe was readily available, but the four-inch was a special order that would hold the job up for weeks if not months. Or, to reduce the argument to its philosophic essence, if a pipe leaks in a wall where no one sees it, does it really leak? In this world of sinners, a surprising number of whom were plumbers and electricians, Mitchell liked having JB&B on his side.

Don Ross, the JB&B partner on the job, was a neat, bland-looking man in his fifties who spoke with great precision and a sardonic turn of phrase. "We're a huge pain in the rear end to architects," Ross says complacently. "Designers are very … I don't want to say arrogant, but maybe that's the best word. It's very important to them whether something is an inch or an inch and a half, not that anyone else in the world would ever notice." Ross himself was an HVAC engineer. The JB&B philosophy was that artificial ventilation and lighting were not just convenient substitutes for the natural items, but an improvement on them. JB&B's own offices, at the prestigious office address of 345 Park Avenue, were exemplars of the mechanical engineer's art: they were in the basement.

The building would be built by the Turner Construction Company. That is, Turner would supply engineers to manage the project; it would coordinate all the millions of details in getting a building built, from obtaining Saturday work permits from the city to leasing portable toilets for the workmen; and it would negotiate, subject to approval by Eichner, the contracts for approximately a dozen major and perhaps two dozen minor trades. In exchange for these services they would receive a fixed fee, under an arrangement known as a construction management agreement.

There were only three or four construction managers in New York at that time that could be entrusted with a $300 million office building. Bruce had already used two of them on his various projects, and had his disagreements with both, making Turner the next logical choice. There were several things Bruce looked for in a construction manager. The quality of the actual finished product was not high on the list. The building would be built to the specifications of the architects and engineers, who would reject any work that didn't meet their standards, so in the end you would get the building you were paying for. What mattered was the pain it took to get to that point. Where Bruce thought the choice of CM could make a difference was in the ability to negotiate a good price with the subcontractors; the willingness of the CM to hold down his own expenses (referred to as "general conditions" and generally billed as a percentage of the overall construction budget); and, above all, tenacity in pursuing claims against the subcontractors.

Contracts with the major trades are elaborate documents intended to cover every conceivable contingency. But circumstances change. The owner has a change of heart about a color, the engineer suffers an attack of conscience, or the pieces specified simply don't fit together right. Or, more frustrating yet, subcontractor A screws up, thereby delaying, interrupting, or otherwise complicating the job of B, who figures out a way to distill from that event a quantifiable money claim. Subcontractors tend to regard such inevitabilities as found money. Once the main contract is signed, the developer is at their mercy for any extras. You sign a contract for something to be painted blue, and a week later decide you want it red, and all of a sudden red paint costs 20 percent more. Developers rightly resent the fact that this is a perfectly legitimate way to steal that someone else thought of first. Their only check against such extortions is the backcharge, a device for holding the subcontractor liable when he does something wrong: liable, that is, not just to fix the error itself, but to reimburse the owner for any additional costs he might have incurred as a result. The owner's object in this game is not to steal every cent of the subcontractor's profit, but to have a weapon of his own to use in the endless war of claim and counterclaim.

Turner faced an enormous logistical task. They would eventually lease a floor in the old Times Tower building just for the engineers working on this project. That didn't include the supervisors who worked at a trailer on the site and the executives in the company's headquarters. The one thing Turner would not do was any actual construction. It had a small crew of laborers on the project, who were responsible for general maintenance and cleaning of the site. But each of the hundreds of discrete tasks involved in actually building a building were parceled out with medieval specificity among the various tradesmen. It was a rare event to see Turner's own laborers doing any work on the building itself. That usually meant something had been done by mistake and needed to be torn down. There was no union for mistakes, common though they were.

Turner Construction was the major operating subsidiary of the Turner Corporation, a great and venerable company, founded in 1902. By 1987 it claimed to be the largest erector of buildings in America, with offices in thirty-five cities. Annually since 1910 Turner has published "Turner City," a brochure showing all the projects it built the year before. The 1987 version showed Murphy/Jahn's celebrated United Airlines terminal at O'Hare; office buildings from Boston, Wilmington, and Washington, and factories, hospitals, hotels, and apartments from all over the country, with a total value of nearly $2.8 billion.

Yet, oddly, in its home city of New York, in the prestigious field of high-rise office construction, Turner was not the leading builder. The only New York office building Turner completed in 1987 was an eighteen-story, block-long structure at the unlikely address of 375 Hudson Street, in Greenwich Village. Among the major midtown buildings that went up in the late 1980s, many more were built by Tishman Construction (identifiable by the crossed beams that formed the "T" of its distinctive logo) or HRH, a division of Starrett Brothers Housing Corp. There was a theory that Turner was at a competitive disadvantage in this world because the people in charge were … to put it bluntly, not Jewish, and most of the developers were (with the exception, to save him the trouble of pointing it out himself, of Donald Trump). Turner built hospitals, schools, and high-minded WASP projects like Lincoln Center and the United Nations Secretariat. In the 1980s it built office towers for IBM, Equitable Life, and Citicorp, but it didn't build many speculative office buildings for Jewish developers. Bruce was Jewish, but his one true god was Rational Process, and at the moment, Rational Process seemed to be indicating the Turner Construction Co.

Turner had a reputation for standing above the chiseling, petty and grand, that characterized its industry. In 1986 the U.S. Attorney in Manhattan, Rudolph Giuliani, indicted more than a dozen people in the concrete industry on racketeering charges. Testimony at the trial showed that the Colombo crime family dominated the concrete industry through Ralph Scopo, the president of the Cement and Concrete Workers. Large jobs were allocated among seven concrete companies who kicked back

2 percent of the contract to Scopo. This may have been one reason that concrete prices in New York City were as much as a third higher than across the river in northern New Jersey. In 1988, Turner calculated that a first-class office building that could be built for $100 million in New York City would cost $56 million in Los Angeles, $59 million in Houston, and $75 million in Chicago. The concrete cartel was finally broken after a trial that lasted for more than a year, ending with the convictions of several of the most prominent executives in the industry. The companies were placed in receivership, and everyone celebrated the end of high concrete prices. Unfortunately, a year later, when 1540 Broadway was going up, the industry was still waiting for prices to come down.

Turner was a remarkable company. It inspired astonishing loyalty among the people who worked for it. No one at Turner ever complained about the organization to outsiders. The field engineers all looked neat and businesslike, in their white Turner hardhats and their clean blue Turner windbreakers over white shirts and neckties. Even the caked brown mud and splashes of gray cement on their boots spoke of honest industry and purpose. Within Turner itself, the New York office had tremendous cachet. People from other parts of the company would come to New York to see how skyscrapers are built. They would see their counterparts wrestling with obscure jurisdictional issues involving unions that don't even exist anywhere else in the country. They would see the logistical problems in scheduling dozens of deliveries a day to a site with only one place for trucks to park. Then they would shake their heads and go back to Nashville and build another nursing home.

Even honest unions in the New York construction industry are characterized by an intransigence that would make a Welsh collier gasp. The miner may strike, but not even he would have the arrogance to put coal back into the ground and insist on being paid for it. An electrician in New York, though, will take it on himself to decide whether a piece of equipment, delivered in working order and ready to be installed, should have been built by him on the site instead. And if he so rules, he will take out his tools and take it apart, and then conscientiously put it back together again, all at his hourly wage. The unions decide whether their men can work overtime, which they may withhold because they want to spread the work around among more men, or they don't like the contractor, or they're looking for a payoff, or they just want to throw their weight around. One of Mitchell's heroes was a vice president of HRH who once was rushing to finish an addition to Memorial Sloan-Kettering Hospital, at a time when the masons decided they had too many men idle and slapped a prohibition on overtime. But the work that remained—closing off the openings left in a wall for access to the outdoor construction hoist—didn't lend itself to hiring more men, because you could only work on a floor at a time. In desperation, the boss suggested going for coffee with the union's business agent, and maneuvered him past the children's cancer ward on his way to the cafeteria. "Look at them, Vinny," he said; "are you telling me that you won't work overtime for them?" With a tear in his eye, the union man consented, just this once. Mitch cited this as an example of creative construction management at work, but the fact is that in most other places in the country, you don't have to show someone a bunch of dying kids to get him to work overtime.

The New York office was staffed mostly by natives, tough Irishmen and Italians from Queens or New Jersey, like Bob Fee himself, a rangy, rugged-looking executive with steel-gray hair, whose father was a boss in the old Starrett company. Fee was the top construction executive in Turner's New York office. Below him was a "job executive," who was responsible for Broadway State and several other jobs. This was Gary Negrycz, a wiry man with a brush of fading brown hair and the genial smirk of a grown-up juvenile delinquent. Gary would lean back in his chair at meetings, smoking unfiltered Camels (which had the advantage, he once remarked, that no one ever asked to borrow one), and wait for a question to come his way with the air of the class cutup who knows he'll be thrown out of school anyway and might as well tell the truth.

Even Mitchell was impressed by the Turner panache. "Those Turner guys are great," he told Andrea once, in the midst of a crisis over a crack that excavation had opened up in the west wall of the Lyceum. "I wish I had six guys like Ellis."

"Then why don't you hire him?"

"They never leave."

"Why? Are they paid so well?"

"It's not even that. It's the Turner esprit. They really believe in that company."

Naturally, over the course of the months, Mitchell would have occasion to revise that opinion, volubly and emphatically, several times. But on balance, most people connected with the Broadway State Project considered Turner a class outfit.

With Bruce's team, half a dozen architects and engineers from Skidmore, JB&B's plumbers, electricians, and HVAC engineers, and Gary Negrycz and John Ellis of Turner, the regular Wednesday afternoon job meetings now packed Eichner's conference room, which was already as stuffy as a rush-hour subway even before Gary and Luk Sun began turning all the oxygen into carbon monoxide. The circle expanded no further, though; although dozens of subcontractors would work on the building, none of them, except in the rarest of instances, would be permitted to see the inside of Eichner's offices. It happened once that the demolition and excavation contractors met at 625 to coordinate their schedules, and when Luk Sun found out about it he blew up. "I don't want any meetings with the subcontractors here," he lectured the staff. "No one here should have anything to do with those meetings. You know what happens? Associated says, 'Here's my schedule,' and Laquila [the excavation contractor] says, 'That's gonna set me back two weeks.' So either Associated is gonna have to put on more people, or Laquila is going to have to go to overtime. And you know what happens then? They turn to you and you reach into your pocket for money!"

The first issue the parties had to settle concerned the very essence of the building, the choice of a material for its structural frame. The possibilities were steel or reinforced concrete. All of Bruce's apartment towers had used structural frames of reinforced concrete, and if the Broadway State Project had stayed a hotel, it probably would have as well. Of the generation of midtown office buildings that went up at the same time as Broadway State, roughly half used steel. Oddly enough, the choice did not revolve around the costs of the two systems, which were close enough that it was hard to predict now which would be cheaper in two years when the building was actually built. The decision had to do with the specific properties of each material, and the way they are used in construction. Both steel and concrete buildings take the weight of the structure in vertical columns—at the perimeter, in the core, and in intermediate locations as needed. Either may have some form of diagonal bracing to stiffen the building against the wind. In a steel frame, the columns are linked by horizontal beams. (Strictly speaking, a beam that runs between two columns is a girder. If the columns are on the perimeter of the building, the girder is a "spandrel." The smaller beams that run between girders are "purlins.") Steel columns and beams typically have the familiar wide-flange **I** shape. They are hoisted into place on the building by a crane and then bolted together. A corrugated steel deck is laid across the beams, and a concrete floor, four to six inches thick, is poured on the deck.

In a concrete superstructure, by contrast, the floors are integral with the columns. Concrete structures are poured in place. A wooden mold, called a form, is nailed together for each level and filled with concrete, which is a mixture of cement, sand, and gravel; when the concrete sets, the forms are stripped away and used to build the next story. Within the form, running through the concrete, is a mesh of reinforcing bars, or "rebar." This is steel rod, generally an inch to two inches in diameter, heavily ribbed to grip the concrete when it hardens. Lengths of rebar run up the columns, overlapping to tie together successive stories; they bend out to engage the concrete floors, and within the floors they are tied together in a dense web that holds the whole thing together, like straw in a mud hut.

Steel is considered a better material than concrete for spanning long distances without intermediate columns, which is why it is often preferred for office buildings. A typical midtown office tower will have uninterrupted spans of at least thirty and as much as fifty feet from the curtain wall to the core. The tenants can divide the space any way they like. But big spans aren't important for residential buildings, where there are lots of fixed walls and almost every room has a window. Concrete saves money in residential construction by eliminating the need for a hung ceiling. The underside of a concrete floor is the mirror of the top, a flat slab. Coat the underside with plaster and paint and it becomes the ceiling of the room below. But an office building, which has overhead lighting fixtures and ventilation, requires a hung ceiling in any case.

These considerations applied only to the office tower, however. This was a mixed-use building, where, as Halvorson observed, "there's a lot of call for piling things on top of one another that don't have any structural relation to one another." In the base of the building, the concrete-versus-steel question broke down into a series of trade-offs. Steel would give more flexibility in the complicated geometry of the retail floors. A retail tenant who took two floors, say, might want to add a staircase after the building was finished. This could be a nuisance in a reinforced concrete building, because the floor is integral to the structure; you can't just make a hole and leave the ends of the rebar dangling. But concrete was *more* flexible in terms of time. Steel had to be ordered six months or more in advance. To modify a beam on the site it had to be heated red-hot over a fire of hundred-dollar bills. But you can change any part of a concrete structure up to the morning it gets built, for the cost of plywood and nails. Steel would probably require fewer columns taking up space in the retail atrium; at $100 a square foot, this could add up to measurably more rent over time. Concrete, on the other hand, took up less *vertical* space. Every inch below grade would have to be blasted out of tough Manhattan schist. Given the urgency of completing the excavation in time for the May 1988 vesting deadline, this was a big plus for concrete.

Luk Sun, naturally, wanted both, as well as ten-foot-high ceilings on the retail floors.

"My preference below is to do it in steel," he announced at a meeting one afternoon, "and to get my ten feet floor to ceiling, and to hold to a total depth of fifty-two feet."

"Physically, you can't do that," Mitch said flatly.

"Don't tell me it can't be done! I want them to do it!" The architects looked away, embarrassed. Don Ross, the mechanical engineer, pointed out that after subtracting for the thickness of the bottom slab of concrete and the height of the garage floor, a total depth of fifty-two feet would leave about forty-two feet for three floors of retail, fourteen feet for each. He needed four feet between each floor for ducts, pipes, electrical conduit, and lighting fixtures. "If you want ten feet clear," he pointed out mildly, "that leaves you with not much room for the slabs and beams. You need a material with structural integrity that's dimensionless."

"Then don't give me four feet of ductwork on each floor!" Luk Sun shouted. "You're designing for a restaurant on every floor. I don't want a restaurant on every floor. Do one floor fourteen, one thirteen. I don't care how you do it! I'm telling you what I want!"

This was one case where he didn't get it, though. As Mitchell observed the next day, "When you tell a consultant to do something that cannot be done, that your own people are telling you can't be done, you don't look that smart. And later on, when he calmed down, the sagacious Oriental one agreed." On the other hand, the tirade was not without its effect, because rather than endure another one, the engineers went back to work and lopped about a foot and a half off the depth over the next couple of weeks.

Just as they fought over inches, they fought over days. Everyone wanted more space for his own part of the job and more time to do it in. Elaborate schedules were drawn up with flags showing all the deadlines and milestones, and people fought fiercely to push their own responsibility as far back as possible. As weeks went on and deadlines passed unobserved, the schedule would get increasingly far removed from reality, and finally someone would sit all the parties down to make a new one. Eventually this would be Turner's responsibility, but in the early days, when the job still existed mainly on paper, it was one of Tom Fridstein's less pleasant tasks to take a timeline of an eighteen-month process and try to fold it, accordion-style, into twelve months.

"You'll get the foundation drawings 6/1 and start excavation 6/15," he told Gary one day in early May.

"You expect me to bid the hole in two weeks? That's crazy!" Gary exclaimed. He looked down at the old schedule in front of him. "What happened to 5/15?"

"It's still between 5/14 and 5/16," Fridstein said testily. "But you won't have your drawings for two weeks after that. We'll issue specifications for the structure on October 2."

"Okay, steel, 8/2," Gary said, jotting it down in his notebook.

"Steel, *10/2*," Fridstein corrected him sternly.

"I can try ..."

Most often, though, they didn't argue at all, but worked with common purpose against the forces of entropy, the vast invisible conspiracy of government bureaucrats and their near cousins at Con Ed who would bury the Broadway State Building in forty stories of paperwork. The building would have to have new electrical vaults—chambers under the sidewalk for the transformers that reduce Con Ed's 13,000-volt street service to the 265/460-volt current that would circulate in the building. First, though, the vaults serving the old buildings would have to be decommissioned. This evidently required a two-thirds majority of Con Ed's shareholders and approval by the College of Cardinals. Gary thought the process could be speeded up if he and Mitch took the borough superintendent to lunch.

"Good idea," Mitch agreed. "I'll eat and you talk, and then you eat and I'll talk."

"I can't eat that much," Gary said.

Nowhere was entropy harder to conquer than in the seemingly simple matter of the Variety chimney.

The chimney, which contained a flue for a small gas furnace, ran up the west wall of that ancient building, where it adjoined the 46th Street annex. Since the annex was higher than Variety, the chimney continued up the wall of the annex one more story to that roof. It did, that is, until Associated began tearing down the annex, and in the process, more or less unavoidably blocked the chimney with rubble. Now it would have to be fixed.

By itself, that wouldn't have been a problem for the architects of the Sears Tower and the builders of the IBM building, but the chimney was only one of a series of misadventures that had caused Variety's general manager, a harried-looking man named Vito, to be extremely wary of his exuberant neighbors. Vito was worried about dust from the demolition affecting the delicate computers in his offices. "We wet everything down," Gary said firmly, when this was brought to his attention, "and therefore, *there is no dust*." Vito was worried about vibration. "Man in that building is crazy," muttered Associated's shop steward, known only by his nickname, Alabama, a rangy, very dark man whose face had a number of scars that didn't look like they came from shaving. "You just *lean* your *back* against his wall and he comes running out to yell at you." That was an exaggeration; you just *back* your *bulldozer* into his wall and he came running out to yell at you. One afternoon in May, an elderly clerk on the second floor of Variety's offices heard a crash and felt a breeze on her legs and looked down and saw daylight coming from a hole about two feet by three feet that had opened in the wall next to her desk. She screamed, Vito came running, and within a few minutes the site was swarming with cops, putting an end to work on that day.

"We did not put a hole in the wall of that building," Mario insisted to Ellis the next morning. "There was a beam from our building sitting on a little ledge in their wall, and when we dropped the beam about a dozen bricks came out with it. The mortar was all just sand. I wish my building was that soft," he concluded, sounding very much aggrieved.

"Who are you sending over to fix it?" Ellis asked.

"A good man," Mario assured him. "I used him on my own house."

"Is he a wrecker or a plasterer?" Ellis persisted.

"In the old country," Mario replied, "he did everything."

The real problem with the Variety chimney, Luk Sun saw right away, was that the new building was going up four hundred feet right next to it. Since they couldn't have the chimneypot adjoining a glass curtain wall, they might have to carry the chimney up to the new roofline, an ugly, stupid, and above all expensive metal flue right up the back of their beautiful new building.

"I just think you ought to know about this problem," he told Bruce one morning.

"I'm glad you told me, but I'm now going to forget about it, because the resolution to this problem is simple. In no way, shape, or form am I paying for a four-hundred-foot chimney for that stupid building," Bruce said.

"That's about what I figured," Luk Sun muttered.

The only thing he had to figure out was where it could go instead.

The simple solution to a chimney that was lower than the surrounding buildings was to move it to the middle of its own roof. But—surprise!—it had to be at least ten feet horizontally from the adjacent structures, and Variety was only sixteen feet wide. The alternative was to run the flue diagonally across the roof and up the wall of the building on the other side. That required only fifty or sixty feet of additional flue. The building on the other side was an old brick loft containing the backstage storage and dressing rooms for the Lyceum theater, and there was no reason to think the Shuberts would object. There was only one tiny problem with the building on the other side, which Andrea brought up at one of the innumerable meetings devoted to this topic. Even though it was a run-down, charmless structure of no architectural merit whatsoever, by virtue of contiguity to the theater's magnificent Beaux Arts façade every one of its dingy bricks took on the sacred aura of an official New York City landmark, as if it had been sculpted by the very hand of Augustus Saint-Gaudens.

"This will have to go before the Landmarks Preservation Commission," Andrea announced, to a pall-like silence. "We should try for a Certificate of No Effect, but I don't know if we'll get it. We may need a Certificate of Appropriateness."

"What's the going rate for one of those?" Gary asked after a moment.

"I don't know, only because I can't predict what they will deem appropriate for this wall. In theory, anything they want. They could require a flue of hand-beaten copper and make you attach it with bronze screws."

"Just to put up a chimney? On the back of the building? We're not even over their property line."

"You're touching their building," Andrea said. "If you can figure out a way to run a chimney up fifty feet of their building without touching it, you're home free."

"Mitchell, make it so it doesn't touch the Lyceum," Howard ordered. "Make it a free-standing chimney."

"Howard, there's *physics* involved here. These things can *lean*. When you need a lawyer, you don't go to me. When I need an engineer, I don't go to you."

The Variety chimney, so seemingly inconsequential, so maddeningly complex below the surface, came to symbolize all the frustrations and delays that New York City in its dumb obstinate density placed in the way of development. "This is where the game is won or lost, guys," Luk Sun exhorted his staff, and week after week they wrestled with its intricacies. Should they sound out Landmarks on the idea, or just do a drawing and file it and see what happened? When and how should they bring this up to Variety? Vito seemed like a reasonable person. But Luk Sun regarded it as only common sense to approach him as if he were as crafty and unpredictable as Stalin. This seemed confirmed when Lydia brought up at a meeting in early June that Variety now wanted $6,800 to pay for relining the chimney.

"That's an absolute gift!" Luk Sun erupted.

"Yes, it is, and the question is, do we want to make any kind of gesture toward them as an inducement to let us move their chimney?"

"They have to be induced to let us move their chimney for them?"

"Well, we don't know, but they might very well regard this as our problem, which it is."

Luk Sun groaned. He clenched his fists and his face turned red at the thought of spending nearly seven thousand dollars on Variety. But he knew he had no choice except to see how much he could bargain them down. While everyone argued about who should write the letter to Variety—Lydia wanted Howard to do it, but Howard was reluctant because then Vito would take it to *his* lawyer—Luk Sun looked to the heavens to explain why he should be condemned to live in a world where every other person he met wanted money from him. The heavens held no answer, only the promise of more trouble to come, of endless wrestling with innumerable petty details, so that the building didn't so much seem to get built as disentangled—pulled painstakingly from the tendrils of greed that spring up like kudzu as soon as you turn a shovelful of the worthless, but precious, soil of midtown Manhattan.

Well, to be fair, he thought, we're as greedy as the rest; otherwise we wouldn't survive.

14

Increasingly absent from these deliberations was Bruce himself. He had conceived the project, put the people in place to get it done, and brought it this far into the world; now there were more interesting things he wanted to do with his life. What could be more interesting than a $300 million building? Only one thing: a leveraged buy-out of a public company worth five or ten times as much. The skills that had brought Bruce this far in the world of real estate—the knack for spotting value, the guts to take big risks, and the sense to lay them off on someone else as fast as possible—were, he believed, destined to find their next expression on Wall Street. He flew out to California to meet Michael Milken, prompting Howard to mutter darkly about "Bruce and Henry going off to play in traffic." Bruce reported on the meeting with pleasure. Milken said his qualm about doing business with a New York real estate developer was that the handshake signals the *start* of negotiations. Bruce admitted that could sometimes be true. Milken went on to wonder how Bruce got where he was, with no family money or contacts. "When I was a kid," Bruce replied, "if you didn't do what you said you would do, you were marked lousy. Now, the standards of society have eroded to the point that just by doing what you say you'll do, you're hailed as some sort of genius and you rise to the top of the heap." The junk-bond genius appreciated that remark. But nothing came of the meeting.

Of course, Bruce was not losing touch with the project; far from it. All the financial stuff still to come, and there were thousands of hours of it, he handled directly. He spared himself a lot of technical wrangling over where to put the men's rooms, but if a dollar bill fell he heard it hit the floor. Luk Sun was his vicar and inquisitor-general for the extirpation of unnecessary cost. Bruce considered this an essential part of Luk Sun's professional education. "I'm trying to sit on my hands," Bruce said. "I'm in my cabin. The blinds are drawn. I peek out periodically, go to the door and put my hand on the knob and open it a crack … and then I stop myself. The project has got to be Wong's. There are certain things I bring to the table—perspective, balanced judgment, an overview of the process. We were going to build a hotel. The ship was foundering, and someone had to turn it around. I had to say, 'Hey, guys, we're heading for the rocks here. It's a big ship, and they're big rocks.'"

Admittedly, people who did not share Bruce's global perspective sometimes found this a frustrating way of doing business. "We have all these meetings," Fridstein observed pointedly, "but no one's in charge, and if you need an answer on something it always has to be next week."

Already, although the building was still in the early stages of being designed, Bruce was giving thought to the other end of the process, which would be income. The building would not produce rent for three years at least, but signing a tenant now would be a major coup in convincing the bank to loan money for the project. Some developers won't go ahead with a building at all without a commitment from a major tenant. The notoriously conservative Durst told the *Times* that if United States Trust backed out of his building, he would leave a hole in the ground. But these tend to be the developers already sitting on $2 billion portfolios. If he hoped to catch up to them, Bruce had to push on, with or without a tenant, but better with than without.

He was an optimist by nature, and nothing in his business experience had given him reason to be otherwise. He had started in real estate in the 1970s in the depths of New York's worst crisis since the Depression, when the city found itself unable to borrow or to meet the payments on its bonds, when businesses, fleeing the crumbling city for office parks by the sides of highways, pushed the vacancy rate in prime Manhattan office buildings from 4 percent to 16 percent in two years, and he had made money right in the teeth of it. He moved from Brooklyn to Manhattan just in time to catch the wave of the city's great recovery. All through the 1980s the great engines of commerce churned on, colonizing acre after acre of the insides of big, square glass-and-granite buildings. In five years, from 1980 to 1985, developers built and rented over 18 million feet of offices in midtown. The vacancy rate plummeted to below 5 percent, and rents in a few years went from around twelve dollars a square foot to almost forty dollars, where they stayed for most of the decade. People who owned or built Manhattan office buildings in those years made astonishing amounts of money. In 1977, the Reichmann family of Toronto (Olympia & York) bought eight New York office buildings that had been part of the Uris family real estate empire for $320 million, only $50 million of it in cash. Within five years (after some additional millions were invested in improvements) the properties were worth $2 billion.

Directly or indirectly, most of this expansion was related to the financial markets, to the creation, marketing, and exchange of ever larger and more imaginative forms of debt. Local employment in the field known to labor statisticians as FIRE (finance, insurance, and real estate) grew by more than 100,000 jobs between 1977 and 1986, to 526,000. (That was just half as many jobs as the largest category, "services"—but, of course, many of the "service" jobs, from messengers to law partners, were ancillary to the financial industry.) At an average density of one employee per 250 square feet, that created a demand for 25 million feet of additional office space, nearly thirty buildings the size of the Broadway State Project. Foreign banks alone—of which Cushman & Wakefield counted 356 that year, up nearly 50 percent in the decade—employed more than 30,000 people in New York. A whole skyscraper full of the purse-lipped purveyors of sports shirts at J.C. Penney slunk off to a suburb of Dallas, and after a brief nervous spasm the city shrugged: their places in the city's economy (if not necessarily the J.C. Penney building itself) would be filled by a British merchant bank, a Hong Kong investment group, a regiment of fresh curly-headed lawyers to throw into the takeover wars. The lights burned late in the new buildings; the air conditioners hummed all night long, carrying off the sweat of so much concentrated acquisitiveness.

So it was not surprising that the first potential tenant Bruce courted for the building was an investment bank. The bank was Morgan Stanley & Co., which had been planning to consolidate its Manhattan offices in the Solomon Equities building at 1585 Broadway. Exactly why that deal fell through is a mystery. Perhaps David Solomon was right, and bankers didn't want to work in a building with billboards on it, and that it was they who prompted David Solomon's agitated assault on the Times Square zoning. Bruce heard about the deal's collapse one Friday morning in early spring. He mentioned it to Henry, who made a call and added a crucial piece of intelligence: Morgan was now considering moving to Westchester, outside the city altogether.

Characteristically, Henry saw this development as a setback, the loss of a tenant who was going to "anchor" the whole area, while Bruce regarded it as a wildly favorable opportunity. This took more than his usual quota of imagination and audacity. Fifteen eighty-five Broadway was a 1.2 million-square-foot building, and Morgan had intended to take, immediately or for future expansion, virtually all of it—nearly half again as much space as Bruce's building would have. Morgan would probably require several trading floors of 40,000 or more feet. The only way to get these into the Broadway State site would be tilted on their sides. Hemmed in by streets on three sides and existing buildings on the fourth, there was no obvious room for Bruce's building to grow.

Bruce found room, though.

He looked south to what was generally known as the Bond's site, the blockfront between 44th and 45th streets. The development firm of Tishman-Speyer, which held an option on the property, was planning an office building in its place. If that building could be linked to Bruce's by wide passages on several low floors, each of the joined floors would have more than 50,000 square feet. If, moreover, the two sites were merged into one zoning lot, it might be possible to talk the city into letting him put all the signs on one of the structures, and make the other the executive offices.

There were only a couple of obstacles to this beautiful scheme. Gerry Speyer of Tishman-Speyer would have to agree. Bruce considered that the easy part; he never doubted his ability to persuade people to pursue their rational self-interest, once he figured out for them where it lay. Morgan Stanley would have to agree that such a building met their practical, economic, and psychological needs. And there was the matter of eighty feet separating the two building lines, eighty feet that Bruce didn't own, could never own, because it happened to constitute the right-of-way of West 45th Street.

Late that same day, past six o'clock, Bruce convened a small gathering of Howard, Luk Sun, Alice, Mitchell, and another engineer on his staff, a brooding gray-haired man named Pat Rafter. Bruce sat in his secretary's chair, feet on her desk, worrying a paper clip as he spoke; the others stood or leaned against computers and Xerox machines still warm from the day's race against the banks.

"It's a great idea, Bruce," Howard said, "but I can't see closing the street while you put those things up there."

"Forget it, that's nothing," Mitch announced.

"Forget it?" Howard asked, incredulous. "You think the city's going to let you close a street in Times Square for three months?"

"The erection is easy," Mitch barked. "You use T-plates, put them up with a crane, tie them in to the two structures. The hardest part is the mechanical interconnects between the buildings."

"Can I get some numbers here, guys?" Bruce interrupted. "What are we talking about here? Is this putting a man on Jupiter or only the moon?" Mailman jotted down some numbers and came up with a figure of $1.2 million for each of the spans.

"Okay. Pat?"

Rafter scribbled some numbers and said he thought that was pretty close. "Maybe, on the conservative side, it would end up more like $2.5 million," he added.

"You see what it's like in the construction business?" Bruce said, rolling his eyes. "Two point five million is close to $1.2 million."

"Look," Mitch said, "you don't have to build these things at all. If you want a trading floor, take over the basement of the Lyceum, merge it with your hole, and make that your trading floor."

"But that doesn't give us even a million feet total," Eichner objected. "Why should they want to shoehorn themselves into less than a million square feet with no room to expand? No, the bridge is the right way to go. We have to think about the practical problems. We might have to merge two lots here. The lots are not contiguous. The question is, is this going to take an act of Congress to fix, or does someone have a better idea?"

"That's the simple part," Howard said. "You buy the streetbed from the city and then you lease it back to them for a dollar." He looked pleased with himself. After a moment, Alice asked, "Has anyone ever actually done this?"

"Offhand," Howard said, "I couldn't say. Not that it matters. The thing that will make it happen is that Morgan is talking about leaving the city. If we were going to do this tomorrow, I'd call [Deputy Mayor] Bob Esnard. He'd say, 'Okay, give me a one-page memo on it.' We'd have a meeting in the Hall. I would prep Morgan very carefully on what to say.

They've got six thousand jobs, half of them minorities, they want to stay in the city but they need the following things. And the mayor will lock himself in with his people, and they'll ask themselves, 'How much do we want to do this, how much heat will we take from the Municipal Art Society?'"

"It will take forever," Luk Sun said sourly.

"For six thousand jobs," Howard replied dryly, "the city moves fast."

Still, the idea was daunting. It was daunting in part because it meant that the project could no longer proceed "as of right." Instead of breezing through the halls of government with a few nominal signatures and stamps, the project would enter into that unique bureaucratic torture known as ULURP, for "Uniform Land-Use Review Procedure." The project would have to go before the Community Planning Board, an appointed body of distinguished civic leaders (when they agreed with you) and petty demagogues (when they didn't). Although the community planning board was an informational and advisory body only, it had the ability to make you sit through hours-long harangues from any neighborhood busybody whose cat was once run over by a cement truck. The project would have to pass the City Planning Commission and the Board of Estimate, a unique body composed of the city's leading elected officials, which wielded far more power than the nominal legislature, the City Council—at least until 1989, when the Supreme Court declared most of New York City's government unconstitutional.

The project, moreover, was coming at a time when the balance of power in the city appeared to be shifting away from the developers. Things had gone pretty much their way for a decade—ever since Ed Koch had taken office in 1978, a year in which more office space was built in suburban Morris County, New Jersey, than in all of New York City. The boom of the 1980s, fueled by lenient tax and zoning policies, was starting to give way to a backlash, led by the Municipal Art Society and enlisting a small but influential constituency that included Jacqueline Onassis and the *Times*'s distinguished architecture critic Ada Louise Huxtable. Huxtable wrote a long article around this time under the headline "Creeping Gigantism in Manhattan." "What is new and notable in New York City's unprecedented building boom," she began, "is that all previous legal, moral, and esthetic restraints have been thrown to the winds, or more accurately, to the developers, in grateful consideration of contributions to the tax base and the political purse." That was one of the milder expressions of indignation to find print that year. A few months after the stock market crash in the fall of 1987, *New York* magazine's

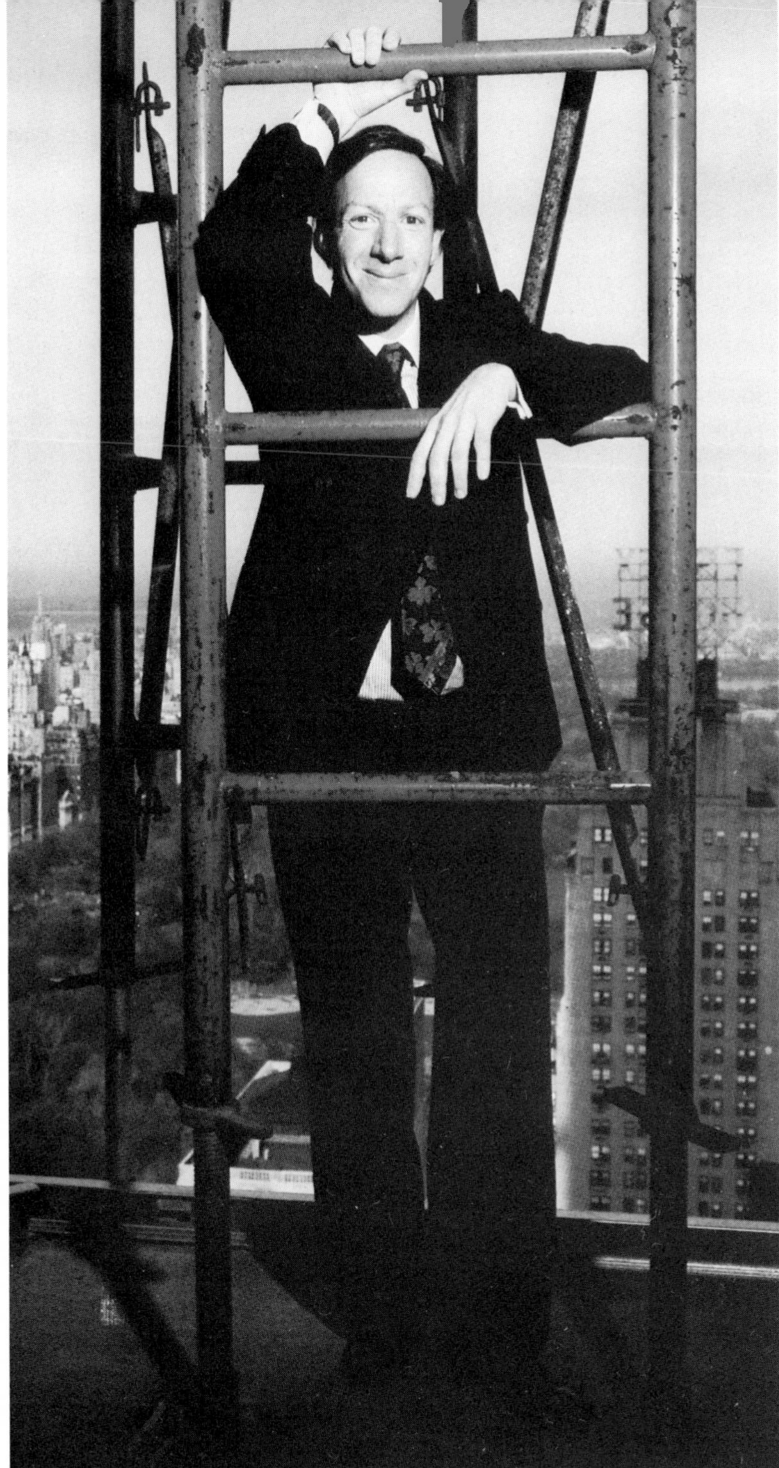

(Theo Westenberger)

At the age of 40, Bruce Eichner told an interviewer: "I have more money than I ever thought existed in the world."

(Skidmore, Owings & Merrill)

Pinning the bowtie: The building's most distinctive feature, its triangular prow, began as a flat, vertical sign (top right), marking the "bowtie" where Broadway and Seventh Avenue cross. The architects liked it so much it grew to the whole height of the building (middle), then turned into a lattice of steel trusses (bottom). It was a short leap to having the building itself come to a point (left).

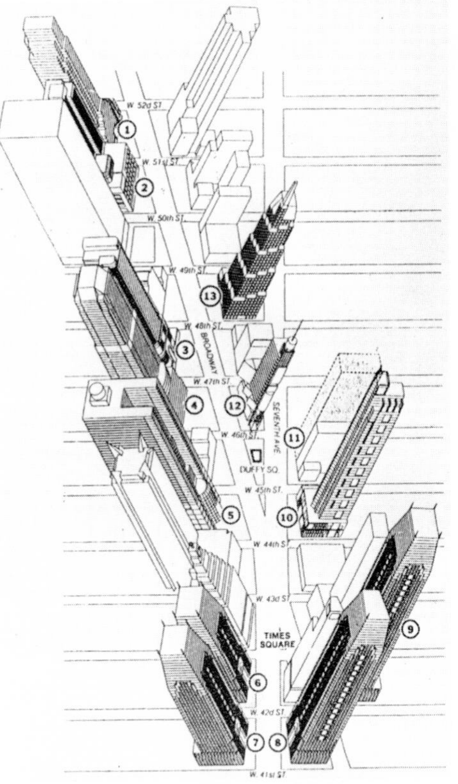

(New York Times)

:hanging face of Times Square: 1540 lway—#10 on the map and in the center of te model below—was one of a dozen planned ings that critics feared would turn the Great e Way into a copy of Park Avenue. But it t quite turn out that way. The four big towers corner of 42nd Street (#6–9) were never built.

(Skidmore, Owings & Merrill)

The new building's foundations were dug nearly 60 feet into the ground, within inches of a subway tunnel and a landmark theater.

Once the ironworkers got a rhythm going, the building went quickly, sometimes two full stories in a week.

Audrey Matlock (top left) always wanted to design a skyscraper, and Skidmore gave her chance. But she was gone even before 1540 Broadway was finished. A building needs engineers (John Ellis and Mitch Mailman, to right; Sal LaScala center photo, left) almost much as it needs lawyers (Howard Hornstei center photo, right). Project managers Luk S Wong (bottom left) and William Tung (bott right) kept the building going up, and watch every dollar going out.

(*Jacques Chenet*)

(The Jerde Partnership)

on Jerde's idea for the atrium was to turn it into a "habitable sign," an electronic xtravaganza that came to be called the "Whiz Bang."

(Addison Thompson)

(Jacques Chenet)

The Bertelsmann Building (also known as 1540 Broadway), formerly the Broadway State Building and One Broadway Place.

Carter Wiseman wrote that it might have been a blessing in disguise if a few developers went broke as a result. Several strains of civic outrage came together in this movement. These included indignation over the illegal demolition at the Macklowe site; revulsion at the vulgar posturing of Donald Trump; and esthetic queasiness over the influence of Post-modernism on the city's skyline, especially directed at the famous "Chippendale" top on Philip Johnson's AT&T headquarters. But there was nothing, short of throwing a blanket over it, that the city could do about the AT&T building, and the same went for Donald Trump. So the backlash concentrated on the one thing the city could control, the size (and especially the height) of new buildings in Manhattan.

One building that ran afoul of the city's new mood of iconoclasm was, as it happened, Cityspire. One chilly spring afternoon in 1987, Cityspire's topping-out party convened on the dusty concrete slab of the tenth floor. A topping-out party celebrates, of course, the erection of the building's topmost structural member (not the completion of the building, which could by no stretch of sales rhetoric be considered finished for months, or sometimes years). Originally this was a party for the workmen to mark a job on which no one died, paid for with a safety bonus from the insurance company. Nowadays topping-out parties for a major building can be elaborate catered affairs filled with bowing Japanese bankers, silk-suited contractors, minor city officials, and hangers-on from the press clustered around the buffet. The topping-out party for Trump Tower attracted both the then-governor of New York, Hugh Carey, and Mayor Koch—before his feud with Trump—who saluted the developer's enterprise thus: "As my mother used to tell me, it's better to be rich, if you have a choice, than to be poor." But the party for Cityspire was a modest affair, with hero sandwiches for the workmen and a few dozen executives from the various contractors, some of whom didn't feel much like celebrating anyway because their trials were starting in a few weeks. Bruce did not want to call attention to the topping-out of Cityspire just then, because it was topping out at a bit over 813 feet, eleven feet higher than was specified in the zoning variance that allowed it to be built.

Eleven feet in 800! Who, in Bruce's view, could possibly care—except as a way to stop him from building at all. As he tirelessly pointed out to reporters over the next two years, the additional height, which was attributable to thickening the floor slabs for structural reasons, contributed no additional floor area to the development, and therefore represented no additional profit. The issue revolved around how and when

Bruce should have notified the city of the change. His opponents contended that as soon as the change was decided on, Bruce should have filed his plans over and gone through the entire approval process again before starting to build. This would have cost only a few million dollars in interest. Bruce contended that the effect of the eleven feet was *de minimus.* He held that if he had applied for the taller building in the first place, it would have been approved. He was just anticipating that approval. Unfortunately, a few developers had adopted the deliberate strategy of exceeding the zoning restrictions and then presenting the city with a nonconforming building as a fait accompli. Bruce was caught up in a wave of civic outrage at that shady practice. Cityspire's eleven feet of concrete became a convenient symbol of what the average newspaper reader might have been led to assume was an unprecedented crime wave among real estate developers. And when the commission later voted on retroactive approval for the taller building, it was voted down.

To Bruce, this episode only served to remind him why he had left the public sector in the first place. To deny him his eleven feet was "a perfect example of irrational processes at work. Any judge would throw it out in a minute, so why go through the exercise?" But this was the uncongenial atmosphere in which Bruce was proposing to request a very large zoning variance to erect a very conspicuous structure above a public street in the very prominent location of Times Square, and the question was, Was he dreaming, or just kidding? Surely it would have been folly to attempt it without Howard, or some equally knowledgeable and well-connected power broker, on his side. A tremendous mystique has understandably grown up around people like Howard, the shadow rulers of what Jack Newfield of the *Village Voice* dubbed "The Permanent Government": the banks, insurance companies, developers, and lawyers who rule New York no matter who holds nominal elective power at any given time. Howard insists his job is far less complicated and sinister than the *Village Voice* makes it out to be. Go back to his analysis, and you will see that the decision about bridging 45th Street would be made by the mayor on political grounds, but "political" only in the highest sense of weighing competing public interests: keeping a major employer in the city, versus keeping a major street open to the sky. In that sense, Howard's contribution was not in his connections, but in understanding how the political process works, seeing how to frame an issue so that the city's interest can most clearly be seen to coincide with that of Howard's clients.

Of course, the scenario began with Howard placing a call to the deputy mayor, and the deputy mayor picking up the phone to talk to him.

Now, is there something wrong with this? Could just anyone call up the deputy mayor, and have his proposal on the mayor's desk within the week? No, but why should they? Howard was a respected lawyer whose client was a prominent developer with a record of getting major projects built. By their accomplishments, they had earned the right to be listened to.

But was it just their accomplishments that opened these doors? From 1984 to 1986 Bruce and Howard gave more than $40,000 in campaign contributions to the mayor, the City Council president, and the Manhattan borough president. Other developers gave even more. The developer Joseph Bernstein gave more than $100,000 to the same three officials and to City Comptroller Harrison Goldin—a demonstration of civic interest made more remarkable by the fact that Bernstein didn't even vote in the 1985 mayoral election. (Bernstein's company, New York Land, was later identified as a front for the American real estate investments of Philippine dictator Ferdinand Marcos.)

In 1988 a state commission on "government integrity" investigated the astonishing generosity that the real estate industry displayed toward members of the Board of Estimate. Though the commission tried mightily, it never succeeded in establishing a link between a particular contribution and a specific benefit obtained by the donor. In testimony to the commission, Donald Trump maintained that he gave money mostly out of friendship, which explained why—since he had so many friends—he sometimes contributed to more than one candidate running for the same office. Bernstein testified that he did not expect favors in exchange for his generosity, but that he was afraid he might be "punished" if he didn't give. (A few years after Bernstein's checks cleared, the city sold him the air rights from a high school for his Americas Tower project on Sixth Avenue and 45th Street.) Interviewed by commission staffers in his office, Bruce asserted that "it would be bad business judgment to stop contributing to campaigns in this city." But by the time he was called to testify a few months later, he had decided that was an "ill-conceived" answer. "I thought to myself that that is an argument one person can make," he told the commissioners, "but it was not my motivation in contributing money. ... In an effort to answer a question, I inadvertently blundered into the area of philosophy." He pointed out that although he did a lot of business in Brooklyn, he did not contribute to the Brooklyn borough president's campaigns. He rebuffed suggestions that his service on a fund-raising committee for the mayor was related to his seeking approval for Cityspire at around the same time. Toward the end of his testimony, a commission member brought up a narrow Board of Estimate vote approving Bruce's residential project at 86th Street and Broadway: "Mr. Eichner," said Richard Emery, "I am asking you seriously for your hypothetical opinion on a point. If you had never embarked on a program of campaign contributions along with all your colleagues in the real estate industry, do you think you could have won the six to five approval on 86th and Broadway?"

And Eichner replied, "Absolutely. How's that for ultimate arrogance?"

And Howard added, "On the merits, we should have won eleven to nothing."

So perhaps Bruce could have won a franchise from the city to build a bridge across West 45th Street. The world will never know. Bruce called Gerry Speyer the next morning and told him his plan, and Speyer seemed interested. Bruce called an executive of Morgan Stanley and outlined the idea to him, and he said he would bring it up to the directors. Bruce got as far as mentioning the idea to David Childs, without authorizing Skidmore to do any billable work on it. And there matters stayed. Who knows what goes on in the minds of an investment bank? Morgan Stanley never even came around for a proposal. Two years later, they were still in the same offices, with no announced plans to move anywhere. This sequence of tantalizing opportunities, great excitement, and anticipation followed by the letdown of a deal that not only didn't work out but turned out to have had no basis in reality in the first place happens all the time in the real estate business. It happens in other fields, too, of course, but not many individual commercial transactions are as big as a major office lease, which can run for twenty years at $30 million a year.

The office tower was only one part of the Broadway State project. Although the retail accounted for only a small part of the building's leasable space, it would ideally make a disproportionate contribution to its income. Bruce was expecting to rent the office space for around forty dollars a square foot (gross, including taxes and operating expenses passed along to the tenant). Rentals in the shopping atrium were projected to average nearly $100 a square foot. The choicest locations, with street frontage on Broadway, might command as much as $165. This disparity reflected the reality that retail frontage on the city's streets was in finite supply, while office buildings had the whole atmosphere to fill. That wasn't even top dollar for retail space in Manhattan at that time. The priciest retail space in the city, on Fifth Avenue in the Fifties, rented for as much as $400 a square foot. The tenants included some of the city's most fashionable jewelers, but also, to New York's perpetual embarrassment, what were known locally as "Going-Out-of-Business" stores, tourist traps selling cameras, small appliances, and "Oriental-design" rugs for whatever was in the customer's wallet.

In the retail atrium Bruce would be attempting something that had almost never been built successfully in New York. Paradoxically, New Yorkers, in the most vertically oriented city in the world, clung to the habit of walking in off the sidewalk to do their shopping. New York Land Company had developed a 260,000-square-foot mall in an old department store just across the street from Macy's. It was supposed to bring the sophistication of upper Madison Avenue to Herald Square, but what it brought instead was the desolation of the Bronx; for years it remained nearly three-quarters empty. The "festival market" concept that was so successful in Boston, Baltimore, and other older cities never fully caught on in New York; its local incarnation, South Street Seaport, was thronged with young stockbrokers getting drunk after work, but otherwise, the *Times* noted, "has failed to find its niche within the cutthroat retail marketplace of Manhattan." The glamorous marble-and-brass atrium at Trump Tower was an exception, although real estate brokers often muttered that the stores there didn't do as well as Trump claimed; whether out of envy or conviction is impossible to say.

The lesson Bruce took from these examples was the importance of visibility from the street. Bruce demanded that the atrium be brought right out to the building line, where a glass wall on the sidewalk would make it visible to anyone passing by on Broadway. A tremendous amount of effort went into tinkering with the dimensions of the atrium so that shops on all three lower levels could be seen from the sidewalk. SOM made charts showing lines of sight from the various points along the sidewalk to the shop windows inside. They constructed elaborate models, and everyone would take turns crouching down and squinting critically through the plastic windows. Luk Sun's usual reaction was that the space looked cramped and the atrium hole needed to be made bigger. The problem lay in making the hole bigger without making the surrounding floor area smaller, because the other thing Luk Sun insisted on was maximizing the rentable retail square footage. The initial pro-forma to the bank specified 120,000 rentable square feet of retail, and even after SOM told him that would be impossible he pressed them to come as close to that number as possible.

One morning early in 1987, Steve Berini got a visit from an old friend and protégé, Al Corti, director of leasing for the Hahn Company. The Hahn Company, of San Diego, claimed to be the largest developer of shopping centers on the West Coast, and one of the largest in the country, with (at that time) close to fifty centers in eighteen states. Berini told Corti a little bit about his own retail troubles on Broadway, and Corti offered to look at the plans and offer any criticism he thought might help.

Corti did indeed have some criticisms to offer. He thought the retail atrium was "sterile" and "rigid"; it lacked "identity" and "visual interest." He thought there was far too little public space, especially in the "food court," and that the second subcellar was too far from the street to be useful for retail. He suggested putting the movie theaters down there instead, because the theaters would do business no matter where they were.

Berini passed these remarks on to Bruce, who found that they encapsulated a lot of his own uneasiness with Skidmore's work on the atrium. Bruce suggested that Hahn could come aboard as a consultant. Corti, after talking to his boss, Vernon Schwartz, said they didn't do consulting as such, but might be interested in a deal if Bruce gave them an equity stake. Bruce's reply stuck in their minds a long time. "I don't give anything to anybody," he said. "But I don't mind if they earn it."

There was one other area of revenue to be explored at this early stage, and that was the outdoor signs. Alice Hoffman had a meeting with Mel Starr, the president of Artkraft Strauss, which built almost all the major illuminated signs in Times Square. Starr was a man in his sixties with a bushy gray mustache, wearing a sports jacket in oversized blue and brown checks, a brown shirt with an embroidered apple on the collar, several impressive gold chains, and a gold Star of David at the level of his navel. Starr had very clear ideas about what the Times Square of the 1990s should be like, which was remarkably similar to the Times Square of Artkraft Strauss's heyday in the 1940s and 1950s. He arrived with a completed sketch of a sign he proposed to erect on the Broadway façade of the building: virtually the entire Broadway façade, approximately 75 feet high and 175 feet long. It was a sign for Budweiser beer, and it contained a monumental Budweiser logo, flanked by two illuminated fifty-foot-high cans, surrounded by animated Clydesdales and flapping neon eagles and a traveling message sign carrying sports news. With Eichner's permission, he was prepared to fly out to St. Louis on the next plane and sign up Anheuser-Busch.

"Won't this make us known as the Budweiser building?" Alice asked doubtfully.

"Of course it will!" Starr replied exuberantly. "It will give you *presence.*"

A pause ensued.

"Can we get a million dollars a year for that?" she finally asked.

"A million dollars?" Starr asked expansively. "In fifteen years, I can get you two million dollars."

"What about in three years, when the building opens?"

Another pause. Starr looked deflated. "I don't think that's in the cards," he said at last.

"What *is* in the cards?" she persisted.

A much longer pause. "Two hundred thousand," he said at last.

"I've got to tell you, your numbers are scaring us to death," Alice told him as he rolled up his drawings. "Two hundred thousand dollars is nothing to us."

15

Even while demolition continued, preparations were under way for the next phase of the work, which would be excavation. A hole fifty-four feet deep (as was then envisioned) covering 37,000 square feet worked out to an excavation of 74,000 cubic yards, minus the volume of the existing cellars. A rough estimate of the material that would have to be actually dug was 60,000 cubic yards. This may not sound like much in comparison to other great construction projects of the past (the Great Pyramid of Cheops, 3.3 million cubic yards; Grand Coulee Dam, 10.6 million cubic yards), but it was quite enough to have to remove in eight months, considering that the average dump truck carried only between ten and fifteen cubic yards.

The question was, 60,000 yards of what?

In a general sense, the geology of midtown Manhattan held few surprises. There would be dirt, and below that clay giving way to weathered feldspar, and then increasingly dense layers of Manhattan schist—that ancient gray, foliated, metamorphic rock, often flecked with shiny chips of mica, that has been the foundation of more great fortunes than all the rubies of the Orient. But the contour of the rock varied greatly even over short distances, so that it was impossible to predict the conditions below ground at any specific location. Data from nearby excavations was as useless as a dowsing rod. All one could do was hope. Unfortunately it wasn't even clear what one should hope for. The excavator preferred dirt, which was easier to dig, while the engineers were hoping for rock, which was preferable as a support for the foundations. In particular, the footings of the building, where the major columns come down to ground, should rest on "sound, hard rock" capable of bearing no less than forty tons of lawyers (approximately 500) per square foot without crumbling.

Hard rock was also intensely desirable on the west side of the site, adjacent to the subway tunnel that ran beneath Broadway. This was not, Gary pointed out, because rock was necessary to stabilize the tracks during the intensive blasting and digging that would be going on just a few feet away. Rather, it would help stabilize the Transit Authority's civil engineers, whose permission was required for blasting near a tunnel. "We're not going to harm a hair on the head of a single fare-paying passenger," Gary assured Luk Sun. "All we have to do is convince the Transit Authority that the subway won't fall into our hole if the earth tilts on its axis and starts rotating around the equator, and for that, it would be nice if we could point to a piece of rock the track is sitting on that hasn't budged in 600 million years."

Unfortunately, a series of test pits dug by men with jackhammers and shovels showed that the rock was highest where it wasn't needed, in the southeast corner. As one moved west, toward the subway, the rock fell off to as low as thirty-six feet down, which was below the level of the tracks.

The one thing one didn't want to find, of course, was water. Nineteenth-century maps indicated a small stream in the general area of the site. This said nothing about the likelihood that water was still present underground, but it was an unwelcome discovery nonetheless. Where water has been, the rock left behind is often decomposed and crumbling. In more recent times, a small stream of water had been observed from time to time running along the concrete floor of the bottom cellar of 1540 Broadway. Ellis had filled a jar from this source and sent it to a laboratory. The report was that it was full of coliform bacteria, indicating a leaking sewer as the source.

"So," said Mitchell, "does that mean I ask the city to fix its sewer?"

There was a moment of silence while everyone contemplated the absurdity of this suggestion.

"You could try," Gary said judiciously. "You never know what will happen. I dug four basements when I built IBM, pumping like a maniac all the way down, and when I finally got that sucker as dry as it could be humanly made, the city came and fixed the sewer anyway."

One sunny morning in June a flatbed truck pulled up to the site and drove onto the carpet of dirt where the Howard Johnson's had been. Two men erected a boring drill on the back of the truck—a very complicated and dirty piece of machinery at whose business end was a hollow bit and a length of pipe a couple of inches in diameter. The pipe went down in five-foot segments and returned with a cross-sectional sample of the subterranean environment. The men started the engine, threw a lever, and then commenced to lounge morosely against the side of the truck and drink coffee. On some invisible signal they stopped the rig and hoisted the pipe to the surface. When they tapped it with the head of a heavy wrench, a cylinder of slimy gray-green rock, in broken sections of about six inches, slid out. An engineer, a small, precise, brown-skinned man in a gleaming white hardhat, materialized and examined a crumbling yellow patch on one section.

"Feldspar," he muttered. "Crummy rock."

Suddenly a chunk of concrete, a piece no bigger than an apricot, came spinning out of the air and landed by his feet. Then another landed at the edge of the sidewalk and skipped across the pavement and into the gutter. A pedestrian cleared it by a short hop as it skittered past, but neither he nor anyone else hurrying along Broadway that morning paused to see what new urban disaster was heralded by a fall of stones from the sky. One of the drillers looked up. He saw a small shower of debris burst from a shattered window high up on the north wall of 1540 Broadway.

"Hey!" he yelled. Alabama, the demolition shop steward, came running over, looked up, and yelled, much louder, "HEY!"

Another, larger chunk came down and punched a jagged hole in the roof of a van parked nearby. Mario, whose van this was, appeared, looked up, and yelled "HEY!!!"

"Hey, what is this fucking shit, they're throwing stuff out of the windows," one of the drill operators bellowed. "If one of them pieces of rock hits me, I'm gonna fucking sue."

He struck a defiant posture with his arms folded across his T-shirt.

"Let's get the fuck out of here," his partner said. "If one of them bricks comes down on your head that hardhat won't mean shit ... you see what it did to the roof of that car?"

"They're gonna stop," Mario said.

The debris stopped.

"Never a dull moment," Mario muttered.

A family of tourists had edged in off the sidewalk and was staring wide-eyed at the devastation around them. Mario hurried over to shoo them. "Please," he implored, "if something came off that building and hit one of those kids you'd never forgive yourselves."

"We're going," the man said apologetically, but the woman looked annoyed and snapped, "You should have it closed off!"

Mario lost his beseeching tone. "You should know better!" he yelled back.

Meanwhile, another problem was looming at the opposite end of the site, where the Lyceum stood. On blasting in that area, the Landmarks Preservation Commission would have final say, and the care the Transit Authority exercised for the lives of its passengers was nothing compared with the zeal Landmarks brought to the protection of stone cornices, carved wooden balustrades, and plaster egg-and-dart moldings. Early in April, Howard and Andrea met with the staff of the commission, including the executive director, Gene Norman. At the next project meeting in Bruce's office, Howard announced that the commission was taking the question very seriously. It was imperative to draw up a protection plan for the Lyceum. "Or as sure as I'm sitting here," he warned, "there will be no blasting on this job."

"They're rubbing their hands together," Andrea added.

The protection plan began with an exhaustive survey of the Lyceum theater as it existed in A.D. 1987. This document, in four volumes including two of photographs, represents one of the most comprehensive records of plaster fatigue in the annals of civil engineering; no crack visible to the naked eye escaped notation, because no crack would go unpunished unless it could be proven to have been there before.

The theater would be monitored for vibration during the blasting. This is commonly done with seismographs, the same instruments used to detect and measure earthquakes. Of course, the Richter Scale is a relatively coarse device for measuring the effects of construction blasting. Or so one hopes. Blast effects are described in terms of the peak velocity, in inches per second, of the vibrations induced in the building being monitored. A commonly used ceiling, below which it is assumed no damage can occur, is two inches per second. But the Lyceum was an old building with long, unsupported spans, and in the opinion of the commission this made it particularly vulnerable to the effects of nearby blasting. They suggested reducing the limit to 1.5 inches per second.

"That's a crock of shit!" Gary objected, when Andrea relayed this view to him.

"I wouldn't know but I'll take your word for it," Andrea said dryly. "If you can put that into technical language I'll try to make that case with them."

"What we need is a rock star," Mitchell put in briskly.

Andrea looked surprised. "A rock star? You want my daughter to suggest one?"

"I've got one already, thanks."

The man Mitchell had in mind was Charles H. Dowding, professor of civil engineering at Northwestern University, author of *Blast Vibration Monitoring and Control,* winner of the 1981 Outstanding Applied Research Award in Rock Mechanics from the National Committee for Rock Mechanics, among seven pages' worth of additional honors and publications. What made Dowding so valuable was his theory of frequency-dependent blast monitoring, which gave a rationale for accepting higher vibration limits than the industry standard under certain conditions. On a day in late spring, Howard, Andrea, Mitch, John Ellis, and Dowding came to make their case to a half-dozen officials of the Landmarks Preservation Committee.

Dowding's theory was that velocity alone did not accurately predict the potential for danger from a given blast. Equally important was the frequency of the vibrations induced by the blast, especially in relation to the resonant frequency of the building. A structure, like a guitar string, has a resonant frequency at which it will naturally vibrate. A blast wave at or close to that frequency will cause the greatest damage. In the case of the Lyceum, Dowding determined that, owing to its long unsupported span, it had an unusually low resonant frequency of around five cycles per second. He determined this by putting a seismograph on the balcony and having Ellis jump up and down on the balcony to set it vibrating. If his theory was correct, vibrations of much higher frequencies would leave the structure relatively unaffected. He illustrated this with a ceramic coffee mug that he held suspended from a long rubber band. With a slow, rhythmic motion, corresponding to a low-frequency wave, Dowding set the cup oscillating wildly up and down. Then he jiggled the band rapidly, mimicking a high-frequency shock wave, and the cup twitched slightly but stayed essentially in the same place. Happily enough, high-frequency waves are just those produced by close-in blasting, which also gives the highest particle velocities. Dowding therefore recommended a sliding scale of maximum particle velocities, depending on the frequency, of up to 3.0. Finally, since he was one of the few people in the world who understood this stuff, he offered to supplement the on-site seismic monitors by monitoring the blasting telemetrically from his office in Chicago.

"We will look carefully at the plan," said the commission's counsel sternly, "but the best plan in the world doesn't enforce itself."

"Know that we will be in the field," added Norman ominously, "monitoring to see that the plan is observed. And if there are violations, we will shut you down."

The demolition was picking up speed now, in spite of all the obstacles that were constantly put in its path. There was a steady drizzle of summonses from the city's building inspectors. Artie Baris's nephew Kevin would periodically devote an entire day to sitting around a sweltering municipal office to contest these, at the end of which he would have to pay a fine anyway. There were two on successive days for the crime of placing building materials in the street—namely, a plank of wood to discourage civilians from parking in front of the sidewalk cut used by the dump trucks. "I mean, we paid the city for the cut anyway, so what's wrong with trying to keep people from parking there so we couldn't use it—especially since it's a no-standing zone anyway?" Kevin complained. Fine: $100 each. He got two summonses for failure to produce a permit for the use of water from two fire hydrants. They had the permits, but they were in Mario's truck, and Kevin didn't have a key to open the truck when the inspector came. Fine: $100 each.

A natural question is whether a twenty-dollar bill directly in the hand of the inspector would have saved a lot of this trouble. It is a matter of record and common knowledge that, as a state organized-crime task force report said in 1987, "bribes, grease payments, and tips are a way of life in New York City's construction industry." A few months later, a federal grand jury in Brooklyn indicted twenty-five contractors for allegedly bribing inspectors to overlook violations in the way they removed and disposed of asbestos. Several big demolition companies were named in the indictment, but Associated was not among them. It would be naïve to think that no money ever changed hands on the Broadway State site. Once in a while Kevin, checking trucks out on their way to the dump, would be asked as a "favor" to sign a driver out for one more load than he actually took in a day. "I don't think my uncle would like me to do that," he would say innocently, and the driver would grind his gears and lurch off as if he'd just seen the ghost of Bobby Kennedy.

But it would be wrong to imagine that corruption was so commonplace that no one thought twice about it. On the contrary, people were sensitive about the matter to the point of paranoia. This was especially true among city inspectors, who out of self-preservation had to regard everyone they encountered on a job as a potential witness for the prosecution. Around this time Ellis and Gary Negrycz were in Turner's trailer on the site, wrestling with a problem over the excavation permit. Ellis put in a call to a Fire Department official who had authority over blasting on the job. "Just a minute, chief," he said, "I'm going to put you on the speaker phone so Gary Negrycz can hear this." Instantly the line went dead. Ellis looked up, puzzled, but Negrycz was unsurprised.

"Don't ever put a guy from the city on the speaker phone, John," he said quietly. "He doesn't know who else might be in the room. I would've done the same thing myself."

As the weather grew hotter and the job grew dirtier and the columns they had to take down grew heavier, Mario's mood seemed actually to improve. Between twelve and twelve-thirty the men would sit in the shade of the sidewalk bridge on Broadway and try to cool off and eat their lunches. Mario would pace restlessly up and down, looking for banter.

"We're making good time now," he would say. "Gonna get another floor tomorrow, then work all day Saturday and spend Sunday sitting on the lawn and watching the flowers grow. Hey, Horse, what's your favorite flower?"

"Ain't got one," growled Horse, a man as big and dark and forbidding as a Kansas thunderhead.

"Well, then, what's your favorite verse of Scripture?"

"Ain't got one of them, neither."

"How about the Twenty-third Psalm? John three-sixteen? 'For God so loved the world that he gave his only Son, that whoever believes in him should not perish but have eternal life.'"

"Do you have a verse for walking on high steel?" Mario was asked.

"I do!" he replied enthusiastically. He paraphrased Matthew 4:6: "'If you fall, God will surely bear you up, and your foot not be injured.' I know it's true because I fell five stories and God surely did bear me up. Five *loft* stories. I hit a pile of rubble and walked out the cellar, without a scratch on me. My shoelaces was still tied. The doctor looked at me and said, 'I don't know how many lives you've got left but you just used one of them.'

"Of course, in the Bible there, that's Satan talking to Jesus. But maybe even Satan tells the truth sometimes."

On a sunny Tuesday in June, two Caterpillars were seen to be hard at work in the dirt of what had been the theater, sorting through the masses of rubble. One took up a bucketful of debris, and, backing slowly across the yard, spread it out with a touching delicacy, like a jeweler spilling stones onto black velvet. A line of pickers followed, bent over like peasants, gleaning the odd nugget of copper or tin. Another machine roared up to a thick section of wall that had fallen more or less intact and pulled it apart by dragging the teeth of its bucket across it, like a predator flaying a kill. Alabama directed a hose into the creature's dusty maw. The bulldozer took a deep bite of the disordered heap of bricks, lurched around in a half circle, and then charged across the yard to dump its load onto a sloping pile that was gradually taking shape in the area of what had been the orchestra.

Mario was getting ready to wreck the proscenium wall. This was a seventy-five-foot-high wall of reinforced concrete, with attached brick-work, running about eighty feet east and west down the middle of the block. The theater had been ground to dust except for this one monumental wall. There are two ways to wreck such a wall. You could erect a scaffold alongside it and send up men with hammers to break it apart from the top down, which would be slow, expensive, and fairly foolproof. Or you could pull it over all at once in one mighty apocalypse, which is quick, cheap, and also pretty much foolproof, depending on how fast you can get out of the way of it when it falls.

The tool for this job is the rake, a piece of equipment so primitive and ferocious in appearance that it is astonishing to see it in use on the streets of New York City. It consists of a heavy steel claw about four feet long mounted on a forty-foot length of thick steel pipe. The pipe fits into a socket on the bucket of a Caterpillar, turning an ordinary bulldozer into a long-necked yellow-bodied prehistoric monster on treads. The procedure is for the driver to hook the top of the wall with the claw and then tug in reverse until a large chunk of the wall breaks off and comes flying down in a thick cloud of rubble. Because the wall was higher than the rake could reach, the men were building a steep, two-story-high ramp on the south side for the Caterpillar to climb.

The operation was scheduled for the early evening, when it would still be light but Variety's delicate computers would be slumbering. At five-thirty, Alabama was stationed on 46th Street, waiting for Variety to close for the night. George Atkinson, a burly, soft-spoken engineer, stood on a tread of his machine, sizing up his concrete adversary. The wall ran east and west and he would pull it over from the south. On the north side there was the back of 1550 Broadway off to the left and Variety over on the right. On the south side, where he was, there was just the wreckage of 1540 on his left, and on the right, the wall of the Lyceum. He would have to be careful not to drive into it when he came roaring backwards off the ramp.

"How come everybody is so damned particular about that building, anyway?" he asked.

Someone pointed out the bas-reliefs to him.

"Shit," he said, incredulously, "you mean that stuff on the front? We knock down buildings like that all the time."

On 46th Street, Alabama saw Vito leave Variety and lock the door behind him, and he walked to the corner to put up a barricade to close the 46th Street sidewalk to pedestrians. Atkinson climbed into the cab of his machine. The rake was lying on the ground; he lowered his bucket and drove forward until the pipe meshed in the socket, and a man ran up and secured it with a pin the size of a milk bottle. He raised the bucket and the rake elevated itself shakily into the air.

Atkinson drove his bulldozer up the ramp. He hooked the brick and pulled off a chunk perhaps five feet across and three deep.

"My stomach's jumping!" Mario confessed. He bawled encouragement to Atkinson. "Get a big piece!" he shouted. "Not a little piece! A big piece! Come on, man! Do it!

"If I stood over there he'd hook a piece," Mario muttered. "He wants me to hold his hand." He ran across the yard, stopping to pick up a fistful of gravel that he flung at the cab's window to get Atkinson's attention. With big gestures he motioned Atkinson to start pulling the wall on the left.

"Mario!" Ira called from the sidewalk. "Get back up here!" The rake tugged at a forty-foot slab of brick. A crack opened at the corner, then grew as the Caterpillar grunted and strained. Finally the wall began to lean. "Man, that wall is hard," Mario commented; and just then it surrendered, and a huge irregular chunk came crashing down, while the bulldozer came charging backwards off the ramp, carried more than halfway across the yard by its momentum.

"Now I can uncross my fingers," Mario said. "No, that's not right, I keep them crossed all the time."

"What are you building here?" a man asked from the sidewalk.

"Skating rink," Mario answered with a big grin.

"You ever find anything interesting when you dig in here? Bodies or anything?"

"Bodies? Oh, yeah, we found three of them right here, only the machines ground them up so much there wasn't much sense in telling about it."

Finally the big concrete wall itself was the only piece left standing. Atkinson got a grip on the top of the wall and began to pull. The bantering group on the sidewalk grew silent. A few chips flew off the top as the rake's teeth seemed to slip for a moment. Then they dug in and held, and with a tremendous crash the whole wall buckled and tumbled in a great cloud of gray dust.

"I knew he could do it!" Mario exclaimed. "Come on, let's take a look!" He started walking toward Atkinson, who had climbed out of his cab and was standing alongside his machine, looking down toward 46th Street. A police siren started up nearby. "I'll bet someone called the police," Mario said, grinning. "Always happens when you drop a building, someone calls the police and says the building fell down."

He gained the embankment. Atkinson was still staring steadily down. The grin left Mario's face as he followed the engineer's gaze to the wall of 1550 Broadway. "Shit!" he exclaimed. "They took the whole back of that building off!"

Not exactly, but bad enough. When the wall went over, a chunk of it didn't fall neatly in a pile but by some freak of mechanics went flying off, hurtled sixty feet across the yard, and smacked into the back wall of the Short Lines bus tour office. It made a hole ten feet high and fifteen feet wide in the masonry-block wall, and the force of it coming through blew out the plate-glass window. Shards were scattered halfway across 46th Street. Luckily, the office was empty—although the camera store in the same building was still open—and Alabama had stopped traffic, so there were no injuries. By the time Mario reached 46th Street, the street was full of confused-looking cops. He occupied them while Alabama headed up a small detail on the other side of the block, quickly, quietly, burying the rake in the dirt. By the time the TV crews arrived there was nothing to see, except the broken window and the gaping hole in the wall. But this time, when the job was shut, it stayed shut for five days.

16/16

Disagreements between architects and clients are fought on notoriously shifty and treacherous ground. The client has a program, which describes the building's size and function; the architect has a parti, the idea that he wants to express in the building's design. The apparent equivalence of these positions is subverted, however, by the fact that the former hires the latter. Thenceforth, the architect's duty is to fulfill the client's program. It would be unprofessional for an architect to argue for a design that did not advance the program, no matter how beautiful or intellectually satisfying it might be. Most architects would never do anything so irresponsible, except when they've designed something really, really terrific that the client is just too cheap, ignorant or stubborn to appreciate. What distinguishes successful architects is the ability to convince themselves that even the most benighted client will eventually recognize great architecture. If the profession had a coat of arms, it would say, "They'll love it when they see it."

To be fair, the client, especially a speculative developer, is also a slave to the program. He has partners and banks to answer to, a pro-forma that must be met. The architect likes to imagine that he alone has been invested with the sacred trust of bringing forth the building, but from the point of view of the developer, he is just another consultant.

"Lawyers come in, and their word is golden, they utter the word 'risk,' and a whole series of architectural opportunities are gone," Childs once griped.

Some architects, of course, win arguments with clients. Frank Lloyd Wright lived for decades off people who wanted a Frank Lloyd Wright house more than they wanted one with walls and doors. Helmut Jahn's implacable insistence on having things his own way has worn down more than one developer. Childs is by nature a more agreeable man. Most often when Bruce suggested something, Childs was quick not just to implement it, but to endorse it as a concept. "Bruce's heart is in the right place," Childs said early on. "If someone had described Bruce to me, I would have said, 'There's a guy I wouldn't like,' but I'm fascinated by him. I think he's got special stuff in him that will make special projects. I have worked with clients who seem intent on bringing out the worst in you, on finding out what you would most like to build so they can go in exactly the opposite direction, and Bruce is nothing like that."

But Bruce's "process" placed its own peculiar demands on the architects. After David's confrontation with Bruce over the prow, he came back to the office and eloquently described the humiliation of having his design critiqued by a real estate broker. It was clear he would have been less offended if Bruce had consulted a hot dog vendor from Central Park. "In a way," Audrey mused, "it's easier to work for someone who pounds the table and says, 'This is what I want!' because even if he's wrong you know where you're going."

The following day, Tom Fridstein scheduled a meeting with Luk Sun to talk about "process."

"Something has gone wrong with the process," Fridstein mused on his way uptown. "We thought we had tacit approval on the direction we were taking. To be told now after all these weeks that it's all wrong is terribly demoralizing. This is a creative effort. You have a team, and when you have to go back and redo six weeks of work, you can't just throw more people at a project; the people there just have to work harder. And after a while it burns the people out. I can't ask them to stay up all night again because the client showed the drawings to a real estate broker who didn't like them.

"We'll survive, we'll pull together. We haven't lost six weeks, Bruce has. If we go on from here, we can still get the foundation in by next May. But Luk Sun wanted working drawings by October to bid the job, and he's lost any shot at that. It just can't be done.

"I think that despite what he says, at heart Bruce doesn't want a great building. And he's wrong. Nobody wants to go into an ordinary building, not clients, not staffers, not secretaries. People want quality architecture. It will be tough enough to get people to take space in Times Square. If Bruce puts up less than a great building he'll be dead. And we can't afford to do that, either. We wouldn't want our names on it. We have twenty or thirty projects going on in Manhattan right now. If we walked away from this job, it wouldn't bother us any. But it would certainly hurt Bruce."

The next day, Wong was asked if he had tried to smooth things over with the architects. He looked incredulous. "I told Fridstein I don't want to hear that his people are demoralized and going to stew for a week because there's a change in the design. They're paid for this. If we lose time, it's our problem, not theirs."

Luk Sun shook his head.

"Prima donnas," he muttered.

A certain chill characterized the atmosphere at the job meeting the following week, which both David and Bruce missed.

"Because we're still looking at the massing, we don't have new office floor plans to show you today ..." Fridstein began.

"Why, Tom?" Luk Sun asked softly.

"Well," Fridstein answered, "without the nose, the whole expression of the building changes."

"If your nose is removed, you might want to redesign your face," Bill Hellmuth added.

"Especially if you cut it off yourself," Gary put in.

Luk Sun threw him a frosty look.

"Thanks, Gary," Tom said. "I was waiting for someone to say that."

This was a clever ploy by Fridstein to conceal what the architects were really up to, a subversive masterstroke of literal-mindedness. Bruce's instructions to take the prow, the trusswork, off the building, represented a clear-cut case of *force majeure*. But they hadn't surrendered, merely retreated to fight another time. When they returned the following week, they brought new sets of plans and a new model. The trusswork had indeed disappeared, but in its place, the building itself now came to a point on Broadway: "a crease, a bow," David said, "which we think creates a very dramatic and impressive space with views up and down Broadway; and on the point of the crease ..."—David paused almost imperceptibly—"we have kept the spike."

"That's a metal pole," Bruce said.

"Yes, or it could be glass, or it could be lighted," David said, adding hastily: "And now it's really more like a pinstripe running up the side of the building."

The architects had also applied some ingenuity to the curtain wall. A series of recesses had been chiseled into the building in vertical strips, on the 45th Street elevation and on the Broadway face of the tower, on either side of the prow. The recesses were three feet deep. They were large: twenty feet across and three stories high. They were in a pattern that repeated every four floors—that is, with one unrecessed floor between them. These did multiple duty as an architectural feature. They provided an intermediate visual scale between the large-scale massing of the building and the details of the mullions and spandrels. They promoted verticality. They drew attention to the office entrance on the south elevation. And they drove the structural engineers crazy trying to figure out how to support the three-foot-deep overhang of the unrecessed floors. Nothing that drives engineers crazy can be all bad, Audrey reasoned.

"I have two questions about this design," Bruce said. "I definitely like the fact that it now looks like a building I understand. To me, it's now more elegant-looking than avant-garde. You may not like this comment ..."

"I've never objected to elegant," David put in.

"... but what I like about this building is, it doesn't scream Times Square at you. It doesn't respond to what the planners believe is the nature of Times Square, 1987, that they want to see frozen in aspic.

"I just want to think about how usable that space at the point of the building is going to be. I'm worried it's going to be a kind of screwed-up room."

"Do you want us to do a layout for you?" Bill asked. "This could lay out in different ways, as a conference room, a reception area, a chairman-of-the-board suite."

"Yes, fine," Bruce said. "But assuming that works, I'm still not sure how I feel about that pole down the front. I see it as unpainted, weather-worn."

"Well," David said, "bear in mind, looking across the street is no treat, so you want to look up and down Broadway, and this creates a natural division from inside the space."

Luk Sun had been staring at the floor plans for some time. He was looking at the core. The hard work of designing the core was still in the future, but the architects had sketched in locations for the elevator shafts and stairs. The elevator cars were arranged in facing rows on either side of a north-south corridor. This worked well on the ground floor, where as one entered the building from 45th Street, the elevator corridor lay straight ahead across the lobby. The lobby, squeezed by the through-block passage to the west, was not as large as the architects would have liked, so the corridor on the far side made it seem larger and gave it a visual focus.

But on the office floors it seemed to Luk Sun that this did not work so well. The elevator corridor ran perpendicular to the strong east-west axis of the building, an axis now made even more pronounced by the building's prow. That seemed ungainly. The offices would lay out awkwardly. What would happen, he mused, if the core were given a quarter turn? You probably wouldn't have one long corridor then, but two shorter ones side by side. If one of these were on axis with the prow, someone stepping out of the elevator onto a vacant floor could just look to one side and be looking straight out at the prow, "which I gather is going to be a major marketing point," he added.

David, Bill, and Audrey immediately came up with reasons why that would be impractical, why it would screw up the lobby and make them throw out six weeks' worth of work on making the movie theaters fit around the core, but Luk Sun was adamant.

"Okay, we'll try," Childs agreed, "but I can't promise anything."

"David, try."

This turned out to be a major turning point in the design of the building. There was no design meeting the next week, but on Friday Luk Sun went to Skidmore's office to go over the drawings. "We spent a lot of time studying your suggestion about the core," Tom said, "and at first we were extraordinarily upset ... but in some ways we decided it really works better. Bob Halvorson [the structural engineer] says he's been staring at these drawings for months trying to make something happen. Turning the core did it. We can put six steel columns in the core, a very stiff core that takes almost all the wind load of the building."

The one place where the rotated core posed a problem was on the ground floor, where access to the elevators was now from the far right-hand corner of the lobby as one entered from 45th Street, rather than straight ahead. Straight ahead was the blank back wall of one set of elevator shafts. Eventually, something would have to go on that wall. There would be time for that later. Luk Sun offered only one cautionary note. "I'm not going to spend a hundred and fifty grand for a fucking Lichtenstein," he warned them.

Now, and only now, the engineers could work their magic of breathing life into the shell the architects had handed them. Conceptually, the elevators are the starting point in designing the core. This is not just because they take up the largest amount of space, but also because they have to be in the same place from floor to floor. Any of the other components that run vertically through the building—plumbing, stairs, even structural columns—can undergo a horizontal displacement (called a "transfer") between floors, but elevator shafts can only go straight up. So they must be in the right place the first time.

The elevators had their own consultant, a former Otis engineer named Kevin Huntington. Huntington's job was to calculate the most efficient arrangement of elevators to move 3,000 people in and out of their offices four times a day. There is no simple formula for this. Or, rather, there are simple formulas, but they don't give the best answers. They tend to err on the side of excess capacity, because the consequence of underelevatoring—riots in the lobby by lawyers forced to wait a whole minute to start making money—is too awful to contemplate.

Huntington approached elevator design as an art as well as a science. With the plans of the building and a few crucial facts about its location and occupancy, he would conceive an elevator scheme—so many cars of given dimensions and speed serving a stated number of floors. That was the art. Then he would try it to see how it would actually function in the building; this was the science. The key to Huntington's business was proprietary computer software that could simulate a five-minute segment in the life of the building, drawn from any desired part of the day. The computer would set the hypothetical elevators moving and fill them with imaginary people. Ghost vice presidents would cluster in the lobby at nine-ten, jabbing impatiently at the "up" button; at noon, ectoplasmic secretaries would gravitate toward the elevators, where the "Down" buttons glowed red with the promise of the pleasures of lunch and shopping. The computer would dispatch cabs to answer the imaginary calls and monitor each phantom trip. Then the computer would spit out pages of data on every important parameter of elevator performance, and Kevin would see how close he had come to the ideal balance of efficiency and cost.

To do his job, Huntington had to become something of an expert on the culture of the American office building. He once spent nearly eight months studying a single bank of elevators serving twelve floors of the Exxon Building. The peak time for elevator use in midtown Manhattan is at lunch, specifically 12:20 P.M. In other cities it is usually at the start of the day (eight-fifteen in Des Moines, for example), but the uncertainty of rush-hour transportation in Manhattan flattens out the morning peak to a half-hour blob. The most important factor in passenger satisfaction is the length of time, on average, spent waiting for an elevator to answer a call. The degree of crowding in the car is second most important. Total trip time, the sum of waiting and traveling time, is third, illogically enough; total trip time ought to be more important than waiting time alone, if what matters is how fast you get to where you're going. But Kevin had stumbled on the psychological truth that people are less impatient of time spent actually in motion than of waiting. He had calculated the threshold of frustration very precisely, and determined that a first-class office building in midtown Manhattan should have an average waiting time at the height of the morning rush of no more than thirty-one seconds. Twenty-seven seconds was "good" and twenty-four seconds was considered "excellent." Peak lunchtime waits were permitted to be exactly seven seconds longer. These figures vary from place to place, and predictably were longer in cities where the majority of inhabitants don't bill their time in five-minute segments.

As far as crowding goes, Kevin assumed a theoretical maximum density of one person per 1.65 square feet, or twenty-three people in a typical office cab seven feet wide by five and a half feet deep. Actual average loads, in his opinion, should not exceed 2.75 square feet per person. Corporations liked to put their big executive offices on the top floors, which were correspondingly less crowded, so Kevin had to account for that. He also had to make some assumptions about who would occupy the building. A building with just one large company in it requires more elevator capacity than if it had many smaller tenants. This is partly because people at a big company will tend to arrive and leave at the same time, and partly because they move around more between floors during the day. "The larger the company, the more random movement," Kevin explained. "Some of it is relatively aimless. Some people in big companies seem to spend a lot of time just going from floor to floor, hiding." The type of business also makes a difference. Accountants tend to stay put a lot. In Kevin's study Morgan Stanley had four times as many floor-to-floor trips as Price Waterhouse.

Meanwhile, JB&B's mechanical engineers were at work. They had two floors devoted entirely to their equipment, the fourth and the forty-first. In addition they would need large chunks of space in the cellar, where the electrical, gas, and water services came into the building, and in various rooms scattered through the retail areas and in closets in the core on every office floor. There was a whole team of engineers, too:

Anthony Montalto for plumbing, Bob Gruter for electric, Mike Jelic for HVAC, all reporting to Don Ross, the JB&B partner. Even a subject as mundane as plumbing takes on unimagined complexities in a high-rise structure. Two entirely separate systems were required just to supply water to the sink taps in the building. The pressure in the street mains would bring water up to about the fourth floor of the building. The rest of the building would be supplied by a 4,000-gallon tank on the roof, to which water would be pumped through a vertical rise of nearly 600 feet. Waste water from the toilets on the lower floors would drain down to a sump and then be pumped back up to the sewers. Montalto also had a whole separate system of fire sprinklers, standpipes, and pumps to design. The building's "life-safety" systems were of staggering complexity and cost. Even the HVAC system was enlisted in the battle against fire; it was designed to make it possible, say, to simultaneously exhaust smoke from any floor and put the adjacent floors under positive pressure to prevent the fire from spreading to them. Later, when the building was marketed, embellishments such as these would be a big selling point to tenants.

Gruter, subject to Con Ed's approval, issued the designs for the transformer vaults under the sidewalk on 46th Street. Four 13,000-volt cables would enter these vaults from the street; out would come, in thick braided hanks, the 265/460 volt three-phase power that would circulate in the building. Local transformers on each floor would supply 120 volts to the wall outlets. Gruter had to design the "network protectors" that would fill a good-sized room in the basement next to the vaults. The lives of Con Ed's workmen might depend on these devices, whose function was to isolate each of the four feeder cables. If one of these cables were to be shut off in the street for repairs, the building would still be powered by the other three; the network protectors would assure that current didn't flow back through the building's wiring and out into the supposedly dead cable. One floor below was the main switch room, where rows of gray steel cabinets would hold fuses the size of a rolling pin, and 4,000-amp switches with lever throws as long as a jack handle.

Gruter added up all the electrical equipment in the building, including an estimate of all the lamps, typewriters, computers, copying machines, refrigerators, and coffee machines the tenants would plug into the walls. He then wrote a letter kindly requesting Con Ed to provide service in this amount, approximately 15 million watts. This was merely an opening gambit. The utility was aware that this figure—"total connected load"—was a hypothetical number, which assumes that every fax machine in the building is running, the elevators are all ascending at once ... and the building is on fire, so the fire pumps are working. It knocked it down by approximately a third to arrive at what it considered a realistic estimate of "peak demand"—which might be experienced, say, on a hot Friday afternoon when the major tenant has just been advised that Saul Steinberg is preparing a hostile offer for its stock.

The building's electric-power consumption had a direct bearing on its air-conditioning requirements, since virtually all that power ended up as heat. Modern office buildings are air-conditioned year-round, even when they are simultaneously heated. Only the perimeter offices have radiators; the interior of the building must always be cooled. Jelic calculated the heat load at four watts per square foot of standard office space, to cover lighting and general office equipment. He added a margin of extra capacity for high-heat-output tenants such as mainframe computers. Then he had to take into account the people.

Metabolism is the hidden adversary of the HVAC engineer. The average office worker, assumed to be essentially at rest, has a heat output of seventy watts. Eight lawyers could bake a potato in an hour, but of course they'd have to bill $2,000 for the job. The Broadway State Building (counting the office tower only) would be designed to exhaust approximately 500 kilowatts of human waste heat, the equivalent in calories of *three whole pizzas every minute.*

Like so much else in New York, air-conditioning technology has had to adapt to the ways of Tokyo and London, namely their perverse insistence on working when it's past midnight in New York. Until a few years ago, buildings would typically be cooled by a central air-conditioning plant on the roof. If an office within the building needed to work late, the building engineer would have to be on hand to keep a compressor operating. This might cost several hundred dollars an hour in salaries and electricity, an amount large enough to conceal a nice profit margin for the landlord as well. But that was in an era when most office buildings kept what were called office hours. The modern financial industry no longer shuts down as long as there is a stock market open somewhere in the world. Tenants, as a result, have gotten smarter about their leases, and less inclined to ignore such fine-print items as after-hours air-conditioning charges. Ross advised Eichner to put smaller air-conditioning units in the machine rooms on each floor for tenants to control directly, and pay for themselves. Luk Sun, cursing his misfortune to live in an age so mean-spirited and penny-pinching that tenants will stoop to any trick to save money, reluctantly agreed.

The building would still have to provide centrally for the dispersal of the heat generated by these machines. The laws of physics do not permit the mechanical production of cold, only the transfer of heat from one place to another. The medium would be ordinary water, pumped through the building to evaporation towers on the roof, where it would trickle through an elaborate aluminum baffle and allow the already sopping atmosphere of New York to carry away its heat.

"Ross," Mitchell asked at one point during JB&B's presentation, "have you thought about what happens if a tenant asks for operable windows? What is the implication of that?"

"The implication is that the tenant is an idiot," Ross replied succinctly. "Anyone who wants to bring the outside air of New York City into his office has to have a screw loose."

"It could be a big selling point," Luk Sun said. "They read all these magazine articles about the sick-building syndrome, it makes them want to breathe natural pollution."

"It wouldn't sell me," answered Ross. "For me, it does nothing except to confuse the air-conditioning."

But then Ross's office was in a basement.

Several months had gone by since the decision to build the Broadway building out of steel rather than concrete, and Skidmore had yet to come up with a scheme, a design, for how the building would stand. This, too, was work that could only really begin once a core was settled on. There are several components to a structural design for a skyscraper. The first obligation of any building, naturally, is to support its own weight, or "dead load," and the weight of its occupants and their furniture, the "live load." Collectively the two constitute the "gravity load." Structural engineers regard gravity with a certain condescension. The calculations for live and dead load are tedious, but usually straightforward: beams big enough to span a bay (the distance between successive columns) without sagging; columns light near the top of the building, heavier at the bottom as they have progressively greater weight to support; thick concrete footings to spread the load onto the rock. This reveals engineering at its most basic, the application of mathematics to common sense.

The true art of the structural engineer is in bracing the building against wind. Unlike gravity, the wind is constantly changing its strength and direction, and it exerts its force on the building in many different and interesting ways: by attempting to overturn it, bend it, shear it, or twist it. In theory, there is no limit to how strong the wind can blow. In practice, engineers use meteorological data to decide what the likely dangers are; they design typically for a "fifty-year wind," defined as a condition expected to occur no more than once a half century, or a "100-year wind." The Broadway State Building was designed for a 100-year wind. At that location, the 100-year wind from the north implied a peak velocity of 105 miles per hour. This would exert a force on the building of thirty pounds per square foot at the top, ranging down to around twenty at the bottom. In terms of what engineers call the overturning moment—the force that must be resisted to keep the building from toppling over—this was the equivalent of 2.7 million pounds acting at the midpoint of the wall. (Or, to use the common engineering unit, 2,700 "kips," a kip being equal to 1,000 pounds.) As is well known, tall buildings bend in the wind. A typical design criterion calls for a maximum deflection at the top of one five-hundredth of the building's height. In the case of Broadway State, this was a little more than a foot.

There are several things an engineer can do to stiffen a building against the wind. Consider a structure consisting of four pieces of lumber nailed loosely at the corners to make a rectangle. Stand it up on one of the short sides and push on a long side; the corners bend and the rectangle collapses into a parallelogram. One way to prevent this, clearly, is to strengthen the corners. With sufficient care and given enough nails, it ought to be possible to fashion four joints that will remain rigid. (Yes, in theory even one perfectly rigid joint among the four would keep the rectangle intact.) Another way to accomplish the same thing would be to nail an additional piece of lumber as a brace between diagonally opposed corners. The rectangle now functions as two right triangles with a common base. The great thing about a triangle, unlike a quadrilateral, is that it cannot deform except by changing the length of one of its sides. The structure is now inherently rigid; to collapse it, you would have to push hard enough not merely to bend the joints but to completely rupture them.

Structural engineers with a 500-foot-high rectangle to stabilize would be happy to take advantage of this simple Euclidean wisdom, but for the fact that developers usually don't like giant diagonals crisscrossing the walls of their buildings and getting in the way of the views. (Although "expressing" the diagonals on the outside of the building can sometimes be a very chic move, oddly flamboyant and functional at the same time—see Skidmore's John Hancock Tower in Chicago.) Alternatively the engineer can design the wind bracing into the core, where it can be hidden in the interstices between elevator shaft walls, stairways, and closets. This works best in a nice square building with a nice square core in the center. Many buildings have been designed this way, especially in Houston, where Bob Halvorson had been practicing until he came to New York. But the Broadway State Building was not in Houston; and its plan was not a square.

In late May, Skidmore and Turner came to 625 Madison to outline three alternative structural schemes for the office floors of the building. (The base floors presented their own engineering problems in spanning the atrium and the theaters, but there was no "scheme" for dealing with them, just a series of ad hoc solutions.) There was nothing to choose among the three designs on purely structural grounds. Engineering a building is an all-or-nothing proposition; a structure either meets the design criteria or it doesn't. Cost would be a consideration, naturally. In direct costs for materials and labor, about 10 percent—something over $1 million—separated the most expensive scheme from the cheapest. The other considerations were ease of construction (which in the end came down to money, because slowing the job meant more interest expense) and the impact of the different schemes on how the office floors would lay out, which in turn would affect their leasing desirability, so that came down to money, too.

The most straightforward scheme used a moment-connected frame on the perimeter of the building—that is, beams and columns joined at rigid right angles, not with nails but with full-penetration welds and dozens of heavy bolts. This was the most expensive of the schemes; there would be eighty moment connections on a typical floor, and Turner estimated that each would cost $225 to build, against twenty-five dollars for a shear connection designed merely to hold two pieces of steel together. It also presented some architectural difficulties around the deep, three-story-high recesses Audrey had designed into the curtainwall. The recesses created the unusual situation of a single building elevation lying in two different planes. To develop enough rigidity, columns would have to follow one plane or the other; they couldn't just jog in and out every four stories. But they couldn't follow the outer plane, because in that case they would lie outside the curtain wall when a recess occurred. If they followed the plane of the recess, on the other hand, they would fall three feet *inside* the building on the unrecessed floors. While technically feasible, it was hard to imagine where the unlucky person who had that office would put his desk.

What the moment frame had in its favor was familiarity and simplicity. It was good enough for the Empire State Building, Mitch pointed out. In fact, "If you were building the Empire State Building today, you'd probably do it the same way, except that back then they riveted steel instead of bolting it. Bob Fee's father built the Empire State Building, come to think of it. I'll bet you a quarter that when all the shouting is done, and we've looked at every scheme imaginable, that's what we'll end up doing, because that's what you always do."

The second scheme was a variation on the moment-connected frame intended to be more compatible with the architecture. In this scheme a full-story-high Vierendeel truss would span between the columns at each unrecessed floor and across the bay of the prow. A Vierendeel truss has the shape of a ladder lying on its side. For maximum rigidity the trusses would be fabricated out of welded plate steel and trucked to the site as one huge piece. Their stiffness meant that fewer moment connections would be needed, so even taking into account the cost of the trusses, the whole job would be cheaper. And by holding the unrecessed floors in their rigid grip, the trusses would permit the columns to transfer around the recesses, eliminating the problem of columns running through the middle of offices.

On the other hand, the engineers pointed out, the vertical elements of the trusses would partially block some windows on the eight to ten floors where they were used, which could make those offices less desirable.

As far as construction went, Turner had a strong preference for anything that didn't require a truss. Ordinary beams and columns don't always fit together perfectly as they arrive from the fabricator. The ironworkers fine-tune them as necessary by banging them into place with a hammer. But if a shop-welded, full-story-height truss gets hoisted up 300 feet in the air and is discovered not to fit, you have a serious problem.

The third scheme did away with any bracing around the perimeter at all. Instead, it achieved an extremely stiff core by encasing six major columns in a thick jacket of concrete. This was not at all the same thing as a concrete building. There would be real steel columns inside the enclosures, not just rebar. Technically, these were known as composite columns. Halvorson called them "globs."

Since concrete costs less than steel, for a given unit of compressive strenth, the glob scheme was the cheapest. Architecturally, the glob scheme had no impact at all on the views from the windows. But the globs themselves would be as much as eight feet on a side at the lowest floors—that is, in the retail atrium, where rents would be highest. Luk Sun kept multiplying sixty-four square feet by six columns, by five floors, by $100 a square foot, until he couldn't stand it anymore. Finally he thanked everyone and asked Skidmore to come back in a week with a recommendation.

They couldn't do it. They got as far as throwing out the moment-connected frame, and then deadlocked hopelessly over the choice between the composite columns and the Vierendeel truss. They returned for a three-hour presentation, exhaustively cataloguing the advantages and disadvantages of each, and when Luk Sun asked for their recommendation, he was answered with what amounted to a shrug.

"You're telling me Skidmore doesn't have a recommendation?"

"Of course not," Hellmuth replied. "We have *two* recommendations."

"You want us to resolve this for you?" Luk Sun asked.

"We want you to make a decision."

"When do you want it?"

"Immediately."

"When is immediately?" Luk Sun asked.

"Next week," Susanne Churchill replied, with a sigh.

Halvorson wanted to do the globs. Halvorson, like many engineers, believed there was as much creativity and genius involved in designing the structure of a tall building as in the architecture. It just was harder for laymen to appreciate, because buildings as a rule stood up. But the engineering profession had its own standard of beauty, which consisted of achieving the maximum strength from the smallest weight of steel. Steel in 1987 in New York was running at around $1,200 a ton, so this was not just an academic consideration. The glob scheme, Halvorson estimated, saved as much as five to six pounds of steel per square foot of occupiable space. Admittedly it achieved this savings by partially substituting concrete, which is not free. "But," Halvorson told Luk Sun, "in the end there's no way all the things you're adding will amount to anything close to the cost of the steel you're saving."

But there was a whole other level to the debate that had nothing to do with economics, but was intellectual, esthetic, philosophical. The architects and engineers disagreed about the structural system because they disagreed about the nature of the building. The globs concentrated the wind-resisting structure in the core and allowed the perimeter columns to take only a gravity load. This division of purpose struck Halvorson as simple, elegant and efficient. The bumps and corners and recesses that Audrey had designed into the building were just arbitrary complications as far as he was concerned. For himself, he would prefer a nice square, flat-planed building every time, but if the architects wanted complexity, they could have it. Let him design a core as rigid as he wanted, and then the building could turn a corner every six feet if they wanted.

For precisely the opposite reasons, Audrey was drawn to defend the Vierendeel truss. To her, the complications of the building's massing were not arbitrary at all, but the natural, logical, organic expression of the building's unique site and program. The four-floor pattern of recesses was chosen because of the specific proportions of the south elevation. The trusses every fourth floor therefore would be the literal embodiment of the idea behind the building. If Halvorson thought she would be pleased by the freedom to make the wall any shape she wanted, he was dead wrong; it was precisely the implication that the wall *could* take any shape that she found insulting.

"People see different things in the beauty of a building," she mused. "Structural engineers try to minimize the weight of the steel, and I guess this other scheme does that. But so what if it's a little cheaper to build: you can't get any revenue out of the area taken up by the columns, and you've got these six elephant feet coming through the middle of your retail space.

"If it turns out that the glob scheme makes sense for the developer, then so be it. It would be irresponsible of me to push something like that because I believe in it conceptually. *I just believe that something that's conceptually right will probably be programmatically right as well.*"

This debate was well-hidden from the client, naturally. As far as Eichner Properties was concerned, the only issue was which scheme made the most economic sense. Luk Sun couldn't decide. He would stare at the drawings, and make a suggestion, and a day or two later a new set of drawings would arrive with the columns in a different configuration, but they never went away. He asked whether it would be possible to shape the globs for architectural effect as they passed through the retail space. "Absolutely," Hellmuth replied. "You can make them round, you can make them bullet-shaped, you can make them cruciform, you can make them anything, except smaller."

"Maybe we should look at the moment frame again, guys," Luk Sun murmured.

There was silence.

"If I said to you I want to go with a moment-connected frame and I can't live with columns three feet inside the building, what does that do to the skin of the building?" Luk Sun asked.

"It's a whole new building," Bill said.

"Suppose we don't have two planes. Suppose we manipulate the curtain wall to give the effect of the recesses, but do it all in one column line. You'd get, say, eighteen inches instead of three feet. How would that look?"

"Like you took decals of the design and stuck them on the building," Audrey said bitterly.

"I can't live with those globs, I can't live with stuff blocking the windows," Luk Sun said heatedly. "Once you're finished you're gone. I'm stuck with the building. This is my decision. We will have the moment-connected frame. The columns will run in a single plane. The recesses will be dummied in the curtain wall."

"You lose the whole expression of the building if you flatten out the wall," Audrey retorted. "You've got to be able to read these recesses from the street. At eighteen inches you won't know they're there unless a pigeon is sitting on them."

Halvorson was disappointed as well. "There's nothing wrong with what we're doing," he said in his soft, diffident voice, "but it will never make headlines in *Engineering News Report.*"

Luk Sun considered it a good two weeks' work.

"You've got terrific architects on this job, and Halvorson is a very good engineer," he said later, "but you can't expect them to do your thinking for you." Luk Sun knew this firsthand, being an architect himself. He knew the awful temptations of the field—of any creative field, for that matter—to fall in love with what you've done and close your mind to the alternatives.

"You've got to push them and push them to do better. They come to you and say, 'Look at this, we've got a terrific ... Buick for you.' And you've got to say, 'No, sorry, I want a Jaguar.' And so they go away and come back in two weeks and say, 'You're gonna love this, we've actually been able to get you a ... Lincoln.' And you've got to shake your head and say, 'Nice try, but I really have to have a Jaguar.' And then they'll go off and sulk and mope for a while, but if they're any good, they'll come back eventually and they'll put the drawings up on the boards and bring you in and say, 'We didn't think we could do it, nobody else in the world could have done it, but believe it or not, here it is, a Jaguar.'

"And that's when you've got to be able to turn to them and say, 'Okay, good, I'll take it ... *but* I want it at a Chevrolet price."

17

In May, Bruce and Luk Sun flew to Las Vegas for the annual convention of the International Council of Shopping Centers, where they met with officials of the Hahn Company. It was immediately apparent that the two parties were wildly divergent in corporate philosophy, negotiating strategy and personal style, and that they were destined to make a deal, because each had something the other wanted. For the Hahn Company, it was risk-free access to the richest and most prestigious consumer market in America. Ernest Hahn had made his fortune in the simple trade of paving over cornfields and putting four walls and a roof in the middle. In 1980 he sold the company to Trizec, the multi-billion-dollar Canadian real estate firm, precipitating a crisis of identity for the company he founded.

"We thought of diversifying outside of retail," Al Corti said, "because how many more cornfields are there? And in the end we concluded we'd stick with what we know, because whatever cornfields are left, we'll find them first." But by the late 1980s, cheap suburban land was disappearing from the countryside, and Hahn turned its eyes to the richest cornfield of all, the one between the Hudson and East rivers. But desire was tempered by fear. Corti had actually grown up in the Bronx, but like everyone else in California he had been infected with the notion that to stick a shovel into the dirt of Manhattan was to bring down on your head an ancient and terrible curse that would make you wish you'd chosen to build on a toxic dump site instead. Hahn had come within forty miles of midtown, to a place called Bridgewater that sat on the intersection of two interstate highways in central New Jersey. From "Bridgewater Commons" they could almost see the green glow over Manhattan from the cash registers that never sleep. But they also imagined they could hear the curses of sullen bureaucrats awakened from their afternoon naps and smell the blood of developers being tortured to death for paying off a Teamster with the wrong brand of Scotch. You had to be insane to try to build there, Hahn executives believed. That was what Bruce offered them: the power of positive insanity.

From Bruce's point of view, Hahn supplied something he had felt all along was lacking in the New York retail environment: vertical integration of design, marketing theme, leasing skills, and mall management. He envisioned a deal in which Hahn would in effect lease the entire retail area of 1540 from Broadway State and then sublease it to individual tenants. "Say the pro-forma number were $100 a foot, to make up a number, then I'd press them as close as I could to 75 or 80 percent of that number"—in other words, on 100,000 square feet of leasable area, Bruce would expect to be guaranteed between $7.5 and $8 million. You didn't need to be a rocket scientist to figure out that this by itself was roughly a quarter of the total income the building would eventually have to generate.

Vernon Schwartz, Hahn's executive vice president, describes Bruce's position in their first meeting as "If you're interested, let's make a deal, if not, forget it." Schwartz was interested, but also wary. The Hahn deal, so simple in conception, began to reveal its complexities as soon as the principals commenced to negotiate. Legally, the deal was complicated by the fact that Hahn wanted an equity interest in the retail space. This required breaking the retail out as a separate condominium within the building, and creating a new corporation which Hahn and Broadway State Partners would own equally. So Bruce was a landlord, but also a partner; and Hahn would be a partner, and a tenant, and also (for a fee) the manager of the shopping mall. This gave Bruce a whole new repertoire of negotiating postures to add to his accustomed one of insatiable attack. With a nimbleness that Schwartz found perpetually disconcerting, Bruce could switch between his role as partner and that of a shrewd, implacable adversary, eternally poised to stalk from the room at a moment's notice if he suspected he was getting anything less than everything.

In all their years of buying up cornfields, Hahn had never encountered anyone quite like Bruce. Strategically, he was brilliant for his ability to analyze a position from both sides of the table, to grasp instinctively what concessions the other side might be willing to make and which points they would never surrender. Tactically, he was indefatigable, a master of the mock tantrum, which served as punctuation for a demand, as demurral, as distraction. Sometimes he and Luk Sun would work as a pair, like shoplifters. While Bruce held everyone's attention at the door, out which he was threatening to walk at any minute, Luk Sun would enter into a quiet conversation in the back and fill his pockets with everything he could carry.

Schwartz was about Bruce's age but opposite in temperament—measured, reserved, and scrupulously polite—though also a very tough negotiator. Corti sat in on some of the sessions. Once, in New York, he had dinner with Berini afterwards and told him, "I don't even think these two guys are going to live through this." The issues were money, of course, but money in a dizzying variety of forms: capital investments, guarantees, preferences, loans, and repayments of loans. In the end the agreement would send millions of dollars on roundabout voyages back to the pockets of the people who spent them in the first place.

Each side had its priorities. Bruce's original goal was for Hahn to guarantee a certain minimum rent. But such a defensive strategy was alien to Bruce's nature, so he quickly decided that if Hahn collected rents above the minimum guarantee, he wanted a share of those, too. Schwartz was mainly concerned that the agreement be so worded that no one from the Hahn company would ever have to be in the same room with a New York City electrician or plumber. He seemed to believe they could rob you by telepathy. Bruce agreed to bear the risk of construction cost overruns, because with Luk Sun in charge *there would be no cost overruns.* But the black hole at the center of the negotiations was this: Hahn was being asked to lease a space that not only wasn't built yet, it wasn't even designed. Since the cost wasn't coming out of their pockets, Hahn had no incentive to economize on the design. Bruce obviously did. "We have got to box in this cost somehow," he would warn Vernon. "We've got to make a distinction between overruns in construction cost, which risk I am prepared to bear, and budget increases as a consequence of gold-plating the design, because I'm not stupid enough to sit back and pick up the check for you to build the set of *20,000 Leagues Under the Sea*!"

"No, but look, we can't do business like this, if you always scream and threaten us ..." Vernon would begin in his most reasonable tone, only to be interrupted by a roar from Bruce: "Vernon, it's not your money!"

The obvious way to settle this difference was to pursue the design until its cost could be reasonably estimated, and then conclude—or abandon—the partnership. Unfortunately, Bruce had neither the luxury of time nor the freedom to walk away from the deal. Not long after he began discussions with Vernon, he mentioned the prospect of the Hahn deal to Alan Rosenstein of Citibank. As Bruce had hoped, Rosenstein thought that was a terrific idea that would go a long way toward making the bank comfortable about lending money for the project. Unfortunately, Rosenstein liked the idea so much that he made it a condition of financing the building at all. So Bruce was negotiating with his back to the wall. He had to make a deal; Hahn didn't. And it seemed to Bruce, as time went on, that Hahn must have either discovered or guessed that fact as well. This was negotiating with his back to the wall and a gun to his head as well.

Physically, the design of the retail atrium began to change almost as soon as Hahn became involved. Hahn's first requirement was to bring in a new architect for the retail atrium. Skidmore, Owings & Merrill knew how to make a building beautiful, but not how to make it sell sweaters. At bottom, they didn't care. Luk Sun had been pressing Skidmore about their choices of materials and colors for the atrium, and Audrey had given a perfunctory presentation of black slate floors, white ceilings, and polished stainless steel accents. "I'm not happy with the black and white, I'm not happy with the stainless," Luk Sun said. "This is Times Square. I want something with more life and color."

"We were thinking of something a little more stark ..." Audrey began, only to be interrupted by Tom Fridstein:

"This is a marketing decision," he said. "I hate to say don't listen to the architect, but this really is a decision for you to make"—which gave a pretty good idea of Skidmore's priorities.

The architect the Hahn Company wanted was Jon Jerde of Los Angeles, best known for his work on the 1984 Summer Olympics sites. In almost every respect, Jerde was the antithesis of SOM. Where Skidmore disdained to make mere "marketing decisions," to Jerde that was what architecture was all about. "Earning the right to do something," he would tell his staff, "is as important as doing it." Where Skidmore was restrained, Jerde was eclectic and anarchic. He would borrow themes from his favorite places—the back streets of Tuscany, the cliff villages of the Anasazi Indians—and put the results down where the spirit moved him. "When you make wine," he liked to say, "it doesn't taste like the grapes it was made from." His mentors weren't other architects, they were movie art directors or science-fiction writers. If modern architecture sought to inspire humanity to live up to the ever-more-perfect purity of its buildings, Jerde seemed to believe that humanity would improve on its own if it just had a decent place to go for an ice cream cone.

Jerde was in his late forties, with a square-jawed, rugged face under a sleek helmet of graying hair. He commanded that essential tool of the great architect, a resonant baritone, which he would use to mesmerizing effect on a client, spouting aphorisms as his vision took shape in bold marker strokes on the very conference table before him. Opinion was divided on the propriety of this habit. Andrea Kremen was caustic on the subject of "the great master striding up to the canvas with his disciples gathered around in a reverent circle." But Howard found it admirable. "I like a guy who takes out his pencil and draws right in front of the client," he said. "That takes guts. You don't see David Childs do that."

Jerde had an astonishing tale of woe to account for his winding up as the most famous shopping-center architect in America. After graduating from U.S.C. in 1964, he was tempted by a Los Angeles firm with that dream of every young architect in those days, a five-figure salary. He planned on spending a year there and then living off what he had saved, but his wife had other plans and at the end of the year handed him divorce papers. The settlement essentially trapped him in his high-paying job indefinitely. Over the next decade Jerde directly or indirectly was responsible for millions of square feet of shopping centers, all of them deplorable. "Hissing, grim tubes," he called them, down which shoppers were made to trudge until, with nothing left to spend, they were spit out into the parking lot.

Yet gradually an idea was taking shape within him for a different kind of shopping center. It would be a celebration of civic life instead of a cynical machine for evacuating wallets. It would be open to the community instead of isolated in its asphalt meadow. It was around this time that the Hahn Company felt the need to make a belated homage to the American downtown. They had come to this position reluctantly, at the behest of San Diego's powerful mayor, Pete Wilson. The city acquired a large site in its decrepit downtown of pawnshops and tattoo parlors and virtually gave it away to Hahn, on the condition that they do something useful with it. For a long time Hahn acted as if they hoped the city would build another freeway interchange on the site instead. Every study they did of the site convinced them it would be a disaster. Finally Ernie Hahn himself called in Jerde and said, "Jon, I hope to God some of those things you've been saying are even half true, because that's the only thing that's going to save us here."

Jerde quit his job and opened his own practice, with Hahn as his first and for a time only client. Horton Plaza, as the project was called, became Jerde's revenge on the shopping center. He set about conscientiously breaking every rule the Hahn Company had. It was axiomatic in shopping-center design that you created an environment with as few references as possible to the world outside, where there were things to do besides shop and eat. Exits were as obscure as the fire code allowed, it being assumed that shoppers were too stupid to leave unless they smacked their noses on a door. Jerde did the unthinkable and opened the mall to the city around it; he flayed off the roof and took its venerable H-plan and twisted its spine like a sadistic child. He slathered the walls with phony Tuscan mosaics and absurdly rusticated stucco in pale blue-greens and desert pinks and ochers. This reflects Jerde's peculiar contempt of buildings, or "mere objects." His own interest, he says, is with "the spaces between the buildings." "To the traditional architectural palette of structure, form, and color," he elaborates, in his typical vein of passionate obscurity, "we've added an experiential dimension that has to do with issues of use, of vitality, of pitches of energy from cool to hot." *Architectural Record,* in a generally favorable, if somewhat puzzled, appreciation, described Horton Plaza as "either an appropriately idiosyncratic response to San Diego's quest for a sense of place [or] Postmodernism gone amok."

Jerde had little firsthand experience with Times Square. He toured the area one Sunday with Luk Sun and came away with the impression that Times Square was a little like Hollywood, a place that had been outstripped by its legend. It wasn't as dense or vivid as it looked in photographs, he thought. The signs are spaced a little farther apart; they don't set the night on fire in life the way they do in Kodachrome. His idea was to distill this slightly disappointing stretch of cityscape to its essence, to crystallize it and concentrate it on a single place, a point on the map where the real geographic Times Square would miraculously coincide with the iconographic one of fabulous memory.

In late May, Jerde's first drawings arrived at Bruce's office. They came at a time of transition for the Broadway State team, marked by the hiring of a new project manager to work under Luk Sun, a young architect named William Tung. Tung was a very handsome, polished young man, who had been born into a wealthy Hong Kong family and educated at American boarding schools and at Princeton. He had worked for his family business for a while, and at Skidmore, and when Tom Fridstein ran into him at a job meeting he said to Bruce, "That's the *second* right choice you've made on this project." Luk Sun made it clear that Tung would be in charge of the project on a day-by-day basis, which was the role Alice Hoffman thought she would be playing. His hiring, Alice believed, marked the beginning of a campaign by Luk Sun to get her to quit. Mitchell had long since stopped talking to her.

At the end of a staff meeting one Wednesday morning, William unrolled Jerde's first efforts. The atrium, which Skidmore had drawn as a rectangle, was now a semicircle. Its flat side was the sidewalk on Broadway, and its curve was bounded by a horseshoe-shaped walkway. As nearly as could be told from the drawings, the atrium and walkway were open to Broadway. This reflected Jerde's belief in making retail spaces extensions of the street, open like a bazaar to the life around them. "Times Square is a very corrugated space," he said, "with all kinds of lateral pedestrian texture on a horizontal plane. New Yorkers seem to resist going into a box, which is why we're trying to make this appear to be just a blip in the street."

Unfortunately, without Jerde there to explain it, the drawing lost much of its power. Also, as Andrea saw immediately, it violated zoning in several critical respects, including the signage, streetwall, and height-and-setback requirements. "I strongly doubt the City Planning Commission would accept signage on that horseshoe instead of out at the building line," she said.

"They don't want recesses or urban plazas," Alice added.

Luk Sun turned on her.

"Alice, we'll change the law! This makes the retail work! The way they wrote the text, you can't make the retail work."

Alice pointed out that if the atrium was open to the outside it couldn't be heated or air-conditioned. This was true; Jerde seemed to have forgotten that he wasn't in San Diego.

"Well, we'll have to give something up, then!" Luk Sun retorted angrily. "Have you got a better idea?"

"I'm not an architect," Alice said. "I like the Skidmore plan."

"Defend the Skidmore plan to me."

"It obeys the zoning," Alice said simply. "We forced them to obey the zoning."

"Are you going to sell the retail in Skidmore's plan?" Wong bellowed.

"Hahn is prepared to put a guarantee on the retail. A *guarantee* on the retail!"

It was apparent that Alice was pursuing a losing argument, but she was too honest and stubborn in her own way to drop it. As far as being fair to SOM was concerned, there was no greater irrelevancy. Luk Sun refused to acknowledge that SOM's pride was in any sense a consideration. The transaction between Broadway State Partners, client, and Skidmore, Owings & Merrill, architects, specified the payment of cash in exchange for drawings; any other compensation the party of the second part might derive was not part of the deal.

There were several other changes to the original retail design that became apparent as Jerde's drawings began arriving over the next couple of weeks. The most obvious was that the four Loews theaters had been moved down to the second subcellar, where Skidmore had been planning stores. Hahn's experience was that nobody would go down two flights of stairs, or even escalators, to shop. This made room for a two-level "food court"—areas of tables surrounded by fast-food counters—on floors two and three. Unfortunately, the theaters had to be several feet higher, floor to ceiling, than the retail floor they replaced, so the move had the effect of making the excavation deeper, wiping out several months' work by the engineers directed at making it shallower.

The other change was a slow but steady decline in the square footage of rentable space, as distinguished from common areas such as the atrium and food court. This was an unexpected development. Bruce had pressed Skidmore to extract every inch of rentable space, and after much pain they had gotten the total up to almost 100,000 square feet. The assumption was that Hahn would want the same thing. But pretty quickly it became clear that Hahn's interests actually lay in the other direction. Their guarantee to Bruce would be based on the rentable area. The smaller the rentable area, the smaller the guarantee and the less Hahn would be risking. This of course would limit Hahn's own profits as well. But they would still get all the same benefits of corporate prestige and experience in the New York market. And in any case Hahn would only make money if they could lease the space. From the point of view of leasing, the atrium and common areas were a cost-free amenity to dangle in front of potential retail tenants. The leasable area began a downward trend toward 60,000 square feet. As a direct consequence the guarantee, which Bruce had hoped would be around $7.5 million, looked like it would settle out closer to $4.5 million.

Meanwhile, Skidmore was still working away at the retail drawings, along with the rest of the building. There was no point in demoralizing them until the Hahn deal was a sure thing, Luk Sun reasoned—especially with the deadline nearing for filing the zoning drawings, a prerequisite for the all-important building permit. As luck would have it, though, the Skidmore team found out about Jerde sooner than Luk Sun had intended. Tung and Audrey had been coming to 625 Madison so often that they had dispensed with the formalities of the reception desk. One afternoon, as Luk Sun and Bill were going over a new set of drawings with two of Jerde's associates, the two Skidmore architects bustled into the conference room for a scheduled meeting. "Just give us a couple of minutes, guys, okay?" Luk Sun said coolly, and they retreated; but there was no doubt of what they had seen. "I guess I'd better lay things out for David," Luk Sun said gloomily at the next day's staff meeting.

"David will understand," Howard assured him. "He's a partner, a money man. It's the Audreys of the world you have to watch out for."

The next morning Luk Sun went to Skidmore. He called the team together in a conference room and explained the financial history of the project, emphasizing that it was at Hahn's insistence that Jerde was brought aboard. He didn't mention that he agreed with the choice. When he took questions, he was relieved to see that they all had to do with the technical details of coordination between the two architects. He didn't know that Audrey was actually relieved to discover that Jerde had been brought in just for the retail; she had spent a day thinking they had been kicked off the job entirely.

A few weeks later the collaboration began in earnest when Jerde himself flew to New York for a meeting at Skidmore's offices. Fridstein introduced the team and explained the building as it had taken shape up to that point.

"This is about the fifteenth time we've been in a joint relationship with Skidmore," Jerde said expansively, "and we've found them everything from terrific to horrifying … and I'm sure this will be terrific."

"I was going to say, I'm sure we'll fit in that spectrum somewhere," Fridstein said dryly.

In fact, Jerde decided, if he had to work with the heirs to Gordon Bunshaft, he could do much worse than the team designing the Broadway State building. "The Skidmore esthetic had to bend a little when it met Washington, D.C., and Childs was the man to do it," he observed.

"And that young girl designer," he added approvingly, "is very un-Skidmorean."

18

By early June, 1987, with around eleven months to go before the zoning deadline, 1540 Broadway had been ground down to a ten-story nubbin and was falling at the rate of a floor every few days. The eastern half of the site, where the theater had stood, was a level desert of rubble. Work had been stopped for more than a week following the accident in pulling down the proscenium wall, but eventually was allowed to proceed. The damage to the bus-tour office was patched in a day, but for several years thereafter lived on as the subject of an arcane and increasingly meaningless lawsuit between Broadway State Partners and the owners of 1550 Broadway. Skyscrapers, whose birth should be attended by beams of glory, almost invariably come into the world trailing cobwebs of legal papers instead. But the time was in sight when nothing would be left standing at the corner of Broadway and 45th Street, making it time to think about the foundation: the concrete walls, slab, and column footings, and the hole they would go in.

In mid-June Turner sent an invitation to bid to a half-dozen of the major excavation subcontractors. Bidding the job is the highest art of the construction manager. He has to allow the subcontractor to make an informed bid, even while the building is still being designed. He has to use all his wiles to get the best possible price, while at the same time holding the owner's greed in check, so that the subcontractor does not lose so much money he goes broke in the middle of the job. And he has to make sure that the wrong bidder doesn't win. "I've been through this a hundred times," Gary said, "where you put in one guy you don't want as a rabbit for the others to chase, and then when his bid comes in a million below everyone else you say, 'How can we not give it to him? Look at all the aspirin we can buy with the money we'll save.'"

But the problem with the foundation of 1540 Broadway was finding anyone at all to do it. There were a lot of new buildings about to go into the ground, and none of them had foundations as deep as fifty-seven feet below street level. There was the zoning deadline to consider. Strictly speaking, this would be Eichner's risk, not the subcontractor's. The wording of the contract required only the subcontractor's "best efforts" to complete the foundation by the deadline, not a money-back guarantee. But subcontractors knew that if they took a job like this and missed the deadline, their pride would be hurt, their reputation would suffer, and the developer would probably try to wriggle out of paying them anyway.

Five bids eventually were received. The spread between the highest and lowest was unusually large, more than 40 percent. In part, this was because the requirements for supporting the subway tunnel were left undefined while the Transit Authority engineers decided, so Gary intimated, between solid ivory brackets with bronze screws and beams of hand-carved mahogany from the island of Timor. Only one bid was under $10 million, and that was quickly withdrawn when the company won the contract for another Times Square building. The next lowest bid was thrown out because the company didn't think it could make the May 13 deadline. That left Laquila Construction Company, in Brooklyn, low man. By coincidence, Laquila and Turner were also building Americas Tower, a big office building at the other end of the same block. Mitch was happy to see them get the job. Laquila had plenty of trucks and its own rock-crushing plant, which reduced its reliance on finding dump sites in New Jersey. And Laquila had a schedule that showed they could complete the job on May 13. Not *by* May 13, but *on* May 13. If there were an eclipse on May 12 and the men stopped working to watch it, they would finish a day late. Only after the contract was signed did Ellis get a copy of Laquila's schedule, seven pages of closely spaced printout, and discover that their plan for meeting the May 13 deadline included working on Christmas, Thanksgiving, and New Year's Day.

Laquila was awarded the job on July 9. That same day Turner obtained a permit for Phase One of the excavation, covering the area away from the subway, east of a line that roughly paralleled Broadway fifty feet from the sidewalk. The next few weeks were devoted to mobilization. A Caterpillar 973 bulldozer made its appearance on the site. Along the foundation wall of the Lyceum, three drilling rigs were jockeyed into position for "line drilling"—defining the perimeter of the site with closely spaced holes. The bits were three inches, and they left the equivalent of two diameters between holes. The drills were air-powered by a compressor parked in the street; they made a noise like a hundred ripsaws on a hundred oak knots. The bits went down eight feet in about three minutes, producing for each hole ten dry quarts of pulverized rock that coated everything in sight with a layer of fine gray dust.

The nature of the site began to change almost immediately with the beginning of excavation. Contours emerged, as the top layer of undifferentiated dirt was scraped away to reveal a varied substrate of weathered schist, clay, and more dirt. One morning in early August Gary stalked down to where a backhoe was clawing away at the ledge of rock that had supported the Variety building through its decades of tribulation. He watched glumly as the teeth on the bucket clawed the rock, leaving long white scratches on the brown face. "Shit rock," he said, kicking over a grapefruit-sized chunk, which revealed a face of orange flecks of iron oxide and gleaming chips of mica. "Manhattan schist. Only problem with it, it disintegrates when exposed to water or air. Other than that it's fine. Just our luck, it's vertical, too." He pointed out some faint striations in the rock, actually about twenty degrees off the vertical, indicating the planes of foliation along which the rock would be inclined to break and slide. "Schist" comes from a Greek word meaning "easily cleft." "You don't worry about those things if they're horizontal," Gary said. "The building is not gonna slide sideways. When they're nearly vertical like this, though, it makes you think about doing something so the existing buildings don't fall into your hole."

In addition to the topography of nature, there was that imposed by man. Part of the art of excavating lay in sculpting the remaining terrain. Laquila as it dug couldn't simply throw the dirt over the side, so until the very last bit was dug out, there would have to be a ramp for the dump trucks to drive down onto the site. Laquila's principal earthmoving tool was the backhoe, a Caterpillar 245 with a three-and-a-half-yard bucket at the end of an arm that could reach up or down two stories. The backhoe had a large square cabin mounted on wide-set treads. The driver sat in a glassed-in cab at one corner. The bucket digs with a motion like a child digging in the sand, scooping toward itself with the bucket bent inward. It has other functions as well. Before a blast, it would drape the area with blasting mats of thick, woven steel cable, whose purpose was to contain flying pieces of rock. By smashing on the ends of fifteen-foot-long I-beams, it drove them vertically into the soil adjacent to the 46th Street sidewalk to keep the dirt face from collapsing into the hole. When the job was slow, the operator would sometimes amuse himself by picking up the larger unbroken pieces of rock lying around and see if he could get them to shatter by dropping them fifteen or twenty feet. Occasionally a workman would hitch a ride in the bucket and be carried halfway across the site in one dizzying swoop.

With the start of excavation, Ellis and Michael Danberg began spending all their time at the site. They made their headquarters in a battered trailer containing a desk and telephone, a table for unrolling blueprints, and a water cooler. For a while the trailer was parked in the street on Broadway, but eventually Turner built a shed over the lane of traffic nearest the sidewalk and moved the trailer atop the shed. This shed, or bridge, would remain in place almost until the building was complete, and millions of people would pass underneath it rather than take their chances with the taxis by crossing the street. Turner's own engineers, though, will go around the block to avoid walking underneath a construction job, unless it's one of their own. "We do the right thing, according to the code," Gary said. "Two-inch planks, sitting on four-inch I-beams, with a layer of corrugated metal, so that the poor pedestrians don't get dripped on, the fact that if the bridge wasn't there it would rain on the pedestrians anyway notwithstanding. If they drop even a 200-pound beam it will go through the bridging, through the sidewalk, through the subway tunnel, through the rock ... if we can find the rock."

In addition to Ellis's spartan accommodations, there was a trailer for Laquila, and one for the Working Teamster Foreman—a comparatively deluxe affair, with an Oriental rug (bought on the street for fifty dollars), a sofa, and a stereo. A boardwalk, accessible by a rickety wooden stair, connected the trailers and gave an excellent view of the whole site, looking east toward the Lyceum. Often on sunny mornings the Working Teamster Foreman and the Master Mechanic could be seen leaning over the railing, calmly taking in the scene of grimy toil below.

As the machines scraped away dirt, the contours of the rock on the eastern half of the site began to emerge. Beginning about three feet from the rock face, the drills made a grid of holes, two to three feet apart. As each hole was completed the driller marked it with a wad of rolled-up newspaper. In preparation for blasting, seismographs were installed in the adjacent buildings. First, the seismic consultants, John V. Dinan Associates, set up a machine in a corridor in the basement of the Lyceum. The machine detected motion in all three physical dimensions. The respective velocities were squared, and the square root of the sum of the squares was the index of the strength of the shock wave at a given location.

A technician sat at the machine throughout the excavation. This was a job with all the glamour of a night watchman and none of the opportunities for leisure. The technician sat under a 200-watt bulb in a gloomy cellar and waited for an explosion to go off, which sounded like anything from a heavy book falling off a shelf in the next room to someone swatting the back of his chair with a two-by-four. The technician kept a log of all the explosions and their vibration levels, although more than half the time, the blasts registered as "TSM"—too small to measure. On rare occasions, he would measure an excessive level of vibration. Then he would go out and hope to find the blaster in a good mood and issue him a warning.

"Excessive" meant a particle velocity of more than two inches per second, which was the customary standard. BSP had gone to a lot of trouble to convince the Landmarks Preservation Commission that this figure could safely be exceeded in certain instances. The commission had considered Professor Dowding's argument that the frequency of the wave was more important than the instantaneous velocity. Unfortunately, the commission did not have final say in the matter. Blasting of any kind was regulated by the Explosives Unit of the New York City Fire Department. The chief of the Explosives Unit, Joseph Venditto, was not impressed with the equations in Professor Dowding's book. Dowding's theories were never put to the full test because the Chief insisted on enforcing the two-inches-per-second standard he was comfortable with. But having advertised Dowding to the Landmarks Commission as the Vladimir Horowitz of seismography, BSP discovered they were stuck with having him monitor the blasts as well. In mid-August he came to install his own machines in the Lyceum, which would be linked by telephone line to his office in Chicago. Dowding was disappointed to discover Dinan's machines already installed in the choicest locations. Professional courtesy among seismologists requires setting up machines at a respectable distance from one another. This avoids embarrassment when they give divergent readings.

A powder magazine made its appearance on the site, a red steel box like a large doghouse. There are places in the country where almost anyone can walk into a general store and buy a box of dynamite, but New York City regulates explosives as stringently as if anarchists still lurked behind every post office. The permit for 1540 Broadway set a limit of 750 pounds of explosive a day, all of which had to be delivered to the site that morning and detonated before dark. Boxes of explosives were transported in a small red truck with comically oversized rubber bumpers and a locked compartment lined with wood to prevent accidental sparks. Then they would be unloaded and carried for the last hundred feet of their journey on the shoulders of the powder monkeys, humped across the treacherous terrain of the site and dropped casually on the ground where they would be used.

When the weather turned cold, the men would light substantial bonfires to keep warm and to thaw the frozen valves on their drilling machines. Newspapers and paper bags would occasionally take flight from these conflagrations and waft across the site, burning merrily. This would make Danberg apprehensive. As part of his training to be an assistant site superintendent for Turner he had been shown a safety film whose most enduring image was of a man with his hand blown off by careless handling of dynamite. In reality the men had little to fear. The explosive was Tovex, a formulation designed to be even safer than dynamite. When DuPont introduced it in 1974 it sent around an advertising film that showed it burning harmlessly in a fire, while sticks of dynamite erupted in an impressive blast. Later the films were withdrawn when the company admitted that they couldn't get dynamite to explode in a fire either, and the sticks in the film had been detonated with an electric blasting cap.

Tovex came in tubes of bilious pink, wrapped like a sausage in plastic, flabby to the touch of the only people who were supposed to touch it, the two blasters and the powder monkeys. The powder monkey would pick up a stick, jam a blasting cap trailing blue and yellow wires into the gel-like mass of it, loop the wires around the stick, and lower it into the hole. As many as four additional sticks might go into the same hole, followed by a layer of the ubiquitous gray drilling dust, tamped down with a long wooden staff. A single blast may have only a couple of sticks of dynamite in one or two holes, or it can be many times that size. One explosion involved 300 pounds of explosive in twenty-four holes, but thirty to fifty pounds was more typical.

The purpose of blasting, obviously, is to break the rock into pieces small enough to remove. Broken rock takes up more space than solid rock, so there has to be room for expansion. If you set off a blast in a hole in the middle of a field of rock, you would shake it up and give it a good scaring, but you wouldn't open up many useful cracks. Therefore, when possible, the blaster works on a ledge with an open face. The ledge will have rows of boreholes at regular increments from the edge. The blaster loads as many as five rows, and sets the caps so they go off at twenty-five-millisecond intervals, beginning with the row closest to the face. Thus as each successive row detonates, the rock adjacent to it has already been shattered. Of course, the delays are too small to be detected by ear, the individual blasts being subsumed into a single teeth-jarring boom.

When the shot is ready, the blaster walks off and smokes a cigarette until the backhoe operator takes notice of him and lumbers across the broken terrain in his direction. Men attach the blasting mats to a hook on the bucket, and the backhoe drapes them over the loaded holes. The blaster bawls a command, and one of the drillers pulls a handle on his rig and sends a short, violent blast of compressed air through a horn. The men working nearby walk purposefully to the far side of a piece of machinery. If there's a man in a suit in the hole, the more superstitious drillers may go and stand by him, on the theory that only poor people get killed in construction accidents. Then a double note on the whistle, and the powder monkey swats the plunger on the detonator.

There's a dull, muffled thud; the mats jump as if someone had punched them from underneath, and a thin cloud of gray smoke filters out from between and beneath them. The backhoe roars up and drags the mats away, laboriously, like an amateur magician pulling the handkerchief off a trick that he's not sure quite worked. Then the work of the blaster stands revealed in all its majestic entropy, rock lying in broken clumps and sheets, fodder for the gravel mill.

In contrast to the generally blithe spirit of the men who knock buildings down for a living, the atmosphere in the hole was grim and purposeful. The constant roar of machinery precluded all but the most urgent conversation, but even during breaks the demeanor of the blasters and drillers varied approximately from remote to sullen. It is not clear why this should be so. Demolition and excavation are both dangerous, although blasting, when done properly, is less unpredictable. Blasting is one of the only trades that offers an opportunity for creative self-expression. The most skilled electrician only builds what the drawings tell him to build, but there are an infinitude of ways to blow up 750 pounds of explosives in a day. Blasters write their signatures in the air. Once, when an explosion rattled the windows of the trailer, Mitch, who was there meeting with Ellis, looked up and said, "That must be Flowers."

"No, he's digging Americas Tower," Ellis said. "We've got Barnes here."

"Neither one of them are gentle guys."

"You can believe it," Ellis agreed. "We're not letting Barnes anywhere near the Lyceum. We drew a line across the middle of the site from north to south, and told him, 'You stay on this side of it.' Jesse Palmer's taking that rock out."

"He's a good man," Mitch said.

Palmer was a rangy, dark, grizzled man with a voice like a dump truck coming up a hill, who learned his trade as a coal miner in West Virginia. He was neither proud nor insulted to be chosen for the comparatively delicate end of the job; it simply recognized his philosophy of blasting, that if you work your way down, a few sticks at a time, at the end of the day you'll take out just as much rock, and you can sleep at night. Having blasted for subway tunnels, highways, dams, and countless foundations, Palmer did not consider this hole exceptional in any way, except that it went down a little deeper than most, but he didn't expect to find anything at sixty feet down that was different from what he'd seen at thirty. "To me it's just another damn hole," he said.

From the cabin of the backhoe, Rocco Tomassetti drove the men hard, and himself hardest of all. In addition to operating the biggest and most elaborate piece of equipment at any given time, Rocco was the general superintendent on the job and a principal in the company. Laquila was a family company. Rocco's father, Dino Tomassetti, had come to America from Italy after the war and gone to work as a laborer on a sidewalk gang. He began his own business pouring concrete patios for friends on Long Island. In twenty-five years he had built Laquila, named for his hometown outside Rome, into what Ellis estimated to be a $100 million business.

Blasting quickly loses whatever thrill it possesses and turns into production work; the production of nothing, of negative space. Summer turned to autumn, autumn turned to bleary winter, and the blasting went on. Rock was scooped up in the backhoe, dropped in the bed of a dump truck, shaking it like a fat man sitting down in a sports car. Dump trucks lumbered reluctantly up the ramp, sometimes with a nudge from the bucket of the backhoe, an oddly human gesture like a coach patting a football player on the fanny. They reached the street and turned south on Seventh Avenue heading for Brooklyn, while the next truck was already backing down the ramp, number 50 or 75 or 100 for the day.

Whistles sound, thumps resound across the site and three or four large dark objects fly forty feet in the air. It takes a moment to recognize them as the shadows of startled pigeons on the blank side wall of 1550. Senior citizen, chalk-faced, walks over to Michael Danberg on Broadway.

"That was some *fucking* boom," the man yells. "It got me right in the fucking nuts. Are you trying to knock my dick off? You want me to call the mayor?"

"Move along, sir," Mike says politely.

"You skinny little bastard, what the fuck are you trying to do to me? I'll take a shit in that white hat, you bastard."

Danberg says something about calling a cop. The man stalks off, muttering.

"I'm starting to miss school already," Danberg says.

19

By early summer, Eichner Properties was in full headlong rush on the Broadway State Project. There were phone calls back and forth to Berini in California and meetings virtually every day with Skidmore, JB&B, Turner, Hahn, Jerde, or Citibank. There was a presentation to a potential office tenant, who appeared with the suddenness of a phone call in the night, and then slowly slunk off into the twilight of vanished deals. There was a stream of letters and phone calls to the city officials overseeing the project, followed by urgent meetings with the consultants who bridged the gap between the city's regulations and common sense.

And still, Luk Sun had a long list of all the things that he was afraid weren't getting done. He called Alice and Bill into his office one July morning for a combination pep talk and dressing-down. "Is anyone focusing on the back-office space for this building?" he probed. "Lockers, building manager's office, mailroom? What about security? It affects your doors, your elevators, a lot of things. And we've got to focus on three big items. The elevators. The curtain wall. Structural steel. There's big exposure there. Lots of money. You should be banging Turner. *Banging* them. Because whatever you save on those trades, that's the ballgame."

In all this excitement, no one was allowed to forget the Broadway

State Project's sinister bogey, the Variety chimney. Andrea had convinced the Landmarks Preservation Commission that moving the Variety chimney to the side wall of the rear annex of the Lyceum theater would not measurably detract from the public's appreciation of this treasured landmark. Now all they needed was an architect to design the new chimney, subject to approval by Variety and the Shubert Organization. Then, with an engineer's certification of safety, an asbestos inspection report, notification to the Community Planning Board, and a very long form whose purpose was to assure the city that they weren't demolishing a single-room-occupancy hotel, they could apply for a work permit. Luk Sun was not satisfied with this rate of progress. "Listen, I said to you guys, if we can't organize this little project, we're in trouble. We get someone to do the work, he's gonna want to put up scaffolding. What's the scaffolding going to sit on? Laquila is taking his ground away."

Meanwhile, Eichner Properties prepared for its momentous move from 625 Madison to new quarters on the eleventh floor of Cityspire. The new offices were far more in keeping with Bruce's growing stature and ambitions. In his design Jahn had sought inspiration in that treasured symbol of his homeland, the Black Forest, and decorated the offices in deep arboreal greens and a loamy black. Bruce admired the elegance of these colors, but they weren't exactly his taste, and for his private office he specified a pale Brooks-Brothers-broadcloth blue. Some longtime employees contended that around the time of the move to Cityspire, success seemed to stifle Bruce's anarchic spontaneity. He seemed increasingly inclined to conduct business in private meetings with Henry, Howard, or Luk Sun rather than company-wide shouting matches. No one, though, seemed to connect this with the fact that as soon as he stepped over his own threshold he was surrounded by green. Bruce's office was in the southeast corner of the building, overlooking the tiled dome of the City Center theater. He had a private conference room that was larger than the one that had served the whole company at 625 Madison. The new company conference room could seat sixteen people at a table of polished black granite. Henry Miller, Luk Sun, and Howard all had nearby offices. Mitchell, by choice, was in the distant northwest corner.

In the last week of June, the project faced two major milestones within three days: delivery of a "zoning set" of drawings to the City Planning Commission, and a presentation to a potential tenant, the law firm of Proskauer, Rose, Goetz, and Mendelsohn. The zoning set was a prerequisite for transferring the Lyceum air rights to the site. The air-rights transfer was a matter of right; as long as the project met the specified conditions, the city had to approve it. Nevertheless it had to be referred for hearings to the local Community Planning Board and also to a body called the Theater Advisory Council, representing theater owners, producers, and actors, and chaired by the actress Ellen Burstyn. Howard estimated the process would consume ninety days to reach its foregone conclusion. "Bill," he warned Hellmuth at a meeting in late May, "we've got to have a complete zoning set by June 29. I will call Mr. Fridstein, I will call Mr. Childs, I will call Mr. Skidmore, Mr. Owings, and Mr. Merrill, but we have to have it."

The zoning set comprised detailed floor plans, roof plans, building elevations, sign elevations, zoning maps, and pages of calculations to show that the project met all the requirements of the zoning text. Eichner hired a special zoning consultant, a former city planner named Michael Parley, one of whose major tasks was just to make sure Skidmore got all this stuff right. The end product would be seventeen sheets of three-foot-by-four-foot blueprints, each folded into quarters lengthwise and thirds horizontally into a neat packet showing Thomas Fridstein's stamped signature on top. BSP had to provide eighteen copies.

"Do you have any idea what the printing bill for this project is going to be?" Luk Sun muttered darkly.

June 29 was a Monday, and Skidmore worked all through the weekend to get the zoning set ready. On Monday morning, Andrea called Audrey and told her she could have another week. To secure the air-rights transfer, the zoning set had to be accompanied by Shubert's covenant to maintain the Lyceum. By an oversight, no one had bothered to secure this document. "I'm sorry, and I'm not sorry, because I think by focusing on it this way we worked out all the kinks and I think for all our purposes this shouldn't go to them with a lot of red flags," Andrea told her. "Now go take the rest of the afternoon off."

"Sounds great to me," Audrey replied evenly. "Just cancel the tenant presentation on Wednesday, and I'm out of here."

"Ahhh ... that's not my department," Andrea answered dryly. That afternoon, there was a meeting at VMS's offices on Third Avenue to prepare for the presentation. Proskauer was a major law firm looking for about 300,000 square feet, plus an option to expand, and if Bruce could sign a lease with a tenant of that caliber now it would obviously make a very favorable impression on the bank.

Howard knew several of the partners, and they weren't telling him no. "They're going to make a decision by July 15," he said, "and it's between us and David Solomon's building. I think they would like to do a deal with us, but they're a little frightened of the retail. I told them, you could live your whole life in the building and never know the retail was there. They want to be reassured we're not going to have peep shows in there. Okay, no problem, we don't want peep shows, either. A point in our favor is that we're closer to Grand Central. I'll bet three-quarters of the partners live in Westchester."

"Well," said Fridstein, "if I were signing a $30 million lease I wouldn't make my decision based on 500 feet."

"Yeah, but when I was on the Planning Commission, people used sillier arguments," Howard said. "The CEO of a billion-dollar company would say, 'I'm leaving New York unless I get a place to park my limousine.'"

They went over the drawings carefully. Skidmore had done an interior layout to show how a law firm could use a typical office floor, with senior partners in the prow and lesser partners around the perimeter. BSP had also commissioned the first artistic rendering of the building. Until now, the building had been seen whole only by the architects, and by them only in their minds. For everyone else it was a constant struggle to integrate the elevations, sections, and plans into a mental model of what the building would actually be like. To be sure, Skidmore had computers that could produce drawings from any perspective known to Euclid, rotate them, and slice a section along any desired axis. But computers lack the subtle art of the renderer. Their colors are too intense, their shadows too crisp. The building inevitably looks like something that was assembled out of a box.

The rendering was done by an architect named Lebbeus Woods. His perspective, a seven-eighths south view from the corner of 45th Street clear back to the full width of the Lyceum, emphasized the sober corporate face of the building, while foreshortening the billboards on Broadway to insignificant blurs and reducing 1550 Broadway to total invisibility. The conventions of rendering did not preclude such a perspective, even if it could be achieved in life only by tearing down most of the existing block between 44th and 45th streets. The windows already dedicated to a Riese hamburger joint were drawn with almost Classical severity as a row of solemn gray rectangles. The shadows on the building suggested a fall or spring afternoon, but the sidewalks were almost empty and the traffic (composed entirely of different colors of 1974 Pontiacs) was so sparse that the nonexistent traffic lights and street signs wouldn't even be missed.

The Skidmore team worked most of Tuesday night getting the drawings ready, as well as a new model for the occasion; David had a meeting in Chicago Tuesday evening but flew back on the first morning flight and breezed in in time to dazzle the lawyers with his witty, learned, and impassioned pleading for his building. "A great presentation this morning," Luk Sun told Fridstein as the job meeting got under way that afternoon. "Pass the word to all the troops."

"As soon as they wake up," Hellmuth put in.

"The materials were great, and David Childs' metaphors were outstanding."

The following Monday, a week after the original deadline, the zoning set arrived at Eichner Properties. It took three messengers to carry it. Alice and Bill spent most of Tuesday delivering the copies to various offices around the city. At the job meeting Wednesday, Luk Sun made the mistake of referring to the one-week delay as a "reprieve." "It wasn't a reprieve," Fridstein said testily. "We were ready to go. The sleep was already lost."

Capturing the building in a rendering did not mean that the work of designing it came to a stop. On the contrary, the rendering had gotten ahead of the design, incorporating some details that Eichner had not yet seen or approved. This was especially true of the top. One of the most conspicuous effects of Postmodernism has been to totally discredit the International Style helipad roof, the geometrically perfect, logically impeccable termination of the building at its own highest floor. This was actually the second time such a development had occurred in the history of the skyscraper. The very earliest tall buildings, built before and just after the turn of the century, exemplified the famous dictum of Louis Sullivan, "Form ever follows function." They were rectangular boxes whose flat roofs were if anything emphasized by their typically heavy overhanging cornices. What we think of as quintessential skyscrapers—the Empire State, Chrysler, or RCA buildings, crowned with spires that just barely pierce the firmament—represent a later development, the romantic eclectic style of the 1920s and 1930s. So history was repeating itself in the 1980s, although not necessarily to advantage. The tops of many Postmodern buildings were all vainglory and histrionics, calling attention to themselves rather than the sky: emphatic yet arbitrary gestures like the Citicorp building's famous slump, which helped give rise to a whole generation of sloping, angled, or pyramidal tops, or the bizarre keyhole-in-the-sky of the Texas Commerce Tower in Dallas, which inspired nothing.

The Broadway State Building, though, was destined to have a spire. The prow, begging to be carried up beyond the roofline, called it forth; any other resolution would have been unthinkable. At one point, the architects, in their endless quest to find a way around the setback rules, tried putting a bowsprit at the top of the building, a spike cantilevered out from the prow, like a spear held vertically at arm's length. At the next meeting it was gone. "The bowsprit was shaved off by zoning," Hellmuth explained. "It invaded the setback, which is a no-no even six hundred feet in the air. To make it legal it would have had to be a sign and say 'Eat at Joe's.'"

"A hundred years from now," Childs added, "scholars will be going over these drawings with chemicals to see the building that might have been."

"We'll put a time capsule in the building," Luk Sun suggested.

"Make sure you put in one of Bruce's ties," Audrey said.

"Can you put in all of his ties?" Childs asked.

Skidmore's new scheme called for three silver mullions to run the length of the building, at the apex of the prow and its two corners. At the roofline, these turned into metal poles that ran up another forty or so feet, with the central one rising highest; they were linked with horizontal struts and diagonal braces in a graceful, airy structural lattice. "It is the same as the mast of the Empire State Building, except that it is a design for the next century," Hellmuth said. "It rises with the curtain wall at the three corners, then the curtain wall dematerializes and the mast rises like a sculpture, like the flèche of a medieval cathedral."

Behind the spike, there was a three-story box on the roof, which held the water tanks and several sets of stairs.

Hellmuth: "The stairs are nonfunctional. It's all fantasy up there, it adds some complexity. You walk around New York and see these wonderful rooms at the top of buildings like the San Remo [a spectacular old apartment house on Central Park West] and you wonder what marvelous things go on in there. The stairs are for the people in the street, to look up at and dream about what it would be like to be up there."

Luk Sun looked extremely unconvinced by this speech, but he held his tongue. Further east on the roof was a low, narrow penthouse that held the machinery for the high-rise elevators. On each side of this structure, three or four columns rose from the surrounding roof and then bent back horizontally to form a row of flying buttresses. Luk Sun expressed some doubt about the practicality of that arrangement. "They're not really flying buttresses," Hellmuth explained, "they're expressed piers. They have a definite structural function. They're structural steel, not decorative iron, and if we don't use the steel there, you'll have to use it somewhere else."

That was part of the problem, though, Luk Sun pointed out: if they served a structural function, they had to be fireproofed, and if they were covered with fireproofing, they couldn't then just be painted, but would require some more elaborate cladding, such as a sleeve of ornamental metal, or a box of curtain-wall glass. If Hellmuth wanted to add complexity, Luk Sun thought grimly, he'd succeeded: figuring out how to pay for all this stuff was going to be the most complex thing he'd done all year.

The curtain wall was to be the most unusual feature of the building, because of the recesses and because it was to be in two colors, green and blue. The idea for the wall was inspired by the very hip architectural style of Deconstructivism, which just then was being hailed as the logical successor to Postmodernism. Peter Eisenman, for whom Audrey had worked when she first came to New York, was a pioneering Deconstructivist. Deconstructivism was a subversive attack on the common-sense verities of architecture, such as gravity and the impenetrability of solids. Deconstructivist architects designed walls intended to look unfinished, or even crumbling; they put columns in the middles of rooms and staircases that led nowhere. Obviously not many office buildings got built in this style, and the term certainly never crossed Audrey's lips in the presence of anyone from Eichner Properties. But there was arguably a Deconstructivist influence on Audrey's parti, which was to create the visual impression of a blue building superimposed on a green one. The tower would be primarily clad in the blue glass, except for the prow and the recesses along the sides, which would be green. The bustle, off to the left side, as one viewed the building from Broadway, would also have the green skin. The impression therefore would be of a green-glass building somehow inside a blue one, visible in the recesses and where it pokes out to form the prow.

For this scheme to work, the two walls would have to look as different as possible, not just in color but in the detailing of the mullions (the vertical strips between panes of glass) and the spandrels (the horizontal bands between floors). Audrey envisioned the blue skin as very slick and uniform, with narrow mullions painted to blend in with the glass. The green wall, for contrast, would be highly articulated, with prominent silver mullions and spandrels and a "supergrid" of metal strips lying outside the plane of the glass. Working against this ambitious agenda was the budget for the curtain wall, which had been fixed at thirty-five dollars a square foot—or, since the building was designed with a little more than 300,000 square feet of wall, around $10 million for the entire job. That included manufacturing the wall at an outside plant, shipping the panels, erecting the wall, and caulking it. Eichner regarded thirty-five dollars as a reasonable compromise between the goal of economy and the danger of driving the architects to suicide.

Turner was at that moment building a fifty-story office tower for Citicorp in Long Island City, Queens—the tallest building in New York City outside Manhattan. That building—also designed by SOM—had a curtain wall priced a little lower than thirty-five dollars, based on a simple, repetitive green-glass module. In his heart, Bruce probably thought he ought to get a wall at least twice as good for essentially the same price, because he would work twice as hard as Citibank at it. But one way or the other, that was all he was going to spend. The curtain wall was one of the few major costs that Bruce really controlled. He couldn't do anything about the cost of steel or concrete. As a matter of practice he refused to cut corners where it would hurt the marketability of the building, in the elevators or HVAC equipment, say. But Bruce did not believe that tenants asked much more of a curtain wall than that it keep out the rain. "I'm telling you this now," Bruce warned Skidmore. "This is not gonna unfold like a bad play, where the villain unmasks himself in the third act. A thirty-five dollar range doesn't mean forty-one dollars. It means thirty-five dollars, or maybe $35.25, if you give me a good reason to go the extra quarter."

For their part, the architects felt that this was late in the day to discover that they had to design a building covered with aluminum siding. "If I'd known it was going to be a thirty-five dollar wall, I would never have taken the job," Fridstein muttered, one of several occasions on which Bruce provoked him into quitting retroactively. Bruce was unmoved. His stubbornness forced the architects to search for alternative solutions. Since the thirty-five-dollar figure was based on the Citicorp wall, someone suggested, why not take that as a starting point, and see if it could be modified to work in the Broadway building? A curtain wall is a fairly complex structure of metal strips and angles designed to suspend a large piece of glass on brackets embedded in the concrete of the floor above. By adapting a wall that was already in production, a fabricator might be able to save a lot of money and shop time.

The Citicorp wall was being built by Flour City Architectural Metals, and in midsummer Flour City's Oscar Drucker came to New York to discuss the job. He returned two weeks later with drawings of what he thought a thirty-five-dollar wall ought to look like. The recesses had been reduced to vestigial patches identifiable by a different color of glass and by somewhat wider mullions. The architects were appalled. "Look," Childs explained, "designers are optimists. We already know, intellectually, that the building isn't going to live up to our drawings. The colors won't have the same contrast we've shown here, the delineation won't be as sharp. But if we lose the remaining elements that give the wall some definition, it's not going to be a building we're going to be proud of. It's going to be an embarrassment, architecturally speaking."

Only Gary remained calm; he had been through this process scores of times. Contractors feared what they didn't understand, and what they feared, they charged more for. It was mostly a matter of education. Take the question of how to treat the curtain wall where it fell in front of columns and spandrels. Drucker had assumed Skidmore wanted shadow boxes at these locations. These are shallow pans that create an illusion of depth behind the glass, contributing to a uniform, monolithic appearance, at least until the lighted office windows reveal themselves at dusk. But the architects didn't want a shadow box; they wanted opaque spandrel glass at those locations, which was cheaper. So it might be possible to trade off the shadow boxes for things they did want.

The designers had already lost one battle over the recesses when Luk Sun rejected the Vierendeel truss scheme, which would have permitted true structural cantilevers as deep as three feet. It had been decided then that the recesses would be created within the curtain wall itself. Now they were about to lose another struggle over how that effect would be achieved. Audrey had assumed the depth would be roughly halved to around eighteen inches. But to do that required the curtain wall to jog in and out at each recess, with all the expense of turning the mullions and forging a waterproof joint at the corners. Oscar's counterproposal was to create the recesses within a single mullion line. This would limit the recesses to slightly less than the depth of the mullion itself. The maximum that could be achieved in this way, he announced, was nine inches.

As for the supergrid, they could forget about that as well. The added cost of that was twelve dollars a square foot, for the entire green-glass section of the building, or about $2 million all told.

"There's no way you can take the money out somewhere else and put some of it back into the wall?" Susanne Churchill asked Luk Sun plaintively.

"No," he said briefly.

"But you wouldn't object if we tried to find it for you?"

Luk Sun brightened. "Certainly not," he said emphatically.

Susanne realized she had made a trap for herself. "We'd better not do that," she said hastily, "or you'll take it out of both places."

That was so obvious, Luk Sun didn't even bother to deny it. When Hellmuth and Fridstein presented the final rendering of the curtain wall, Bill left out all lyrical metaphors and simply described "the best combination of things Oscar is willing to give us for thirty-five dollars." The depth of the recesses was fixed at nine inches. The blue skin would have painted mullions intended to recede into the field of glass, while the green would have a more assertive, articulated treatment, with wide, shiny—but flat—mullions.

"This happens all the time," Hellmuth remarked. "The designer puts some texture in the building and the developer flattens it out. Unfortunately, buildings don't have little footnotes down near the bottom where you can explain to people how great it started out to be."

In essence, even as the building was being designed, it was being undesigned. This was called "value engineering." Value engineering is a technique for comparing the costs and benefits of alternative design and construction choices. It is a fashionable discipline in engineering schools, but invariably the exigencies of development in the real world mocked its presumptions to neutrality and scientific precision. The architects preferred to refer to the process by the less glamorous but more honest term, "cost-cutting."

Turner had a whole department for this function, represented on this job by Lee Tsangeos, whose title was "estimating engineer." The first estimate of "hard" (or construction) costs for the Broadway State job had been prepared back on April 1. This of course was just an exercise, based on Turner's calculations of typical costs for first-class office space, since the building then was little more than four elevations on Audrey's sketch paper. But it was a necessary exercise, because on a fast-track project, design and construction—and therefore expenditure—proceed simultaneously. To wait for the building to be designed before figuring out what it would cost would be like waiting until a child is full-grown before measuring him for clothes. The budget Lee established for ten major categories of expense would be a benchmark to measure future profligacy, or even, should it occur, economy. As the designs were refined and the bids came in, adjusted expenses would be compared to these estimates, and the total job cost revised accordingly, almost invariably up.

The hard-cost estimate prepared by Turner on April 1 came to $109,605,000, or $113.62 per square foot for a building of 964,675 gross square feet. That did not include demolition (which was outside Turner's contract), or the work letter—the interior construction and fixtures that the landlord customarily provides for incoming tenants. (It did include nearly $14 million for "general conditions" and Turner's profit on the job.) Mitchell offered a demurral to this figure. "Negrycz, you bastard, this is gonna be horrible if we have to pay this amount of money," he said. "I assume that when you decide to get serious about this job, you will show us how you're going to build it for $100 a foot." But while Skidmore had been designing castles on the roof, Lee had been quietly adding up numbers. Kevin Huntington had reported that the office building needed fourteen elevators, six in a low-rise bank running to the twentieth floor and eight for the remaining floors. The engineers were starting to come up with estimates for steel, and JB&B was looking into what it would take to air-condition, ventilate, and heat the atrium. By July the figures in Lee's notebook had reached the alarming sum of $120 million.

Luk Sun's instructions were to reduce this by $15 million. In early August, Gary convened the first of many meetings for this purpose. "What we're down to," he told a sober-looking team from SOM and JB&B, "is there's a piggy bank here, and when we put enough pennies into it, we can build the building. We can't afford to put anything onto this building that's not necessary. There's a lot of hard items here. But we're being told if we don't get that money out, we can fill the hole back up and go home. And Turner has a very selfish interest: if we don't build the building, we don't make any money … of course, we also don't lose any money."

Lee had drawn up a list of suggestions to achieve around $8 million in savings. The first, and by far the largest item, was "tower remassing." Lee didn't pretend to know much about architecture, but he knew what it cost. One key measure of the efficiency of a design is the ratio of exterior wall area to total floor area. Obviously, the more regular the plan, and the larger and fewer the floors, the better this ratio will be. Lee had demonstrated this by drawing the tower as he thought it should be, as a simple rectangle with no prow and no recesses. As a kind of homage to the idea of the prow, he had sliced off isosceles triangles at the northwest and southwest corners of the tower; then, for symmetry, he did the same along the eastern face, resulting in an octagonal tower with four long faces parallel to the streets and four short angled ones. Since the floors were also bigger, he was able to make the building two stories shorter with the same FAR. This, he announced proudly, saved a total of nearly 41,000 square feet of curtain wall, plus perhaps as much as 500 tons of steel, and possibly one high-rise elevator. And, as a bonus, since a regular tower like this didn't seem to require the elaborate top the architects had wanted, Lee had chopped that off as well.

Value engineering! Audrey could hardly believe her ears. Once more the architects resorted to their inexhaustible supply of metaphors. The bowtie! The spike! The prow, moving through space like a ship through water! The buildings reading through each other, interpenetrating, dematerializing into the great firmament that revolves around this very point on the globe, Times Square, Manhattan, U.S.A.! Luk Sun sat impassively. He had no intention of letting the estimator design the building. But he was perfectly willing to have Turner soften up Skidmore for an assault in the areas where he felt Skidmore deserved it, such as the rooftop. "They're going to fight you tooth and nail," he had warned Lee before the meeting. "You'd better be prepared for an intensive few weeks, because they'll have to be dragged kicking and screaming."

Kick and scream they did, but Skidmore was at a disadvantage at this critical time: David and Tom were on vacation for much of August, and Susanne Churchill was leaving to take a job in SOM's London office; it would take awhile for her replacement, Dale Peterson, to learn to stand sideways when Mitchell cranked up to gale force. Many of Lee's suggestions did find their way into the design. The ornamental stairs on the roof disappeared quickly. The architects put up more resistance to the idea of eliminating the flying buttresses, on the grounds that they were necessary to brace the top of the building against the wind. "If you take the bracing off the top," Phil Murray warned them, "you'll save a quarter pound of steel [per square foot of floor area], and have to put back a pound and a half somewhere else."

"Yeah," Gary agreed. "Bear in mind, Mitch, this is a very windy location. It blows on Broadway when it's still everywhere else."

"That's funny," Mitchell barked. "I got the same speech when I built a building on 85th and Second, and when I built this building on 56th Street."

The beams stayed, but they were reduced to pilasters in the wall of the penthouse (the structure holding the elevator machinery). Lee had suggested reducing the live-load specification in the building to fifty pounds per square foot from eighty. Fifty pounds is suitable for general office purposes, but law offices and a few other uses may need stronger floors. (This is due to the weight of the law books rather than the lawyers themselves.) After much debate, Luk Sun delivered Bruce's verdict: no compromises that could affect the leasability of the building. In the same vein he rejected a Skidmore suggestion to reduce the floor-to-ceiling height by three inches, to eight foot nine, saving $300,000 from the steel and curtain-wall costs.

"We advise you strongly to do it," Fridstein said. "Nobody does nine-foot ceilings anymore."

"No," Luk Sun said doggedly. "It's a marketing issue."

"Okay," Tom said testily, "we found the money for you. If you want to put it back, I assume you'll find a way to pay for it."

The tower design stayed essentially as Skidmore had drawn it, but after some study Audrey reported that it would be possible to eliminate one or possibly two floors by making the existing lowrise floors a little larger. There was a small architectural penalty, she noted, in compromising the definition of the tower and prow, but Skidmore could live with it. Preparations were made for dropping one high-rise elevator.

At this point Hellmuth spoke up to remind Luk Sun that they were still carrying structural steel in the building to support the extra FAR represented by 1550 Broadway. "You have to roll the dice and decide if you're gonna get that holdout building," he said. "You can't make a cheap building and plan for every contingency."

Luk Sun asked for another couple of weeks to study the issue. Then he promised an answer in another week. Finally Tom said he needed a decision immediately, or the steel drawings would be delayed.

"Okay," Luk Sun said. "No 1550."

"You want us to take the steel for 1550 out of the structure," Phil Murray repeated.

"Yes."

Bill pressed him: "No 1550, done, gone, ain't gonna happen, is that right?"

"Right," Luk Sun said firmly, adding under his breath, "as of today."

But even as that decision was being taken, another development that would end all possibility of saving an elevator was taking place at the other end of the site. "In a move that likely surprised the entertainment industry," *The New York Times* reported on July 14, "the Cahners Publishing Company said yesterday that it had agreed to buy *Variety*, the trade publication known as the bible of the industry." Cahners, a division of a British publishing company, was estimated to have paid between $45 and $60 million for the magazine. A few days later, by coincidence,

Audrey was working on the area around the truck docks and garage entrance on 46th Street, which had always been one of the most difficult and cramped parts of the building. On a whim, she drew a revised plan that incorporated the extra sixteen feet of frontage from Variety.

"You can see how much better this works," she told Luk Sun when she presented the drawings.

"Audrey," said Luk Sun, "I have no reason to believe that Variety is for sale."

"Gee," she said. "Even if we show them this drawing?"

"All right," Luk Sun admitted, "they are interested. At what number, we don't know."

"Does that mean we can stop working on moving their chimney?" Alice asked.

Luk Sun glared at her. "You can stop working on the chimney," he rasped, "when the building starts to come down."

20

By and large, the cost-cutting at this stage spared the atrium, only because not enough of it had been designed yet to cut. It was assumed, though, that once Jerde's imagination was turned loose in California, there would be a festival of value engineering in New York. What little was known of his plans did not discourage this view. Jerde indicated he wanted a skylight in the setback roof along Broadway, giving a view from the atrium of the prow of the building above. This reflected a grave misunderstanding of the engineering problems involved. All the rain runoff from thirty-five stories of building above would come crashing down on this skylight, which could not be even slightly pitched, because then the high end would protrude above the setback line. Consequently, Turner, which as a matter of professional discretion rarely made guarantees, came as close as it ever did to guaranteeing that this skylight would leak.

What was Jerde up to? Occasionally a hint would be dropped at a meeting, or Luk Sun would pick up a rumor from someone at Hahn. A flume ride. A dolphin pool. A round elevator—"not a cylinder, he means a sphere," Luk Sun explained to Fridstein, "that would pop up through the roof and then ride the prow to the top of the building." Jerde and some of the Hahn Company brass came to a meeting in New York in July to talk about concepts. Jerde proposed glass-enclosed kiosks cantilevered out from the walkways into the atrium. "You could link the kiosks with tubular glass columns," he mused, "and fill the glass columns with colored liquid." He started to sketch a giant Wurlitzer. "I've wanted to do bubble columns for the longest time," he said wistfully.

As long as they didn't have to build it or pay for it, the Californians were endlessly inventive about how to improve the project. They were frightened of New York City, but at other times they seemed to treat it as just a big San Diego with Jews. At one meeting, Luk Sun brought up the triangular traffic island between Broadway and Seventh Avenue. He thought it would be nice if it could be dressed up a little, especially if the Marriott across the street would help pay for it.

"I've been thinking about that myself," Al Corti replied. He proceeded to outline a plan for a pedestrian bridge across Broadway. Stairs could lead up to the bridge from the traffic island. This could be just the first link in an entire network of elevated walkways that could someday stretch to the Javits Convention Center, more than a mile away on Eleventh Avenue.

"It sounds like Minneapolis," William said dubiously.

"Exactly!" Corti agreed enthusiastically. "It would be *better* than Minneapolis!"

This suggestion left all the New Yorkers speechless for a moment. "If our idea was to make the atrium attractive from the street," Andrea finally said, "I don't think we accomplish that by putting the entrance in the shadow of a bridge ..."

"That's no problem!" Jerde interrupted exuberantly. "We'll tunnel out from the basement to the triangle in the middle of the street, then bridge from there to the Marriott!"

"There's a subway in the way," Alice pointed out.

"Oh, well, we can move them, right?" Jerde responded lightly, but then suddenly his eyes lit up: "We can have the subway run right through the project! That would be great!"

In the embarrassed silence that followed, William finally spoke up and said, "I don't think that's really the kind of retail mix you want."

Jerde did most of his creative work at his home in the Santa Monica Mountains, an eccentric, romantic old place built of massive stone walls and redwood beams salvaged from the old Venice Pavilion. One summer night he sat down there with Richard Orne and a bottle of wine. If it is nine o'clock in Brentwood, it is midnight in Times Square. The theater crowd is now safely buckled into their Volvos northbound on the Saw Mill River Parkway, leaving Broadway to the night people, the three-card monte dealers shuffling and spieling wherever there was a wide spot in the sidewalk, the teenagers ogling the shop windows with their meretricious booty of gold chains, silk shirts, buck knives, and cheap steaks. A police car, idling at the curb, suddenly stirs to life and hurls itself, howling like a fiend, against the wall of traffic. The tingle of danger is never far from anyone's mind, and even the barbecued chickens lie under the hot red lights like accident victims.

Overhead the signs pulse and swirl in pinwheels of Coca-Cola red and Kirin gold.

The buildings themselves, Jerde thought, disappear into the night, leaving behind their outlines in light. And they weren't exactly missed, when you think about what they look like in the daylight.

Why, he wondered, are we so hung up on architecture, on planes and angles and masses, in this place of no architecture?

The real architecture of Times Square is the signs. That's right. Who said architecture had to have three dimensions, anyway?

Right! We'll do the world's first two-dimensional shopping center! This will be the first building in the world to employ ... virtual architecture.

A world of total illusion! You can have ... Regent Street. You can have the Nile. You can have the Moon.

No. Wait. There is a third dimension.

Of course there is.

Time.

Yes!

You can do a projection of the Piazza San Marco, but you've got to have ...

Pigeons flying over it.

Exactly.

This was the birth of the concept that Jerde would eventually call the "Whiz Bang." Another architect, Craig Hodgetts, and Jim Dow, a movie special-effects and lighting designer, also played a role in its early development. Jerde described his idea as a "habitable sign." He wanted to create the illusion of walking in off the street to the secret heart of Times Square. Sometimes he would liken it to a big rectifier tube in an old-fashioned table radio, pulsing with all the energy of New York. Mysterious electrical gear would sputter and crackle forbiddingly, almost as if you were somewhere maybe you weren't supposed to be. His nearest analogues were the set of the movie *Blade Runner*, or the first floor of

Bloomingdale's, "laid out with black aisles and sculpted with light." It would be nothing like "a banal shopping center with carpeting and Radio Shacks," but equally far from the benign, Disney-esque fantasy world that had been Jerde's trademark at Horton Plaza.

In September, Jerde's team came to New York to present this concept. He brought plans and elevations and a plastic model the size of a picnic hamper that traveled with them on the flight from California and arrived somewhat the worse for wear, so that Orne and his associate Bob Gilley had to spend a good part of the night in their hotel rooms gluing it back together.

Jerde had retained the idea of the semicircular atrium. "It is part of the exciting nature of curves to be self-revealing, to make you want to see ahead," he explained. But he had surrendered the notion of wrapping the sidewalk around the atrium. Now there would be a flat glass wall at the property line, interrupted by columns and by glass doors. Inside the doors would be a continuous walkway around the atrium, lined with storefronts on the far side. All the floors would be open to the atrium and linked by escalators.

This work, said Jerde, "marks the end of the armature phase. We have located all the lease lines and the circulation patterns on which the decorative, or thematic, elements are superimposed.

"We will have interior signage at three different depths. The signs will be related to the exterior signs at street level, but not identical, like the ectoderm and exoderm of an embryo." At the storefront line there would be neon store signs, either in the plane of the storefront or "bladed," meaning perpendicular. Suspended from the second-floor slab, he proposed a "video wall" of ganged television monitors, creating a mosaic that could be fragmented, repeated in countless different variations or blown up and spread as one vast image across hundreds of screens. And in front of that, hanging within the atrium itself, would be "a gossamer veil of light," a wall of glass that could be transparent at one moment, opaque at another, erupting into a sunset or ribbons of pure color, giant logos spinning and twirling through space in a display that had never before been witnessed in the entire glorious history of the enclosed shopping mall.

This was easy to do, Jim Dow assured them, with LCD (liquid crystal diode) panels, larger versions of the number displays in calculators or portable-computer screens. LCDs are plastic plates that are opaque in their natural state but turn clear when a voltage is applied. In their clear mode, people could look through them to the stores and the neon signs and the video wall. Opaque, they would function as a screen for the projection of still or moving images, wall-writing with fast-moving laser beams, or innumerable other special effects. Treated as a matrix of thousands of individual pixels, the wall itself could form block-letter messages, images, or geometric patterns, materializing, expanding, rotating, traveling, and then disappearing in seconds.

Jerde went on to outline some of the ways the Whiz Bang could be used. It would serve as both an attraction for shoppers and an advertising medium for tenants—or even outside companies, who could book time on it like a television station. There would be a library of prerecorded effects that could be programmed to play throughout the day. But he expected that most often the Whiz Bang would be operated in real time, with live shots from remote video cameras in the atrium itself, network newsbreaks, and special effects that would feed on and amplify the excitement of the crowds. Video artists would clamor to perform, or you could charge people five bucks a minute to run the machine, fulfilling every kindergartner's dream of splashing paint on a wall thirty feet high, and have a line stretching out to Sixth Avenue.

"This," Jerde concluded portentously, "will be what it would be like to shop in a space station! This will be the biggest piece of urban theater ever done. If you put one in Tokyo and one in Los Angeles, and hooked them together, you'd really have something. It's inevitable that the whole world will someday be wired together like this, and that it should start right here in Times Square."

A world linked by shopping! Teenagers buying T-shirts in Atlanta watching couples slurping cappuccino in London watching the same Nike logo bump as secretaries on their lunch break in Brasilia! And at the heart of it, the Broadway State Building, Times Square, U.S.A.!

By definition, a genius is someone who is ahead of his time, and Jerde was perhaps farther ahead than most, so it probably came as no shock to him, having finished this elaborate and impassioned presentation, that those to whom it was addressed chose to critique it on the most mundane and narrow grounds conceivable.

After a long pause, Luk Sun finally spoke: "Even if the Buildings Department agrees with you that this is the most wonderful attraction in the city, the safety requirements will cost a fortune."

"You mention the word 'laser' to a plans examiner, and he sees his whole life passing before his eyes," Howard added.

"Local 3 [the electricians' union] will have a field day with this," Luk Sun said glumly.

"Local 3, nothing," Alice put in. "You'll have to use stagehands."

"This means, I assume," Bruce put in, "we have to have somebody there running it twenty hours a day."

"This is a profit center," Dow replied. "It has its own little office tucked in the building, and there's a guy there like a disk jockey; he runs commercials for your stores, and then he sells commercials to outside entities and he pays you your cut. It won't cost you anything."

"Except if he finds he can't make any money on it," said Bruce, "and then it becomes our headache for the next hundred years."

"We're investment builders," Luk Sun said. "One thing investment builders don't want to be is guinea pigs. There's too much at stake. This is a forty-story office building being built by ironworkers who wear construction boots, and when something doesn't fit, they hit it a couple of times until it does. I want to see where this is working. Show me an application, let me touch it and kick it."

"Well, the technology is proven, and it will work," said Hodgetts. "But we're designing this to be architecture. Mute, in its fail-safe state, it's glass and metal and it's beautiful."

"That," said Bruce, "fills me with a *great deal* of confidence."

The presentation had lasted for most of a day, and the sun was low in the sky when people finally piled into the elevators and out into a balmy summer evening. "What gets me," said Fridstein, "is that we're all hunched over our computers trying to shave $50,000 worth of steel off the building, and those guys in one swoop just went ahead and added a million dollars' worth of glitz."

But Fridstein was wrong. The Whiz Bang didn't add a million dollars to the price of the building, although no one had any way of knowing that at the time; it would add $7 million to the price of the building.

To Bruce this was no laughing matter. His problem was that there was no obvious way to separate the business agreement with Hahn from all these ridiculous questions of dancing lasers. His problems were personified in Hahn's leasing director, Al Corti. Corti had one of the hardest jobs of anyone in the project. He had to convince shoe-store chains with 400 outlets that you couldn't tell apart without a microscope to come to this tiny little mall at rents that would look to them as if they were being quoted in yen. He looked on the Whiz Bang as his big selling point, and he insisted that it be built with every refinement and elaboration Jerde could concoct. "You have to get past all these threshold issues," he explained. "'I'd never come to Times Square.' 'If I did, I'd never be off the street.' 'If I were, I'd never be in the back.' It's doable, but you've got to give them a reason to come. You can sell somebody the Brooklyn Bridge, but he wants to make sure Brooklyn is on the other side."

Corti had a unique negotiating style. Most participants in a business negotiation will, as soon as they figure it out, concede the basic premise that underlies their opponents' position. Bruce was usually happy to let his opponent win all the debating points, as long as he got the substance of what he wanted. But there is also a desire on the part of people in a business setting not to appear dumb. If something is assumed by everyone else at the table to be an obvious and incontrovertible fact, it tends to go unchallenged.

But Corti didn't seem to care about appearing dumb. He had seized on Jerde as his savior and the Whiz Bang as the instrument, and he clung to them with an obstinacy that at times seemed to embarrass even his colleagues in his own company. If Bruce was operating from the premise that the Whiz Bang was only worth building to the extent that one could demonstrate a positive relationship between returns and cost—well, Corti simply didn't recognize that argument. If Luk Sun pointed out that some of the things Jerde wanted might be simply unbuildable under New York building and zoning codes—well, that wasn't Corti's problem.

Summer wore on, and still there was no deal with Hahn, only an unsigned draft of a "letter of intent," which Citibank agreed was nice to have, but not enough to persuade them to issue a loan. Citibank did, however, proffer their own "letter of intent" for a loan of $280 million, subject to the following major conditions:

1. BSP providing $40 million in equity, cash, or a letter of credit. This was in the works. Berini had arranged to borrow $10 million from one of the VMS investment trusts, the "Strategic Land Trust." This was a fund that sold shares to the public and invested the proceeds in VMS's own projects, for a guaranteed rate of return. The other $30 million would be borrowed from a bank. If worse came to worst, Berini assumed that European-American Bank would lend it to them—because if there were no construction loan, EAB might never get back all the money they had already advanced on the land loan.

2. A signed deal with Hahn, satisfactory to the bank. Bruce believed he could achieve this.

3. Citibank's own ability to syndicate $205 million of the loan amount to other lenders, reducing their own exposure to just $75 million. This was something Bruce had no possible way of influencing.

Were these conditions onerous? Hardly. Once, banks were stuffy enough to demand a leasing commitment from a creditworthy office tenant before financing a commercial building of this size, but no more. In lieu of office tenants, 1540 Broadway offered theaters (already leased to Loews), retail (presumptively leased to Hahn), and 100 parking spaces that would never know a vacant instant from the moment the door opened. This, on paper, was an unusually solid project by the standards of the mid-1980s. And there would be $40 million in equity. True, it would probably all be borrowed. But it would be borrowed against VMS's outside assets, so as far as Citibank was concerned, it was essentially the same as cash—unless, that is, you believed as a matter of principle that someone seeking to borrow $280 million should come up with $40 million out of his own liquid assets. But Citibank was in no position to make that demand, since at the same time they were loaning to other developers who had no equity in their projects at all.

Still, no deal was no deal. After nearly two years of effort by Eichner, Skidmore, Turner, and the rest, Bruce assessed the chances of the project going ahead as seventy-five–twenty-five. "If I get Hahn to sign the letter of intent," he mused, "that goes up to ninety–ten. Then I just have to hold everyone together. I've been down this road; I'm used to a certain amount of pain and suffering. I've got a good relationship with the lender, and the project is inherently a good one, by the numbers.

"But the deck of issues is pretty complicated. You're not playing with a computer, you can't feed in a set of numbers and get an answer. The management of EAB is trying to buy the bank. They're so pissed because what was supposed to be a favor to Bruce Eichner turned into an eighteen-month loan that they're all alone on for $70 million, that I don't know if I can go back to them for anything."

On September 1, the land loan matured, and EAB told Berini they were prepared to begin foreclosing on the property. The project was dead out of money, and the one bill that could not be postponed was coming due: the Riese Organization's monthly tribute for "lost business." Anyone else, Bruce was willing to stall, but the assumption was that if the check didn't arrive at the Riese Organization on the first of each month, Murray Riese would end up owning the project and everyone at Eichner Properties would spend the rest of his life working behind the counter at a Roy Rogers. So Bruce did something he hoped never to do. He put $20,000 of his own money into the project to help meet the payment. That's how desperate things were.

Of course, EAB had to be pretty desperate, too, and in that fact

Bruce saw an opening. He and Berini went to EAB and waved Citibank's letter of intent. "I understand your patience is at an end, and I don't blame you," he told Dempsey, EAB's president. "But the simple way out of this for you," he went on, "is not a foreclosure. It's for EAB to help put up the equity for the project." Berini agreed to put together a package of collateral from VMS's portfolio that would support a loan of $30 million; based on that EAB would issue a letter of credit for the equity. EAB's fate would no longer be tied to 1540 Broadway, because their security would come from VMS. The waters could cover Manhattan as high as the roof of Grand Central, but EAB's credit would be safe in places like San Antonio and Grand Junction. The Broadway State Building, which in so many ways was a quintessential urban project of the late 1980s, would be built on a foundation of suburban condominiums, shopping centers, hotels, and office parks whose only real address was an interstate exit.

Bruce was pretty pleased with this job of work; provided he brought all the other pieces along, it meant that he and Berini had essentially placed all the equity and debt themselves, something that an investment bank might well have charged them $2 million for. And, once EAB agreed to these terms, with a final, ultimate, not-to-be-extended extension until the end of the year (for another 1 percent fee, amounting to around $700,000), VMS was able to raise $3 million to help carry the project for the next couple of months. So Bruce, naturally, prepared to pay himself back the $20,000.

"No way," Berini said. "If you can't come up with $20,000 until the end of the year, screw you."

Something else happened, that fall of 1987, that would eventually affect the project, although at the time no one was sure just how. On Monday, October 19, following a hundred-point loss on Friday, the stock market went into complete panic and lost more than five hundred points, about a quarter of its value. This crash was widely heralded as marking the end of the fabulous boom of the 1980s, and people who had made their fortunes in that decade grimly prepared to hoard them against the coming famine. But Bruce wasn't finished making money yet, not by a long shot. As the market closed he was literally jumping up and down with excitement: companies that he had been following for months as their stock spiraled up out of his reach suddenly became available at pushcart prices. "I have to believe this is the greatest opportunity I've seen since I've been in business," he said, "—unless you believe in a depression. But if it's 1929 all over again, what difference does it make?

You're stuck in the economy anyway. You'll go down the tubes with your real estate instead of your stocks, and in the end it won't have mattered.

"You've got to keep thinking rationally. People are so emotional. They look for stability all the time … and you can't find it. It's not there."

Henry, who had a fair amount of his own money in the market, punched up quotes on the terminal in his office with a horrified fascination. "IBM is down more than thirty points," he says, "or a quarter of its market value. It was capitalized at $100 billion, so that's $25 billion that disappeared in a day."

Someone asked Bruce what stocks he owned.

"Nothing," he said; then corrected himself: he had some AT&T that he'd bought for income. Henry looked it up; it had closed at around twenty-four, down six.

"I bought it at twenty-four," Bruce said, with a shrug.

Before the end of the week, Bruce and Henry had begun accumulating shares of a big retail chain they had been eyeing for some time as a takeover candidate. But it was about the same time, as New Yorkers began to poke around in the wreckage of the stock market to see if anyone was still alive in there, that the first wave of articles began to appear, speculating on the end of the great real estate construction boom of the 1980s.

21

The person who truly held the fate of the atrium in his hands was neither a banker nor a businessman, though. This was Jerry Gillman, of the firm Cole-Gillman, whose role was to expedite the architects' plans through the bureaucracy of the Department of Buildings. Gillman was perfectly suited to this occupation. He was a middle-aged man with a horse-collar of springy gray hair, a peremptory manner, and a pungent New York bray that could cut through a roomful of murmuring architects like a taxicab scattering joggers in Central Park. He wore short-sleeved shirts in the summer, ocean-blue slacks, and shiny neckties that ended a button and a half above his belt. This was a uniform carefully assembled to enable him to get off an elevator in any municipal office in the city and appear instantly at home. Jerry Gillman was the one person connected with the project whom no one dared to contradict or second guess. There was an almost superstitious aura about his work, as if any interference risked throwing the project into a bureaucratic limbo from which it might never emerge. Nearly every meeting now ended with a list of questions for Jerry Gillman, who unfortunately was one of the busiest and most inaccessible men in New York. His days were spent in constant transit between Department of Buildings headquarters downtown, architects' and developers' offices in midtown, and sites that could be anywhere, until by midafternoon he had accumulated an inch-thick wad of phone messages.

What Gillman essentially offered was his access to the borough superintendents who made the key decisions on what was acceptable under the building code. This saved the architects weeks wasted in filing plans, waiting for the examiners to find something wrong with them, and then trying to figure how to satisfy the objections—all accomplished, in the ordinary course of things, at the end of a long and infinitely frustrating line of fellow practitioners seeking the same things. There is nothing necessarily sinister about this line of work. But to the city administration, expediters were an embarrassment, proof of the slur that New York's bureaucracy was so glacial that an entire profession had grown up around it trying to speed it up. In November, 1987 Mayor Edward Koch and Buildings Commissioner Charles M. Smith, Jr., circulated a letter to developers and architects, addressing "the concerns expressed ... over the purposes for which fees are paid to expeditors who are often retained to do little more than stand in lines at the Buildings Department." The mayor was upset by reports that an unidentified expediter had tried to pass along to a client the cost of bribing a plans examiner. Unwilling to credit such a vile slander against a city employee, Koch denounced this as "a subterfuge against the client to extort higher fees." The mayor went on to outline two pages of improvements in Buildings Department procedures—such as letting architects phone ahead for appointments, instead of making them appear in person to wait on line—intended to eliminate the need for expediters. Three years later, though, there were just as many expediters as ever, and some of them were so busy that they had taken on assistants whose main job was to stand in lines at the Department of Buildings.

In the mid-1980s Gillman had observed an interesting development: a number of the Buildings Department's plans examiners were being drawn from the ranks of former firefighters, who naturally were extremely conservative on issues of fire and smoke. This spelled trouble for the atrium. A fireman looks at an atrium and he sees a big chimney. The atrium would have absolutely state-of-the-art life-safety features. It would have powerful exhaust fans, roof hatches that would pop open to allow smoke to escape into the atmosphere, close-mounted sprinkler heads. But that probably wouldn't be good enough, Gillman warned. The new theory called for enclosing all but the lowest levels of an atrium with a continuous floor-to-ceiling glass wall, to prevent smoke spreading from floor to floor.

Skidmore's Joe Blanchfield explained all this at the next job meeting.

"There's a building across the street [the Marriott] with a forty-story atrium," Luk Sun objected.

"That was built in the 1970s; this is now," Blanchfield answered. "Many of the atriums you see around the city could not be built today."

Luk Sun sank in his chair. "What about the escalators?" he asked.

Blanchfield said that in order to preserve a continuous glass wall, the escalator landings would have to be enclosed in glass-walled vestibules. Luk Sun sank even lower in his chair. Apart from the expense, this was sure to mean trouble with Hahn. The whole idea of an enclosed shopping mall was to put as few obstacles as possible in the way of a dollar trying to find its way into a cash register. Now, traffic would back up behind the vestibule doors. Shoppers would experience an infinitesimal hesitation in which to ask themselves whether they really needed a maple-walnut frozen yogurt cone. Most people would answer yes, naturally. But Hahn didn't get rich selling things only to people who actually needed them.

"Could we use fire shutters?" Orne asked, referring to steel gates that would drop from the ceiling in case of a fire to make a smoke-tight seal.

"Let me play devil's advocate," Blanchfield said. "What happens to the people on the escalator when the shutter drops?"

"Ahhh … they get cut in half."

"Well, that takes care of them, but how does everyone else get off the escalator, except to jump?"

"You could put the escalators in glass tubes, like gerbil tubes," Alice suggested.

"I don't think we want gerbil tubes," Orne said dubiously.

"You could go back to your flume-ride concept," Luk Sun suggested.

The issue of smoke enclosure for the atrium became one of a number of points of contention, any one of which could at any moment prove fatal to the deal that Bruce was struggling to hold together in his sessions with Vernon Schwartz. If Bruce thought he was building a forty-story skyscraper with stores, as far as Hahn was concerned this was a shopping center which happened to have some office space upstairs. When Jerde's plans were overlaid on a structural diagram for the building, Phil Murray, the SOM structural engineer, realized that four major building columns at the corners of the prow came down right through the middle of the atrium. To Jerde and Hahn, this was outrageous, insufferable. The columns would destroy sight lines to the stores from the sidewalk. They would hopelessly interfere with views of the Whiz Bang. They would overwhelm the romantic, exotic atmosphere, its evocative shadows and electrifying lights, with a gross reminder of the dead weight of offices above.

"I don't think we can live with those columns coming down through there," Bob Gilley said.

"You're going to have to," Luk Sun replied heatedly.

"Then I would ask Skidmore," Gilley went on calmly, "whether they have tried every solution."

"We can take a look," Murray said cautiously. "We looked at the logical ones."

"Do an illogical one," Gilley urged.

Surprisingly, that turned out to be good advice. Simply by refusing to accept an answer they didn't like, the clients forced the disinterested equations of engineering to yield up a different result. Murray and his associate Tim Kaye designed an immense steel truss to carry much of the weight of the west face of the building. The truss would span across much of the fourth floor, which was dedicated to machinery anyway. Thousands of tons of compressive and tensile force would zigzag up and down through the gloom of the machine rooms. The connections among all these bracing elements, when they were drawn months later, would form an array of gussets and flanges resembling a vast iron model of a virus, dumb but potent, bristling ominously with hundreds of high-strength bolts.

"I assume this is gonna work," Mitchell barked when Murray outlined the scheme to him, "or you wouldn't have designed it this way. I would just remind you, this building is being built by ironworkers, not by watchmakers."

When the question of buying Variety arose, Bruce was receptive, but not as much as he might have been two years earlier. It would mean a bigger building, naturally, and all things being equal, a bigger building was a more profitable one. But the project was already racing against the vesting deadline, and adding to the site would only push the finish line further off. And the last thing Bruce needed at this point was to make the project more expensive. He was scrambling just to keep the project afloat; clearly there would be no money to buy another building at least until the construction loan was in place.

On the other hand, how could he turn it down? Variety's new owners planned to consolidate its offices with their other publications. The former owners, who still had the building, had no other use for it and offered it to BSP for $1.5 million. This worked out to a little less than sixty dollars a FAR, compared to seventy dollars Bruce had paid for the Loews site, two years earlier. But he had no intention of spending even that much. He instructed Lydia to offer an even million, and they settled at around $1.1 million, but with financing terms that in effect made it even cheaper. Howard warned Variety that the sale might not close until the end of the year. They said that would be fine.

"As long as you're moving," Howard added casually, "why don't you apply for utility shutoffs in the building?"

"No problem," they said. "Happy to do it."

"They're so nice," Howard reported back later, "and so dumb. There will be an empty building, no utilities, no one to bother us about blasting. They couldn't give that building away to anyone but us. It makes you wonder how much better we could have done. This would be the time when you could really play hardball," he said, almost wistfully. "But of course," he added briskly, "we won't."

Skidmore proceeded to incorporate the Variety site into the project, which brought the large floors up to just over 22,000 square feet. But the first thing Gary said when he came for the job meeting the next day was, "No, I am not going down sixty feet under Variety. You haven't got a prayer."

"Your problem is demolishing it, or excavating it?" Luk Sun asked.

"My problem is, I've got a piece of land sixteen feet wide and I've got to put drills and blasting mats on it, and I've got to have a place for a drill to turn around and I've got to have a place to dump the rock, unless I dump it in the hole, and then nobody works in that corner of the site."

"Gary, you've got to try," Luk Sun urged. "I really want this."

"Yeah, and I want a Mercedes gullwing," Gary sighed, "and my chances of getting one are about as good as yours of making that hole. All right, I'll talk to Dino. I'm sure he's been thinking about this already. It's been all over the street since Friday."

In the trailer on the site, one wall of John's tiny office was given over to a large chart of the progress of Laquila's assault on bedrock, plotting rock removed against time. One line showed an idealized schedule; the other represented the actual cumulative amount of rock removed each day. On September 30, with 14,000 cubic yards of rock excavated, the lines crossed for the first time. With the hole down more than thirty feet at its deepest point near the back wall of the Lyceum, Laquila was ahead of schedule.

Unfortunately, the sheer volume of material removed was not the full measure of progress, since there was almost no excavation taking place on nearly a third of the site. The parapet of 1550 Broadway, especially along the 46th Street side, was showing signs of cracking under the stress of twenty-five explosions a day next door. The bus company hired an engineer, who warned that the parapet might at any moment decide to end it all in a plunge to the sidewalk. It took more than a month of legal wrangling to resolve that problem, and in the interim blasting was prohibited within twenty feet of 1550. Nor was there blasting being done along Broadway. The Transit Authority had finally approved a scheme for bracing the subway tunnel with thirty-foot-long vertical soldier beams. Only when those were in place could blasting in that part of the site begin, subject to monitoring by a third firm of seismic consultants, and requiring the services of a flagman who would stop train traffic in the tunnel when a blast was imminent.

On a morning just before Thanksgiving, one of the technicians manning the seismograph in the Lyceum came to the theater early, as usual, switched on the light in a basement dressing room, and saw a crack that was not in the four-volume catalogue of Lyceum cracks that had been compiled before the start of excavation. It was not a "hairline" crack, but more like log-splitting size. It ran along the base of a wall to a corner, turned up, and disappeared into the ceiling. The technician ran out to find Ellis.

"That's a crack, all right," Ellis said calmly. "Let's see where it goes." He climbed to the darkened stage wing, turned on a light, and saw it emerging from the floor, hideously full-blown, black and ugly. Ellis called Andrea. He was about to leave for a ten-day holiday in England. Later he would confess that he checked the American papers every day for a story about the Lyceum theater collapsing, in which case he wouldn't have bothered returning to the United States. The last thing he did before leaving was to stop blasting within thirty feet of the theater.

Not only did the blasting stop; the whole operation went furiously into reverse. Instead of trucking rock away, Laquila began heaping it up into a huge berm against the sheer rock wall below the Lyceum foundation. Rocco insisted that the theater had not been damaged by Laquila's blasting. Instead, what had occurred was the accident foreseen by Gary Negrycz back in July: the rock under the Lyceum had slipped along a plane of foliation, and a wedge of it had begun to slide northwards into the hole, taking with it part of the back wall of the theater. That was the reason for building the berm: it was holding the rock back, like sandbags heaped against a dike.

The important point, said Dowding, who came in from Chicago in the first week of December to consult on the problem, was that the accident was not caused by blasting, but by removing the rock; you could have dug the hole with teaspoons and the result would have been the same.

"Well," said Andrea, "you'll get a chance to test that theory, because I presume that teaspoons will be what we'll have to use, once Landmarks finds out about this."

There was a meeting in the trailer to decide what to do about the crack, involving Mailman, Ellis, Laquila and Laquila's engineer, someone from Shubert, and Shubert's engineer. Tension was running high. You could look out the grimy trailer windows and see the crack, a faint but unmistakable line in the bricks, starting at the foundation and tracing a jagged path about halfway up the wall. If you looked up from that point, you would see a 10,000-gallon water tank sitting atop the roof; if the wall started to slip into the hole, forty tons of water would give it a good shove on its way. Someone suggested draining half the water out of the tank to reduce the load on the wall. Laquila's consultant, Irwin Toporoff, leapt to his feet as if he would hurl himself bodily at the perpetrator to prevent any such thing from happening. "That's the very worst thing you can do!" he shouted. "The last thing you want is water sloshing around in there."

Besides the berm, Laquila had attempted to stabilize the rock with rock anchors. Laquila drilled eight holes at an angle down into the rock, forced cement to the bottoms of the holes, and stuck in forty-foot lengths of steel rebar. After the cement set, the bars were stretched and capped with steel plates welded to their free ends. In effect, the rock had been pinned together, as if by eight giant safety pins. Inside the theater, a telltale had been mounted on the wall to keep track of the size of the crack. This was a two-part plastic gauge, about three inches long. One half had a clear window with red crosshairs that overlaid a grid on the other half. The halves were glued to the wall on either side of the crack, and any change in the width of the crack would show up as a displacement of the crosshairs. For the past week there had been no change, indicating that the rock had been at least temporarily stabilized. Toporoff also proposed a series of trusses inside the theater to hold the corner together. "I don't know about those trusses," the Shubert engineer began. "You're depending on the rods not pulling out of the walls, and I've seen it happen so many times ..." He closed his left fist around the forefinger of his right hand and then yanked them emphatically apart, and shuddered.

"Look!" Toporoff erupted. "I have as much to risk as anyone because if anything happens to that building, I might as well retire, and I'm a couple of years short of retirement. If we do what I've shown here I have no worries. What do you want me to do, guarantee that if a Martian *spits* on the wall it won't get wet?"

Eventually the meeting broke up. Shubert's engineer promised to study the plans and get back within a few days.

It was time to notify Landmarks. As it happened, that night was a birthday party/fund-raiser for Mayor Koch. Howard, Andrea, Bruce, Mitchell, Luk Sun, and William attended, courtesy of Eichner Properties. Howard was careful not to buy tickets in the name of an entity that had business before the Board of Estimate. Eichner Properties did not have business before the board. Fifty-sixth Street Associates, which owned Cityspire, did have a pending matter before the board—approval of the additional eleven feet of height—but that was a separate partnership.

The dinner was held in the ballroom of the Grand Hyatt Hotel, a matter of some amusement to reporters who pointed out that the hotel's landlord was the mayor's hated enemy Donald Trump. Between the fruit cup and the soup, Howard saw Gene Norman.

"We have a little problem with the Lyceum you ought to know about," Howard said. "Let me get Andrea to explain it to you."

Andrea told him about the crack and what Dowding said that exonerated the blasting.

"I understand," Norman said, smiling. "I don't believe you, but I understand. It was your guy from Chicago. I should have known not to trust him."

The next day Alex Herrera and William Cary of Landmarks came to look at the crack. It loomed hideously large, in a powerful theatrical spotlight set on the stage. It was an unmistakable, classic, jagged crack in the black-washed wall, like the crack a cartoonist would draw in the Iron Curtain. At eye level, it was three-eighths of an inch across, and although for some reason you couldn't see daylight through it, you could feel the cold wind coming through.

"That," said Herrera, "is a *huge* crack."

Ellis and Andrea rushed to assure him that it only looked that way, because of the big expanse of wall, the black paint, the strong spotlight.

"I think," said Cary, "that from a procedural point of view, it would have been better if you had called us down when Dr. Dowding came to inspect it."

"Well," said Andrea, "we didn't want to say, 'Here's a crack,' and stand around scratching our heads. We wanted to wait until we had a plan for dealing with it so we could discuss this intelligently."

"Could you, architecturally, avoid taking out the remaining rock?" Cary asked.

"No, believe me, I wish we could," Mitch said quickly. "I wouldn't be racing the May 13 clock. I'd much rather face you guys with a problem for which I know there is a solution, than be up against it on May 12."

"You know," Herrera said to Andrea, "I really could close the whole job down." He paused, and Andrea held her breath. "But I'm not going out to call the police," he went on. "As long as you stay thirty feet away, and nothing more happens to the building, we'll wait and see."

22

The stock market crash of October in the end proved not to be the boon Bruce had envisioned. Within days he and Henry were ready to mount a raid on the assets of a major supermarket chain, but the swashbuckling bankers they had been counting on to join them were nowhere to be found. There is such a thing, Bruce realized, as being too visionary. "Every bone in my body says there's a gigantic hole in the market," he said, musing in his office one afternoon. "But I have to convince the guys at the investment banking houses. They're so nervous. There was a company we liked at fifty-two, fifty-three. By the time we completed our analysis the stock was in the low sixties. We saw a breakup value in the seventy to seventy-five range … and before we could put a deal together the stock went to eighty and split two for one. It is now, as we speak, four days after the crash, eighteen (thirty-six on the old basis) and I can't get an answer out of the investment bank, the same one that said it was worth seventy-five."

As far as the project was concerned, Bruce didn't regard the crash as anything to become alarmed over, yet. He was not about to lose sleep over the possibility of a recession three years down the road. You have to keep going, shut that possibility out; you can't fill the hole back up and go home. A more immediate danger was that the crash would throw a monkey wrench into the financing. There were two ways in which this could happen. One was if interest rates shot up. No one was sure why they should, although out of any given set of economic conditions it was possible to construct a scenario in which interest rates went up, or for that matter down. The interest rate in the loan was not fixed, but would be adjusted periodically with reference to LIBOR, the London inter-bank rate, which essentially reflected Citibank's cost of funds. A construction loan, unlike a consumer loan, is not amortized, and the borrower makes no interest payments as he goes along. It is all repaid in one lump sum out of the proceeds of a permanent mortgage after the building is finished and earning income. But interest accrues, naturally, as money is spent each month, and in effect the borrower borrows the interest as well as the principal from the bank. The $280 million face value of the loan included approximately $47 million in anticipated interest costs, known as the "interest reserve." If interest rates increased markedly before the loan closed, the bank could become nervous about the adequacy of the interest reserve.

The other danger was that Citibank would be unable to line up co-lenders. Since Citibank's commitment was contingent on syndicating the bulk ($205 million) of the loan, that would kill the deal, unless Citibank decided in the end to take a bigger share for itself. For several months, Citibank had been trying to market the loan in Japan. There was a theory that Japanese investors might be open-minded about Times Square, because the comparable district in Tokyo was the Ginza, which comprised some of the most valuable real estate in Japan. Japanese firms, despite their impressive acquisitions, were still relative newcomers to the business of financing new construction in Manhattan. If they wanted to learn that game as well, it would have to be on the West Side, because that's where the buildings were going up in 1987. Henry had given Citibank a list of banks, real estate syndicates, and "trading" companies to receive offering memoranda for the loan. The offering packages made a stack of documents five inches high.

No one pretended to understand the psychology of Japanese investors. Their thoroughness was legendary. It was almost as if, at a time when the eight biggest banks in the world were all Japanese (Citicorp, the parent of Citibank, was ninth), they were taking extra precautions to avoid being played for a sucker. Citibank, as the lead lender, hired an engineering firm to go over the drawings for the building, and, later, to keep track of the money as it was spent. Ordinarily, participants in a syndicated loan would be satisfied to let Citibank worry about this stuff, but not the Japanese; from the other side of the globe came a steady stream of telexes seeking details on the structural framing, the capacity of the stairs and fire exits, the insulating properties of the window glass and the rank, reputation, and creditworthiness of the Turner Construction Company. The deal was so complicated that a Citibank vice president later used it, in a speech to a Chicago real estate group, as an example of how to do business with the Japanese. She quoted an official of the Bank of England: "We are in a football game where the Japanese keep score by different rules. Other people count the number of times they score a goal; the Japanese count how often they kick the ball."

Citibank got a lucky break when the Industrial Bank of Japan agreed to participate; the imprimatur of the sixth-largest bank in Japan was a big help in bringing other investors aboard. In less than two months, $165 million of the loan had been syndicated. Then came what one Japanese company referred to as the stock market "crush." Suddenly interest in the project began to dry up. Polite letters began arriving in New York, full of gratitude for the opportunity to consider the deal, of regret for the circumstances that unavoidably made it impossible to pursue it, of hope that the sender would receive the honor of an invitation to consider Citibank's next project.

They were $40 million short. It wouldn't pay to sit around and worry about this, though. Bruce still had to negotiate the loan with Citibank, and as a prerequisite to that, he had to conclude his deal with Hahn.

Considerable progress had been made since May. The outline was in place for a ninety-nine-year master lease of the retail atrium. BSP would build the raw space, finish the public areas, and contribute a sum (later fixed at $7 million) toward the expense of leasing and finishing the tenant spaces. Hahn would find tenants for the mall, manage it (for a management fee) and split the rent with BSP, subject to the terms and conditions of the agreement. The agreement would be like a valve, turning the cash flow first on one party up to a specified amount and then the other. A list of preferences specified the order in which the partners could be repaid for various kinds of advances and capital expenses, and any income left at the end of this game would be shared fifty-fifty. For a term of seven years after completion of the space, and subject to a whole list of other conditions, Hahn guaranteed a minimum payment to BSP of $4.5 million a year.

This summary, however, begged a whole series of questions, which had to be exhaustively, obsessively negotiated one at a time, often by several successive sets of negotiators: Bruce with Vernon, then Wong and Tung with one or more of the Hahn executives, and finally, when the outlines of an agreement had been sighted, by the respective lawyers. When would the space be finished? How would the rent be phased in—bearing in mind that it would take months, from the time the space was turned over to Hahn, to build out the tenant spaces and get the mall open and operating? Was Hahn forbidden to do another deal in the Times Square area? For how long? What *was* the Times Square area?

It didn't help, in Bruce's opinion, that lawyers were now involved. Partly this was just because he hated paying legal bills. But his aversion to lawyers went deeper than money. Bruce's lawyer was Barry Ross, a partner in Robinson Silverman Pearce Aronsohn and Berman. Bruce considered Ross a tremendously smart man, which was a mixed blessing in a lawyer; the smarter lawyers are, the more sides to a question they see, and the more complicated they want to make everything. Bruce drew a distinction between his world of "business points" and Ross's realm of "legal points." The former had to do with money in the here and now: who spent what, who got how much. The latter had to do largely with the what-ifs, the potential for things to go wrong and the remedies and sanctions that could be applied. It wasn't that Bruce didn't believe that things could go wrong. On the contrary, he knew that thousands of things would go wrong, most of them totally unpredictable, unforeseen, and beyond the scope of even the most comprehensive legal draftsmanship. And in that case the solution would be found in the real world and not in the carefully crafted and scrupulously numbered paragraphs of the agreements. Ultimately he would be thrown back on his own resources, to rant and deal as best he could. To spend $200 an hour pretending otherwise struck him as an expensive form of voodoo.

His other objection was that since lawyers were by training tacticians, they didn't always grasp the nuances of Bruce's grand strategy. With the papers in front of them, they lost sight of the fact that the Hahn deal was not an end in itself, but a condition for getting the building built at all. One morning early in November Bruce walked in to Henry's office to show him a swollen right hand, which he had injured pounding a desk in frustration during the previous day's negotiations. "They were meeting for three hours on four points and settled one of them," he said, still seething at the memory, "which was that Vernon would waive his objection to rent control, that we wouldn't have to hold them harmless in case some time in the ninety-nine-year history of the project the city instituted commercial rent control. Before that they spent forty-five minutes arguing about what happens in the event of losses not covered by casualty insurance, like a terrorist blows up the building and you have a terrorism exclusion on your policy. I finally had to say, 'Let's pass on that and get on to something important.'

"The reason I banged my hand is, I said to myself, How do you go into battle with these guys and not let them see that all you're carrying is a toothpick? In my mind I've made a decision, I'm going to give up every nonessential business point to close the deal. And when I negotiated one of these things, my lawyer said to me, 'You're giving something up!'" Bruce described to Henry a complicated exchange over handling rent abatements in the event of a construction strike. "I wanted to give up enough so that we could get off the goddamn point," Bruce explained, "but not call attention to the fact that I'm limping. And then my lawyer speaks up at the meeting and says, 'Do you know what you did?' And I said, 'I know what I did, please shut up about it.' I was trying to take a piece of Scotch tape that was completely transparent and put it over a hole and say, Okay, it's fixed. And my lawyer says, just in case everybody in the room hadn't noticed already, 'Hey, *don't you want to do something about that hole?*' So that's why I went into the next room to bang a desk."

There were two points on which the deal came close to foundering. One of these was a straightforward business point, a classic zero-sum game. The issue was common-area-maintenance (CAM) charges. Hahn's standard shopping-center lease required individual tenants to pay a share of general upkeep and cleaning expenses, prorated according to the size of their stores. Schwartz pointed out that the movie theaters would draw several thousand people a day through the mall and therefore ought to share in this expense. But Bruce's lease with Loews had no provision for passing along such a charge. Luk Sun proposed going to Bernie Myerson of Loews with this problem. "Fine, go to Bernie Myerson," Bruce said. "When you have this conversation, I want to be standing a block away. Then in the end we'll eat the theaters' share." Based on Hahn's simple formula of prorating the area of each tenant, this would amount to a whopping 43 percent of the total CAM costs. Nobody, least of all Hahn, was sure how much that would be, but the estimates began at twenty-five dollars a square foot annually and grew bigger each time they looked. That implied a potential liability to BSP of over $600,000 a year.

Note that Hahn was not offering to clean the theaters, their lobbies, or their restrooms for this sum. Loews itself would receive nothing. The charge Hahn proposed to levy would cover only the wear and tear on the doors, floors, and escalators of the atrium by the customers on their way to watch the movies.

"They can't do this to us!" Bruce exclaimed to Luk Sun.

"Isn't this what we would do in their shoes?"

"Of course, but we wouldn't get away with it either."

Luk Sun called Vernon. "Vernon, you can't do this to us," he said. He used every argument he could think of. The real maintenance expense, he argued, was in the food court. He discovered that CAM is not always prorated on a strict cost-per-square-foot basis; the big "anchor" tenants rarely pay their full share. The theaters deserved the same consideration. And how much could it cost to sweep a damn floor, anyway?

"We can't be on the hook for a cost we have no control over," Bruce told Vernon. "Give us a dollar figure, not a percentage," he pleaded, "and we'll negotiate it that way." Hahn refused. Since they had never swept a floor in New York, they had no idea of the cost, but if it were like everything else in the city they would need a crew of three on each broom. For weeks this question cast a pall on the entire negotiations. The problem was there was no theory on which a compromise could be struck. Hahn's position was that BSP should pay 43 percent of the CAM costs, based on the theaters' share of the total leasable space. Bruce, ideally, wanted to pay nothing. The solution would be found somewhere between zero and 43 percent, but there was no obvious way to get there. Finally, someone discovered that if you took the theaters' area as a proportion of the *total* area of the mall, including public as well as leasable spaces, it came to around 21 percent. This was roughly halfway between 43 percent and nothing. Logically there was no reason to advance this formula. In terms of Hahn's argument, it made no sense. In terms of Bruce's desire to fix his obligation in dollar terms, it didn't accomplish that either. It was a convenient way to split the difference, which just happened to work out arithmetically. Sometimes in business you just have to look the other way and get on with the deal.

The other big issue was of a very different sort, an open-ended question, almost philosophic in its implications, and demanding a far more creative solution. It concerned Bruce's exposure for the cost of building the public spaces in the atrium—the floors, ceilings, lights, escalator railings, and finishes. Until Jerde finished his design, there was no way to specify how much this might eventually cost. "They said, 'It's gotta be what it's gotta be,'" Bruce told Henry, "and I said, 'Bullshit. I can't leave myself open to this.' I proposed a sixty-day clock after the agreement is signed for Jerde to produce design drawings, then another sixty days to price it. At the end of that process, if we don't like the cost we can walk away, and if they don't like what we propose to build, they can walk.

"What the bank will say when they see it, I want to be standing a block away when it happens. I decided not to raise it with the bank. Their lawyers will read it anyway, and the shit will hit the fan. I know exactly what they'll say, they'll say, 'You don't have a deal, you've got an agreement to agree.'

"I asked Vernon Schwartz to give me a number. A notional number, a parameter, something we know we're shooting at. And he said, 'Okay, $18 million.'"

"Eighteen million!" Henry exclaimed.

"That's nuts," Luk Sun put in. "That's a ploy. It's like going in to buy a suit and asking for a size fifty-six, so the salesman can bargain you down to a forty-two."

Bruce spent the next weekend brooding about the problem. It was apparent that the solution lay in giving both sides time to study and price the drawings before committing themselves. The 120-day clock did that, but it was too awkward. It drew the bank's attention precisely to the weakest part of the deal. He needed simple, clear but unobtrusive language that said the same thing. Simple, so there could be no misunderstanding between himself and Vernon. Clear, so no one could dispute the meaning in case Hahn eventually did go south. Unobtrusive, so it didn't frighten off the bankers.

Monday morning, Bruce put in a call to Schwartz in California. "Look," Bruce said, "we're never going to resolve this issue until we've got a set of drawings in front of us, but we can't wait that long. Let's come up with an outline of your requirements and a provision that makes final drawings subject to your signoff."

"And if I don't sign off, then what happens?" Schwartz responded.

"Then nothing happens," Bruce said. "Look, obviously, if you make something subject to approval, and you don't approve, then there's no deal. But I can't put that in the language. I can't go to the tallest building in New York and take a can of red paint and write a big sign that says, 'There's a giant hole in my deal with the Hahn Company.' The bank is never going to approve that. You want a loophole, Vernon, I'm giving you a loophole, I'm just trying to make it small enough so that the whole deal doesn't fall through."

All of this effort, of course—as well as everything else that had been done on the building up to this point—would go to naught if Bruce couldn't make a deal with Citibank. The project was once again running out of money. Skidmore's bills were overdue to the point that Fridstein threatened to withhold drawings. At one point he actually shut the job down for two days, giving all the architects a furlough, which Audrey used to paint her loft. "You don't like to do this, because you want to think you're all on the team together and you know they're gonna come up with the money eventually," she said. "But there's also a part of me that says you've got to stand up for the profession. Is Laquila going to dig the hole for no money?"

Berini came up with some money, and the crisis passed, but the problem would remain until the construction loan closed. The history of a commercial building is a tale told in three loans. First, the land loan, from European-American Bank, which financed the purchase, the tenant relocations, and whatever development work and physical construction had been done to this point. The construction loan, now under negotiation with Citibank, would repay European-American and carry the building through construction and leasing. After five years, it would be replaced in turn by a permanent mortgage. The size of the permanent mortgage would be determined very simply. The bank would add all the rental income from offices, retail, parking, theaters, and signs, and subtract taxes and operating costs, to arrive at net operating income. It would knock this down by around 10 percent, as a cushion, and then calculate how big a loan that income would support, based on interest costs at the time. For example—rounding off some of the numbers in the actual Broadway State pro-forma (before the Variety area was added in)—the project when fully leased in 1993 was expected to generate net operating income of around $36 million: $27 million from the office space, $7 million from the retail, and the rest from theaters, parking, and signs. Rounding this down to $32 million to provide a safety margin, and assuming a 10 percent interest rate, that would support a permanent mortgage of $320 million.

Subtracting what they had spent to get to that point, Bruce and Berini would then have the difference to put in their pockets—$20 million, if everything went according to the pro-forma. And they would still own the building. Whatever income the bank left on the table would be theirs. And they would be in the happy position of sitting back and letting inflation work for them. Office leases usually provide for rent increases at periodic intervals, typically every five years. If rents went up an average of just 1 percent a year, they could refinance in a decade and split another $30 million all over again. Commercial leases in the 1980s typically escalated by between 2.5 and 3 percent a year.

That is an example of leverage at work. If you started out with $300 million in cash, and bought a building with it, after 10 percent general inflation the building would be worth $330 million, but you wouldn't be any better off, relative to the cost of everything else. If the building was worth ten $30 million Picassos when you started, it would now be equal to ten $33 million Picassos. If, on the other hand, you started with nothing and borrowed the $300 million for the building, and it went up in value by 10 percent, *voila,* you would now be worth $30 million. The deal, as Bruce hoped to structure it, would have approximately the leverage of a cigarette lighter in a nitroglycerin factory. The tiniest spark of inflation would set off an explosion of value for him.

That is how you get rich in real estate. It helps, of course, that these profits receive favorable tax treatment, because the government indulges the fiction that real estate is a depreciating asset, while in fact it usually grows more valuable each year. If Bruce kept his 50 percent of the project, he would be entitled, on even the most conservative depreciation schedule, to write off around $5 million a year in income—not just from the building itself, but from any source.

Not all developers operated this way. Some preferred to take a small equity position and get most of their money in the more secure form of a flat fee paid directly out of the development budget. Bruce did not take a development fee as such. All of his projects paid an administration charge to Eichner Properties, Inc., for the work done by Luk Sun, Mitchell, William, and everyone else in the office. Starting in 1988, Bruce paid himself a salary as well, but it was only $200,000 a year, which was modest. The big money would only come if the project itself turned a profit.

This was, naturally, the riskier course. Bruce was gambling that he could finish the building on schedule and within budget. This at least he had some control over. He was gambling on the real estate market three to five years down the road, which one couldn't control but could perhaps predict in general terms. And he was gambling on interest rates over the same period, which was not much different than putting down $300 million on whether it would rain on Yom Kippur in 1993. If rates were not 10 percent when it came time to refinance, but 12 percent, then $32 million would support a permanent debt not of $320 million, but of $266 million. In that instance, there would be nothing for Bruce and Berini to split. Less than nothing, in fact, because Citibank would be waiting at the door, wanting to know where the money was coming from to repay their construction loan.

Henry and Bruce devised strategies to deal with these contingencies, too. You could seek a "participating mortgage," in which the lending institution got a share of the project's equity in exchange for a low interest rate. If conventional rates were 10%, a participating mortgage rate might be as low as 6%—in which case the building could be financed out, not at 10 times net operating income, but 15 or 16 times. Still, in Henry's darker moods, he would remind himself that most of the great Manhattan real estate fortunes were not built in a decade by one audacious entrepreneur, but over a lifetime of buying, building, and accumulating. Traditionally it took a generation for an office building to really pay off. The last ten years had been very untraditional times in real estate, when people like Bruce and David Solomon were able to take a shortcut through the traditional path of completing one building every three or four years. But maybe those days were coming back, he thought.

The size and structure of the construction loan was determined by the project's "total development cost," which was set at $300 million. "Hard" costs—the actual construction of the building—represented only a third of that. Land costs, including the various purchases, tenant buyouts and interest on the EAB loan amounted to about $75 million. The interest reserve for the construction loan was $47 million; Citibank and the participants also took an up-front fee of 1 percent of the face value of the loan, or $2.8 million. The balance was "soft" costs, including the architect's fee, administration, taxes, insurance, legal fees, and leasing commissions. There was a $16 million item for the "work letter," the cost of transforming raw floors into habitable office space (or an equivalent payment in cash to the tenants). There was a contingency reserve of just under $9 million. As of the end of October, two months before the loan in fact closed, the contingency fund already showed expenditures of $667,889.71.

Of this $300 million, $280 million was the face value of the loan. BSP would contribute $10 million in cash equity—borrowed from one of the VMS limited partnerships—and $30 million in letters of credit, which were not intended to be drawn. After two and a half years, BSP would come up with an additional $10 million in cash, and the letters of credit would be reduced by that amount. Citibank would hold the remaining $20 million l.c. as a hostage against completion of the building. If everything went as planned, BSP would get it back at the end.

Behind that simple scenario was a document of surpassing complexity. The loan was to carry a nominal interest rate of around 10 percent (actually, to be precise, 9.783 percent). That, though, was just the arbitrary figure Citibank used to calculate the size of the interest reserve, representing a guess as to the average cost of money over the life of the loan. They were by no means obligating themselves to loan money at that rate, or any rate. Each month as bills came due BSP would draw down the loan to pay them, and each draw would in effect be borrowed fresh. The rate would be fixed at 1.5 percent above whatever LIBOR happened to be on that day. For each of these individual loans, or tranches, BSP could select a maturity date one, two, or more months away, up to a year, each bearing a slightly different rate. The rate would be fixed for that period, at the end of which the tranche would have to be borrowed again ("rolled over," together with the new money drawn that month) at whatever rate then prevailed. Thus BSP could lock in a favorable rate for up to a year, or, alternatively, take a short maturity and gamble that rates would fall. And, for its own convenience, the bank limited the number of tranches that could be outstanding at any one time.

Obviously it would help if Lydia knew with some precision the project's cash requirements several months in advance. She wrote a memo explaining this to Mitchell and asking him to set up a system for forecasting the construction draws. Mitchell predictably felt the need to lecture about the idiocy of this idea. "It's a fucking administrative nightmare," he bellowed. "Who dreamed this up? Obviously someone who never built a building before. You know what this is? It's a full-employment project for Henry Miller."

Henry was fully employed as it was. He was thinking about what would happen if interest rates strayed above that magic figure of 9.783 percent. For the moment, that seemed remote; LIBOR in the fall of 1987 was around 7.5 percent, implying a rate for the loan in the vicinity of 9 percent. But that could change very easily. In a highly leveraged deal Citibank would be sure to seek protection against this contingency. There were ways to protect against a floating interest rate. You could make an offsetting investment in something that increased in value when rates went up—put options on T-bills, say. Or you could find a third party to underwrite the risk and guarantee you a fixed rate. Neither of these appealed to Bruce. To hedge the market himself would put him in the commodity speculation business. He didn't want to spend the next three years checking bond prices every half hour. To buy the protection would cost a lot of money, and in the end all you got was very expensive peace of mind. Henry thought it would help them all sleep nights. But Bruce had no trouble sleeping at night. He told Henry he would think of something else. After a couple of weeks he thought of it; he described it to Henry and then left for a two-week trip to Paris and let Henry and Lydia work out the details.

Bruce's plan had the advantage that it didn't cost any money, and the corresponding disadvantage that it required him to bear all the risk himself. In calculating the interest reserve, the bank used a nominal rate of interest (9.783 percent) and a projected schedule of construction draws. It could therefore calculate at any time how much cumulative interest should have accrued up to that point at a constant rate of 9.783 percent. Bruce proposed comparing that ideal figure with the actual interest cost accrued at regular six-month intervals. If actual interest had exceeded the projection, Bruce would give the bank a letter of credit to cover the shortfall. If rates had stayed low, and actual interest costs were below the projection, Bruce would get a credit for that amount, which could be used to offset a subsequent shortfall. After three years the game was declared over, and if any letters of credit were still outstanding, the bank presented them for cash. Henry explained this in an eight-page memo, including several pages of charts. He didn't explain where the letters of credit would come from, because he had no idea. Luckily, the bank never asked.

"This is so complicated," Henry said, "that I don't know if even I understand it. We meet with the bank every day and talk about it, and then the lawyers go back and write it all down, and the next day we can't even decide if what's on the piece of paper is what we all agreed to twenty-four hours earlier."

On and on it went, endlessly, repetitively, the bankers' work of parsing risk, dividing, assigning, and subassigning it. Not a dime passed through the agreement that did not have to justify itself to the Risk Police: Rosenstein, a slender, very precise, and humorless man with brown hair and a neatly trimmed beard; his colleagues from Citibank; his consulting engineers from the firm of Merritt & Harris; and Citibank's lawyers, from Mudge, Rose, Guthrie, Alexander and Ferdon, Richard Nixon's old law firm. The nation's finest legal and financial minds were bent toward the task of conjuring up ever more elaborate and farfetched disasters and then arguing for hours about who would pay for them. To Bruce it was like having to sit through an argument over the order of seating at his own funeral. And invariably, in his experience, the disasters that struck were the ones not covered by the agreement.

Take the question of change orders in construction contracts already signed. There were sure to be hundreds of them, on a fast-track job of this size. How much could BSP change on its own?

Rosenstein proposed a limit of $100,000 per item, or an aggregate total of $1 million; beyond that the bank's approval would be needed.

"What would you expect the change-order budget to be on a job this size?" Mitch asked.

"For a $100 million job, around $8 million," one of the Merritt & Harris guys replied.

"Then why not put it at that?"

"Because," said Rosenstein, "if you spend $8 million, you're going to be over your construction budget."

"Not necessarily," Mitch shot back. "We can make it up somewhere else on the job."

"If you can do that, fine," Rosenstein replied. "You've got the right to reallocate money within your budget. We've always given you that right."

Luk Sun pounced. "To reallocate without your approval?"

Rosenstein looked at him as if he were crazy. "*With* our approval."

"Not to be unreasonably withheld," Luk Sun stipulated. "I want that in the documents."

"I'll have to let you know," Rosenstein responded cautiously. The perfect posture for a banker: standing on his *right to be unreasonable*.

If any of these innumerable provisions were violated anytime in the course of the loan, Citibank had the right to declare a technical default. This sounds more ominous than it is in fact. The documents prescribed an elaborate mechanism for curing defaults. The ultimate penalty, and the only one that really mattered, was foreclosure, but this was the H-bomb of debtor-creditor relations, as dangerous to the side that launches it as to the target. The last thing in the world the bank wanted was a half-finished project on its hands. "The documents are written so you're in technical default the minute you close on the loan," Lydia said. "It just makes the bank feel better if they have something they can hold over your head."

The trickiest part for Bruce was meshing the Hahn deal with the bank loan, and the most intractable issue concerned Hahn's guaranteed minimum rent. This was nominally $4.5 million a year, for the first seven years after completion of the building. On close inspection, though, it turned out to be something less than that. Once they actually began leasing the space to tenants, Hahn could begin escaping the guarantee. Leases with so-called credit tenants—essentially, branches of major chains—reduced the guarantee dollar-for-dollar. If Hahn signed, say, a $500,000 deal with B. Dalton, the guarantee went down immediately to $4 million. The argument came over the treatment of "noncredit" tenants, which meant everyone without a major corporation standing behind him. Hahn wanted to get off its guarantee on those leases also, after they had proven their ability to pay their rent over a certain period. Hahn wanted that period set at a year. Bruce had reluctantly agreed, although he would have preferred a longer term. So he was neither surprised nor too disappointed when the bank demanded three years.

It is useful to recap the situation to which this dispute pertained. The building is finished, the mall is open and doing business, so what by common assent are the riskiest passages are already past. Hahn is collecting rent and sharing it with BSP. We have now, let us say, an empanada counter occupying 600 square feet in the food court. This establishment has been in possession of its space for a year and has met its rent obligation of $5,000 a month. The question is who, over the next two years, should bear the risk that an outbreak of salmonella wipes out the empanada counter, and that a mass abandonment of the custom of eating results in the inability of the Hahn Company to rent that space to anyone else, so that their total obligation to BSP falls below $4.5 million a year? Should it be the Hahn Company, with fifty shopping centers around the country? Or should it be Citibank, the largest bank in America—bearing in mind that Citibank requires only that the project generate enough income to support the loan until refinancing, and that between the empanada counter and the bank stands the entire Broadway State Project, with 850,000 feet of office space and all the other state-of-the-art assurances and guarantees and protections the bank has imposed on it?

The problem in debating this proposition was that there was no appeal either to logic or equity; it was simply a question of who was going to back down first. The arguments descended in a steep spiral toward utter circularity. Vernon asserted that a year was ample time to determine that a retail tenant was going to survive. Rosenstein was smart enough to turn that around and reply, "If you're so sure of that, why are *you* so anxious to get off the guarantee at a year?"

Early in December, Hahn's financial vice president, Roger Birks, came to New York to close the deal with Bruce. There was a full day of meetings devoted to the various issues still on the table. Luk Sun,

William, Birks, and Hahn's lawyers met in the large conference room; Henry, Lydia, Berini, Alan Rosenstein, and Peter Shuldiner of Citibank, plus the bank's lawyers and Barry Ross, gathered in Bruce's office. As they dealt with a whole range of questions, big and small, Bruce moved between the meetings, and somehow each side formed the impression that progress was being made on the guarantee issue in the other room.

At six o'clock, all the parties gathered in Bruce's conference room to deal with the guarantee. Bruce evicted Hahn's lawyer Gene Pinover from his chair next to Roger, making a big display of sitting next to his partner—to counter the accurate impression that he would actually prefer the bank to prevail here. Peter Shuldiner of Citibank, who had been in the room all day, left to make a phone call, and everyone sat quietly and waited for him to make his entrance. He came in and stood behind a chair. "Well," he said, "we've done a lot of hard work today, and we're ready for the breakthrough that will close this deal, so where are we?"

Roger Birks seemed to blush slightly as he said, "Well, you've read the documents."

No one spoke for a moment.

"Let me get this straight," Shuldiner said. "You mean, the deal as outlined in the papers we read is what's on the table now?"

"That's right," Birks said quietly.

Another silence. Shuldiner appeared to be very angry, although with whom would be the subject of much subsequent speculation: With Hahn's obstinacy? With Bruce, for letting him believe that a breakthrough was in the works? "Well," he said softly, "we can't live with that."

Roger seemed embarrassed. "I don't want to be the bad guy," he said. "But we've already given up a lot."

Bruce spoke up for the first time. "Peter," he said, "let me make sure I understand your demand here. Your position was that you wanted a noncredit tenant to be in possession and paying his rent for three years before the guarantee went away. If we give you that, does that solve the problem?"

Peter looked at Alan Rosenstein, Rosenstein shrugged, and Peter nodded.

"Well," Bruce said, "there's an obvious solution that will send us all home early. Let's settle this at two years."

And Birks said, "Look, we have to talk."

The meeting broke up. Berini, Luk Sun, Barry Ross, and a few others walked down the hall to the big conference room. After a few moments Bruce came bustling in. "Well, partners," he said genially, "where do we go from here? Peter pulled me aside just now and said, 'Three years or no deal.' He told me, 'Get rid of Hahn, fuck them, do the deal without them.' I've never heard Peter say that. He's not bluffing. This deal won't get done at one year, it won't get done at two."

"How serious was he?" Ross asked. "Will they really close the loan without Hahn?"

"Yes," Bruce said.

"No," Berini said. "And I don't think we want to go that route now ourselves."

"I'm going to have dinner with Roger," Bruce said. "What deal do I try to cut with him? I suggest we hang tough with Hahn. I said, 'Peter, you know what's gonna happen? We're gonna backstop it. Hahn couldn't have picked anyone better than you to do their negotiating. I've been going into battle with a toothpick all along, because you made Hahn a condition of the loan.'"

Bruce had to go. He had to be at Christie's, where he intended to bid on a piece of jewelry as a present for his wife on their fourth anniversary. (He got it.) On his way back he picked up Roger at his hotel and headed off to dinner.

The parties, absent Citibank, reconvened at ten o'clock at Barry Ross's offices in the Helmsley Building. Three separate meetings went on here. In one, Luk Sun and William Tung were engaged in a long call to California over various technical points in the lease. In another room, the lawyers were going over the documents point by point and negotiating every clause and comma. Bruce had to bite his hand to keep from bursting in on the lawyers and snatching all the papers off their table, tearing the papers into tiny pieces, and making them eat the pieces. Not that the lawyers wouldn't do it, but he would pay for the pleasure at $600 an hour.

The third meeting was a speaker-phone call, with Bruce, Berini, and Birks in the room, and Vernon Schwartz at home in California. Bruce seemed uncommonly on edge. Berini characteristically displayed the tense anticipation of a man sitting with a drink on his deck, waiting for the sunset.

"Vernon," Steve said, "I think the whole situation has turned around on us, so that what started out as a credit enhancement deal is now being viewed by the bank more as a credit risk."

"I don't understand," Vernon replied. "You've got a deal with a tenant for 64,000 feet. That tenant is the Hahn Company. This is a risk? If the bank isn't satisfied, we'll change the documents to satisfy the bank, and you make us whole for any added risk we bear after a year."

Bruce's prediction from earlier in the evening was coming true; BSP was going to have to pick up some of the guarantee. Now it would be a fight to see how little they could get away with. Vernon obviously wanted them to bear the whole thing.

"I can't let you do that, Vernon," Bruce said sharply. "You pick the retail tenants, I'm stuck with them. Why should the risk have to come back to me?"

"But you already agreed to one year in our deal," Vernon pointed out. "You're in no worse position this way. If we were only on the guarantee for a year, and the shit hit the fan, it would be your problem. This way it will still be your problem."

"Then the bank is going to ask us to prove we can come up with it," Berini said.

"Why does the bank have to know about it?"

There was a pause. "All right, Vernon, Steve and I will talk for ten minutes and then we'll have an answer for you."

Birks left the room. The two partners were alone. "Mousetrapped!" Bruce said.

"No, we're not mousetrapped," Berini said. "We're in a lousy position, but we're not mousetrapped. I think if he's smart, he'll bluff and say no deal tonight."

"Let's think this out rationally," Bruce said. "We've got to take the position, we're in this fifty-fifty. The flaw in his argument is saying we're no worse off. We are, because we don't have a payment guarantee to the bank ourselves. If the retail goes into the tank after the first year, the project doesn't look so good, but we're not on the hook ourselves for the retail rent, and he's trying to put us there. We've got to say, 'You offered one year, the bank wants two more, you take one, we'll take one.'"

"And if not," Berini said, "we've got to be prepared to walk."

"Absolutely."

They left after midnight and met again the next morning to work out language they could take to the bank. It called essentially for a two-level guarantee. Hahn's guarantee to BSP would run for seven years under the terms originally proposed—they could get off it immediately with credit tenants, and after a year for all others. A separate guarantee, incorporating a version of the stricter three-year test the bank sought, would run only to Citibank; that is, it would be nullified as soon as Citibank was financed out. And in a side agreement, Bruce and VMS agreed to share with Hahn—"joint and several," in the legal terminology—the additional risk of the Citibank guarantee. That was what it all came down to, the perfect circle at the innermost center of the deal: Bruce and VMS were guaranteeing the payment of rent to themselves.

The absolute, final, not-to-be-exceeded deadline set by European-American Bank to be financed out of the land loan was set at Friday, January 15. The first draw under the Citibank loan would be the biggest, because it would repay the land loan, and the rate they got would go a long way toward determining whether Bruce's self-hedging interest scheme was a masterstroke of finance or a prescription for slow strangulation. A terminal at his desk gave Henry real-time updates on the world's credit markets. Just after the first of the year, nine-month LIBOR was running at 7.625 percent, implying an interest cost under the loan of 9.125 percent. That was well below the nominal rate. But Treasury prices were down, meaning that rates were up. Henry noted that this hadn't been reflected in LIBOR—yet. He punched up numbers obsessively and prayed for the loan to close.

But the agreements so painfully hammered out by Bruce and the others were just a semi-finished product; the end product would be the hundreds of pages of dense legal prose that would be bound into two thick volumes to sit on Bruce's credenza, unopened for all eternity. The first two weeks of January were weeks of fourteen-hour days for the Broadway State team, as three teams of lawyers obsessively combed the language in the tripartite agreements for clauses to dispute. The lawyers from Mudge, Rose went over the development budget with Alice and Lydia. The budget was two pages of small type, and had lists of projected expenditures under half a dozen column headings. The lawyers changed each one of the column headings. At the end of the budget was a paragraph which read in its entirety:

Note: Portions of the following budget line items are allocated for the Hahn $7,020,400 initial leasing amounts as follows:

Base building, $2,400,000
Leasing commissions, $2,600,000
Leasing income, $2,020,400

The lawyers changed "Note" to "Notes." They insisted that "initial leasing amounts" be capitalized—capital letters, that is, not capital expenses. And they put numbers (1), (2), and (3) in front of the three items.

"Are those little i's, or numbers?" Alice asked, bent over her copy.

"Numbers."

"Do you want periods after the numbers?"

"Parentheses."

This would have bothered Bruce less if BSP weren't paying for the lawyers—not just their own lawyers, but Citibank's as well. On Wednesday, January 13—two days before the loan was to close—Mudge, Rose submitted a bill for around $400,000, including $50,000 for a partner Henry claims he saw only once at one two-hour meeting. Henry is on most matters a far more reasonable man than Bruce—that was virtually part of his job description—but he shares some of Bruce's feelings about real estate lawyers. "In the final analysis, there are only three possible outcomes to this. Either the loan will work pretty much as we think it will, in which case the papers won't matter. Or we have a problem, and either we work the problem out, or we don't and they get the building. We spent a million dollars and seven months to write that down in more words than the *Encyclopaedia Britannica.*"

Luk Sun came into Henry's office, looking more lugubrious than usual. "I just got a call from Alan Rosenstein," he said heavily. "Bruce refused to pay the Mudge, Rose fee and he left the office, and Alan is refusing to fund unless it's paid. He said he's going to be at the lawyer's for another fifteen minutes, and then he's going home."

"Oh, great," Henry said. "Wouldn't it be wonderful to get this far and blow it all on this? Where's Bruce?"

"We can't find him," Luk Sun moaned.

"You know we're going to have to pay it eventually anyway."

"You want to just do it on your own?" Luk Sun asked hopefully.

Henry hesitated. "Bruce would kill me," he said, shaking his head.

Bruce arrived a few minutes after ten the next morning, having already met with Rosenstein, and listened with amusement to Henry's account of this conversation. It was a never-ending source of wonder to him that people as smart as Henry and Luk Sun, people who knew him as well as anyone in the firm except for Howard, still could miss his point so completely. Of course he was going to pay the damn Mudge, Rose bill. He made a big deal about it, naturally, because he wanted something back, a concession on the timing of the administrative fee to Eichner Properties. The bank wanted to spread it out over three years, and Bruce wanted the same amount of money paid over thirty months. He had stormed into his meeting with Rosenstein, ranting about how never in his years in business had he seen such unconscionable piracy, slapped his hand on the table, and said, "Okay, if that's your Mudge, Rose bill, then this is my administrative budget, and that's final!"

"And everyone said, Yeah, okay, calm down, there's nothing to get excited over. Also, I shamed them into allocating a million dollars from contingency to cover the legal bills, because otherwise I would already be over budget on my legal, and it puts me in a bad light to be over budget when the loan hasn't even closed yet, even for something they made me spend."

Since all Bruce had done was agree to pay something he had no choice about, this is known as cost-free bargaining.

So everything was in place for the closing Friday. Bruce went home in a good mood. That evening he took a call from Vernon Schwartz. The Hahn deal had been physically signed by all the parties, but the papers were being held in escrow by Kaye, Scholer, pending the final signal from both parties to put them into effect. And Schwartz was having second thoughts.

As Vernon was to explain it later, he and Roger had been growing more and more worried by the common-area-maintenance costs, the cleaning and upkeep expenses that get passed on to tenants in their rent. The share of these costs that BSP would have to bear on behalf of the movie theaters had been one of the major sticking points in the deal earlier. Hahn had started estimating CAM at around twenty-five dollars a square foot and each time they learned a little more about labor costs in New York the estimate went up. Now they thought they might be fifty dollars or more. Most New York merchants were accustomed to stores on the street, and would have to be educated to the idea of spending money to improve the environment immediately outside their own doors. And if it looked like the cost might exceed 50 percent of their nominal rent, Vernon was afraid he would never rent an inch of that space.

So he wanted Bruce to bear some of that risk as well. After the guarantee was met, he wanted BSP to give up a portion of its rent to help offset maintenance costs if they exceeded a certain amount.

Of course, he didn't expect Bruce to reopen the documents at this point, so he would settle for a side letter spelling out that agreement. Without it, he wouldn't authorize the lawyers to execute the papers, which meant no closing.

Around the same time, Al Corti was giving the same message to Berini in California.

"I could have killed him," Berini said, when Bruce, white with anger, called him the next morning—Friday, the day the loan was to close. "This guy's my best friend, and to spring this on me like that ... I wouldn't have even known, except that I called him to tell him I had a son, and after he congratulates me he stabs me in the back with this."

"I couldn't have made the call Vernon made," Bruce said. "I think it must be the difference between working for a corporation and working for yourself. This isn't Vernon's reputation as a human being on the line, it's the Hahn Company. If the deal doesn't make money, they're going to look to him and say, 'See what you got us into?'"

He hung up with Berini and had his secretary place a call to Hahn.

One more call; one more round of the game he had been playing for seven months.

"Vernon, I can't give you that piece of paper. The bank has to know what our arrangements are, and I can't have an agreement out there that materially affects my obligations that the bank doesn't know about."

Schwartz suggested making the arrangement take effect only after Citibank was financed out. But of course that didn't change Citibank's perspective, because the permanent lender would have to be told about it, and anything that affects the permanent lender affects what is most near and dear to Citibank's heart, getting its money back.

"I'll tell you what I'll do, Vernon," Bruce said urgently. "I will work with you over the next few months to come up with an equitable solution to this problem that we can both live with. And I will give you a gentleman's agreement that down the road, if you're hurt by this thing, I will bear it equally with you. I have spoken to Berini and he agrees. This is as far as I can go."

Vernon gave his assent. Bruce hung up and turned to Luk Sun. "A nice piece of work," he said; it wasn't clear if he meant his own performance, the deal as a whole, or Vernon Schwartz. Schwartz, later, defending himself against the charge of taking advantage of his partner's desperation, pointed out that Bruce had been saying for months that it was the last day to close the loan, and how was he supposed to know he really meant it this time?

"It's over," Luk Sun said. "Now the fun begins."

Bruce stood and the two men hugged. He called Berini on the speaker phone and explained what he had done.

"Well," Berini said, "we have a gentleman's agreement. Are we gonna be gentlemen or scumbags?"

"I vote for scumbags," said Luk Sun.

Early the next week, Henry and Lydia closed the first tranche of the loan, for $55 million at 8.94 percent for six months. Interest-hedging was off to a very good start.

And not long after, the bill for closing costs came from Robinson Silverman. It was for $435,000 in time, plus $38,000 in expenses, mostly for word processing and messengers. The largest item was for Barry Ross's time. He had put in 428 hours on getting Bruce his loan, and escaped with his life.

23

Of all the disasters envisioned by Rosenstein, few were as terrifying as the prospect of missing the May 13 deadline for vesting the foundation. He had Luk Sun describe to him in detail the vesting process, the avenues of appeal, the option of filing a lawsuit that, if they lost, might leave them with several floors of the building that could never be legally occupied. As a last resort, they would put up a smaller building. Rosenstein dwelt at length on this possibility in all its horrifying detail, until Mitch was moved to remark, "Gee, Alan, you're painting it a little more sinister than it is, and that's not like you." Citibank had good reason to be concerned, though. A smaller building would be a different building, with a different pro-forma, and the loan would have to be modified accordingly. When this was explained to the Japanese participants, they insisted on their right to reapprove—and, consequently, to disapprove—any such restructuring of the loan. That, of course, was intolerable to Citibank. The building would be well along by the time the zoning appeals were exhausted. For a bank to pull out of the loan at that point would be like the steel mill pulling out of the job and taking back the columns. The common good of all the lending institutions required that they bind themselves to the project through thick and thin.

Or so it appeared to Citibank. But the issue revealed a deep-seated difference in the business culture of the two nations. If a similar question came up between American businessmen (leaving lawyers out of it, for the moment) it would most likely be framed in terms of loyalty. But an appeal to an intangible quality such as loyalty simply was not recognized by the Japanese. Their position was that the deal was what was written down in the documents; if the project no longer corresponded to what was in the documents, then there was no deal and no presumption of a deal, and they would not obligate themselves to make a new deal, although of course their head offices in Tokyo would be happy as always to consider any new proposals.

Finally Citibank hit on the strategy of invoking *force majeure*. If the building failed to vest, it would have to be smaller. This was a matter of obeying the law. Everything in the deal had to be subject to law. If tomorrow the building code changed to require fire sprinklers to spray ginger ale, that was a risk all participants agreed to share. Once it was cast as a question of obeying the law, the Japanese conceded the point. But it's not surprising that Rosenstein had been feeling the pressure.

"Look," Luk Sun reminded him, "if we didn't think we could make the vesting, we wouldn't be attempting it in the first place."

"Yes," Rosenstein prodded, "but what might make you not make it?"

"If there's a construction disaster, if we get twelve feet of snow this winter ..."

"But there's nothing specific hanging out there that you're worried about?"

"Only that we found a Phoenician galley in the rock," Mitch replied, but there are some things that even a banker recognizes as a joke.

The Lyceum crack had not yet achieved the status of a disaster, but it had some of the makings of one. More consultants had been retained—the geologists Woodward-Clyde, engineers from Lev Zetlin Associates. This placated Landmarks, but it did not make the job any simpler, because if enough people look long enough at a belt, someone is bound to suggest reinforcing it with suspenders.

Laquila put in more rock ties. The corner under the Lyceum looked like a knee that had been in a bad accident, held together with pins and plates and iron straps that in turn were rigged with cables and turnbuckles to anchors in the rock. Finally, around the end of January, Laquila was permitted to resume digging along the west side of the Lyceum. (William Tung was later to estimate the total cost of the Lyceum crack, including all the consultants and the actual repairs to the theater, at more than $500,000.) In February new trades began appearing at the site, lathers and carpenters. A rough wooden trough took shape along the south face. Laquila was preparing to pour the first concrete footing of the first stretch of foundation wall. From sixty feet below the level of the sidewalk, the building was at last starting to rise.

There were some other new faces around this time. Turner appointed a project manager, Sal LaScala, who had just built the Saatchi and Saatchi headquarters at 375 Hudson Street. Sal was a protégé of Gary's, and carried himself with the same streetwise insouciance, looking warily out on the world through watery, pale blue, heavy-lidded eyes as if wondering whether the day would bring some new disaster, or only the familiar ones. A Turner project manager is a perpetual gypsy, inhabiting a succession of makeshift offices in trailers and vacant storefronts. Sal established a field office on the twenty-first floor of the old Times Tower. The space had been swept bare to the concrete and furnished to standards that would embarrass the campaign headquarters for a minor-party congressional candidate. The office had a terrific view of Times Square, looking north, into which 1540 Broadway would eventually rise, although for now, Sal pointed out, all there was to look at was a hole, which you couldn't see anyway because of the buildings in between, and who had time to look out the windows anyway?

A new machine made its appearance on the job, a sixty-five-ton Grove crane that squelched ponderously through the mud on heavily ridged tires. Laquila had bought the Grove especially for this job. Sitting at the bottom of the hole, the Grove could extend its boom to unload trucks parked on 45th Street. The hole soon became cluttered with stacks of lumber, rebar in untidy heaps, coils of wire, and, incongruously enough, a small pile of something that looked very much like hay. It was hay, as a matter of fact; it would be heaped atop the poured concrete to keep it warm while it cured. "The same stuff you feed to horses," Ellis said complacently.

In the southeast corner of the site Laquila built a stair tower to the street. Three or four men in suits and topcoats walked carefully down the ninety-six steps to the muddy floor of the hole in the early afternoon of Friday, February 5, a clear and bitterly cold day, to witness the first pour. The perimeter of the footing was outlined with rough boards, forming a trough eighteen inches wide, about two feet deep and some sixty feet long. This was the form for the footing of the south foundation wall. To ensure a firm bond with the concrete, men were bailing water from the trough with buckets, scraping it with shovels and scouring the rock with compressed air, until it was clean save for an apparently irreducible residuum of mud. Every twenty feet or so along the trough was a wider and deeper spot where a building column was to come down to ground. Men stood inside these, fashioning intricate meshes of rebar. Each column footing was marked by four anchor bolts sticking straight up in a cluster near the center. The bolts would hold the columns down against the tendency of a tall, flat-sided object such as a building to blow over in the wind. The big core columns, whose footings were cubes of concrete the size of delivery vans, would have four-inch anchor bolts. These on the perimeter were two inches, but even they had washers as big as saucers and nuts the size and shape of a filet mignon.

Skidmore had specified that the columns should rest on "sound, hard rock" with a bearing capacity of forty tons per square foot. A firm called Testwell Craig was retained to inspect the rock. The test instrument was a length of number-eight (one-inch diameter) rebar. The inspector dropped the bar on the rock and then listened. Rock in its original state of virtue rang with a pure, bright note. Rock that sometime in its billion-year history had come into contact with water or another agent of degradation gave a sodden thunk or thud. If that doleful note was sounded, Skidmore would have to decide whether to make Laquila dig down deeper, or increase the area of the footing, or attempt some other solution.

The cold in the rocks at the bottom of the excavation had been concentrating since Christmas. It quickly penetrated the leather soles of business shoes and continued up the legs. Various thoughts preoccupied the men as they stamped up and down in the hole. Phil Murray was anxious. If he had been asked to build a sixty-foot hole in the ground, he would have called on his years of training and practice and taken days to figure how strong the walls needed to be, and then the city's gimlet-eyed engineers would have pored over his calculations in search of a misplaced decimal point. Which was as it should be. But the random and invisible processes of geology did not operate under the same constraints. Phil nervously glanced up at the gray rockface, festooned here and there with icicles. "Do you know what's behind those walls?" he demanded. "I don't. No one designed them but Nature." He indicated a large patch of concrete about halfway up the far wall. Three weeks earlier, one afternoon between twelve and twelve-thirty, a chunk of rock had fallen there and left a hole that took thirty-two yards of concrete to fill. The men discovered it when they returned to the hole after lunch. Half an hour earlier someone was working right below it.

Sal was thinking ahead. He imagined where the job would be in a year's time: structural steel finished, the decking a few floors behind, and the curtain wall up around the twenty-fifth floor. The job was represented in his mind by a series of intersecting bar charts representing the various trades. Each milestone along the way inevitably led to the next task.

Rocco just tinkered and fidgeted in the cab of the Grove, waiting for the concrete.

The concrete arrived in three trucks, spaced over two hours—large, noisy, filthy vehicles churning their contents in canted ellipsoid barrels. Rocco swung a bucket the size of an armchair up to the street and the first truck filled it with a sludgy gray mix. Then Rocco lowered it until it hung suspended by cables a few feet above the trough. Two men tugged on a lever and the bucket opened from the bottom and the concrete fell out, lightly steaming. As it slithered into the form, it buried, along with rock, mud, and rebar, two new pennies that Sal had tossed in for luck, one for each of his girls.

Over the next few weeks the pace of construction began to pick up. The footings spread out in both directions from the first pour. The men began preparing to pour the foundation walls. It is impractical to pour sixty-foot-high walls in one operation, so they were poured in segments, called lifts, each fifteen feet high and of varying lengths. First the bare rock was swathed in strips of white plastic with innumerable small coils on the rock-facing side, like giant sheets of Velcro; the loops were supposed to collect any water that dribbled through the rock over the next hundred years and direct it down to drains in the footings. (The drains would run to a sump under the garage floor, from which a pump would lift the water some fifty feet up to the level of the sewer.) Then the men knocked together a scaffold; lathers erected rebar, and the plywood walls of the forms were nailed into position, ready to receive concrete.

With the start of foundation work, the hole underwent a startling transformation. The excavation face, craggy and fissured, full of secret drips and faults and glittering facets of mica, was a window into the natural world, a rare glimpse of the great rock beast that slumbers beneath the foundations of Manhattan. Now there would be a wall instead of a window, and the volume enclosed by the wall had lost its magic; it was on its way to turning into that most ordinary of spaces, leasable space.

The entire concrete operation testified to the insanity of trying to build a skyscraper in midtown Manhattan. Clearly the only sensible way to build walls around the perimeter of an excavation is to drive a mixing truck to the edge of the hole and dump concrete directly into the form—

provided, naturally, you can get to the edge of the hole. But hemmed in by the Lyceum, by 1550 Broadway, and by the pedestrian bridge on Broadway itself, Laquila didn't have access to even half the site. So Rocco designated a spot along 45th Street for the concrete trucks to unload. A long chute, called an elephant trunk, was built from the side-walk to a hopper at the bottom of the hole. The trucks would pour their contents down the elephant truck into the hopper. The men would fill a bucket from the hopper and Rocco, in the Grove, would swing the bucket over to where it was needed—approximately tripling the man-power you would need to accomplish the same thing in, say, Plano, Texas.

All this took place in a controlled race against the chemical reaction that began when water was added to the dry mix in the concrete plant, the reaction known as setting. If the Grove blew a cylinder head in the middle of a pour, Rocco could sit and watch as the contents of the hop-per turned slowly to stone, entombing his profit. The drivers, for their part, lived in dread of having their load set up inside the truck while waiting for the light to change at Sixth Avenue. The concrete plant was at 127th Street along the East River. This was only about five miles in a straight line from Times Square, but in the event of a major civic disaster such as a fire, a water-main break, or a presidential visit, in terms of travel time it might as well be in New Haven. The setting time of con-crete depends on several factors, including the ambient temperature and the ratio of water to cement, but in all cases there have been traffic jams in the history of New York City that were longer.

Drivers, being no fools, will sometimes attempt to retard the setting time of their loads by adding water en route. Unfortunately this reduces the strength of the finished product. Concrete in a high-rise building must be mixed to exact proportions within tolerances that are surpris-ingly strict, given the casual nature of materials such as sand, gravel, and cement. Five different concrete mixes would be used just on the founda-tions and slab of 1540 Broadway, each with characteristics appropriate to its task, and the formula for each had to be empirically derived each time. For most of the foundation walls, Skidmore specified concrete with certain chemical and mechanical properties, capable of supporting 4,000 pounds per square inch. This is a very modest strength by the stan-dards of modern technology; some high-rise buildings in other cities are designed with 20,000 psi concrete. The concrete contractor made up four different samples composed of varying ratios of Portland cement, water, sand, coarse aggregate (or gravel), and fly ash (a waste product of coal combustion). The source of each ingredient was specified, down to the power station that would supply the fly ash. The samples were tested in a laboratory, and the cheapest one that met the requirements was chosen.

Unfortunately, concrete suppliers occasionally deviate from the mix, invariably erring in the direction of adding more of the ingredients that don't cost much, like sand and water. Accordingly concrete is monitored with a zeal that society lavishes on few other products. Testwell Craig had an inspector at the concrete plant itself, watching the trucks as they were loaded, and inspectors on the site for each pour. Every load of concrete had to pass the "slump test." A metal cone, like a small megaphone, is filled with concrete from the truck, and the contents dumped onto a board. The height of the resulting mound is compared to the cone. The difference—the amount by which it slumped—gives a rough indicator of the proportion of water in the mix. In addition, the inspectors took samples of concrete from each pour. Plastic cylinders about a foot high were filled from the trucks. The cylinders, arriving at Testwell's laboratory in Queens by the hundreds each day from jobs all over the city, were allowed to set under optimal conditions (72.6 degrees, 95 percent humidity) and then tested for strength. The test consists of putting the concrete cylinder in a hydraulic ram and squeezing until it breaks. The testing machines have polished steel jaws (behind doors of heavy steel mesh) and can deliver a force of up to 400,000 pounds. At their limit of compressive strength, the cylinders fly apart, leaving stubby, ragged cones surrounded by shards. The records of thousands of these routine shatterings accumulated in John's cramped trailer like old college term papers.

As foundation work progressed, there was a noticeable increase in general civilian traffic onto the site. One morning in March a middle-aged man in a brown suit, a sweater, a vest, and an overcoat pushed his way through the fence door on Broadway and stood at the railing at the edge of the excavation, looking meditatively into the hole. After a few moments he pushed on the railing gingerly with his finger and dourly observed the degree of give. This was a building inspector. Shaking his head, he trudged up the staircase to the boardwalk where Ellis's trailer was parked and yanked on the door.

John reacted as if nothing short of a visitation from his sainted grandmother could have pleased him more. "How are you today?" he exclaimed solicitously, and when the man grunted "Cold," John offered to make a cup of tea. The inspector shook his head irritably. He sat down at a desk and spent a long time examining logs, safety reports, permits, and other documents. Finding everything in order, he put on an expression of stoic disgust, suggesting an employee who has been asked to clear out the desk of a detested and suddenly deceased colleague, and went out to inspect the site, Mike Danberg tagging along.

"You need a midrail here," he said, indicating the guardrail around the hole. OSHA required twin safety railings around the hole, but only the upper one was in place. Danberg launched into an explanation of why the lower rail was missing. "Just get it up," the man said wearily. He walked out the gate and around the corner to a patch of craggy and lumpy asphalt paving, overlaid with a carpet of newspapers glued down by frozen coffee. "You should put something down here so people can walk without tripping," he said. Mike explained that they had laid fresh paving that very weekend, but it had buckled under the heavy traffic.

At the southeastern corner of the site was the stair tower, whose landing was about five horizontal feet from the sidewalk; anyone passing by could walk out onto a broad, swaybacked plank above sixty feet of nothing. "You should have some kind of railing here to keep people out," the inspector muttered. Mike replied that he personally had put one up earlier in the day, but the men must have removed it for their own convenience. He found it on the landing and jammed it across the opening. There was a "Keep Out" sign nailed to the board and the inspector examined that for what seemed to be a very long time. Danberg had done the job with scaffold nails. These have a skirt of metal about a half inch below the head to prevent them from being nailed home, making them easy to remove when it's time to take down the scaffold.

"Better hammer those nails home," the inspector said finally.

"Aah, they're scaffold nails," Danberg murmured. The inspector shot him a look. "I'll do it," he said hastily.

The inspector's visit was followed, coincidentally, by an appearance by Kathleen V. Hopkins, Turner's regional director of safety, a formidable woman with the stern bearing of a former operating room nurse. Construction work is inherently dangerous, although statistically not any more so than several other trades, such as mining. And it was more dangerous in New York City than anywhere else in the country; a survey by the *Times* counted eighty-one construction-worker deaths—and eight of civilian passersby—between 1979 and 1986. This was a rate more than double the average in the *Times*'s survey of the thirty-five largest cities. The summer before, a piece of lumber had fallen off a high story of a Zeckendorf project under construction near Columbus Circle, killing a man crossing the street below. As a result, the city passed a regulation requiring plastic netting around all unenclosed floors under construction—a requirement that Gary calculated would add over $100,000 to the cost of 1540 Broadway.

The workers, unlike passersby, are supposed to be protected by hardhats. A modern hardhat has a shell of high-impact plastic and a complicated suspension that holds it several inches off the skull and is intended to absorb the impact of anything falling from above. As protection, naturally, a hardhat is only useful when worn atop a head. Compliance among Turner's own employees, and later among the ironworkers, was universal. In the other trades it ranged from conscientious to adolescent defiance.

"This has been a pretty good site," Hopkins said. "You can't do everything by the book, though, because this is New York. See those guys standing over there on the rebar?" She indicated a group of carpenters building a form for the third lift, thirty feet off the ground. "They're supposed to have safety harnesses on. Anywhere else they would, but not in New York. See those lathers working on the bending rig?" Four or five men were huddled around a piece of machinery on the ground, wearing all manner of headgear: hooded sweatshirts, knit watch caps, old tweed hats jammed down over their ears. "They won't wear hardhats. You could fire every one of them and get a whole new crew from the union, and they wouldn't wear hardhats, either. So what are you going to do? A year or so ago a lather was killed on the ground by a piece of formwork falling off a building. The next week I walked by the site and I saw half a dozen lathers standing around, and not one of them had a hat on. I said, 'Did you know Charlie?' And they all said, 'Yeah, it was a terrible thing that happened to him.' And I said, 'You idiots, how can you stand around like that in the exact same spot he was killed and not put a hat on your thick heads?' And finally one of them said, 'Well, a hat wouldn't have helped Charlie much, the wood landed next to him and then bounced up and caught him under the ear.'"

Occasionally people came onto the site uninvited. There was a high wooden fence around the area, but the door was unlocked and, as a rule, unguarded. Tourists sometimes wandered in with their cameras. Shortly after lunch one afternoon the gate swung open and about twenty young black men came streaming onto the site and up the stairs to the bridge, where they milled around, chanting and raising their fists into the air. "We want a J-O-B!" one would intone; and the rest would chorus back: "So we can E-A-T!" Nobody paid much attention to them. This was what the construction industry referred to generically as a "coalition." The coalitions had been formed in the 1960s to combat the widespread racism of the New York City construction unions, which maintained, then as now, a monopoly over hiring in the most desirable trades. After a series of demonstrations they won the right to place some of their members in apprenticeship programs, and over the years some of the groups had done quite a bit of good; others, though, had the reputation of being primarily shakedown artists.

Several of the men pushed into the trailer, where Sal happened to be meeting with a subcontractor.

"I don't talk to the coalitions," Sal said, with reasonable politeness for someone whose office had just been invaded. "You have to deal with Mike Carbone at the head office."

"We don't want no Mike Carbone, we want jobs," one of the men shot back.

"I don't have no jobs to give you."

"Let us talk to Rocco."

"Rocco's in the hole, and I'm not letting you inside the hole. That's trespassing," Sal said firmly.

The men grumbled, muttered, but left a card and marched back out the door. Sal turned back to his meeting.

"I heard them say they wanted a job," he said dourly. "I didn't hear them say nothing about wanting to work."

As the vesting deadline approached, Rocco drove his men even harder, and himself hardest of all. As the days lengthened, so did his workday, from seven in the morning until the last light of dusk, six and seven days a week. Each week somebody from Turner had to go down to the Buildings Department to apply, pay for, and obtain a permit to work after normal business hours. "He's taking this as a personal challenge," Mike Danberg observed. "He's gonna get this done or die trying." Inevitably, the city conspired against him. Vice President Bush visited New York for two days in April, and that meant no blasting, because of the risk of a crazed terrorist hijacking a dynamite truck and driving it into the middle of the vice presidential motorcade. "That does it," Sal said disgustedly. "I'm not voting for the guy." Two weeks later Sal was stomping around the trailer, waving a page torn from the *Daily News*. "'Saturday,'" he read in an aggrieved tone, "'Sikh Parade closes 47th Street at Broadway at 1:00 P.M. and proceeds down Broadway to Union Square. ... Sunday, Armenian Day Rally closes Broadway from 1:30 to 3:00 P.M. at 44th Street.' That's great. Tomorrow it starts at one o'clock and lasts for how long? I've been on the phone all morning to the police and they don't even know. Who are the Sikhs, anyway? Those are the crazy Moslems from India, right? How am I gonna get a truck across Broadway in the middle of them?"

And, as a final insult, the Lyceum booked a show. The Lyceum had been dark for more than a year, and would be dark for virtually the rest of construction, but for a few weeks in the spring of 1988 it would be the setting for one of the luminous events on the musical calendar of New York, a solo performance by the pianist Michael Feinstein. The significance of this event, as far as Sal was concerned, was that he would have to stop blasting at seven in the evening and one on Saturday afternoons, unless Rocco could time his blasts to the crescendos.

The last bits of the excavation were the hardest, as well. With the ramp all but gone, dump trucks could no longer drive down into the hole. Rocco brought yet another crane to the site and used it to haul rock up in buckets. This was a tedious operation, involving Rocco in the crane on the street, Angelo in the hole filling the bucket with a bulldozer, another man tugging on cables to steady the bucket as it ascended and yet a fourth worker to relay hand signals to Rocco in the cab. A truck, which Rocco could load with the backhoe in less than five minutes, took fifteen or twenty minutes to fill at this pace.

Variety was still standing, for all the predictable reasons. It took Bruce longer than he expected to find the money to buy it, the asbestos-removal certificate was delayed, and so on, in the familiar chain-reaction-in-reverse by which the development process fizzles out without the constant application of energy and money. Taking into account the time it would take to demolish the Variety building, they had no hope of finishing the excavation and foundation beneath it in the time remaining. Luk Sun reluctantly agreed not even to attempt it. The loss of a few thousand feet of retail space, in the far back corner of the site, was not too significant. But Skidmore had been counting on part of the space underneath Variety for the garage. In fact, they had determined that the garage would be impossible to operate without it; the cars wouldn't be able to get out of the elevators. So Luk Sun authorized blasting out a shallow notch, about three feet deep, five feet wide, and running all the way to the bottom cellar, on the west rock face under Variety.

The bank stepped up its scrutiny as the vesting deadline approached. When their engineers came to inspect the site in late April, they were met by a full honor guard of Howard, Andrea, William, and Mitchell. But there was no hiding the fact that the corner of the foundation beneath Variety would not be finished in three weeks. The bank engineer pointed this out.

"Of course it won't be finished!" Mitch expostulated. "It won't even be started. There's no point in doing anything there because I have to notch out a piece of the rock, and I can't do that until the building is down. Understand, this is not a case of my not being able to do something I said I would do. We made a conscious decision not to do that section of the foundation before May 13."

"Then," the guy said doggedly, "you could make a conscious decision that you *are* going to do it, couldn't you?"

"But that wouldn't make any sense. Why spend a lot of money on overtime to get the building down, when we'll have all the time in the world later? Once we get the rock out, I think we could win an appeals case with just what we've done on the foundation so far, don't you think, Howard?"

"Oh, yes, once we take all the rock out, no question," Howard agreed.

"Right, once we get the rock out," Mitchell repeated.

"Then I'd feel very confident," Howard said.

The bank guys wandered off. Howard stood for a long moment watching a bucket full of dirt slowly wind its way up toward street level. "Why can't we have two damn buckets?" he muttered.

Howard and Andrea, meanwhile, were planning strategy. The process was this: on May 13, Charlie Smith, the Buildings Commissioner, would rule on whether the foundation met the requirements for vesting. There were three: an approved building permit (which they had); a completed excavation (which was barely possible, but unlikely, because they couldn't dig the notch under Variety until Associated finished the demolition); and "substantial completion" of the foundation wall (which would be subject to interpretation). If Smith ruled against them, they would bring their case to a body called the Board of Standards and Appeals. The BSA was permitted to take into account such elastic parameters as intent and effort. Before he was a member of the Planning Commission, Howard had sat on the board, and he and Andrea were old friends of the chairman, Roger Bennett. They had lunch with Bennett, which was perfectly proper since they did not have a case before him at the time. Andrea reported at the next staff meeting her impression that a strong good-faith showing would suffice.

"That's great," Luk Sun said tersely, "and the next time you see Howard, tell him to stop saying that around Turner."

Andrea looked miffed. "Am I my boss's keeper?" she asked. "Since when am I responsible for Howard?"

There was one tiny catch, however. The appeal would take at least a month to conclude. If the foundation failed to vest on May 13, the zoning would revert to 15 FAR. Thus the project would be out of compliance with zoning, because the building permit was for a structure with 18 FAR. The outcome would be a stop-work order from the Buildings Department, pending the appeal. Thus they would lose a month's time—worth a million dollars in interest.

In Howard's estimation, this was absurdly unfair. Even if they somehow lost their appeal, a 15 FAR building would still need a foundation. The work they would do during that month—mainly finishing the foundation and digging a network of trenches and sumps to collect water under the slab—would have to be done anyway. This was so obvious and logical that Howard and Andrea actually had hope that the Buildings Department would agree on the merits.

But the city had other ideas. Certain developers had made a practice of taking the most liberal interpretation of the zoning rules and then hoping for the best. Once they actually reached the stage of a completed building, they would throw themselves on the mercy of the courts and claim "hardship" unless the city let them use what they had built. The law, in its abhorrence of arbitrary state power—or, depending on your point of view, its deference to politically connected developers—held numerous precedents for the city to be mousetrapped this way. Howard and Andrea met several times in late April with the deputy commissioner of the Buildings Department, Neil Dennis, seeking assurances that they could keep working during the appeal. Howard even offered to stipulate to the commissioner that no work they did during this period would be used in a subsequent "hardship" appeal. Dennis was skeptical.

"What happens in a year," he said, "when you're up to thirty-eight stories, and you're supposed to stop at forty, and you've got your concrete trucks circling in the street? Are you really going to stop? Or are we going to have to arrest you?"

Howard considered this a moment. "Okay, fine, you can arrest us," he responded.

"Is that how you want us to treat our friends?" Dennis said with a smile, turning them down.

That was in the last week of April. Now everything would come down to completing the excavation by May 13. And that, in turn, meant that Variety would have to come down right away. The building was about ready to fall down on its own anyway. If Associated could clear away the debris by the following Monday—May 2—they would have a little less than two weeks to finish digging.

Gary convened a lunch meeting with Sal at a pizza place, elaborately disguised in blond wood and quarry-tile floors but offering the same oily pizza served the length of Queens Boulevard. He had bargained a favor with a commercial trash hauler, who would cart away the wreckage of Variety so that the building could be demolished over the weekend—taking into account, naturally, the performance schedule at the Lyceum.

"So," Gary began, "I think what you got to do is get Associated working from one o'clock Saturday morning until …"

"Seven o'clock Saturday evening when the fucking piano playing starts. Unless someone gets to him and breaks his fingers first."

"And then from one o'clock Sunday morning until …"

"The matinee at three."

"Which ought to be plenty of time," Gary concluded. "Now, you got any other problems?"

"There's a hydrant out front," Sal noted.

"Hydrants have a shutoff valve under the sidewalk. That's because they break occasionally. If this one breaks, make sure it's shut off first, and it's put back bright and early on Monday morning."

Gary walked back to the site and stood in the sun for a few moments, watching Rocco work. Mitchell joined him.

"Are you gonna push the plunger on the last shot?" Mitch asked.

"No, I'll leave that to Sal," Gary said.

"I never go to the ceremonies, if there are officials around," Mitch said. "I'll go to the parties with the workers, sure. But not to listen to a lot of speeches."

"When we topped out 52nd Street," Gary said slowly, "we really topped it out. We brought a real piece of steel down from the building so we could put it back up. And afterwards people came around and said, 'Where were you?' I went and took a bottle of Scotch and sat off in a corner and cried."

"Why is that?"

"Because after that, they weren't gonna be mine anymore. Not in the same way. I used to go into Bob Fee's office and he'd sit in his chair and chew my ass out, and then I'd go out, and the job was still mine. Now I sit in the chair. And the Sals of the world, they get to build the buildings."

Working all Friday night under the lights, and again after the show on Saturday, Associated reduced Variety to rubble. Mike Danberg told Mario to remove the hydrant if it got in his way, but Mario replied that the last time he removed a hydrant he had a fire, so he just worked around it. Dawn on Monday, May 2 revealed a bare site, ready for Laquila to go to work on the notch.

Unfortunately, it also revealed the wall of the Lyceum annex that had been hidden all those years. Ellis took one look at the wall and called Sal to come down to the trailer. "That building is just dying to fall down," he said glumly. "It's got exposed cast-iron columns sitting on top of beams with no bolts holding them in. I'll bet when they built it they couldn't get their hands around behind the columns to bolt it up because Variety was there, and they figured it didn't matter because Variety would always be there. Only now it's gone, and what happens if I set off a shot and one of those columns slips off the beam? The whole bloody building falls down, that's what."

"So we don't blast," Sal said.

"And we don't get the rock out," John said bitterly.

"Look," Sal said, "we did everything we said we'd do. We gave them their extra foot when they moved the theaters below grade. We took Variety down. If they didn't buy the building in time, it's their problem."

"But I hate to do all this work for a year and somehow leave it unfinished ..." John said.

"Yeah, but ..."

"Yes, I know, that's got nothing to do with Turner. That's just me talking."

On Friday, May 13, the foundation wall was complete all around the site, except for a stretch of about sixty feet under Variety; the last lift was poured that very morning. The excavation was complete except for the notch under Variety and the trenching. Gary estimated the remaining rock at 300 cubic yards out of a total excavation of some 65,000 yards, or about 0.5 percent. All the column footings had been poured, and Laquila was drilling holes in them for rock anchors, owing to a last-minute decision by the structural engineers to attach the building to China. It was a beautiful spring day, with temperatures approaching eighty degrees, "a day to knock off early," Mitch said. "The only thing left to do is to give this to Dino." He reached inside his briefcase and extracted an unmarked brown glass bottle with a screw-on cap. He unscrewed the cap and sniffed. "Peach grappa," he explained. "The best. Somebody makes it, but I can't tell you who. Dino deserves it. He did a hell of a job."

The inspection of the site did not take place until the following Tuesday. This was a gray, pouring-rain day that saw Howard, Andrea, Mitchell, Gary, Sal, and John huddled damply and anxiously in the trailer, awaiting any sign of Neil Dennis. Around ten o'clock, Howard spotted him across the site, standing in a slicker at the stair tower.

"Can you see the expression on his face?" Gary asked.

"He's smiling."

Dennis bustled into the trailer. He looked at some drawings, then out the window at the hole.

"What are they drilling for out there?" he asked suspiciously.

"Rock anchors," Gary answered. "Thirty-foot-long prestressed Dwidags [a trade name for a kind of threaded rebar] for the overturning moment, they take 120 kips each."

Dennis looked troubled. "Well, you know your foundation is supposed to include all pilings …"

"What pilings?" Mitch interjected. "There are no pilings. These are Dwidags …"

"I know what they are."

As soon as Dennis had left, Mitchell turned on Sal. "You could have finished the rock anchors, you know," he said bitterly. "You should have done the whole hole and foundation, but it would've been real easy to do the rock anchors."

Sal looked away, but his jaw was set.

"All right, guys, thanks," Howard said quickly. He put on his raincoat. "We'll talk to you later." As they left, Mitch banged the door behind him.

"That guy's the biggest windbag I've ever seen," Sal said bitterly.

"Right," Gary agreed. "And you know what you do in the wind, don't you? You let it blow over you. You don't piss in it."

"They could've bought the fucking building a month sooner, too."

"All right, don't get your Sicilian up," Gary counseled. "Let's see what we're gonna do about the trench drains. Let's talk about what we're gonna do, not what's done or not done."

Charlie Smith called Howard the next morning. "Howard," he said, "you didn't make it." Howard wasn't surprised; he just asked for the stop-work order to be issued as soon as possible, so he could get on with his appeal to the BSA. "Howard," Smith said, "that's the first time in the history of this department that a developer has ever *asked* for a stop-work order."

But in the end Howard didn't do so badly, because when the stop-work order was issued, it contained a clause permitting work to continue that was essential to the public health and safety. On the theory that the sooner the building was finished, the healthier and safer everyone would be, Gary constructed an argument that covered most of what they would have done anyway. In order to keep the Lyceum from falling down, they would finish the excavation and foundation wall under Variety. In order to prevent stagnant water from accumulating in the hole, threatening innocent citizens with malaria, they would finish their trenches and drainage system. And so on; the month passed with hardly any noticeable interruption of work.

And in ten minutes on the afternoon of June 14, at a sparsely attended session of the Board of Standards and Appeals, the five commissioners, one of whom sat in the chair Howard once occupied, voted unanimously to vest the Broadway State Project at the full FAR.

"We won, guys," Howard said calmly, once they were outside.

"This is great," said Gary. "I can have three more meetings this afternoon. I had five already today."

24

The winter of 1988 also saw some changes in the development team at Eichner Properties. Alice Hoffman left to take a job at a state agency that built and renovated mental hospitals. Her fate had been sealed one day in January when she had sent a letter to Gary Negrycz, by hand, advising him in formal language that there was a crack in the wall of the Lyceum that Turner would be responsible for fixing. This was a formality for insurance purposes, but it happened to arrive on Gary's desk in the middle of what he calculated was his twentieth meeting on that very subject. Amused by the coincidence, he called Mitch to tell him that he was aware of the crack in the Lyceum, that he intended to deal with it, and that if left alone he certainly would.

Mitch chose to interpret Alice's letter as a slur on the entire Turner Construction Company and a grave insult to his good friend Negrycz, whom at other times he would have cheerfully strangled just to set an example to the rest of the company. With a bellow of rage he came charging out of his office in search of Hoffman, who fortunately was out at a meeting somewhere. "That *bitch*!" he howled. "The man is working *day and night* to solve this problem for us, and she has *hand-delivered* to him, through the *snow,* this absolutely asinine, insulting, ridiculous piece of *trash*!" Not long thereafter Alice took her new job. A year or so later she bought an apartment house in Park Slope, where Bruce himself had gotten his start a decade earlier, and began converting the apartments to condominiums.

A few months after she left, Mitch hired a tall, soft-spoken, prematurely gray-haired Yale graduate named Scott Lewis as the owner's representative on the site, essentially to keep an eye on Turner. And Luk Sun brought in a young woman named Janeen Bateman to work with Bill Tung. Janeen was the heart of the project. She compiled the monthly "draw," the document requesting Citibank to put money in the project's account to pay the bills.

This was a busy time for the architects and engineers as well. One winter day Mitch and Joe Blanchfield of Skidmore took an early-morning flight from LaGuardia to Toronto, and then drove about 100 miles to the city of London, arriving in time for lunch at the University of Western Ontario. Their destination was one of the leading aerodynamic research centers in North America, the Boundary Layer Wind Tunnel Laboratory. The "boundary layer" is the portion of the atmosphere closest to the earth. For a month the engineers here had been studying the 1540 building in miniature, surrounded by a scaled-down midtown. This work had nothing to do with the behavior of the structural frame, which had been calculated mathematically; it was intended to determine the pressures and suctions on the building's outer surface in response to winds from different directions. These could be studied only empirically. To calculate them would be akin to predicting the effect of a car crash on the individual hairs of a driver's head. Someday supercomputers may perform these calculations, but that day hasn't arrived yet and, like most advanced technologies, it will undoubtedly arrive last in the New York City construction industry.

The pressure and suction figures would determine how strong to make the spandrels, glass, and mullions of the curtain wall. Or, more precisely, since the contract with Flour City already specified these strengths (forty-five pounds per square foot for the glass, fifty-one for the metal), they would be used to prove that those values were adequate. If the outcome was any different, Mitch (who did the driving) advised Blanchfield (who had recommended this laboratory over another one in Fort Collins, Colorado) that Blanchfield could walk home.

The wind tunnel was a brightly lit corridor 120 feet long and high enough to stand in. A huge ten-bladed fan at one end pulled air over the building model, which sat on a turntable, surrounded by a scale model of its aerodynamic environment. By rotating the turntable and varying the speed of the wind, the engineers were able to simulate the whole range of fifty- and hundred-year recurrence winds of interest to SOM.

The model was of clear acrylic plastic, honeycombed with 403 holes in arrays on each elevation. Each hole was fitted with a thin brass tube, and in the hollow center of the model each tube joined a plastic hose that ran out the bottom. Nick Isyumov, the manager of the lab, chided Mitch about the difficulty of fitting all those holes into the complex geometry of the building's prow and top.

"Just remember," Mitch responded, "we have to build it in real life."

"Ah," said Isyumov, "but you have all that *room.*"

Isyumov summarized his findings. In a hundred-year wind, the highest reading obtained was forty-three pounds per square foot of suction at the southwest corner of the tower just below the roof. The overwhelming majority of the readings were far below that, mostly in the teens and twenties. "The building sits really in a forest of other buildings. We have found, generally, in a city like New York, the more buildings around the more protected you are. Sometimes you have only one tall building, and someone puts up another one at just the right distance away, and they will cause problems for one another, but in New York you don't often get that effect."

"Well," said Mitch, "the results are certainly helpful, because we would be in dire straits otherwise, with our eight-foot windows."

As soon as they left the lab, Mitch turned to Blanchfield. "Now, I got a serious question," he said. "What do we tell Flour City?"

"We tell him to stay at forty-five."

"Do we share all the low values with him?"

"Why not? What will he do, thin down the mullions? He'll design it to spec. That's why we gave this job to Oscar."

Before Flour City could build the curtain wall, though, they had to settle on a color. Some weeks later, Audrey and Bill came to Cityspire with samples of the materials they had chosen. There was a profusion of them: blue and green window glass, mullions in both colors, blue and green spandrel glass. No one was completely happy with all of them, but for once no one, including the architects, had a firm suggestion for what to change. Luk Sun thought the blue was too dark, but when Audrey said she wanted to avoid "candy colors" he had to agree that she had a point. Bruce thought that the green spandrel had a bit of a "milky" quality.

"That's just because you're seeing it under artificial light," Hellmuth said confidently. "You'll like it a lot better up on the building."

"Architects always say that," Bruce observed.

"Well, it's probably true at least half the time."

Skidmore returned a few weeks later with a darker sample of green spandrel glass and two choices for the green mullions, a very drab gray-green and a brighter medium-green that Hellmuth called "Interstate green." Luk Sun and Bill trudged through an unfinished floor of Cityspire and out onto a seventh-floor setback, which had the nearest approximation of daylight. The setback was littered with construction trash, and the day was bleak and gloomy.

Luk Sun stood on this ledge covered with broken glass and tile, rusted pieces of metal and rotting lumber, and stared lugubriously at Hellmuth's samples, which were reflecting the trash around them. "I don't know, guys," he muttered. "We're closer, but we're not there yet. I still think the spandrel glass needs to be darker. On the mullion, it needs to be either lighter or darker. Or maybe both."

"Well, at least that gives us something to work with," Hellmuth said.

They returned again, a few weeks later. It was a sunny spring day, and this time they brought Luk Sun to the street and set their samples up on a low ledge outside Harry Macklowe's Metropolitan Tower. "I think we've finally got it, Luk Sun," Audrey said. Luk Sun glanced at the squares of glass and painted aluminum gleaming in the sun and gave an emphatic nod. "That's it," he said. "You were close before," he conceded, "but now you're right on target."

It was the same glass. Nobody knew. Audrey had started to tell David, but he cut her off, saying, "Just leave me in the dark, please." In her mind, it wasn't unethical, not like showing the client one thing and then giving him something else. Wong looked at the glass under the right light, in the right conditions, and he accepted it. And he was right. Should she have shown him something *worse* just because it was *different*?

All it proves, she thought, is that you should leave the choice of this stuff to your architect in the first place.

The massing and elevations of the building being set, SOM turned its attention to the interior of the building, which meant, principally, the entrance lobby and elevators. Actual inhabited office space would be built to the specifications of the future tenants, who might or might not use SOM as their architect. Luk Sun kept pressing Skidmore to hurry up with the lobby design, so that the materials weren't chosen at the last minute when the project was out of money—"which means," Audrey grumbled, "that they want us to design something nice so they can cut it later and congratulate themselves on how much money they saved."

But, in fact, the lobby was a part of the building Bruce was disinclined to skimp on. The real-estate industry had come to regard lobbies as a crucial amenity in attracting tenants. For several decades before the 1980s this had not been the case. Lobbies had been reduced to their minimalist essentials of walls of blond travertine and floors of terrazzo (a composite of coarse stones set in colored cement and polished to a smooth finish). Dozens of buildings had been built like that all up and down Third and Sixth avenues and their owners were now frantically laying down marble wainscot, planters, fountains, and rugged stumpy Brancusis to disguise the banality and cheapness of their conception. Bruce wanted his lobby to be impressive yet inviting, elegant but not overbearing, memorable without being flashy. David said that would be no problem.

Waiting for Bruce to arrive before the first presentation of the lobby design, Luk Sun suddenly turned to the architects and asked, "Are we happy with this building?"

"It depends on if you don't cut it anymore," Audrey replied.

"There are two things," David said. "One, you can't cut any more off the top. And it will depend on how well it's built."

"Yes," Luk Sun agreed, "finish is going to be crucial for this building. Durst, Solomon, all those buildings are glass and stone, very symmetrical, very ..."

"Pompous," Fridstein put in.

"... very stately," Luk Sun finished.

"What's the matter, Luk Sun, are you getting cold feet?" Audrey asked with a chuckle. "We can still change it."

Bruce bustled in, and David took the floor to show off the lobby design.

"We've got a grid for you," he began, "a straightforward, harmonious simplification of the outside of the building. What we're proposing is to have glass walls and a stone floor and have the grid of the building go down through it."

David showed his choice for the floor, Regal Gray granite, flame-treated to a rugged texture. This made for a handsome surface but not an especially opulent one, and was a mildly surprising choice in the luxury-drenched 1980s. William Tung privately derided the material as "1972 art museum lobby." The Museum of Modern Art had a floor of flame-treated granite. The floor was to be divided into ten-foot squares by a grid of marble strips, in the resoundingly named African Black Absolute. David brought a chunk of this ebony stone to the presentation.

He set it down on Bruce's big conference table, which it precisely matched.

The walls were a surprise. Marble and granite were the usual materials for 1980s office lobbies. SOM had chosen to cover the lobby walls in translucent glass, with a shadow box behind them, overlaid by a grid of metal strips echoing the grid on the floor. "It's brand-new," David said, "very different, could be quite striking and, get this, quite inexpensive."

"Ah," Bruce said, "he pricked your prurient interest, Luk Sun."

Wong, as always in the presence of novelty, approached it cautiously from the direction of the strictest practicality.

"Is it backlit?" he asked.

"No," Bill Hellmuth replied. "It's lit by transmitted light reflected from the backing; it will have a kind of milky, underwater quality that will convey a lot of depth and richness ... and then if you don't like it you can fill it up with dirt and have an ant farm."

"One of the things that concerns me," Bruce put in, "is the trendiness of lobbies. I'm not worried about a hundred years down the road but I worry about people in five years scratching their heads and wondering why we did it. I have to think about the glass. If it doesn't come off ... you could have a real stinker on your hands. It could look like Plexiglas with fingerprints all over it."

"I like the glass," Luk Sun said. "It's a very sensitive design. Like a little jewel box. Walking into this space off a busy street should be exquisite. I'll tell you what troubles me, though. I asked some brokers to show me lobbies that sell office space. They took me to Zuckerman's building at 53rd and Lex. I personally hate that lobby. I said, 'What do they see in this?' And they said people like the high ceilings, the marble. He said people like the idea that marble comes from Italy. It's imported, it's expensive and impressive."

"It was probably Vermont," Fridstein said.

"Yeah," Luk Sun said, "but the point is that to get something equally impressive in the glass you'll have to detail the hell out of it, and in the end we'll spend just as much, and the only people who'll know how great it is are the six of us here."

Architecture is a sacred undertaking, and sustained at all times by faith. When the Greeks built a temple to Athena they told themselves what architects have said down through the ages; she'll love it when she sees it. The alternative—that she'd hate it and slay all the builders—

didn't bear thinking about. Thus Skidmore refused to give up hope for the glass-walled lobby. They returned several weeks later with a number of refinements of the design and a new shadow-box model of the wall, which substituted a sea-green textured glass for the gray-white frosted panes previously shown.

"Let me get to the big issue, the wall," David began. "We still favor glass, the riskier but perhaps extraordinary solution. That's our favorite proposal." He took a breath. "We also have an alternative material, bleached wood, white, which we also think could be extraordinarily beautiful. There is, certainly, a risk factor with the glass. People might think you're nuts."

"I'm not worried about people thinking I'm nuts," Bruce said. "I'm worried about it as a design element. My reaction is that it's a little cold, somewhat antiseptic, and that is reinforced by the geometry of it. You have a pattern almost stark in its simplicity on the floor. I look to the walls for relief and they don't give me any. It's not even Germanic, it's Swiss."

"What you say is absolutely true," David responded. "The color is cool, and glass always looks cool anyway. You have a tactile memory of touching a cold window and you always expect glass to feel that way. But I think the real note we struck is not so much *cool* as *elegant*. This is not a space you sit in, that has to be inviting. You pass through it on the way to someplace else.

"What about the bleached wood? It's a wonderful material, halfway between wood and silk."

"You're too clever, David," Bruce said ruefully. "You knew I'd feel the glass was too cold, so we'd turn to wood for warmth, but you bleached it all out."

Audrey: "Bruce, this space reminds me more of a Japanese space than a Swiss one. The translucent panels ... to me it is not so much a cold space as a religious one."

"I'm not troubled by the glass, I'm troubled by the coldness," Bruce replied. "But if we can't design the coldness out of the glass, then we've got to be prepared to think about other materials."

The architects packed up their samples. "We'll never get around Bruce on this issue," Audrey said in the car going back to Skidmore. "Bruce has a certain kind of reservation that never goes away, and we can either spend the rest of our lives dragging samples of glass in here, or bite the bullet and give him what he wants. I think we've got to go back to the candy store." This was the nickname for the SOM materials department, with its thousands of samples of fabric, tile, painted metal, glass, brick, stone, and every wood in a bountiful God's creation. They selected a crossfire-grained sycamore, a blond wood ingeniously cut so that the concentric swirls were superimposed with a light tracery of lines at a ninety-degree angle—"as if you were seeing the wood through the wrinkles in a fine silk curtain," Bill explained. This precipitated a twenty-minute lecture that David later described, with a grimace, as "Eichner on colored wood." Bruce wanted a stronger grain to relieve the severe geometry of the space. He wanted a richer color to make the space more inviting. He was having a piece of furniture built of English harewood, and he recommended that Skidmore track some of it down, as an example of what he thought the lobby needed.

It was several weeks before another presentation could be scheduled; Bruce had to cancel one meeting and then David Childs was mysteriously unavailable. The mystery was cleared up in the next day's *Times,* which announced David's selection as the new architect for a huge new project at Columbus Circle. Now it was Skidmore's turn to try to speed up the process. "Time is of the essence," Dale Peterson warned everyone at the next presentation. "If we leave here with these items still open, it's going to be hard to get the drawings out in time."

"Gee, if memory serves, we were ready to look at it last week, but David Childs was busy with another client," Mitchell gibed.

"The week was time well spent," Fridstein responded.

"Not if what you did gets rejected, it wasn't."

Bill Hellmuth announced that after extensive research the SOM materials department had secured a sample of English harewood.

"And did you like it?" Bruce inquired.

"We *loved* it."

"Why are you flattering me?" Bruce asked.

"Because we found out that English harewood is sycamore grown in England."

"Mousetrapped! Well, in my feeble defense, all I can say is, what I saw described to me as English harewood was a similar color but had a more pronounced grain ..."

"Yes, that can be in the treatment, or the individual tree."

"Well, then I think we're going in the right direction, as long as you find the right trees."

But then several weeks later Bruce had a change of heart about sycamore. He explained to the architects that he had seen his English harewood furniture and that in the finished product the grain was not nearly as strong as in the samples he had seen. "It's making me worried about the lobby," he said. "It feels antiseptic. If you can't bring out the crossgrain, it's boring. I'm concerned that as soon as you're done we're going to be shopping for a Kandinsky to hang on the wall."

Bruce then departed for another meeting, leaving the architects and Luk Sun staring solemnly across the table at one another.

"Lobbies are supposed to be cold," Audrey exclaimed. "They're places you pass through, not somewhere you sit down and have a cigarette."

"Audrey, that's not the issue. I've worked with Bruce on four lobbies, and he's very meticulous about them. I said to you, when you first went to wood, you're gonna spend the rest of the job coming in here with Brazilian cashew and Oregon cherry and Australian eucalyptus. You have to go through the pain of exhausting every alternative."

"Maybe it shouldn't be bleached," she mused.

"You'll end up showing him bleached, unbleached, double-bleached, stonewashed, sandblasted, and acid-treated."

It would help, Bill Hellmuth put in hastily, to detail the border between the wood panels. Laymen look at a small-scale architectural drawing and see a pencil line, and to them it looks like a crack. The architect envisions, without yet knowing the details, an exquisite topography of chamfers and reveals. Before the job was done, every place on the Broadway State Building where two surfaces met would have its own precise dimensioned drawings to guide the subcontractors. This is one of Skidmore's great strengths. Their esthetic heritage demanded it. Designing the angle where two perfect planes meet was a responsibility verging on the holy. By contrast, the minor facets of, say, a rusticated Edwardian mansion were far more forgiving, and were apparently often left to the consciences of the individual workmen. David Childs liked to recall that he once saw James Renwick's original drawings for the Smithsonian, and where he wanted grillwork, Renwick just did some cross-hatching with the notation "beautiful grill"—"and it is," David said.

"We should do a real model," Hellmuth said. "I know a place that does the most exquisite models you can imagine, a half inch to a foot, big enough to stick your head in. They're so lifelike that an architect once showed a picture of one to the head of a big Saudi bank and the prince stalked off in a fury and when the architect got his voice back to ask what was wrong, they told him, 'His Highness is very angry with you; you built his lobby without showing it to him first.'"

"I'd like to go that route," Luk Sun said.

"They're expensive," Hellmuth warned.

"How expensive?"

"Forty thousand dollars."

Luk Sun stared at Hellmuth for a moment in total disbelief, as if he had proposed resurrecting Bezalel and Oholiab to build the lobby to the exact specifications of the Ark of the Covenant. He lit a cigarette. "All right, let's try something else first. We'll work with the accents. The reveals, the grid. Get some pieces of wood in here, and we'll move them around until we find some arrangement we like."

"I'd like to keep the wood light," Audrey put in. "It's too small a space to make it dark."

"Fine," Luk Sun agreed, "then we'll go the full circle from light to dark to light again."

A busy several weeks ensued at SOM, as the designers worked on detailing the wall to help Bruce see it in all its complex, three-dimensional virtuosity. The floor, which of necessity was flat, nevertheless achieved at least an impression of a third dimension with a subgrid of white marble strips overlaid on the main grid of black marble. Red marble medallions marked the points where the strips intersected. Audrey did a large-scale rendering of the lobby, and drew in some people to give an impression of bustle and prosperity. Actually she didn't draw them, but copied them from her standard corporate-set passerby figures, which she kept in various sizes in her drawer; she also had a street-people set for homeless-shelter projects. The men were mostly in dark trenchcoats and horn-rimmed glasses, and their postures suggested preoccupation; one well-dressed young woman leaned pensively, not provocatively, against a side wall. In her mind, Audrey had named all these characters. Renderers generally are dated by the figures and cars they populate their drawings with. They learned to do them when they got out of school and mostly haven't changed since. One architect of Audrey's acquaintance automatically drew women lifelike in every respect but with improbably immense breasts. "I assume he thinks that's what women look like," she mused. "That's why I developed these people. At least they look like real people from the 1980s."

Determined to give Bruce his choice of wood, they selected half a dozen samples, including English sycamore again, a maple, a couple of oaks and ashes, and an African wood called anegre, a light honey in color, with a pronounced but even grain.

Bruce chose the anegre. "This works," he said. "The wood works, and you've done the things you had to do to give it a rhythm and a scale.

Any possibility that this would be mistaken for a walk-in refrigerator has been eliminated. I'm pleased with the way you responded to my comments here. I congratulate you."

"We should have known Bruce would like the anegre," Audrey remarked in the elevator leaving Eichner's office. "Look around you." The walls of the Cityspire cabs were virtually indistinguishable from the sample of anegre Bruce had chosen. "I wouldn't have picked it myself, though," she went on. "It's kind of a Milquetoast wood. It's got a fairly even grain, it isn't light or dark ... I don't think it commits. But the main thing is we're going ahead with this now."

"For the time being," Fridstein said.

The decision was announced to Turner at the next job meeting.

"Wood?" said Sal incredulously. "I was all set to go to Italy to buy stone."

The chance to spend a week in Venice touring the nearby quarries is perhaps the finest compensation of building midtown office buildings.

"Forget it, you're not getting a free trip home," Gary said unfeelingly. "There's no stone in Sicily, anyway."

"There's gravestones," Sal muttered.

It was not long after this meeting that Audrey flew out to Pittsburgh to critique a studio by fifth-year architecture students at Carnegie-Mellon. The teacher was a friend of Audrey's named Paul Rosenblatt, and he had given his class a simplified version of the Broadway State Project to work on. It was a six-week project, and many of the students appeared to have been awake for the entire time. Presenting their models and plans, they mumbled invocations of "two-dimensional versus three-dimensional space" and "figure-ground reversal." One very common theme was a cylinder or drum half-emerged from a right-angled mass, echoing the much-despised Marriott across the street. This space was typically described as housing a corporate meeting hall or ballroom.

"I love the fact that my students think corporations are always holding balls," Rosenblatt said. "Next year before we give them a program, I'll take them downtown to see what a corporation actually does."

One young man had created a fantastic building, with an elaborate deconstructivist base and a tower growing out of a giant six-story-high distorted hyperbolic solid cantilevered way out over 45th Street, holding a ballroom. "I wonder," Audrey said gently, "whether you would have had that ballroom in the building if you hadn't thought of that shape. I suspect the answer is, you came up with the shape and fell in love with it, and then searched around for a piece of the program you could stick in there."

The student shrugged and mumbled something about the importance of form. Audrey nodded sympathetically.

"You can't beat them down too hard with reality at this point," she said afterward. "They're gonna get plenty of that later. My idea is that the purpose of school is to help them build up their ideals really high so that at least some little scrap of them is left after six months in the real world."

25

With a few keystrokes, Phil Murray could instantaneously call up on a screen the entire structural framing of the Broadway State Building, 11,491 pieces of structural steel in all, not counting the mast. With another stroke, he could isolate any given section, plane, or floor of it, or show just the columns or beams. He could take four bays across the base of the building and show the effects of differential loading on adjacent columns. One reason that a steel skyscraper is more complicated to design than a wooden barn is that the carpenter usually needn't worry about fractional changes in the dimensions of his materials. Steel stretches under tension and shrinks in compression. So does lumber, naturally, but usually well within the tolerances of the structure as a whole. In a skyscraper one column might be taking just the load of a few floors, while its neighbor carries the height of the entire building—enough, by the bottom floor, to result in a measurable shortening and a corresponding sag in the beam that connects the two columns. The structural engineer has to account for that. He also must account for the tendency of floor beams to bend under the weight of the concrete slab. This deflection—as much as an inch and a half in the center of a forty-foot span—is countered by designing the beam to be slightly humped in the middle, so when the floor is poured the weight of the concrete actually flattens it out.

The engineers had to make each piece of steel just strong enough to carry its load, with appropriate safety factors. To make it stronger than necessary was to commit the sin of overdesign, which Mitchell had consecrated his career to stamping out. Steel beams are described by the depth of their web (the height of the "I" shape) and their weight in pounds per running foot. A typical floor beam for 1540 Broadway was a W (for wide flange, a now almost universal designation) 21X44; that is, a beam with a depth of twenty-one inches, weighing forty-four pounds times whatever its length is—thirty feet, perhaps. The beams at the bottoms of the high-rise elevator pits, which would have to take the impact of a runaway car if such an unlikely disaster should occur, were the biggest beams made in the United States, W36X300's. Yet the main core columns were more than six times as big, built up out of welded plates to a weight of more than 1,800 pounds per foot. The total weight of the steel in the Broadway State Building was 11,628 tons, or around twenty-five pounds per square foot of gross floor area. Given the complicated geometry of the building, Murray considered this pretty good.

In early winter of 1988, bid packages went out to half a dozen steel contractors, and after some negotiations the contract was awarded to Lehigh Structural Steel, of Lehigh, Pennsylvania, for a figure slightly under $21 million. The contract covered both supplying the steel and erecting it, although Lehigh itself was just a fabricator; it would buy steel in the form of plate and rolled shapes, and cut, mill, weld, and drill them into beams and columns that could be assembled with bolts on the site. The erection and assembly would be subcontracted to another company, American Steel Erectors, of New Jersey. Designing the intricate connections between the pieces—the "detailing"—would be subcontracted to yet another company, and the steel itself would come from a few miles down the road, the home plant of Bethlehem Steel in Bethlehem, Pennsylvania.

On the day in June that the first steel went into the hole, the street crane brought out all of Laquila's equipment, except for the Grove. The Grove was to erect the bottom four floors of steel, leaving out enough pieces to make a gap big enough for it to be lifted out itself in turn. When the steel reached ground level, mats of heavy timbers would be laid across the beams to support two big crawler cranes, one on the south side of the job and one on the north. These would build the job up to the fourth floor, which was as high as their booms could reach. The rest of the job would be built by two Favcos, tower cranes that ride on their own superstructure of steel alongside (and braced to) the building itself. As the building rose, the Favcos would lift (or "jump") themselves on hydraulic jacks every few floors. Their supporting towers came in modular sections that the cranes themselves would lift into place. In this way, you could in theory build a tower to the moon.

To take the weight of the two big crawler cranes, the engineers added some bracing in the lower floors and made some beams stronger than was necessary to support the building itself. The bracing would be cut out eventually but the heavier beams would remain. Thus the building would carry forever the telltale structures of its own gestation, like a human navel.

The first piece of steel to be erected was one of the major core columns, weighing nearly thirty tons. More accurately, it was the base plate beneath the column, which distributes the column's weight over the whole area of the concrete footing. This was a steel rectangle the size of a dining-room tabletop and ten inches thick.

("Ten inches, Murrary, you bastard!" Mitch had exclaimed when he saw the specifications. "Do you know what ten-inch plate costs?"

("Yes," Murray had replied calmly. "Build a shorter building next time, Mitchell.")

Around the center of the base plate were eight holes, each four inches in diameter. Sticking up out of the concrete footing were eight bolts, likewise four inches in diameter. These bolts were to pass through the holes in the base plate and then through sleeves welded to the bottom of the column, and, with their accompanying nuts, attach the column to Manhattan. The holes in the base plate had been drilled at Lehigh according to a template, and the template had been shipped to the site and used to align the bolts, so in theory the bolts lined up precisely with the holes, but this self-evident proposition had not yet been put to the test.

Four men stood at the corners of the base plate, which was resting off the ground on a twelve-by-twelve timber. The heavy cable of the Grove dangled nearby. (For steel erection the Grove was also rigged with a light, or "jib" line.) The men slung short lengths of cable, called "chokers," under the base plate. The Grove lifted the plate and swung it over to the footing and down onto the bolts, where it made a perfect match with seven of them. One of the men grabbed a heavy mallet and gave the eighth bolt a couple of sharp whacks. It shifted position by an invisible fraction of an inch and the plate slide down.

The Grove next swung its boom over to the rows of columns and beams laid out on timbers like a jumble of rusted cutlery. Two ironworkers ran chokers through a hole at the top end of a massive column.

Slowly the Grove raised the thirty tons of steel to the vertical and swung it over the base plate. Four men each grabbed a corner and guided the column down onto the bolts.

It remained to unhook the chokers at the top. The engineer in the Grove lowered the jib line; one of the ironworkers grabbed the light cable and stepped onto the spherical weight at the end (called, in a bit of industrial-safety humor, the "headache ball"). The crane hoisted the ironworker until he was level with the top of the column; he stepped lightly onto its smooth surface, unhooked the chokers, and gracefully descended the way he had come.

This was the nucleus of the South Raising Gang, which numbered six, not counting the engineer in the crane. These were a "pusher," or foreman; a signalman, who guides the crane operator, who often cannot even see what he is lifting; a hooker-on, who works the hook and chokers; a tagline man, who guides the steel by tugging it with a rope as you might tug the leash of a large and recalcitrant dog; and two connectors, who join the steel to its adjacent members. The connectors on the South Raising Gang were Danny and Irv, both in their mid-twenties—the one blond and lanky, the other darker and more thickly muscled, with tattooed biceps that had once been the envy of a photographer from a gay magazine who followed him around another site for an entire morning, begging for a pose.

Connectors are the aristocrats of the site. When they have to erect the first girder on a new floor, the connectors grasp the flanges of columns and clamber up by the strength in their arms. When the beam is hoisted into position, they wrap their legs around the columns and wrestle the hanging steel into position by main force. Their essential tool is the spud wrench, whose long tapering handle can be jammed through the ellipse formed by two bolt holes that don't quite match up. Behind them come gangs of bolter-uppers, who fill all the dozens of holes with high-strength bolts and nuts torqued to the specified degree of tightness, and welders who lay the metal deck. All of those jobs have been mechanized to a greater or lesser degree, but in connecting steel no substitute has been found for sheer human musclepower. Connectors bang the steel with heavy hammers, or smash it with the headache ball, or sometimes they kick it or stamp on it; and then, when the piece grudgingly slides into place, they walk to the center of the beam and, like diplomats concluding a successful negotiation, put their arms around one another and step off together onto the waiting ball.

They are tough, proud, virile young men, and, as Ellis says, "you never see a fat connector," which by itself is a unique distinction among the workers on 1540 Broadway. Their shanty, the ramshackle hut in a corner of the site where they hang their tools and jackets, said "Local 40: Real Ironworkers." This was to distinguish them from lesser breeds of ironworker who install stairs or curtain wall. Their attitude does not go unnoticed or unreciprocated. One time a man in a suit, who was writing a book about the Broadway State Building, came by the site at lunch hour, looking for Jimbo, the South Gang pusher. He spotted a man in an Ironworkers T-shirt, blue with a white seal on the chest, sitting in the shade on 45th Street.

"Jimbo?" the ironworker repeated doubtfully. "Never heard of him." On closer inspection, the shirt identified him as belonging to the rival ironworkers' local, 580. "That guy over there looks like a Local 40 guy. Why don't you ask him?"

"That guy lying on the sidewalk over there?" the writer asked dubiously.

"Yeah."

"He's in Local 40?"

"Yeah."

The writer took a closer look. "Then why is he sleeping in the street without any shoes?"

When they are on the ground, they stand on their right to say "Oooh, baby!" to women passing by in the street. They consider it a perk of danger, and it annoys them that members of such mundane trades as steamfitters and tile-setters sometimes assert this prerogative on their own lunchbreaks. Against all common sense, Danny insists that he has actually met and dated women this way. But the women in this part of the city, at least the ones out during the daylight hours, are a big disappointment to the ironworkers. They lack both the glamour of the professional women found on the East Side and the accessibility of the Wall Street secretaries and clerks. Out of range of the sidewalk, ironworkers look for women in windows. Given his choice, Danny would rather work in the financial district, where the streets are narrow and in his memory the buildings all around are filled with with bored young women in short skirts standing on stepstools to water the plants on their filing cabinets. "There aren't any good windows around here," he grumbled. "Not even the hotel across the street."

They appear oblivious to the hundreds of feet of air beneath them. This is not so much a skill as an attitude. Asked whether it was harder when he started out as an ironworker, five years ago at the age of nineteen, Danny scoffs: "The first time was the easiest. It was a big game for me, like the monkey bars in the playground. It gets harder the older you get." Safety rules now require steel deck to come within two stories of the highest floor being erected, so unless a man is unlucky enough to fall outside while working on the perimeter of the building, he can count on landing within, say, thirty feet. Still, this is no job for anyone prone to dizziness or fits of brooding about his place in the universe. Sometimes for no discernible reason a man will come to the job one day and the precipice at which he has been working for a month will suddenly seem more threatening, the air thinner, the ground below bristling with impalements. And he'll be careful for that day, and the next morning he'll be fine. For recreation Danny goes skydiving.

Danger, in any case, does not always take the obvious form of a direct contest with gravity. A month into the job, the last of the big core columns was about to go onto its baseplate when it made what looked like a break for freedom. A timber kicked out from underneath it just as it was being raised to the vertical, and it began swinging and turning, slowly but with the enormous momentum of its 60,000 pounds. Two men dove for the tagline, and a clutch of ironworkers rushed to the side of the column as if to prevent an assassination. "Hang onto that piece!" the pusher called. "Don't let the iron push you around!" Two men, backing up, went crashing into a bucket of bolts. At one point of its swing the column grazed a little eighteen-inch beam lying on the ground on its flange, and the beam tipped over and fell on a man's foot. He went down sitting. The men wrestled the column to a standstill and set it on its plate. Only then did two men lift the injured man by the armpits and carry him to the shade. Charlie Avolio, a Turner assistant who had just come on the job, was in the hole and called up to Ellis on his radio. Ellis ran to the phone in the trailer.

The siren was heard a long time before the ambulance appeared, making its way through the traffic on 45th Street as if rowing against a stiff current. Two cops came to the stair tower where Ellis met them.

"Where is he?" one asked.

"Down there."

The cop looked at the rickety stair tower without relish. "Is he pinned?" he asked hopefully. That would make it a job for the Emergency Services unit.

"Oh, no, no," John said hastily. "Nothing like that. He just can't walk."

The cops started reluctantly down the stairs. Just as they reached the bottom, the engineer swung the jib line over to where the man was lying, and lifted him to the street on an improvised stretcher of wooden pallets.

"Shit," said one cop to the other, as he watched his putative rescue disappear. "Maybe he can take us out that way, too."

"No fucking way," the other one said. "I'd walk out even if both my legs was broken."

The ironworker was in pain. He held his head with both hands, as the medical technicians began to remove the boot from the already swelling foot.

"Anyone know this man's name?" a cop called out to the little knot of men around him.

One of the men was a relative; he started to spell it but kept getting crossed up until finally he removed the hardhat from his own head and pointed to the name written across the forehead.

The technicians hustled the man into the ambulance. It gave a few preliminary whoops before hurling itself against the solid wall of traffic on Broadway.

"Weight of the world on your shoulders," one of the men said to the engineer in the crane. He frowned and gave a little shrug, chewed for a moment on his cigar, and then mashed a lever and set the machine back to work.

Of course, any New Yorker would recognize that the worker with the most dangerous job is the flagman, who has to go out into the street and, unarmed but for a little red flag, stop a line of traffic for as long as it takes the crane to lift a load of steel off a truck and land it on the building. A New York City taxicab can squash you as flat as a four-ton beam, and is far less predictable. One afternoon Danny and Irv were down on the street, slinging chokers around a truckload of smallish beams—eight or so, weighing a total of roughly twenty-five tons. They cautiously signaled the engineer, who took up slack in the line until the chokers went taut and the whole heap lifted an inch off the flatbed, wedged together like a mass of kindling. The two connectors studied it critically for a moment. The light at the corner of Broadway turned green, but the flagman planted himself in front of the nearest vehicle—by bad luck, a delivery van. When you stop a van or a truck, the people stuck behind often can't see what's causing the delay and assume that the driver must have suffered an epileptic fit, which can be cured by noise. A chorus of horns erupted far down 45th Street and made its way west. The van driver stuck his head out the window.

"What the fuck is going on here, anyway?" he inquired.

"They're lifting up steel with that crane there," he was told.

"I don't see no fucking lifting."

"You won't see no fucking steel come down on your fucking fat head if they drop it, neither."

Danny made a gesture, and the crane relaxed the steel back onto the truck. The flagman waved the van on, but by this time the driver's interest had been engaged. Instead of moving on, he yelled something back at the flagman, and then yelled louder as he started to walk away. "You fucking creeps think you own the fucking city!" he bellowed, as the light turned red again and the horns behind him sent a bleat of outrage toward the heavens.

Bobby Sasso, the Teamster, watched all this from the bridge with sophisticated detachment.

"People in this city are like ants," he said. "They'll go anywhere they see a crack. The only ones worse than the drivers are the pedestrians. On another job once I had to grab this old guy in a suit who was trying to walk under a bucket of concrete hanging over the edge of a building, and he said, 'If I was twenty years younger, I'd knock your head off.'" The idea of this quaint threat amused Sasso, but then his face clouded and his voice turned somber.

"I don't like to see nobody get hurt on my job," he said soberly. "Even if they have an attitude and they deserve it."

26

“As large new construction projects move forward in the Times Square area,” *The New York Times* reported in February 1988, “the main unanswered question … is who will occupy the buildings.” Of four big structures under way on Broadway between 45th and 50th streets, the article pointed out, only one had lined up a tenant before construction began: Zeckendorf’s project, on the west side of Broadway at 49th Street, which would house a Holiday Inn Crowne Plaza. Now, the *Times* noted, there was another tenant in prospect for the area: the Hahn Company, whose presence in the Broadway State Building “should enhance the pull of Times Square as an attraction to out-of-towners.” Vernon Schwartz was interviewed for the article. “When the tourists come to Times Square,” Schwartz predicted, “this is one of the places they will want to visit.”

That is an ambitious goal for a shopping mall in midtown Manhattan. True, when tourists come to San Diego, many of them visit Hahn’s mall at Horton Plaza, but its competition is not exactly Fifth Avenue. It takes more than topiary elephants to make an equivalent splash in New York, as Hahn was well aware. All through the first half of 1988 Al Corti and his assistant, a gratingly self-confident young man named Jack Illes, refined and embellished their marketing strategy for the project that, the

Times disclosed, had been given the working name "Crossroads of the World."

Having accepted Times Square as its destiny, the Hahn Company had embraced it with a wide-eyed, provincial fervor. Corti and Illes drew up "design goals" for the project that implied they intended to finish the job of perfecting midtown New York City begun a half century before with the creation of Rockefeller Center:

I) Create a focal point within Times Square; a gathering place for people from around the world (i.e., international flavor).

II) Reflect the dynamic and chaotic personality of New York; express the essence of New York, the core of the apple.

III) Utilize design vocabulary that captures the colorful, animated and eclectic spirit of Times Square.

It takes a certain arrogance to raise chaos and eclecticism to the level of "design goals." This became obvious when Corti specified the stores he hoped to rent space to. He had several dozen of them, grouped by category in all the baffling subspecies of malldom—"showcase retail," "concept shoes," "specialty gift," "specialty sandwich"—but once he got down to naming them, they turned out inevitably to be branches of places that already existed in other malls around the country. This only served to emphasize the gulf between "the dynamic and chaotic personality of New York" and the banality of the actual choice between one fried-chicken franchise or another.

Corti did have some useful insights, though. He recognized that to attract shoppers to the various levels of the mall, the floors would have to be differentiated in some way. He and Illes decreed four "themes" for the respective floors to embody. The lowest floor was designated "Martini Square," an "entertainment district" of nightclubs opening onto a commons. The three levels above—basement, street, and mezzanine—were marked for retail stores under the rubric "Times Square Shops." The second and third floors were reserved for the food courts: on level three, "Cosmopolitan Style" (alternatively called "Talk of the Town"), with "a sophisticated and adventurous approach toward a range of restaurant choices"—in other words, egg rolls; on two, "American Spirit," serving "wholesome and exuberant" food "derived from the American diner era that also saw the development of the American musical theater"—in short, hamburgers. This is marketing at work: the science of applied non sequiturs.

Exactly how much of this thinking was communicated to the Jerde Partnership during the first couple months of 1988 is unclear, but if the retail architects were aware of it, they apparently didn't pay it too much attention. Richard Orne was pursuing his own dream, of space dissolving into a "black box," of an architecture not of stone and metal and glass but of fields of force and pitches of energy, of video images continuously massing and atomizing, vast panoramas erupting into vivid two-dimensional life and then miraculously dematerializing. Toward the end of February the top officers of Hahn came to Bridgewater, New Jersey, for the grand opening of their shopping center there. Then they crossed the river for two days of meetings at Cityspire, where these alternative visions of the mall of the future—total electronic environment or cozy theme park—had their inevitable collision.

Jerde had prepared an elaborate presentation, with colored renderings and dramatic depictions of the Whiz Bang in various states of illumination. "The challenge here," he began, "is that New York doesn't really need another shopping center. We have to transcend that idea. Our inspiration was Le Drugstore, on the Champs-Élysées, and the specific idea was to take the excitement of Times Square and turn it inward so that there was no edge, no boundary between the street and the space.

"We have attempted to define a space with light. Everything that we are presenting today either produces light, reflects it, or doesn't reflect it. Color doesn't enter into it. The analogy is to the inside of a camera, a matte-black box in which night and day are little different, and the storefronts and neon will provide the accents."

He presented some of the materials: a black terrazzo for the floor, which at twenty-eight dollars a square foot would be only slightly more expensive than tile (terrazzo, he noted, costs fourteen dollars in Los Angeles); a perforated metal ceiling, backlit; tinted glass for the elevator trusses to allow a view of the machinery, but "not every nut and bolt."

He called on his lighting consultant, a young Californian named Francis Krahe. "Brightness levels will be dramatic," Krahe said, "focusing attention on the storefronts. The range will be from five to forty footcandles [compared with a uniform seven to eight in a typical suburban shopping center]. The idea is to have nothing brighter than the neon signs or the storefronts." The food-court floors would be studded with small twinkling bulbs; the ceilings would be neutral metal panels, with downlights focused on the tabletops. The walkways around the atrium would have a luminous ceiling of backlit, transluscent plastic. "Imagine walking into this space on a sunny afternoon," Krahe urged; stepping into the cool, evocative near-dusk, and looking up to see the softly lighted arcs of glowing rings on the ceilings above, the electrifying pulse of the neon signs, the fields of twinkling floors below.

This vision failed to have the desired effect. "I thought the idea was those floors would be covered with shoppers," objected Hahn's president, John Gilchrist. "If you can see those little twinkles, we haven't done our job."

A profound silence enveloped the room for a moment as everyone pondered the wisdom of this remark. "Francis, I'm trying to get a feel for the lighting levels," Corti finally said. "Is it something like walking through Times Square at night?"

"It will be lighter than that, but you're in the right direction," he replied.

"In other words," Luk Sun said, "if I'm walking through here with a guidebook in my hand, I'll have to walk up to a storefront to read it."

"What are you doing with a guidebook?" Gilchrist asked indignantly. "You're supposed to be looking at the merchandise."

"The question in my mind," Corti said, "is how this black-box concept advances the themes we want to use in our food courts, and I don't see that it does that at all."

Jerde's expression grew clouded. "We didn't think that putting down boards and sawdust for America and pagodas for Japan made a lot of sense. We think all that should happen back in the tenant spaces."

"But let's think about that," Corti responded. "If we have a tenant with a national chain of sixty-five baked-potato stores and he wants a flagship store in Times Square, he's not going to want it to look different from the others."

The presentation was clearly not going well. Jerde was excused so the partners could talk among themselves. Bruce drew a breath. "I don't know how it works in your part of the world," he said, "but in this company, we don't let the architect drive the process. We would never have come to a presentation for the first time and seen this much work on the walls. It looks to me like he told you he was gonna do what you wanted, and then he went and did what he wanted."

Vernon sighed. "He doesn't think us ordinary people have any right to opinions on this ... but that's an old story. There's a cultural difference here. We're retail developers, you do office and residential."

Bruce: "If you listen to Jon carefully—and you don't have to listen carefully, because he says it five times—he's designed something he calls a theater, a black box. One creates a theater in order to have a performance, so the Whiz Bang is integral to it. And based on the numbers we're seeing, I'm not sure we're going to be getting enough Whiz to do the job."

"The bottom line," said Corti, "is we're not sure a black box is the way to go, and we've got to make that decision soon."

"We've got to make that decision now," Luk Sun said.

The meeting broke up. Bruce, Luk Sun, and William had to prepare for a dinner at Citibank to celebrate the closing of the construction loan. The loan had actually closed several months earlier, but it was the first opportunity to get representatives of all the participants together in New York. In honor of majority taste, the dinner was sushi. The Hahn contingent headed back to their hotels to call their wives, and the architects went out into the night looking for solace. They found their way to the Oak Room at the Plaza Hotel, which had not yet been bought by Donald Trump.

The talk turned, inevitably, to clients.

"We work with some pretty tough people, the French government and all," Jerde said, "but there's nothing like a New York developer."

"I wonder if the French government would like to hire Mitchell," Krahe said broodingly.

Orne came to Mitchell's defense. "You can get used to him once you get past the New York stuff," he said. "You can't take it personally ... even though he directs it at you personally."

Audrey: "Clients always complain, 'You're asking me to take something on trust.' Well, of course you're asking them to take something on trust, based on your professional experience and reputation, which is supposedly why they hired you in the first place. They say, 'How will I know what it looks like when I build it?' And then they don't want to spend the money for the one thing that might tell them, a model.

"Of course," she went on after a bit of reflection, "you don't really know what it will look like, either. You've worked with these materials before, but never in that particular combination, and you know that when it's built, some things will work, some things maybe won't work the way you intended, and the whole thing will be more or less successful. You're not without knowledge, but without total certainty. I wonder if you ever reach the stage where you can know ahead of time what something will look like."

She thought this over for a second.

"No," she decided. "Unless you're doing the same thing over and over. But then why bother?"

The economics of the Whiz Bang were complex even in concept and confusing almost beyond hope when you got down to the details. The agreement between Broadway State and Hahn provided that Bruce would pay the first $4 million in construction cost, the next $2 million would be shared, and Hahn would be responsible for the rest. There were varying provisions for repaying these amounts out of future income. But how would cost overruns be treated? If the Whiz Bang was designed and bid at $6 million, but ended up costing $8 million, would Hahn pay the extra two? Or did Bruce, as the builder, run that risk? Bruce also foresaw trouble from items he took to calling the "but-fors." These were hidden construction expenses that would not have been necessary "but for" the Whiz Bang. Millions of dollars could be buried in such seemingly mundane items as increased electrical demand and cooling for 300 TV sets.

The problem was that Hahn was immune to any kind of cost-benefit analysis of the Whiz Bang. Corti in particular took the attitude that since the Whiz Bang was a prerequisite to the success of the entire project, it would just have to cost what it cost. Bruce saw one possible way out of this morass. If the Whiz Bang attracted enough people into the building, it could become a valuable commercial medium. If he could get an idea of how much income the partnership might expect from it, he would be in a better position to figure out how much to spend on building it. He asked Luk Sun to set up a meeting with some advertising agencies.

The company they came up with was a small agency with a specialization in what used to be called "outdoor advertising," but was now referred to as "out-of-home media," a name evidently chosen to emphasize its distance from its grubby origins in ballparks and on the sides of barns. All three name partners showed up for the meeting with Bruce. Two were creative types, in open shirts and Hollywood tans; one was a business type, in a dark wool suit, white shirt with gold cufflinks. All three wore eyeglasses which were fogged over with the heat of their eagerness to land a major real estate developer as a client. Most New Yorkers retain well into adulthood a superstition that the tooth fairy really does exist, and one day she's going to show up at your door and offer you the chance to get involved with a commercial office building.

Luk Sun showed some of Jerde's drawings and ran a two-minute tape Jerde had prepared to explain the Whiz Bang to potential tenants.

"Unbelievable," breathed one of the creatives.

"Incredible potential," agreed the other.

"You know," said the suit, "if we look at this just as a display, we're not doing justice to it. We have to regard it as a form of communication, a network." He repeated this thought several times. "When I first heard of this, my reaction was that you should be sitting down with people in marketing, media and creative. These people," he concluded portentously, "are within this room."

"Let me ask a question which will set this discussion off in a different direction," Bruce said briskly. "The thing I am interested in is marketing this to users. What kind of revenue can we expect that would help us determine whether we spend $2 million, $4 million, or $40 million? How do we determine that, without building it first?"

A long silence ensued.

"Let me explain why you're here," Bruce went on. "Meaning no disrespect, I am not going to entrust a $300 million project to a company your size. But you have experience in outdoor advertising, and I want you to help us define what the issues are and consult with us on the choice of an agency."

The suit put a look of such total sincerity on his face that Luk Sun had to light a cigarette to hide his revulsion.

"I couldn't agree more," he began. [I knew you were brilliant the moment you called us.] "We are not here to solicit your advertising business. [Modest as we are.] Part of our service to you would be to suggest who you ought to do business with. I'll be very honest with you [but I know you can take it], we could come back to you and say, 'The best company in the world to do this is us.' That may not be what you want to hear [we won't hide the truth just to satisfy a client!], but if we conclude that, we'll say it."

Luk Sun regarded him steadily across the table with half-closed eyes through a haze of cigarette smoke.

"Why is it," Bruce asked mildly, "that every time I ask for advice on marketing it's always the same advice: 'Hire me'?"

"I think," said the suit, "what we have to do is … I hate to use the word 'proposal' … is to say what we think the next steps are and the paths we need to follow. This has been very, very stimulating."

"Fascinating," said creative.

Two weeks later one of the partners, from the creative side, returned with a proposal. In four pages of fourteen-point type, triple-spaced with generous margins all around, it proposed a six-month study of the marketing potential of the Whiz Bang, at a cost of $150,000.

Bruce was disgusted. "If I put this in front of a bank, I'd never do business with them again. We need answers tomorrow, not in six months.

You haven't done anything but repeat back to us the questions we raised last time, and it's obvious you haven't thought about it at all, and I've got to say, we're completely underwhelmed."

Thus ended, for the time being, the efforts to make the Whiz Bang pay for itself. News of Bruce's disillusionment filtered back to Jerde, and a few weeks later Orne showed up at Bruce's office with the latest in what William had come to think of as Whiz Bang saviors-of-the-month, a young man named Bran Ferren. Ferren, the son of the well-known Abstract Expressionist painter John Ferren, was one of the more unusual people to have a hand in the Broadway State Project. He was a pink-cheeked, red-haired, cherubic, squeaky-voiced young man who dressed in black polo shirts, clean white sneakers, and safari jackets. He did special effects for movies; set design and lighting for television, theater, and nightclubs; Defense Department training simulators; optical research; and a recently completed feature film, *Funny,* consisting entirely of non-actors who were filmed in that most intimately revealing of activities, telling a joke.

"Our role," said Ferren, "could be to provide anything from free advice at a distance—i.e., you *don't* want to do this—to a complete design-build turnkey operation. Providing you start tomorrow, the schedule is fine. We're used to doing panic projects because the entertainment industry is based on that.

"My gut feeling is you should either do it like nobody's ever done it before, or save your money. And if we're going to get involved in this, you'd better have a checkbook ready. Because I'm not going to get anyone to build $2 million worth of LCD's that no one else wants by smiling at them.

"Our big selling point is that we understand New York City, a place where truth, honesty, and reality don't apply. We have dealt with the unions and with the code. We can get this thing built."

This was music to Mitch's ears in particular. "You might be the guy who could do this," he announced. "Orne, you son of a bitch, why didn't you find this guy four months ago?"

Orne looked disgusted. "Well, he's here now," he said.

27

One afternoon in the spring of 1988, the Broadway State team gathered in the conference room for a weekly staff meeting, as they had been doing for two years. There had been changes in the team along the way, and more were coming. Andrea Kremen was mulling an offer from a law firm, which she would eventually accept; Luk Sun was turning more and more responsibility over to William Tung, as he prepared to move on to other projects in Bruce's office. But the problems never seemed to change. The printed agenda still listed the Lyceum theater, although the crack had long since been repaired. It appeared that the Shubert Organization was holding off on releasing Broadway State for damages. Howard explained that the pianist Michael Feinstein had complained about noise during his performances, and the Shuberts were waiting to see if he made a claim for lost revenues.

"If they were having such problems, why did the show keep getting extended?" Andrea asked.

"People had to keep coming back to hear the whole thing," Mitch suggested.

"Can we move this item along, guys?" Luk Sun said impatiently.

"No, they're doing the right thing," Howard said. "That's what I would do in their situation. And I think we should go along with them, because of who they are. The Shubert Organization writing letters to the city about what problems we're causing for them, we don't need."

"Where are we on the sidewalk sign?" Mitch asked. This was the billboard on the sidewalk bridge advertising the wonders under construction to passersby, to make them feel better about having to walk out in the gutter.

"You tell me when we're gonna have a leasing agent for this building," Luk Sun responded.

"Why do we need an agent for the sidewalk sign?"

"It's all part of the *marketing*."

"Look," Mitchell said, "the building is ready to start coming out of the ground, and you know and I know there's not gonna be an agent for this building until 1989."

William Tung looked down on his copy of the agenda, where each item for action was marked with the initials of the person responsible for it.

"It says here, 'IBE' [for Ian Bruce Eichner]," he said. "That's about the only thing he's down for, so someone should go in and make him do it."

In fact Bruce was already on the job. As an indication of the priority he gave to leasing, he had recently appointed, with the approval of his limited partners, a new director of leasing for Eichner Properties. This was his wife, Leslie. Leslie Eichner was a vice president of a major bank, a slender, striking woman with long dark hair, very fashionably dressed, whose high cheekbones and wide smile reminded some people of Carly Simon, the singer. New York City real estate development had been a family business as far back as anyone could remember. "Family" traditionally meant fathers, brothers, and sons, but that was just another rule that Bruce's generation was breaking. As far as office leasing went, Leslie had no particular expertise, but she had worked on Cityspire's leasing and would learn fast. Bruce in any case had come to think that a lot of experience wasn't necessarily a requirement for the job. The leasing itself would be handled by brokers, and he needed someone to talk to the brokers. Since the world of office leasing was shot through with jealousies and rivalries rarely encountered outside novels about college English departments, hiring an established broker meant that you started out with twenty guys who wouldn't talk to you if you had the last building in New York—and you'd never even know who they were.

Leslie was charming and smart, and Bruce felt that it sent the right signal to have her in this job: nobody could doubt that she had the ear of the owner.

In April, Bruce met with Marty Turchin, vice chairman of Edward S. Gordon Associates, one of the leading office brokers in New York, at Turchin's office in the Pan Am building.

Marty Turchin at that moment stood at the peak of his powers and achievement. He was a man in his fifties, with a wintry gaze, a fringe of iron-gray hair, and a sleek, conspicuously well-fed body. Even in the company of David Childs and Jon Jerde, he stood out for his exceptional regard for his own opinions and abilities. While the others could adopt, for tactical purposes, a posture of conciliation or humility, Turchin was as incapable of self-effacement as Tyrannosaurus Rex. He was loud in his contempt for his competitors, whom he referred to generically as "the 'Hiya, hiya!' guys." The brokerage business "doesn't as a rule pay a salary to anyone," he explained. "It takes kids just out of school, because they're the only ones who can afford to work for nothing, and gives them a desk and a phone because it doesn't cost anything, and lets them go and canvass buildings until they drop. The ones who get ahead are the ones who call the chairman of some company every day until he finally picks up the phone and he yells at them, 'Listen, I'm never gonna move and if I did you'd be the last guy I'd talk to and you're a prick and an asshole and don't ever come near me again'; and then the kid goes back to the office and says, 'Hey, I've got a great lead.'"

Turchin explained that he, personally, was nothing like that. He disdained even the title of "broker." He was a real estate professional, who knew how to "position" a building, what to put in a lease, how to close a deal. Unlike most other brokerages, which are loose agglomerations of teams each working essentially for its own account, Turchin's company was organized hierarchically. Thus each client had the benefit of its entire staff of dedicated professionals with their long tradition of excellence and their unequaled database (647 buildings on file comprising 328 million square feet, every building canvassed from top to bottom twice a year, 400 major tenants continuously monitored for any change in their space requirements). But that wasn't the real selling point. What Turchin was selling was Turchin, who would bring tenants to 1540 Broadway if he had to go out in the street and bite them on the ankle. At stake was a fee that under standard practice would amount to one-third of the first year's base rent, or, if he should be so lucky as to lease the entire building, as much as $10 million.

And Turchin was hot. He had just won the 1987 Deal of the Year Award from the Real Estate Board of New York, for a lease negotiation so audacious it merited an entire column in *The New York Times.* He had convinced the Sterling Drug Company to renew the lease on their Park Avenue offices even though they had already purchased a hundred-acre golf course in New Jersey for new headquarters. He had been the agent for Mortimer Zuckerman's building at 599 Lexington Avenue, and devised the strategy of "positioning" it as a Park Avenue building. "When we opened, there weren't any buildings on Park Avenue for big tenants to go to. So we said, they'll come to us. The space was sitting empty, we would show it and say, 'This is our number.' It took a lot of balls. But we got some rents north of fifty dollars a foot. On Lexington Avenue." "Location" was still the most important factor in real estate, but Turchin had discovered that it had a psychological dimension as well as a geographic one. By demanding Park Avenue rents, he had "positioned" Zuckerman's building 300 feet to the west. For someone trying to market premium office space in Times Square, this was very good news.

Turchin's approach to client relations was remarkable. Rather than flattering Bruce by telling him what a terrific building he had, he went to lengths to point out all its flaws. Yes, he said, the prow might appeal to some tenants, but when their architects consider how to lay out their offices it will be a different matter. The blue-and-green curtain wall might make a nice picture on the outside, but how will it look to someone on the inside whose office has windows of different colors? Why are there two electrical closets in the core, for Christ's sake?

This attitude did not endear him to the rest of Bruce's staff. "It's all macho posturing," Tung complained. "He's going to make our building look bad so he can claim credit for renting it in spite of us. And he's going to hold off leasing so he can strategize. I can't believe we're going to fall for it." Tung wanted to use Gordon's chief competitor, Cushman & Wakefield. Cushman's officers said exactly the opposite of Turchin: that the building was the best of the West Side developments, with an excellent location, good floor plates, and an interesting feature in the prow. "I said to Bruce, look at who uses Gordon. Zuckerman is from Boston, he's a rookie in New York. Why doesn't Rudin use them? And he didn't want to hear that." As for Mitch, he regarded real estate brokers in general as parasites on the honest labor of the people who actually built the building. He took a dislike to Turchin in particular, as a parvenu who drank French wines because they were expensive (Mitch was the cofounder of an influential private tasting group, California Premier Crew) and a brute who pursued the bloodthirsty sport of shark fishing (Mitch was an ocean sailor).

But Bruce found Turchin an impressive man, and he was not much taken by the competition. C&W had made what Bruce considered a "disastrous" first presentation, offering a team headed up by a broker recently promoted from leasing office parks in Long Island. Bruce was not so impressed, though, that he didn't check up on Gordon. He called Zuckerman's partner, Ed Linde, and got a slightly different version of the 599 story. "Turchin gave them the same speech he gave us," Bruce later reported, "about taking a very aggressive stance and waiting until the right deal came along. He kept telling them the market was about to turn their way, and it took a lot longer than he said it would. What saved them was that interest rates went down. I don't think that strategy is right for this building and this interest-rate climate, so I'm going to bring Turchin in here and see what else he has up his sleeve." Still, Bruce believed the Gordon company's experience would prove useful. He took William's objection and turned it around: if Zuckerman was a rookie in the New York office market so, relatively speaking, was Eichner. He didn't have three levels of staff with years of experience in writing leases. And, in the end, it came down to whom Bruce wanted to work with. "They have a rapport that I don't think anyone else can break through," Leslie observed. "Bruce says, 'What about you know what?' and Marty says, 'yeah' and Bruce nods and everybody else walks out saying, 'What the hell were those two guys talking about?'"

A few days after Gordon was signed to represent the building, Turchin came to deliver his formal critique of the design. The meeting was held at Skidmore, in one of their largest conference rooms, which was filled to overflowing with teams from SOM, JB&B, Eichner Properties, and Turchin's entourage of six men and one woman, none of whom spoke a word. Turchin arrived in a dark blue suit of sumptuous material and cut, whose jacket he immediately doffed and draped over the back of the chair next to his own, which stayed empty although several people had to stand throughout the meeting.

Skidmore had filled the room with drawings, models, and material samples. They had prepared a plan for a law firm to occupy a typical low-rise floor, with offices for eight senior partners, six partners, twenty-five associates, twenty-two secretaries, ten paralegals, a reception area, a main conference room in the prow, three smaller conference rooms, a filing area, library, mailroom, word-processing center, computer room, and a pantry. Turchin gave it a brief, contemptuous glance, seated himself, and began firing questions.

"You've got two electrical closets in the core," he said accusingly. "Does the building need that?"

Bob Gruter from JB&B explained that they had been designed to accommodate up to four meters, so that tenants who took less than a full floor could be billed separately for their electricity.

"How much space do we get back if we eliminate one closet? Forty feet? I want those forty feet."

"What about multi-tenant floors?" Luk Sun asked.

"Rent inclusion, very simple. You pay the bill and spread it out on a pro-rata basis."

"That, sir," Mitchell said commandingly, "is the first time I have ever heard a broker argue for rent inclusion."

"Well, that's what makes horse races," Turchin said equably.

"And if we had designed the building with one meter on each floor, I'll bet you could make a very good case for individual direct metering."

"Say, what did a broker do to you in your previous life?" Turchin demanded.

"Nothing. And compared to most of them, you're not a bad guy. At least you didn't say the building was underelevatored."

"I'm not up to the elevators yet. Now, we have what I call a floating core here, where you've got a section of the core cut off from the rest by a service corridor. And the tenant who takes an entire floor will resent that corridor, because he sees he's paying rent for it but he can't use it for anything. Can we get rid of this condition?"

Terry Bell of Skidmore pointed out that there was bracing in the area, so the space wouldn't be very useful anyway.

"Why is there so much bracing in a building this size?" Turchin snapped suspiciously.

"Because there's nothing but a big hole in the bottom," Mitch replied.

A grim look passed over Turchin's face, and he shook his head ruefully, like a TV surgeon examining the X-rays of an incurable cancer; a look that cried out, *If only you'd called me sooner!*

He went on to criticize the location of the men's room, the design of the air-conditioning units, and a few other technical points.

"All right, next!" Bruce called. "Let's get off the core. Let's talk about the curtain wall. Skidmore's favorite topic."

Everyone took a deep breath.

Turchin: "The simple question is, as the building will read from the outside, does Skidmore have a strong objection to a single glass color?"

A moment of silence.

"The simple answer," said Dale Peterson, "is yes. And I think the way to address it is to demonstrate that it's not a problem on the inside. It's not as if we didn't think about this."

Audrey was prepared with plans for a number of different office layouts, each overlaid with blue and green lines to show the different window colors, "… and in no place," she pointed out, "does a single office have both types of glass. And there's a reason for this. Everywhere there's a change of color, there's a change in plane of nine inches …"

"That's another problem!" Turchin interrupted heatedly.

"… and it's unlikely that any reasonably competent designer would lay out an office to straddle that condition," she concluded.

"What happens if someone lays out an open-plan office on the south side?"

"Well," Audrey said, "it's much more likely that they would do that here in the bustle …"

"I'm not interested in what you think is likely! What if they do it on the south?"

Audrey kept her composure. "Well, then they'll see blue glass, with a thirty-foot green swath in the middle. And I don't think they'll ever notice the difference."

Marty stood and paced over to the plans on the wall. He traced the outline of the building with a thick forefinger, shaking his head. "On the south side, you've got an asymmetric module, changes in plane, changes in color. I have to overcome all three objections in leasing this space, and I think that's asking a lot." His voice grew heated. "I don't even understand how this prow is going to work. What you have here is very nice because you've assumed every floor is going to have two co-equal top executives with 400-square-foot offices flanking a conference room. I've dealt with this situation before, at 599 Lexington, and I had trouble leasing every single floor."

Mitch: "Cut it off! Make it flat! If it was flat, he'd tell you it needed more articulation."

"Hey," Turchin said. "I've got a present for you. I understand you're a great oenophile. I've got a bottle of Thunderbird, April '88 vintage, just for you. Do you drink that?"

"Very nice," Mitch shot back. "I drink it for shark fishing."

"Look," Audrey said, "I think we're making more of this than it's worth. This is more like a bay window in one room. It's not the whole geometry of the building. There are triangular buildings that are very hard to lay out, but this isn't one of those. Be honest, Marty."

Bruce: "Meaning no disrespect, you're asking the wrong questions, Marty. You know that the leasing decision is going to be made by the CEO, the person who is actually going to sit in that prow, or next to it, and we think it's a feature that he's going to fall in love with. We're not gonna change the prow. But we should look at the single color of glass and the recesses. Any time an architect does something that detracts from the use of the building, he makes a mistake."

Luk Sun leapt to his feet to defend the recesses, by showing how they defined and called attention to the office entry below. This, though, set off Turchin on the subject of the office entry. The designers had marked it with a canopy as big and bold and high as they could within the zoning, and still Turchin worried that it wouldn't be conspicuous enough to people walking by on Broadway. He had a deathly fear of potential tenants wandering into the retail entrance by mistake, getting creamed by a roller-skating waitress from the food court, and never emerging to sign a lease. He examined a model of the entrance. "You're saying I'm stuck with that?" he said in tones of deepest dismay.

"I'm saying we thought long and hard about how to make it as prominent as possible," Audrey responded, "and this is the solution we came up with."

"Why can't the canopy come out farther?"

"You can't go out over the sidewalk, by code."

"Can it come up above this line here?"

"No, you'd be invading the setback."

"So you're telling me that's the best you can do? That you've gone to the end of your mental processes, and this is it?"

"It's a tough problem …"

"Maybe we should ask Der Scutt to tackle it then, if it's such a tough problem for you."

Bruce intervened to stop the bloodletting. "What she's saying, Marty, is they have worked hard at this and within the constraints they faced this was their best solution. If you spent your whole life at something, yeah, maybe you could make it better."

Finally Turchin departed, leaving an exhausted team of architects and developers slumped in their chairs.

"Whore!" Mitch spat after him. "Hustler!"

"Just as long as he hustles for us," Luk Sun said. "This is the time we've got to sit here and take it. In 1990 if the building still isn't rented, then the tables will be turned."

He turned to Dale and Audrey. "We're not gonna change the prow, and I'm not gonna buy his argument on the recesses," Luk Sun told them. "But you've got to pick your fights. Turchin has this list of three things he can take out of your hide, and I think he's gonna insist on having one of them. I would urge you to consider a gray tint for the whole building."

"Ooooh," Audrey moaned. "Look, the recesses started out at three feet, and they went to nine inches. And the rationale was, the way people would read the recesses was if we made them as different as possible, including different colors of glass. If we don't have that, you should flatten the whole thing out and make it an Emery Roth box. We're making this decision, and no one has looked at the vision glass together under the right conditions. Before we do this, we should set it up so they can see them the way they'll look in life, and I'm confident they won't see the difference."

"All right," Luk Sun conceded. "I'll give you one shot. But have a fallback position. If they come and see your presentation, it's gonna be thumbs up or thumbs down, and if they say no, I want you to step up to the plate and say, 'This is the color of glass we think you should choose for the whole building.'"

The demonstration Audrey had in mind took place on a hot summer morning at Turner's depot (a decrepit warehouse full of rusting machinery and rotting lumber) in Carlstadt, New Jersey. Bruce drove up in his own car with Leslie and Luk Sun, a few minutes late. A double section of curtain wall—two five-foot-wide modules, one green and one blue, with spandrels above and below—had been erected on a loading dock, complete with Venetian blinds. On the inside the two colors were separated by a column cover, as they would be in the building. Bruce strode into the warehouse and caught sight of Fridstein. Fridstein was in the process of moving to London to help run Skidmore's burgeoning office there. His place on the Broadway State job would be taken by a partner named Don Smith. Bruce had loathed Fridstein ever since he stopped the job over a few thousand dollars nearly a year earlier, and his presence probably contributed to what happened next.

"Did you follow my direction to eliminate any condition where there were two colors of glass in the same office?" Bruce snapped.

"Well," Fridstein said after a moment, "the purpose of this meeting in our minds was to determine whether that situation was really objectionable ..."

"I would find it objectionable," Bruce said brusquely. "I don't want anything that has to be footnoted and annotated before anyone will accept it. I don't want to have to say, Mr. Tenant, go see Audrey, she'll explain the design of the building to you."

He peered at the model.

"Suppose we went, on the vision glass, just blue?"

"It would be very disturbing to us if we did that," Fridstein replied. "It would create a very serious time problem at this juncture. And we don't think you ought to sell the outside of the building short."

Bruce shook his head, asked a few more questions, and then roared back to New York, leaving the clear impression he was inclined to switch to one color of glass.

Audrey watched him go in dismay. "I hate that man!" she exclaimed. "He tore our design into pieces and he just threw the pieces away. The window wall, which we worked our asses off to get for them for their lousy thirty-five dollars, he threw it away. Because the leasing agent doesn't like it. Because he wants to dominate his architects just to show he's the boss. Well, I don't give a shit anymore. Let him have his damn building any way he pleases."

Meanwhile, in the car on the way back to the city, Luk Sun was arguing with Bruce. "I think the building works well with the two colors on the outside," he said. "On the inside, the impact is really negligible. And the time problem is real. If you let the architects jerk you around with the color, we'll never get the damn building closed in."

"We won't be jerked around," Bruce said, "we'll just pick a color and that will be that."

"Bruce, we never 'just pick a color'!"

"I don't like the green!"

"Bruce, the tenant won't care!"

"What if you're wrong?"

"Okay," Luk Sun cried in exasperation, "so take me out behind the barn and shoot me!"

Bruce had made his point. He was disappointed in what Skidmore had done. He was angry at himself for letting it happen; but the one sure way to make him reconsider a course of action was to suggest that he was acting out of something other than cold logic. The next day he sat down with Luk Sun and studied the plans of the building to see where the blue and green glass actually coincided. A letter from Sal LaScala had arrived that morning; written at Terry Bell's frantic request, it warned of "serious budget and schedule impacts" if there were any further delays in finalizing the curtain-wall design. After reviewing the office layouts Skidmore had done, he agreed that the colors were not enough of a problem to warrant the expense of ordering new glass. But he would remember the episode for a long time; like everything that happened to him in building 1540 Broadway, it went into the hopper of "process."

So Turchin did not get his way on the glass. But even coming in at a relatively late date, he did have considerable impact on the design of the building. The core was redesigned to eliminate the second electrical closet, and the lobby desk, which had been placed square on the far wall of the lobby, facing the doors, was moved off to the side elevator aisle. Turchin argued that this improved circulation in the lobby, especially for people entering it from the through-block connection, who otherwise would have to make a detour around the desk to get to the elevators.

And one more thing. After reviewing the lobby materials, Turchin vetoed the wood-paneled walls. "Wood," he said definitively, "is a residential-lobby material. A first-class office lobby has stone. Period." Bruce had been coming around to the same point of view, because the wood in the Cityspire lobby was a maintenance nightmare, forever chipping and discoloring and delaminating or whatever it is that wood does. So the anegre, which the architects had labored so hard to find, went the way of the English sycamore and all the other ideas that didn't work out, from which you could have designed ten, or a hundred, buildings, and found a score of arguments why any one of them was better (or worse) than the building that actually did get built.

28

In the summer of 1988, Mike Danberg left Turner, planning to go to business school in the fall. He had spent a year on the Broadway State project, from demolition through the start of steel erection, and he had picked up some terrific stories for the sheltered suburban pups who had spent their college vacations as cabana boys. He had testified against Bobby Sasso in an arbitration hearing, the question being whether Sasso was entitled to be paid for a weekend day on which Con Ed had disconnected the old building's electrical vaults under the sidewalk on 46th Street. Sasso was supposed to be paid every day the job was working, whether he was physically on the site or not. A dispute arose over whether this covered work on the vaults, which were integral to the job but situated outside its perimeter. Throughout his testimony, Sasso had sat glowering at Danberg, and on the job for the next week he refused to meet his eyes. When Danberg knocked on the door of Sasso's trailer to deliver his check, the Teamster had opened the door a crack, snatched up the envelope, and slammed the door shut. Danberg had learned a lot in his year building a building in New York, and had reached the honest conclusion that you made a lot more money with a lot less aggravation in business.

Danberg's place was taken by a young black engineer named Peter

Crawford, part of a burgeoning Turner crew that would within a few months include a half-dozen assistant superintendents. Steel had reached the level of the sidewalk over nearly half the site. The Grove was gone, and the two crawler cranes had been rolled onto their timber platforms; each of the cranes took a full Saturday to set up, during which 45th and 46th streets, respectively, were closed to traffic. It was possible now for a few days to appreciate the three-dimensional geometry of the building in all its beautiful complexity: the sloping floors of the theaters, the big columns canted away from the atrium, the elaborate webs of cantilevered beams that outlined the curved edges of the walkway. Soon this view would be impossible. Already steel deck was spreading over the lower floors and it would reach the ground-floor level in no more than a week. Later the deck would itself be covered with concrete, and a thick gray hoar of fireproofing would grow over the steel, disguising its raw, elemental strength.

But, of course, none of this was happening quickly enough for Eichner. The big built-up columns had taken longer than expected to fabricate, so often there was only enough steel on the site to keep one crane working at a time. Lying in the midsummer sun, the steel sometimes grew so hot the men burned their arms or hands on it. Gary came by the site, stood just inside the fence for a moment and said to John, "The job doesn't sound right. There aren't enough hammers going." By the first week of September, seven weeks into erection, 1,750 pieces of steel had been put into place, an average of 250 a week; to make the milestone date of November 21 for the fifth floor, the start of the tower, production would have to increase to 350 a week.

By early October, steel was up to the second and third floors, and fireproofing had begun on the bottom cellar. A cementitious mixture was pumped at high volume through a nozzle and blown onto the exposed steel, where it dried to a thick, crumbly crust. (Steel, of course, is itself fireproof, in the sense that it doesn't burn, but it can soften and deform at surprisingly low temperatures. The fireproofing was insulation meant to keep the steel from losing strength in a fire.) The spray-on machine emitted a continuous, penetrating, high-pitched squeal, and covered everything for a considerable radius with a damp, gritty coat. "That must be the worst job in the world," Ellis observed cheerfully.

He had eighty men on the site now, and was preparing for another hundred by the end of the month. Tin-knockers would begin hanging duct; plumbers and steamfitters would run pipe; electricians would lay conduit; ornamental (as opposed to structural) ironworkers would erect stairs, railings, and, later on, curtain wall. Full mobilization would be over 500. Already, though, the men were stepping on each other's toes, or at least their work. A portion of the ground-floor slab had just been poured, right next to the sidewalk bridge at the northwest corner, when it was crossed by a conspicuous set of size-twelve footprints. Ellis was on the phone to the concrete super:

"Listen, you've got to put some barricades up there. I caught an ironworker sloshing through it just like he was at the beach. Those guys don't give a fuck about anyone. I know it gets fill on top of the slab but still, you should have enough pride in your work that you don't leave it looking like that."

A workman eventually appeared with a float and smoothed out the footprints as best he could, and then strung up some rope to block off the area. A moment later, three men carrying a length of pipe on their shoulders came up a staircase, looked disbelievingly at the rope, and began edging their way along the beam at the border of the concrete, skirting a fifteen-foot drop to a sidewalk vault. "Now look," Ellis muttered in an aggrieved tone, "one of those guys will fall in and break his leg and they'll blame me for it."

The vault was a relic of the old 1540 Broadway, a junk-filled crevasse in which an ailanthus tree, several interesting species of ragweed, and a thriving colony of rats had sprung up over the summer. According to Sal's original schedule, it should have been filled and paved over by this time, so that Ellis could drive trucks across it and right into the building. Then they could unload materials right onto two hoists that would run through the atrium. Someone, though, had noticed that the vault was adjacent on the plans to a cellar fan room. If the fan room machinery could be relocated to the vault, Hahn would gain at little cost several hundred feet of leasable retail space. There was only one thing wrong with this plan, apart from how it would complicate Ellis's life: because of its proximity to the subway line, any construction in the vault would have to be approved by the Transit Authority. And so that very day Mitch and Phil Murray were on their way to TA headquarters.

"There are two things you have to remember in dealing with any civil servant," Mitchell lectured as they waited for the subway. "You don't laugh at their suits, and you don't make fun of their offices."

Eventually they arrived at the tenth floor of TA headquarters in Brooklyn. As they emerged from the elevator, Mitch spotted the man they were to see and greeted him effusively. The man gave a grim, tight-lipped nod and continued past them to the toilet. Mitch appeared unfazed and, in an expansive mood, strolled into the office proper. But for the lunatic cheerfulness of the walls, which had evidently been covered with surplus yellow hazard-striping paint, the room exhibited an air of utter desolation. In silence unbroken by conversation or so much as the scratch of a pencil, a score or so of heads, most of them gray, a few bald, several with yarmulkes or turbans, drooped over desks or stared blankly into space. The place was a shrine to retirement. There was a large banner congratulating an employee on his retirement and notices about pension-planning sessions and luncheons for people who were due to retire.

The man sauntered back from the men's room and beckoned them with a curt nod. Phil unrolled a sketch showing the relation of the vault to the subway tunnel. "As you can see," he said, "no matter what we put in here, it is bound to put less of a load on the subway than filling it with rock."

The man shrugged indifferently, stroked his chin, and sighed. After a long moment he jabbed his finger at the drawing and murmured a question.

"We'll get you those figures right away," Mitch boomed. "Nothing is too good for our friends in the Transit Authority."

The man scratched his ear and leaned back in his chair. He understood they were in a hurry. He would like to accommodate their need for haste, but unfortunately it would be inadvisable to file formal plans just then.

"Gee, why is that?" Mitch asked ingenuously.

The man gave a deep sigh. In several weeks the office would be moved to new quarters in Manhattan. Everything would be packed up and shipped across the river, then unpacked into new filing cabinets. Anything submitted before then ran the danger of being permanently misfiled.

Mitch took this news with surprising equanimity. "Well, good luck with your move, and we'll be in touch with you as soon as you're settled," he said effusively. He stood; the man gave them a tired wave; Murray rolled up their drawings, and they strode cheerfully out to the elevators. "What a great meeting!" he exclaimed. "I've never seen that guy in a better mood!"

On alternate weeks now, a handful of men and an occasional woman gathered in Turner's unspeakably cluttered and stuffy field office to nudge the job forward another agonizing increment: Sal LaScala and Pradeep Mehra of Turner, sometimes joined by Gary Negrycz; Scott

Lewis, William Tung, and Janeen Bateman of Eichner Properties; Terry Bell, SOM's job captain, and Phil Murray, the structural engineer; and usually one or two engineers from JB&B. Although in fact very little was ever settled at the job meetings, Sal was a great believer in their disciplinary function. "It's those little dates that they don't make," he explained to Mitch at one point. "I want them to look me in the eye and say, 'I didn't get that to you because I screwed up.' They love it when I cancel a meeting. It's like a holiday to them."

The format of the meetings was always the same: Sal would distribute a printed agenda listing thirty or forty problems to be resolved. Usually this took the form of a decision, a document or a drawing he needed to proceed on a given task. (Requests for money were handled in another forum.) The person whose action was requested would be ready with an excuse for why he was unable to comply. If a mechanical drawing was lacking, for example, JB&B would explain that that drawing required a structural drawing from Skidmore, which in turn was dependent on a decision from Eichner, who was waiting for word from Jerde. They would proceed in this fashion until the finger was pointed at a party who was not represented at the meeting, who was therefore by default nominated to take the blame. Sal would mutter something unpleasant and make a note to himself for next week.

One typically Pinteresque conversation dealt with a $20,000 change order for an elevator stop on the forty-first-floor mechanical room.

"Why are we paying for this?" William demanded.

"Kevin Huntington [the elevator consultant] said you'll need it," Sal said.

"I asked Jerry Gillman," Terry reported, "and he said if you ask the Buildings Department they'll say you need it. If you don't ask, they probably won't require it. So I said, we can't afford to not ask."

"Wrong!" Gary exclaimed.

"What if they make us put one in later?"

"You'll say you've got approved plans that don't show a stop there."

"That won't matter, they'll make us do it anyway."

"Look," Gary said, "why should there be a debate over this? What does the code say?"

Sal: "The code says you need a stop on every occupied floor. If this is an occupied floor, you need a stop. Does anyone work or live on this floor?"

"No," Terry said.

"Then what's the issue?" Gary demanded.

Sal: "The owner's consultant says we need a stop there." The question had now gone full circle and everyone threw up his hands and went on to the next issue. This was the "Critical Items List." Critical Items were the ones that could throw off the whole timing of the job if they weren't resolved. The Whiz Bang, which was supposed to be in place for the opening of the retail, was among the most conspicuous of these, because by definition it had never been built before, and certainly not by Sal LaScala.

"On the Whiz Bang," Sal began with heavy irony, "do we have any drawings, descriptions, sketches on the backs of envelopes, hands waving in the air, or other information that would give us any indication of what's going to be built here?"

"Nothing has changed," Tung replied. "We are proceeding with Bran Ferren."

"You don't mind if I ask you every two weeks, do you?"

"Be my guest."

"On the office lobby, where do we stand?"

"There will be some changes there," Terry Bell said. "There is going to be a presentation to the owner, and then we'll have a direction for you."

"And then," Sal snapped, "we can go ahead and see how that affects the cost."

"Well," Tung said, "we never liked the cost that was there."

"Okay, so we'll start all over."

"We'll make it better ..." Tung said.

"... and the price will come down," Sal concluded bitterly. "I like that thinking."

Somehow, though, the building kept going up, steel laid on steel, bolted and welded and covered with decking. In the fall of 1988, more out of curiosity than anything else, Mitch Mailman and Scott Lewis drove for nearly two hours across New Jersey and into Pennsylvania to visit the plants that made the steel for the Broadway State job. Mitch had put off this trip until the job was well along and Lehigh presumably had hit its stride in fabrication. "You can't get the feel of a job from the first dozen pieces," he explained.

Their first stop was at the home plant of Bethlehem Steel, a complex of foundries, forges, and mills dating from the Civil War, stretching five miles along the south bank of the Lehigh River. The wide-flange beam, the basic structural shape of all steel skyscrapers up to the present day, was first rolled here in 1908. The 1,800-acre plant had a dispirited, slightly uninhabited air. Workers were scattered thinly about the vast enclosures, doing miscellaneous chores like chipping slag out of ladles. In the Basic Oxygen Furnace building, where steel is manufactured in three-hundred-ton batches from molten iron and old cars, even the computers were dirty and neglected-looking. But that appearance was deceptive. The Combination Mill, in which hot steel was rolled, flattened, and extruded into seventy different families of rods, bars, angles, T-sections, H-sections, and other cross sections too complex to bear analogy, was running eighteen shifts a week out of a possible twenty-one.

The steel that would go into the Broadway State Building began with iron ore from the Midwest, typically shipped by barge through the Great Lakes and the St. Lawrence Seaway, down the coast to Philadelphia, thence by rail to Lehigh. The ore was refined in a blast furnace, then transported on the plant's narrow-gauge railroad to the Basic Oxygen Furnace, a bowl the size of a small apartment house inside a vast, dark, and filthy shed. The BOF was primed with two hopperloads of scrap metal, followed by a ladle of 200 tons of molten iron at 2,600 degrees. The ladle was carried by an overhead crane and its contents poured directly into the BOF, as a thick, viscous, cherry-red liquid, its surface heaving and bubbling and sparking into the gloom. A thick prod was lowered into the molten metal to blow pure elemental oxygen into the mix at 20,000 cubic feet a minute. The oxygen burns off the carbon in the iron. Mitch and Scott watched a heat of common structural steel, around .23 percent carbon and .75 percent manganese. "Structural steel," explained the BOF foreman indulgently, "is not a terribly demanding metallurgical product."

As blooms or ingots, the cooled steel proceeded to the mill complex, where it was heated back up to plasticity at 2,400 degrees. It moved down a series of rollers at a fast trot toward the mills that elongate it from a blunt rectangular prism, two by three by seven feet, to as much as 150 feet long. The day Mitch and Scott visited the mill, it was making W24X68's—wide-flange beams twenty-four inches across, weighing sixty-eight pounds a running foot. These are common framing members, of which there were hundreds in the Broadway State Building. The mill shaped the beam in seven passes, the rollers reversing smartly in unison to move it backward and forward. Water cascaded down on the rollers to cool them and wash slag off the metal, sending steam toward the distant ceiling in billows colored orange from the glow of the hot steel. Three men controlled the process from a glassy office high above the mill floor, monitoring the steel's progress through windows and on banks of dials and video screens. From a high catwalk running the length of the building you could hear the steel as it approached with an ominous hiss and sizzle and a rumble like an oncoming subway train, and feel the heat on the back of your neck as it passed six stories below.

From Bethlehem the steel, now in the form of beams of uniform length, traveled six miles to Allentown. Here Lehigh Structural Steel occupied a huge, crumbling plant, consisting of four enormous sheds open at both ends and occupied by a handful of men desultorily tending a few brutal machines. Mitch and Scott were greeted by William Dooley, a Lehigh vice president. He escorted them down a long, depressing corridor of corrugated iron that spanned the yard, decorated with photographs of especially interesting beams. "Here's one of yours, Mitch," Dooley exclaimed, pointing to a photograph of a workman kneeling next to a steel pinwheel of indescribable complexity, an irregular disk from which a half-dozen thick plates stuck out at odd angles. "I forget what we called it, the hub or the knuckle or something ..."

"I would have recognized it anywhere," Mitch responded grumpily. "It makes me wonder if Mr. Murray gave up designing the building at some point. I don't want to go up on your trophy wall, Dooley. It's an honor I'd just as soon pass up."

The men went out to the shops. In one of them, hundreds of pieces of steel were lined up on chocks in varying stages of incompleteness. The plates that would be used to connect the steel were cut to the correct shape by electric torches. Bolt holes were punched (if the thickness of the steel was less than the diameter of the hole), or else drilled by a bit of hardened steel turning on a hollow inch-thick shaft that spurted oil continuously as it rotated. As it augered into the heavy steel plate the drill churned up a thick, silver Medusa head of razor-sharp spiral shavings. Dooley made an expansive gesture with an arm. "Just about everything in here is yours, Mitch," he said.

One crucial part of the building was not to be found at Lehigh, because it hadn't been designed yet. This was the decorative mast at the top of the building. When the steel contract had been put out to bid, the bidders came in with wildly differing prices for the mast, suggesting that the design wasn't far enough along to come up with a realistic estimate. Lehigh costed it at something over $600,000. So Turner had put a $300,000 allowance in the budget for it, with the final price to be determined on the basis of more detailed drawings. Audrey had assumed this would mean the mast would be "value engineered" to invisibility. But it was saved by an unlikely hero: Marty Turchin. Turchin had decreed that the mast would be the identifying logo of the building. He had authorized work on a sidewalk sign incorporating a large cutout of the mast. He had commissioned a leasing brochure that prominently displayed the mast on its cover. This meant it would have to be built. Audrey began to reappraise Turchin in a more favorable light. But it left the engineers with a $300,000 headache.

A series of meetings since then had whittled down the cost considerably, but Turner still didn't have drawings to price. Sal took this up at one of his job meetings. "On the mast," he began, "I was told there was a commitment by Skidmore to have drawings by today. Was I misinformed?"

"There will be drawings by Friday showing typical details, member sizes, connections ..." Murray responded.

"So we'll take those drawings into a meeting with Lehigh and then we'll put this thing to bed, right?"

"Does anything ever get put to bed?" Murray asked.

A few weeks later, on a sunny Friday in October, Sal met John Ellis for lunch at a Mexican restaurant a couple of blocks south of the site. They sat near the back and sipped enormous pink frozen margaritas that were almost entirely ice. Sal had just come from a meeting with Luk Sun where he gave him a September 1989 date for a Temporary Certificate of Occupancy for the retail.

"Just think," he said, "in a year this building will be open. It scares me a little."

"What else went on?" Ellis asked. He was on the site every day and rarely had any direct communication with the Eichner people any longer except for Scott Lewis.

"I gave him the price for the mast. Now, it started out, you remember, at $650,000, then it was 550, 425, we got it down now to $337,000. So anyone else would say, 'Nice work,' but instead Luk Sun says, 'My number is $300,000.'

"So I said, 'That's as low as it's gonna go,' and he says, 'Sal, make it go away.'"

"'Make it go away.' That's good."

"I said, what am I, a magician?"

"Wave your magic wand," Ellis nodded.

"So what am I gonna do? I'm gonna have to make it go away."

"How are you going to do that?"

"He said make it go away, he didn't say make it disappear."

"I see."

"If I make it go away, it's gotta go somewhere else."

"Now I've got you."

This is one common solution to a problem like this. If you have to build a $337,000 mast for $300,000, you build the mast for $300,000, but somewhere else in the building there's a $37,000 screw.

"You wouldn't really do that, would you, Sal?" Ellis asked.

"Nah," LaScala said. "But it would make my life a whole lot easier if I could."

"The whole business has changed," Sal said after a minute. "It used to be, you were building for guys that weren't putting up their cars and houses to raise the cash."

"That's right," Ellis agreed. "When Equitable asked for something to be done, all you had to know was, when?"

"Now you've got to get the Social Security number of the guy who's doing the asking."

"Because he may be backed by a letter of credit from the National Bank of Botswana."

"I heard of one job, the guy had his financing all set, the papers all signed with the bank, and the bank went bankrupt. That never used to happen.

"What can I do?" Sal concluded. "I like to build buildings. I want to build one more job in New York. Columbus Circle. That's the big one. If we get it, and I hope we do, I want that job. I told Gary. He said I'm crazy. You want to build it with me, John?"

"Sure. In a minute."

They walked outside, into the bright sun and vivid life of West 44th Street, and were just about to cross the street when Sal looked up and pulled John back to the curb. He pointed up at the unfinished superstructure of the Hotel Macklowe. From the third-floor windows, bundles of lumber protruded nearly ten feet out over the sidewalk.

"Look up there, would you walk under that?"

"They're supposed to keep that stuff ten feet back from the edge of the building. That's in the other direction."

"If we did that," Sal said, shaking his head, "we'd get a million-dollar fine."

While hundreds of civilians passed heedlessly below, the two engineers carefully skirted the danger zone and headed back to do the only thing they had ever wanted to do, which was build buildings for Turner.

29

By the end of 1988 the building was completely designed, except, of course, for the Whiz Bang, and a few minor details such as the mast and the exterior signs on Broadway, and things that kept getting changed, like the office lobby. Almost a year after the first tentative discussions of glass shadow-box walls, after two kinds of glass and three kinds of wood were finally and irrevocably thrown out at the insistence of Turchin, yet another meeting was convened at Skidmore to consider the lobby design.

Having had many of their favorite ideas rejected, the designers' enthusiasm for making 1540 Broadway the world's greatest office building was beginning to flag just a bit. From the original scheme, they kept one idea that everyone liked: a floor of squares of white granite, separated by black marble strips, with red marble medallions where the strips crossed. Ingeniously, but somewhat supinely, they managed to squeeze two completely different design schemes from this single concept. In one, they kept the white/black/red floor, and made the walls a neutral gray-white stone, above a high wainscoting of black granite. In the other scheme, Skidmore made the walls white, black, and red, and made the floor polished black granite with red marble strips. "We know there are certain parties enamored of a glitzy, slick approach," Audrey said privately, "and this is one, with the black floors. But it's one we think could work, with the walls being what the floors had been, quiet and elegant."

Although Bruce wasn't at this meeting, Leslie Eichner was, representing the leasing interests, along with Helene Saren from Turchin's office.

"Which do we want?" Luk Sun asked briskly.

"Which one makes it look bigger?" Leslie asked.

"The wainscoting," Luk Sun answered.

"I like that one, too," Leslie said. "It gets across the jewel-box idea."

"It's very … architectural," Helene put in.

"Almost a museum quality."

"Settled, then," Luk Sun said happily. "How did you manage it, guys?"

"We've had a lot of practice," Hellmuth pointed out.

"We always get it right the forty-eighth time," Audrey added.

They reviewed the drawings for the elevator cabs. The cabs had been designed at the same time and with the same materials as the original lobby wall. Bruce, who couldn't stand the cool, religious, austere, Japanese/Swiss look of gray-green glass shadow boxes in the lobby, had actually liked it in the elevators, where it seemed to him practical in terms of upkeep and attractive, in an Art Deco way, as a design. Luk Sun, though, thought it would be a good idea to keep their options open.

"Audrey, if the comment came back to you that the elevator cabs lacked *warmth*, what would you do?"

"Gee," she answered, "that's a tough one. This is really intended to be a kind of cool, noncommittal space …"

"Could we achieve a *cool* warmth?"

"You could change the color of the panel behind the glass, I guess. Maybe. I thought you liked the glass."

"I am here in body only," Luk Sun said grandly. "Another's spirit speaks through me."

Audrey took advantage of the moment to bring up a minor change in the elevator cab materials. She wanted to change the metal accent strips and control panels from something called "Satin Polish" (shiny, reflective) to "Imperial Finish" (crinkly, sparkly).

"Is anyone keeping track of the budget here?" Bill Tung asked in alarm. "Are we up to seven figures? Why didn't you know about this when we bid the elevators?"

"I don't know why," Audrey said evenly. "We just didn't think of it. The other was kind of an obvious choice. This is a thousand times better …"

"… And since it's only ten times as much money, you're better off by a factor of a hundred!" Hellmuth added.

"Right!" Audrey agreed. "You can't go wrong like that."

Designing the office lobby, frustrating though it was, was nevertheless a textbook case study of efficiency compared to the way the signs were handled. Given sufficient distance, you can regard any esthetic issue as essentially one-dimensional: you find the point where your taste intersects your budget, and make it exactly that good. The signs, by contrast, were a problem in three, or maybe four, dimensions: their overall architectural effect, their impact on leasing the offices, the amount of money they could be leased for, and, of course, the zoning rules, which were confusing enough to start with and had changed at least twice after Skidmore had filed its original plans more than a year earlier. On those plans, Audrey had drawn six forty-foot-high vertical fins, mounted on the roof of the low setback like giant flags. Keeping this scheme would have several advantages. The city would have to accept it, because the plans had been approved; a revised plan would have to meet the new requirements, which the city had made even more exacting in its effort to beat some damn levity into the developers' thick heads. The fin signs also had the least impact on the views from the office floors, because they presented their narrow edge to the windows. And Audrey thought that if you had to stick advertising on the building, this was about the least offensive way to do it, especially compared to the alternative of treating the building like a giant barn and plastering it with flat billboards.

But it turned out, as Luk Sun and William explored the matter with sign companies, that a giant barn was just what they would have liked to see there. The very cleverness of the fin signs made them suspect: they were too discreet, too abstract, too architectural; huge as they were, they seemed designed to not call excessive attention to themselves. Nobody ever made money in the billboard business by worrying about what the neighbors might think.

So Audrey unhappily drew several large rectangles on poles sticking up from the roof of the setback.

"Wait a minute," Luk Sun said immediately when he saw them, "why are they stuck on poles like that?"

"Because of the sight lines," Audrey replied, with a hint of relish. "That's one of the provisions in the new zoning. Your signs have to be visible at a point sixty feet from the base of the building. If they come down to the roof, the lower part can't be seen."

"But that's crazy!" he expostulated. "The one place on the whole building where the signs won't block a window is the mechanical room [the first floor above the setback] and you're telling me I have to put them on poles to get them higher than that?"

"That's right," Audrey said. "Remember, this is so the signs can be seen from sixty feet away, and it doesn't much matter that anyone standing there sees the sign, because he's only got another twelve seconds to live before he's creamed by a taxi."

But there didn't seem much choice; it made no sense to pass up money now from advertisers to avoid blocking the views of nonexistent office tenants. So Bruce had Lydia send a Request for Proposals to about a dozen advertising firms. Only three responded. The leading contender was Van Wagner Communications, which was interested in the Broadway State Building, but not on Luk Sun's terms. Luk Sun wanted Van Wagner to put up $2 million to build the sign, lease and maintain it, and send Broadway State a rent check twice a year. They proposed, instead, a joint venture, in which BSP and Van Wagner would share according to some formula both the capital expenses and the profits.

Luk Sun saw this seemingly reasonable proposal as a trap of the utmost subtlety and craft. To him it was a way to put BSP totally at the mercy of Van Wagner. The sign company was presumably making similar deals with most of the other leading Times Square buildings. Van Wagner could play off one landlord against the other, and offer the signage on one building as a loss leader to snare a client for another deal that might prove more lucrative. "It's as if we're giving them an exclusive deal on the signs, and *we're* paying *them* for it," he said.

To Luk Sun this was simply how you did business, by assuming the worst possible faith on the part of all other parties. On the other hand, Bruce pointed out, if the signs were as lucrative as he hoped they would be, a joint venture might be very attractive. The trick lay in devising the formula for sharing the profits. You had to leave your partner a big enough share so he had an incentive to make some money for you, or you'd wind up with 90 percent of nothing. Luk Sun realized that, but unfortunately he and Bruce had completely opposite notions of how to structure the formula. Luk Sun, by nature a pessimist, took the conservative course of seeking the largest share of the first dollars in, and a declining portion of the profits thereafter. Bruce, invariably with his eye on the main chance, wanted his share to go up as the profits increased. At one meeting, Van Wagner came in with a proposal for a sliding scale that gave them the lion's share of profits over $2 million, and Bruce—

who had had Tung run the numbers on just such a deal earlier—announced dramatically, "Gentlemen, I accept your proposal, with only one modification. I want to switch the names at the top of the columns."

"Ahh, okay, I guess," the Van Wagner guy said.

"Wait, we've got to talk some more," Luk Sun mumbled.

The Whiz Bang, by contrast, exhibited no forward motion at all. The issues were too complex, the decisions too momentous, the costs too great for mere mortals to grapple with.

For one thing, Bruce recognized that the Whiz Bang was inseparable from the broader question of the atrium design and costs. BSP had to build, finish, and equip the atrium entirely out of its pocket, while Hahn was responsible for a portion of Whiz Bang costs above a certain threshold. If the Whiz Bang costs threatened to get out of hand, then, it would be in Hahn's interests to try to hide some of the work in the overall atrium budget. That is what Bruce suspected was going on. The previous spring, after Hahn rejected Jerde's plans for the two food-court floors, Richard Orne had taken his drawings back to California in a huff and brooded over them for several months. What emerged was a much superior design, but also a much more costly one. The "American Diner" level now was a neon gallery, with bright, highly reflective surfaces and huge, emblematic signs identifying what was for sale behind the counters. The upstairs "Cosmopolitan" level had a wall of edge-lit glass separating the seating areas from the atrium walkway, creating a slightly more formal atmosphere; it was quieter, with more light-absorbing surfaces and pinspots focused on the tables. When Luk Sun saw the specification for edge-lit glass his whole life passed before his eyes. He examined a ceiling plan and discovered that Orne wanted to put recessed lighting fixtures in a metal ceiling. This meant paying electricians to cut holes in the ceiling panels, an extravagance on the order of having a plastic surgeon cut your fingernails.

But what was Eichner's recourse? The agreement between Hahn and Eichner called for BSP to provide furnishings, signs, and graphics "reasonably required for a project of this kind." Was a five-by-six-foot neon sign representing a baked potato with chili, cheddar, and sour cream toppings blinking off and on in a fifteen-second cycle "reasonably required"? No one could say for sure, because no one had ever built "a project of this kind" before.

Bruce knew that in the end he couldn't refuse to build what Hahn wanted, if he hoped to keep them in the project at all. That, though, didn't stop him from screaming about the money. Luk Sun approached the task of cutting Jerde's design with the weary resignation of a cop who sees the same miscreants go free again and again. Edge-lit glass became glass block, stone floors became tile, a whole set of revolving doors on Broadway disappeared between one set of plans and the next, which saved something like $100,000, although Al Corti caught the change and insisted they be put back. Functionally, the purpose of revolving doors is climate control. They act as an airlock between the cold (or hot) street and the temperate space within. Semiotically, they signify "class" and "exclusivity," perhaps because they let in only one person at a time. Corti liked that idea.

"Look," he said, "on the doors, the doors aren't there. They were there when we saw the plans last, and now they're not, and nobody asked us. Has anyone approved this?"

"Yes, Jerde did," Luk Sun said briskly. "And they concluded that if you want the free flow of people in and out you'd be better off without revolving doors. People would be backing up onto the street to get in. Jerde would have liked no doors at all."

"Why does every retailer in New York have revolving doors?" Corti shot back.

"Because they don't want to heat the whole street every time somebody goes in or out."

"Fine, I'm with you on that, give me back my doors."

"All right," said Luk Sun with a heavy sigh; "just remember it was *your architect* who didn't want them there." He shook his head in dismay at the thought of a developer who would ignore the advice of his own architect. What was the world coming to?

All of this, though, was just a preliminary to the real contest, which would be over the Whiz Bang. Bruce wanted the Whiz Bang to come in at a reasonable price, but most of all, he didn't want to be in the position of guaranteeing either its cost or its completion. His nightmare was that the atrium might be finished, rented up, ready to open—and left in suspended animation for six months because some $20 million company in California didn't deliver an electronic part the size of a nickel. In such an eventuality, it was Hahn's position that their rent did not commence until the Whiz Bang was operational down to the last pixel, and Bruce's position that he couldn't allow a $350 million project to be held hostage to something that had never been built in the world before.

"We cannot have an interruption of rent based on inability to complete the Whiz Bang," Bruce said heatedly. "I can't guarantee Sony. I can guarantee plumbing. There's a whole phone book full of plumbers to go to. But what am I gonna do if the computer doesn't work, if the monitors don't get here on time? Stand on the dock in Tokyo and look for the boxes?"

Vernon: "I don't think we can go to a tenant and say, 'You'll have this someday, maybe, by the grace of God, maybe next year …' We can do that, but they'll want to reduce their rent to us, and you don't want that … or, you do want that, but you don't want us to reduce our rent check to you.

"That's the philosophic difference we've always had. You see the Whiz Bang as an added attraction; to us it's integral to the project. We might even choose to pay you rent for six months and not open until the D-Day for the Whiz Bang."

Bruce: "Look, it all comes down to rent."

Vernon: "No, it doesn't. If you came to us and said, 'We'll finish the Whiz Bang in eighteen months, and you don't have to pay rent until then,' I don't think that would be acceptable to us. Because we can't do business with our tenants that way. It's like saying to your office tenants, 'Move in now, there's no air-conditioning, but you can open the windows.'"

Even while this was going on, preparations were under way for the grand press conference to introduce Hahn, and the project, to the world's biggest media (and consumer) market. Hahn had finally settled on a name, after considering a list of no fewer than 111 choices, contained in a memo from Jack Illies to Bill Tung in the summer of 1988. Not all of these were serious contenders. "Apple Hall" and "Gotham Circle" had a flea-market quality that said "Rents in the low $30s." "Worldgate" sounded like "Watergate," and "Ground Zero" had even less happy connotations: Times Square was the usual reference point for the damage-radius assessments of a nuclear bomb dropped on New York City, but why would you want to remind anyone of that in a shopping center? "Metropole" was actually the name of a well-known go-go bar a couple of blocks away. Only a provincial would suggest "Fun City," which had become a term of instant derision after it was first used by former Mayor John Lindsay. In the end they settled on two names: the project was designated "Metropolis Times Square," but the logo was designed around the initials "NY" (for New York), an "X" (the mathematical symbol for multiplication, or "times"), and a square, or "square": NYX□.

"Cute," sniffed Luk Sun when he saw it. "I wonder how many baked potatoes it will sell."

The unveiling of Metropolis Times Square took place at a press breakfast on the sixteenth floor of One Times Square. Ferren, who dressed up for the occasion in an electric-blue shirt and a mauve tie, talked about the Whiz Bang, and John Gilchrist of Hahn described the retail environment he wanted to see: "It's not Gucci-Pucci," he told the *Times;* "It's also not fifteen different shops selling mugs that say 'I Love New York.'" Bruce was the pithiest. "We are a city in which a waterfall is considered exciting," he said. "The rest of the country has gone well past that, and now we're going to catch up."

30

The decision to have Edward S. Gordon represent the building, although it had been made in the spring of 1988, was finally ratified with a contract in the fall—pretty quick work by our standards, Tung thought—and one morning at the end of September Turchin came with a small battalion of consultants for a breakfast meeting to discuss his strategy for "positioning" the building. Mitchell sat at the far end of the conference table, leaning back to display his aloofness from such effete pursuits.

"You ever notice, you almost never see a broker with facial hair?" he muttered. "That's because they're afraid of offending a client. But that still doesn't explain why they have to wear those off-the-rack suits and pale blue shirts every day."

Turchin in fact was wearing a tie with a de Kooningesque splash of color on a chocolate-brown background. Bruce noticed it the instant he walked into the conference room.

"Nice tie, Marty," Bruce said.

"You like it?" Marty exclaimed. "I'll give it to you at cost. Or maybe I'll just leave it here with your secretary for the next time I'm here. I've got a different one in my briefcase for the rest of the day."

"I'd like to talk about how we position the building," Turchin began.

"In terms of location, we represent the southernmost building that faces onto Times Square. The others are thought of more as West Side buildings. We all know there is going to be a transformation of the Times Square area, and we have to see what we can do to push that along, so it's not a significant liability to us."

"You didn't say anything about this stuff last week," Bruce interjected.

"Last week the contract wasn't signed."

Turchin paused for a sip of coffee. A woman sitting to his left tapped his sleeve and whispered something to him.

"What's that?" he exclaimed loudly. "Oh, you want a BAGEL? I'll get you a BAGEL."

The woman blushed deeply.

"What kind of a BAGEL do you want?" Turchin bellowed.

"Why do you shout?" Bruce asked, half-amused, half-appalled.

Turchin turned to him. "Because she whispered," he said simply.

"She whispered to the wrong guy," Tung muttered.

Turchin called on his marketing communications consultant to discuss how to turn the spotlight of publicity on the corner of Broadway and 45th Street. This was the voice of a woman named Jessica, who addressed the group on a speaker phone. She described a contest for real estate brokers. Her company would mail out pictures of ten famous spires, including the Broadway State Building mast, and award a week in Paris (subsequently scaled back to four days at a VMS-owned resort in Boca Raton) to the person who identified them all. This would not only get the brokers' attention, it would position the building in the best possible company: with Chartres and the Empire State Building.

"We're working on positioning publicity," she added. "We'd like to get Paul Goldberger to write something nice about the building. We'll get David Childs to take around some of the writers from the magazines. It says here in my notes, 'socially acceptable architect.' That's good."

"Now," Turchin said, "we've got to deal with question of the address. It is clear a Broadway address does not work for the office building, because the entrance is nowhere near Broadway, and we do not want people wandering into the atrium looking for us. We can use a side-street address. The one I'd like to have is 145 West 45th Street, but I don't think we can get it because we're farther west than the Lyceum and the Lyceum is 149. We can have anything from 151 to 177, and of those I think the best is 175, but it's not exactly as catchy as, say, 666 Fifth Avenue. The other approach is a name address: square, plaza, center, place. This is not the same as the name of the building. That you do after you have your lead tenant in place, if he makes hair tonic and he wants to call it the Brylcreem Building and he's willing to pay you enough for it and you're not worried about getting Vitalis as a tenant, you put the sign up over the door. Or if he doesn't care, you call it anything you want. But we still need an address. We've been struggling with this for a month. Jessica has some thoughts for us."

"The choice must convey an upscale quality, a classy image," she began. "One approach would be to try to create an identity for Eichner Properties with the name 'Broadway Spire.' We also liked the idea of 'Lyceum Place,' tying it in with the Lyceum, which is an elegant and unique identification for your building. One approach we rejected was 'center,' because it seems to have a downscale, shopping-center connotation."

Turchin guffawed. "Don't let the Rockefellers hear you say that!"

Helene Saren produced a list of five suggestions:

Broadway Center
Broadway Plaza
Broadway Times Plaza
Broadway Spire Plaza
Century Place

Three of these names had "plaza" in them, and even by the elastic standards of modern marketing that was a potential problem, because the building didn't have a plaza.

"Broadway Plaza reminds me of a vaudeville theater," Jessica mused. "If you use Broadway at all, you want to elevate it with Tower, or Spire, or something, not something pedestrian like 'Plaza.'

"Century Place has some elegance. Century Center ... no. Century Tower. It reminds you of Century City, which is *the* prestigious office address in Los Angeles. It evokes the Century Club, which is not that far away.

"The Century Club is classy. Free-associate with it for a while. It says Old World, very prestigious, corporate ... I had my first date with Claus von Bülow there. Maybe you could work out a deal with the Century Club, give your CEO tenants memberships there. It's also got a futuristic quality. It says the next century."

A bemused silence greeted this offering.

"Something with Empire?"

Helene pointed out that the Empire State Building would seem to have foreclosed that name for all time.

"Well, let's get back to basics. What exactly do we want to accomplish with this name?"

"We want," Helene said slowly, "to attract people who would really rather be on Park Avenue."

"I've got it!" Leslie Eichner said with a bright smile. "Park Avenue Tower!"

"I kind of like Broadway Spire," Bruce said. "I think it has the built-in advantage of an association with this building. This damn building you can see all over the city."

"The problem is, it isn't an address," Marty objected. "You can't send a letter to a spire."

"Who is this a problem for?" Bruce demanded. "The Post Office?"

"No, they'll deliver mail anywhere. But people outside the city would feel uncomfortable sending letters to 'Broadway Spire.' What is it? Who am I talking to?"

"I think your argument is specious," Bruce said. "You're telling me someone can't send a letter to Broadway Spire Plaza?"

"Aha!" Saren said. "Broadway Spire *Plaza.* You stuck something on there at the end."

"So you're telling me it's just the missing word on the end?"

"Yes."

"You call it One Banana Cake Plaza, how's that gonna help people find it?"

"Take One Astor Plaza," Marty urged.

"Sure. That's the stupidest name I ever heard. The first time I had to go there I had to ask three secretaries where it is."

"Doesn't matter," Turchin said airily. "The thing is, it sounds like a place on the map."

"So," said Bruce, "should we call it 'Broadway Spire Plaza'?"

Well, no. The one name that got around everyone's objections was also the one that everyone agreed was the weakest, because of its tortured length, and the mixed-metaphor quality of "spire" and "plaza," and the fact that *the building didn't have a plaza.*

They argued about it some more, until Bruce finally said in exasperation, "Okay, Marty, tell me what you want."

"Broadway Plaza," Turchin shot back.

"Marty," Luk Sun said, "*there is no plaza.*"

"Broadway Place," Turchin said.

"Broadway Place? Just that?"

"One Broadway Place."

"Okay, Marty, we're gonna call the building One Broadway Place," Bruce said. "I assume this eliminates the last possible objection anyone could have to leasing this building, and I'll look forward to three deals on my desk next Tuesday for me to choose from. Thanks."

"Don't mention it," Turchin said blithely.

The world at large was introduced to this name just a few weeks later, thanks to the unexpected intervention of Mikhail Gorbachev. Howard noticed that the Soviet president's route through the city would take him right past Broadway and 45th Street, and he got the idea of hanging a welcome sign from the building's skeleton. He commissioned a banner twenty feet by thirty, with American and Soviet flags, and a big legend that read:

"Workers and Owners of One Broadway Place Welcome Gorbachev and Wish the World Peace and Prosperity."

"I just want to know, is it fireproof?" Gary said when he heard of this plan. "Because we've got a lot of cutting torches on this job."

"Don't forget, the plumbers on this job are all Jewish," Sal added.

For his part, Luk Sun thought it was a ridiculous waste of money. Howard, more sophisticated in the ways and uses of publicity, couldn't believe his own friends and colleagues could be so cheeseparing. He bet Luk Sun $1,000 that the banner would be on the front page of the *Times* the next day.

The *Times* did indeed run a picture of the sign, but only as part of a story that started on page one. The picture itself appeared on page nineteen, so both Howard and Luk Sun claimed moral victories in their bet, and refused to pay.

On the day of Gorbachev's visit, the ironworkers were erecting the columns in two-floor sections for the eighth and ninth floors. "Now the building's gonna fly," Sal said. "By March we'll be in the sky. We spent a year digging a hole and now, just watch, the thing will go up, poof." Between six and the high setback at thirty-two, the floors were "typical," allowing for some minor differences where the low-rise elevator bank ended at twenty. Erecting the same beams in the same sequence week after week, the men developed a rhythm that sped the job along. The rat's nest of bracing in the atrium and the fourth-floor mechanical room were behind them. For several weeks, the whole front of the building had been sagging by nearly two inches, because it couldn't be bolted up tight. It couldn't be bolted up because a gusset plate in one of the fourth-floor trusses didn't line up with the diagonal to which it was supposed to mate. When Bill Cassidy, the south crane operator, had tried to lift the diagonal into place it had lain crazily against the plate like a book too large to fit on its shelf. The mistake had been made at Lehigh, where the plate had been welded to the beam approximately four degrees out of line. According to the story Scott Lewis heard, the fabricator knew he had made a mistake as soon as he was done, and he left a note on the piece explaining the problem and then went on vacation, but someone lost the note and the piece got shipped by mistake and erected.

The result was to screw up the whole front of the building, because none of the pieces connected to the truss could be tightened until the diagonal could be made to fit. A nearby column was two feet out of plumb and had to be bashed back into place with about thirty blows of the headache ball. A number of already-completed connections had to be disassembled, and as the building code forbade the re-use of the bolts, several hundred eight-inch-long, high-strength, inch-and-a-quarter bolts had to be thrown out at a cost of several thousand dollars. Not to speak of the cost of fabricating a new plate and field-welding it onto the truss, and the additional expenses resulting from the whole job schedule thrown off by two weeks or more. It was Sal's job to keep track of the costs as they mounted into the tens and hundreds of thousands of dollars, so that Lehigh could eventually be made to pay for its error. It was in fact the last one the company would make; 1540 Broadway was the last building fabricated in Lehigh's plant, before the company closed it down forever.

By the last week of December 1540 Broadway was ten floors up, an unsettlingly incomplete object, charged with a muscular, soaring verticality intended to carry it 600 feet into the air, but bizarrely broken off at a quarter of its destined height. The structure gradually dematerialized from bottom to top, as the various operations followed one another skyward in sequence: fireproofing a couple of floors behind the concrete slab, which in turn trailed the metal deck, which followed two stories behind the steel. Most of the upper floors were wrapped in bright orange plastic mesh intended to keep miscellaneous hardware from taking flight off the building. Of the surrounding buildings, Zeckendorf's Crowne Plaza was topped out, and the Hotel Macklowe on 44th Street was up in the thirties. David Solomon's big building at 1585 Broadway was up around twenty stories and the smaller one, 750 Seventh Avenue, around ten. Americas Tower, the other Turner job on Sixth Avenue and

45th Street, was neck-and-neck with Broadway State. For the first time, it was possible to get a hint of the new topography of Times Square. Con Howe, the executive director of the City Planning Department, said he was satisfied. "The deep setback seems to do what we wanted," he observed. "There is enough bulk at the bottom to hold the street line and the towers are set far enough back to give light and air."

Sal hosted a Christmas party at the field office. The menu was the same one for all celebratory occasions in the field: sausage and peppers; fried lumps of breading beneath which the outline of a chicken leg could be dimly apprehended; sheets of lasagna as tough as encyclopedia covers, glued together with white blobs of cheese. Among the guests it was plainly considered a slur on Turner's hospitality to take a plate that could be carried with just one hand.

"Whatsamatter, Vinny," one burly electrician called to another, "your wife don't feed you? I know guys going to the electric chair, didn't eat that much."

"You know guys that went to the electric chair?"

"A few. One or two of them, I woulda wired it myself."

"Yeah," said his friend. "I wish they'd bring it back. That's one switch I'd throw for free."

By midwinter, 400 men (and a handful of women) came to work at 1540 Broadway every day. The task of coordinating all their activities fell on Ellis and his assistants. Just moving them and their gear around the building every day was a major undertaking. The two cranes were dedicated to hoisting structural steel and deck; all other materials had to travel on a hoist which ran in a web of scaffolding up the north side of the tower. The workmen reached their floors on two adjacent personnel hoists that ran outside the tower on the south side, opening onto landings of thick wooden planks. By a quirk of the New York City labor contracts, the men who ran these hoists were among the best-compensated workers in all industrial America. They had to be paid whenever anyone was working in the building, thereby building up monumental overtime credits. On big jobs like this it was not unusual for a hoist operator to make $100,000 in a year. The materials hoist was scheduled more than two weeks in advance, and the right to use it was so jealously guarded that Ellis more than once had to intervene to keep disputes over it from boiling over into fistfights.

All of this was in addition to two hoists that serviced just the atrium; a light derrick for lifting curtain-wall panels, and a separate hoist just for concrete. This was a bucket, holding about a cubic yard, that ran up the south side of the building, in a shaft facing the personnel hoists. When a floor was scheduled to be poured, a hopper would be set up on the landing. The hoist bucket would be filled from a truck, then run up to the floor and its contents dumped into the hopper. From the hopper, in turn, small, self-propelled carts called concrete buggies would be filled; and these, crossing the corrugated deck on tracks of wooden planks, would bring the concrete to the men who would actually apply it to the deck with shovels.

On January 13, a Friday, the hopper had just been filled on the sixth floor when the empty concrete hoist, descending, stuck on something in its shaft. The engineer who controlled it from a shed on the ground noticed slack in the cable and sent two men to investigate. The men couldn't see anything in the way, so they called to the engineer to raise the hoist and let it drop again. Descending, it caught on something at the sixth-floor level and partially collapsed the landing where the men were standing, sending them tumbling to the floor below. The hopper, holding a cubic yard of concrete, sagged as the landing collapsed under it. But it did not fall, because it was secured by brackets to the scaffolding. If it had fallen, it would have fallen on the men, and kept going all the way to the ground.

The men, shaken up but not badly hurt, were quickly helped to safety. Within minutes, it seemed to John, the street was swarming with ambulance crews, police, firemen, building inspectors, and supervisors up to the level of the commissioner himself, plus reporters from every television station between Philadelphia and New Haven. The call had gone out on the police radio as a collapsed floor in a building under construction, which made it sound a lot more dramatic than what had actually occurred. The resulting traffic jam was of sufficient magnitude to call out the traffic helicopters, which in turn brought more officials to the scene.

One of those who heard about it on his car radio was an inspector from OSHA. He arrived late in the afternoon, when the site was beginning to empty out, and went with Ellis to look at the scene of the disaster. There was little to see except a few brackets that had twisted and given way under the platform. The inspector shook his head.

"I don't understand why they didn't go right into the hole," he said of the two men.

"Because it wasn't their time," Ellis said solemnly.

Most of the men on the Broadway State job worked hard, most of them were honest, but some of them weren't, and there wasn't much that anyone could do about it. Eichner certainly had no leverage over them, nor did Turner, nor did even their nominal employers; they owed their livelihoods and loyalty to the union, and the union took care of them whether they were good at their job or not. They inscribed racist remarks with sticks in the concrete, and covered drywall with graffiti rendered in heavy black marker ink. Once the toilets were in place in the second subcellar every accessible surface was quickly overscrawled. "Flush twice," someone wrote, "it's a long way to Turner's office." "The unemployed carpenters of 608 are at home fucking your wife." "Employees must wash there hands, because there's no toilet paper." On this last, a workman of superior education had felt compelled to issue a correction; he had crossed out the first "there" and wrote triumphantly, "It's THIER, you idiot!"

Around noon one day in early spring, a workman having his lunch on the street began berating a passerby who happened to be gay. He spat on the passerby and called him names, and when the man got back to his office he called Turner's head office to complain. Since he happened to be an official of the Urban Development Corporation, a state agency that oversees billions of dollars in construction, he got an unusually sympathetic hearing. A call went out to Ellis.

"I'm in total sympathy with him," Ellis said the next day, "the guy's conduct was disgraceful, but what am I supposed to do about it? Even assuming he was from this job, and he could have been from either of two others on the block, how can I be responsible for 400 men during their lunch hour? What if one of these guys goes home and beats up his wife—am I going to have to be responsible for that, too?"

At nine-fifteen one sunny, cool morning in the spring of 1989, a gang of eight workmen carried a metallic panel approximately five feet by twenty out to the muddy yard on the Broadway side of the building. This was a component of what was generically known as "storefront," the gun-metal-gray curtain wall for the retail atrium. With much shouting and heaving they stood it up on a makeshift cradle, consisting of a couple of scraps of wood padded with fiberglass insulation. They stood there for about ten minutes, holding it. Gradually they began to drift away until only two men were left. The two men stood on the same side of the panel, holding it up with gloved hands, or leaning their shoulders against it, chatting. At around nine-thirty a third man appeared with a canvas sling that he hooked around the panel. One of the first two walked off to talk to a crew of men unloading curtain-wall panels from a truck; that is, they had just sent a pallet loaded with panels up on the curtain-wall hook and were standing around drinking coffee. One of the men pointed to several places where the storefront already in place had been dented by curtain-wall panels as they ascended, and laughed. Bobby Sasso came out to watch them from the bridge. He had on a magnificent white satin jacket, with "Teamsters" embroidered across the back in red and gold, an American flag, a Statue of Liberty, and a few other things. The man went back to help his friend hold up the panel again. At nine-fifty-five he called up to a workman manning a winch on the roof of the setback and told him to lower the hook. Something incomprehensible crackled back on his radio. Ten minutes later the hook came down and the two men attached it to the canvas sling and it rose a few inches off its cradle.

"Hold on, Tommy!" the man bawled into his radio. "We're gonna put a tag line on it." After another few minutes a man appeared with two pairs of locking pliers and a coil of rope. The pliers were clamped onto tabs on the back of the panel, rope threaded through them and knotted, and the panel began to rise again. At ten-twenty it was in place, level with the spandrel beam it was intended to cover, and men inside the building were affixing nuts to the bolts that held it in place. By ten-thirty they were finished. A good morning's work, and everyone got paid.

Graffito inside the hoist: "Even fish know they won't get caught if they keep their mouths shut."

31

In theory, with the closing of the construction loan in January 1988 the financing of the building was complete, at least until the time came to replace Citibank with a permanent mortgage lender. Mechanisms were in place for all the routine handling of requisitions and interest tranches, a budget had been approved and a pro-forma showed with mathematical certainty how everyone concerned was going to make a lot of money. As long as nothing changed, Bruce just had to sit back and build the building.

Of course, things had started changing even before the loan had closed. Bruce had been bargaining with Hahn right up until the last minute, and the ultimate cost of that deal was still being calculated, but it would only go up. In anticipation of these problems, he had also set in motion a parallel process of finding another equity partner. Calls had gone out to various brokers, and as word filtered out to the street Henry got a call from a Japanese-American broker who represented Hazama-Gumi Ltd. This was one of the largest construction companies in Japan, a builder of office buildings, hotels, industrial plants, roads, airports, and tunnels all over the world. This qualified them for an introductory course in building an office building in New York City. There ensued months of some of the most arduous negotiations Bruce and Henry had ever entered into. Every point that Hazama's New York representatives accepted had to be translated into Japanese and checked with Tokyo. Tokyo would often respond with demands so extreme or bizarre that, as Henry characteristically put it, "It makes you wonder if we're speaking the same language. What earthly good does it do for them to make a proposal that they know in advance is completely and totally unacceptable to us?"

Eventually they had settled on a contribution from Hazama consisting of letters of credit that in three stages would amount to $20 million. BSP would use the l.c.'s as collateral for a bank loan to provide additional cash for the project. In exchange, Hazama became a limited partner, with a 5 percent equity share, and it earned the right to call itself the "prime contractor." This meant that all the direct disbursements for construction would actually pass through Hazama's hands en route to Turner. Hazama was to receive as part of its share of the profits a fee of several million dollars for its role in passing the money along. This elaborate arrangement enabled them to list the Broadway project in their annual report as part of their construction work in progress, which made them look like an even bigger company than they already were. But when Henry, joking, suggested that Hazama might actually help build the building, they reacted with shock.

"Oh, no, no. Symbolic, symbolic," they replied.

"In that case," Henry responded, "maybe we pay you symbolic money also."

But the deal also had symbolic value to Bruce. He knew that his fate lay in large part in the hands of the Japanese banks whom Citibank had lined up as co-lenders, and it made him nervous that he had no leverage over them. Now, though, he had a Japanese partner himself, and not just any Japanese partner but one of the biggest and best-known construction companies in Japan. He wasn't sure just how he was going to benefit from that relationship, but he felt in his bones that it might come in handy one day.

And as far as Hazama went, the 5 percent stake was just the first bite of what could amount to as much as 40 percent of the building, if the letters of credit were actually drawn—that is, if BSP, in borrowing against them, either failed to keep up with the interest or couldn't repay the principal when they expired in January 1993. In that case the lending bank would cash the l.c.'s, and for every million dollars Hazama actually had to put up, its equity interest went up by 1 or 2 percent.

But even the $20 million soon began to seem inadequate. In the late fall of 1988, Bruce ordered a complete review of the Broadway State budget, which was continuing to show alarming variations from the version that had been presented to the bank a year earlier. Alarming, that is, to VMS, which sent two officials out to New York at the end of November to find out why the total development cost had increased by approximately $50 million, to around $350 million. Hard costs accounted for about half the increase. Most of this was attributable to the Hahn deal. On the office building, they had also had bad luck on some of the buys. Steel, which had been estimated at $1,400 a ton, actually was bought at $1,800. There wasn't anything you could do about it; that was what it cost. The largest item was the work letter, the money that had to be set aside for improvements to the office space (or as a straightforward cash payment) to induce a tenant to move in. This had been figured at about twenty dollars a square foot, or $17 million over the whole office building, but Turchin was advising Bruce that the market would probably call for double that or more. This was partly just the result of a more competitive market, but it also reflected a growing preference on the part of tenants to get more money up front even at the cost of a higher rent later on. Many of the potential tenants for the Broadway State Building were long-established law firms. These tended to be dominated by partners near retirement age. Naturally, they liked the idea of getting money now and didn't much care what the rent would be in 1998. From the landlord's point of view, Turchin pointed out, it was just moving money around from one pocket to another. Higher rents got capitalized into a bigger permanent mortgage, so in the end you'd come out about the same. It did, though, make it a little harder to *reach* the end. Right now, between Bruce and the end loomed a gap of another $50 million or more over the next two years.

This might have been alarming to Citibank, too, except that they didn't know about it. That is, they didn't know officially. Around the beginning of 1989, Bruce had lunch with a Citibank vice president and alerted him to the possibility that he might need to increase the loan. The man started to choke on his roll. "How much?" he demanded. "I don't know yet," Bruce responded. "I know I'm only going to get one bite of the apple, so let me get the hard numbers and I'll have something for you on paper by spring." Bruce believed you should never come to a lender with problems unless you already had figured out the solutions. By doing the bank's thinking for them, he hoped to harness one of the most potent forces in the American economy, the power of bureaucratic inertia.

Berini, at VMS, had a different strategy in mind: he wanted to look for another equity investor in the building. Eichner and VMS had kept virtually all the equity to themselves, except for the 5 percent they had traded off to Hazama. This served a larger purpose than mere greed; it gave them the flexibility to make a deal for more money should it be necessary. Berini pressed Bruce to bring in a major real estate broker, the firm of Jones Lang Wootton, to try to raise an additional $65 million, in exchange for 49 percent of the equity in the project. JLW drew up a very handsome hard-bound, gold-stamped prospectus, and circulated copies to a number of potential investors. Unfortunately, against Bruce's explicit instructions, they showed it to some Japanese banks, with the result that word quickly got back to the Japanese participants in the loan. Bruce inferred, from Citibank's yawp of outrage, that the Japanese, who don't like surprises, found this a most unpleasant one. So Citibank knew unofficially from at least two sources that the building was over budget, but they didn't do anything about it, because they still didn't officially know, and they probably also hoped that Bruce would solve the problem on his own.

The JLW exercise in the end was a qualified failure. JLW didn't raise any money for the building, but they offered Berini a terrific job in their West Coast office. At this time VMS, which was to be an early casualty of the real estate recession, was just months away from a catastrophic public humiliation, in which several of its top officers lost their jobs. Berini got out in good order and time, leaving his affairs in New York in the hands of a former EAB banker named Maria Cheng. Eichner then began to pursue an increase in the loan. In the spring of 1989 BSP requested an additional $75 million, which together with the $20 million raised from Hazama brought the budget to $395 million. This covered the increases in hard costs and tenant improvements, plus a bigger interest reserve to reflect the fact that the building was not leasing up as quickly as had been hoped. In fact, it wasn't leasing at all.

Perhaps this should not have been surprising. Although stock prices recovered fairly quickly after the October 1987 crash, the damage to the financial industry was severe and long-lasting. The forces that would lead in 1990 to the collapse of Drexel Burnham Lambert were already in motion. In the two years following the market crash, Wall Street lost 15,000 jobs, nearly 10 percent of its work force. Employment in banking declined by around 10,000. Advertising, which went into one of its periodic merger frenzies around this time, declined slightly as well. Of the big glamour industries that had fueled New York's expansion through the

1980s, only lawyers, with their uncanny ability to make money off everyone else's misfortunes, seemed immune to recession. Overall job growth, which had been running at nearly 60,000 annually from 1983 to 1987, had turned essentially flat.

Meanwhile, though, the sorcerer's-apprentice factor was at work in real estate; the spigot of new development that had been opened in the mid-eighties couldn't be turned off in midstream. "A Skyscraper-High Office Space Surplus," the *Times* wrote; midtown office vacancy rates at the end of 1988 were the highest in a decade—10 to 12 percent, depending on which buildings you counted—and over the next year would increase further still, to 15 percent. And as the *Times* pointed out, this didn't take into account several million square feet of office space expected to open in 1990. Just on the West Side, there was Americas Tower on Sixth Avenue and 45th Street, with nearly a million square feet; two Solomon Equities projects in Times Square (1585 Broadway and 750 Seventh Avenue) totaling about 1.8 million square feet; and 1540 Broadway, with 850,000 square feet. For all these buildings, as of 1989 exactly one office lease had been signed, for Proskauer, Rose, Goetz & Mendelsohn—the law firm Eichner had courted unsuccesfully more than a year earlier. Proskauer had taken around 300,000 feet in 1585 Broadway—leaving roughly 900,000 feet vacant in that building alone.

But Turchin insisted that was the wrong way to look at the market. Yes, the vacancy rate was high, but there were a number of companies with leases expiring in the near future who were looking for additional space, cheaper space, better space, or just different space. Others, with a few years left to run on their leases, were seeking to consolidate offices from different locations, or were trying to escape 1970s-era buildings with asbestos insulation, which made virtually any remodeling prohibitively expensive. All you needed was to land one of them for half a million square feet, and your problems would be well on the way to being solved.

Turchin had a list of these companies. All brokers had such a list, and at least some of the names on it were common knowledge even in the newspapers, but Turchin insisted that his list was so special it could never be let out of his possession. Every other week now there were leasing meetings at Bruce's office, at which Turchin would pull his list from his inside jacket pocket and run down the holy roster of names. They included some well-known law firms (Dewey, Ballantine; Coudert Brothers); industrial firms (ITT, Xerox); stockbrokers (Donaldson,

Lufkin & Jenrette); advertising agencies (N.W. Ayer); and media companies (Rupert Murdoch's News America Corp., Condé Nast). The only category he excluded was foreign banks, for whom a New York office was a matter of national honor, cost no object; they would pay fifty dollars a square foot to be in the hottest building on Park Avenue. Each company on Turchin's list had its unique personalities, needs, and problems, which Turchin could discuss in intimate detail. All of them were going to do something eventually, but each for the moment resided in an agonizing state of indecision that could be overcome only with infinite patience and finesse.

And that was okay, Turchin went on. You didn't want to make the first deal, or even necessarily the second or third, because those would be made by the landlords driven hardest by desperation; you wanted to be there when the *tenants* started getting desperate. Bruce endorsed this strategy, at least at the outset. "We are playing a game of musical chairs," he told a reporter for the *Times*. "Just watch what happens after the first two or three big deals are announced."

On the building itself, the first few office floors had been closed in with curtain wall by the spring, and in late May Turner moved its field headquarters from the trailer in the street to the sixth floor. Crude drywall partitions had been thrown up, and fixtures hung on chains from the bare deck above. At the same time, workmen were rushing to finish a much more elaborate suite of offices on the floor above, to be the setting for a series of breakfasts at which Turchin would introduce the building to the brokerage community of New York. The marketing suite took up a few thousand square feet of the choicest space in and around the prow; it was decorated in the most impeccably bland Porto-Corp style of gray and beige. A magnificent model of the building sat in a glass box on a white pedestal in the office; it had been built by hand from SOM's drawings at a cost of $84,000.

At eight-fifteen, on the morning of the first broker breakfast, a jut-jawed, wavy-haired, delicious-smelling man in a light gray suit, with a polka-dot handkerchief poking jauntily from his jacket pocket, picked his way through the mud and debris surrounding the 45th Street entrance, where he found William Tung's secretary in a pretty blue dress.

"Where is the leasing breakfast?" he asked commandingly, and she directed him to the hoist, its wooden doors covered with graphic and appreciative tributes to the pleasures of anal sex.

"*Oy, gevalt,*" he muttered under his breath.

He got on the hoist with a gaggle of ironworkers and looked straight ahead. One of them gave him a hard stare for a moment, and then asked coolly, "You renting this building?"

"Yes!" he said brightly. "How many floors would you like?"

The man seemed to consider this question for a moment. "Aaah, forget it," he said finally. "I'm better off in Jersey." The hoist shuttered to a halt on seven, and the broker walked out, chin up, whistling, past a graffito that read:

> Zebbo-Rapture Say:
> If Life were a thing
> That Money could buy
> Surely the Rich would live
> And the Poor would die.
> So Fuck Them.

It was hot in the suite—Turner hadn't gotten the portable air-conditioning unit to work yet—but the forty men and women sat through Turchin's speech as if they were hearing about relativity from the lips of Einstein. Turchin was a born salesman. As soon as he began to speak it was apparent that the time he had spent criticizing SOM's design hadn't been just an arrogant display of one-upsmanship, but a form of psychological preparation for the task ahead, because it was precisely the things that he had criticized the most that he now singled out as the finest and most desirable features of the building: the elegant and imaginative architecture, the magnificent views from the prow, the convenience of a shopping center right downstairs. Another Gordon broker, David Levinson, talked about "the trademarks of Eichner Properties, function, flexibility, image, and quality." Then Audrey took the floor to talk about verticality, about the two walls interpenetrating around the building, the little jewel box of a lobby. Bill Tung talked about the first-class building systems, with a heavy emphasis, per Turchin's instructions, on security; and Bruce gave a brief pep talk in which he promised that his company would be around to do business with for a long time, and that anyone who wanted to talk about a deal would find that he wasn't the sort of person who let dust accumulate on his phone messages.

Then the brokers donned clean white Turner hardhats and followed Scott out into the building. Turchin drew up a chair next to Audrey. "That was very good," he said briskly. "But I know you can do better. I want more sincerity from you. You designed this building. This is your baby.

"Now," he went on, "you don't refer to the entrance as being on a side street. We have avenues and streets. The entry is on a street. Not a side street, a street.

"Don't apologize for the lobby, that it's small. It was designed intentionally that way. It's a jewel box. Not a little jewel box. Don't call the materials 'precious.' Precious is what a guy buys for his wife. The people who will rent this building buy their suits at Paul Stuart, they're not looking for preciousness."

Audrey nodded her understanding. She was really a very bright young woman, eager to do right for her client. In a few months there would likely be a round of promotions at Skidmore, and she was, in many people's opinions, a leading candidate to become an associate partner. Sincerity. Street. Paul Stuart … Oh, shit, if her classmates from Yale could be here to hear this …

On his way out, Turchin passed the buffet table, laden with fruit, pastries, muffins, and the inevitable bagels and bagel accessories. He speared a slice of pale-green melon from a plate, then watched Mailman apply a thick coating of cream cheese to a bagel and top it off with several letter-sized sheets of smoked salmon.

"You're having lunch, too?" Turchin asked.

"No, I was watching you eat, and it made me hungry."

"I'm not even hungry," Turchin said ruefully. "I went to Arcadia last night …"

"That place! It's a shadow of its former self!"

"I had a bottle of Chambertin, would you believe only seventy-four dollars?"

"That's a good wine, I tasted it years ago."

Turchin sighed deeply. "I've got so much wine, I'll never drink it in my lifetime."

"I know. I stopped buying wine years ago. You run out of space to keep it."

"Oh, I've got plenty of space …"

"And it's expensive to keep. You have to recork it."

"Gee, that's a good point," Turchin said. "My Lafites are twenty-five years old now. The guy from Lafite was here last year, I should have had him do mine while he was here."

Mitch nodded his sympathy, cleaved off a third of his bagel with one bite, and chewed. Turchin spotted Bruce across the room and wandered off to talk business. He had a new client to discuss, a large dress manufacturer looking for several floors of office and showroom space.

"I don't know what kind of a statement it makes to have a fashion business in the building," Bruce said doubtfully.

"No problem," Turchin assured him. "You just have to come up with $100 a foot in tenant improvements to build their showroom space. But they're a very solid business. A very good business, better than real estate."

"Why do you say that?" Bruce asked.

"'Cause you can open on Saturdays for cash."

"A lot of things are better than real estate," Bruce said dolefully.

Over the next two months hundreds of brokers came; they noshed, told jokes to one another, and went away with brochures and fact sheets and information kits, but they didn't bring in any deals. A bottle of champagne stood in an ice bucket at the center of the table through every broker breakfast, presumably in case someone struck a deal right on the spot, but it was never opened. Turchin's air of arrogant superiority, which had served his client so well when 599 Lexington opened in a booming market, turned out to be somewhat less of an asset in the soft market of 1989. His attitude toward clients represented by other brokers seemed to be that they couldn't possibly be serious about wanting to move, or they would have hired him instead. This spirit pervaded the company. Once Helene Saren reported that a broker from a competing firm had called to tell her he was showing the building the next day, but he couldn't name the client.

"Who's the broker?" David Levinson asked.

She gave a name.

"Hah! No wonder! He probably couldn't read the name off the business card. Which he picked off the floor of the subway. He's probably talking to someone who isn't authorized to make the deal anyway. The *office manager.* He doesn't even know he's seeing the building, he's gonna take him to lunch and then shove him inside the lobby and up in an elevator. Call him back and tell him we'll handle it, if the tenant signs, we'll send him a check in six months."

But Turchin's list didn't produce a tenant, either. He had meetings, phone calls, exchanges of letters. The names moved up and down the list in accordance with whatever Turchin had heard last. Dewey, Ballantine had liked the building, but they had three years to run on their existing lease. Donaldson, Lufkin & Jenrette needed two trading floors, and the only floors in the building that were big enough were below the setback, in the atrium. Bruce wrestled with his conscience over whether he could kick Hahn overboard for a 500,000-square-foot office tenant. Meanwhile, just to make it a fair fight, he authorized Turner to get a price on filling in the atrium on the second and third floors. But Turchin didn't think DLJ was serious about leaving downtown.

"I have another idea for you," Turchin said. "You're gonna laugh when you hear this."

"Go ahead," Bruce said. "I haven't had a good laugh since I left government."

"Skidmore."

"I'm not laughing, I think you should call them. Don Smith, the management partner. Not Childs, he's the design guy."

"I know what they'll say," Turchin said.

"What?"

"The office layouts don't work for them."

After several months of this, Bruce got impatient, and told Turchin to stop playing hard to get, and bring him some deals to look at. They would bend over backwards to do their first deal, just to get a tenant in the door. "It's funny," he mused. "Compared to what was predicted two years ago, there are actually fewer buildings under way, and more tenants in the market. And yet everyone is running around saying disaster is at hand, man the lifeboats. There's been a gap of five months, and no deals have been made in Solomon's buildings or Americas Tower. And no deals in our building. So there's a group of fairly nervous developers and fairly nervous tenants."

"And fairly nervous banks," Henry added.

Citibank's response to the new budget Bruce presented in the spring was to refuse to fund a portion of BSP's next requisition—the portion, as it happened, representing what they considered excessive work on the retail atrium, which was precisely the part of the building Citibank had the most responsibility for, having insisted that Bruce make a deal with Hahn in the first place. This precipitated a long and acerbic exchange of letters between Tung and various bank officials, and phone calls (where the real work got done) between Bruce and various bank higher-up officials. A Citibank vice president named John Friel wrote to Bruce in July: "As you know we have discussed with each of the co-lenders your request for an additional $75 million in bank financing. We and the other co-lenders are unwilling to commit to any additional financing. This unwillingness arises in part as a result of a general reduction in confidence of the lenders in the management of this project." There followed a page-long list of questions about how the budget got so far out of whack, when it happened, and why wasn't Citibank told sooner. Bruce had Tung draft a reply, which listed all the meetings they had in which those very issues were discussed, pointed out that Citibank's consulting engineers had gone over the original budget and approved it, and mentioned the offering book from Jones Lang Wootton seeking additional investors, which showed a $350 million budget.

Tung to a vice president named Gregory Nuber: "Your statement that the project has experienced 'major deviation' and 'substantial changes' from the building contemplated by the original loan is incomprehensible to us."

Bruce to another vice president: "If you want to know where most of the money is going, that we have any control over, it's going into the Hahn deal, and I hate to keep repeating myself, but it was Citibank that made Hahn a condition of the loan in the first place."

Since Turner couldn't slow down the building of the building, Bruce had to make up the shortfall in each month's requisition. The money was borrowed against the Hazama letters of credit. But this didn't solve the bigger problem of a $75 million gap that Citibank alone could close—and didn't seem to want to.

Or maybe, in fact, they couldn't. The way the loan was structured, Citibank claimed it needed all its Japanese co-lenders to approve any increase, and the Japanese were not being sympathetic. More than that; they weren't even being communicative. Months went by; there were a series of meetings with the co-lenders in which every detail of the project was rehashed at length. About five meetings into this procedure, one of the participants asked for a clarification of the equity structure of the deal. Maria Cheng began explaining the $30 million letter of credit obtained by VMS, the $10 million loan from the VMS land trust. It took a few minutes, and several baffled questions, for it to sink in, but suddenly it dawned on the Japanese that Bruce and VMS had 95 percent of the building between them without putting up any of their own cash.

"They didn't understand it at all," Tung reported later. "Over there, when you talk about equity, it means you put up cash. I don't know why they never noticed this before, since it's in all the papers, but suddenly they were standing up and denouncing us as scoundrels and cheats. I have a feeling we're not going to have an easy time getting another $75 million out of them."

32

As the building went up, it kept revealing new facets, even to those who thought they knew it intimately. Walking downtown from Cityspire one morning, Scott Lewis crossed 46th Street, looked up at the prow, and was astonished to see shiny metal panels covering the eighth- and ninth-floor spandrels. "I said to myself, did we do that there? And I went and got out the plans and sure enough, there they were. You look at something on paper every day for a year, and you don't really realize what it will look like until it's built." Even Audrey could be surprised. On a crisp morning in early spring, with clouds blowing back and forth across the face of the sun, she walked out onto the low setback with Terry Bell and picked her way through the obstacle course of construction hardware to the parapet, where she could look up at the first few floors of curtain glass. As the sunlight faded in and out the glass panels obediently changed color all at once; the green vision glass, limpid and delicate one moment, the next was an opalescent greenish gray, while the blue windows would alternately brighten and dim, now standing out boldly against the darker spandrels, now fading together into a monolithic wall the color of a tropical twilight. Audrey stood gazing at it a long time. "Boy, look at that," she said at last.

"Is that what you imagined it would be like?" Terry asked.

"Absolutely," she lied. "Down to the last detail."

Around the same time, the architects, accompanied by Sal LaScala, made a field trip to inspect the elevator cabs, which were being built in Maspeth, Queens, an industrial neighborhood just across the East River from midtown Manhattan. The cabs were actually shipped as panels (front, back, sides, and roof) and assembled in the shaft, but the company had put one together for the SOM team to inspect. On the way over, Terry Bell told Audrey that Tung had called to make sure SOM understood that the purpose of the trip was to check the detailing and materials in relation to the specs, not to make any changes.

"Of course, now I *have* to change something," Audrey said.

"That's why they call us SOM," Duncan Reid added. "Spend Others' Money."

But it turned out Audrey was delighted with the elevator. "Great!" she exclaimed the instant she stepped inside the box of cool, milky, greenish glass and gleaming stainless steel. "Extraordinary. The hottest elevator cab I ever saw. You could go to the moon in this." She was even generous about the finish on the accent strips and panels, which had been changed back to the shiny Number Four finish from the more expensive Imperial she had sought. "We didn't lose anything with this finish," she said thoughtfully. "I almost like it better. In fact, I do like it better. Almost."

On closer inspection, she did have a few objections. She stood in the far corner of the cab and peered straight up. The lighting panels were suspended from the roof of the cab on threaded rods, which terminated in washers and nuts. SOM had uncharacteristically neglected to issue a specification for the washers and nuts, and the elevator company had used ordinary industrial hardware. She asked to substitute something fancier. She ran her fingers along the handrail in the back of the car, and realized that the undersides of the brackets holding the rail were unfinished. SOM had never specified a finish, because passengers would never see the bottoms of the brackets, only now it occurred to her that they would feel them. She asked for the surface to be polished.

Elevator cabs are an important but often overlooked aspect of office-building semiotics. No other feature is experienced so intimately by virtually everyone who comes into contact with the building. The cabs for 1540 Broadway were cool, sleek, and "corporate," in the classical sense of standing for the swift, efficient, mechanically precise creation of wealth. This was, however, by the mid-1980s a slightly outmoded paradigm. The quintessential business organization of the decade was not a corporation but a partnership, an exclusive fraternity of professionals, answerable to no stockholders and paying themselves money in quantities beyond the greed or imagination of the "corporate" soul. Architecturally this found its expression in a clubby, antiquarian excess that Audrey in particular found repulsive. In fact, a cab just like that was on display nearby, done up in the Executive Humidor style of sumptuous walnut paneling, heavy brass buttons, and muted indirect lighting from glass sconces. "That's what I'd like to be buried in," she said admiringly. "But I wouldn't want to have to ride in it every morning."

The building was by this time in full stride; the high setback had been reached and the small tower floors were now being erected at the rate of one every three or four days. Soon the topmost floor would be reached, a landmark known as "topping out."

The complexity of modern office-tower construction allows for a certain flexibility in when precisely to decree the building topped out. Can it be said to occur when the men begin erecting the highest floor? Or only when they finish the floor? Or, in the case of 1540 Broadway, was the point only reached when the topmost piece of steel would be erected, which would be the top of the mast, more than 600 feet above ground level? Sal, in his private race with the team building Americas Tower, thought that would be unfairly handicapping himself. So he decreed that the topping-out beam would be a roof purlin from the southeast corner of the top floor. This was the forty-first floor, as far as the architects and engineers went, and would house mechanical equipment serving the office floors below. The next floor down was therefore the fortieth, although the number on the corresponding elevator button actually said "44." This inflation in floor numbers for the sake of prestige, routine in new office buildings, was achieved by having no "thirteenth" floor, and designating the lowest office floor "eight," when it was actually the fifth level above ground. The justification was that the retail and mechanical floors below were all extra-high, and therefore the fifth floor was where the eighth floor otherwise would have been.

Sal scheduled the topping-out party for Friday, June 9. The Americas Tower team, getting wind of these plans, moved their topping-out party to Wednesday, the seventh. "But they still have two lifts to go on the building, so I'm counting it as a victory for the good guys," Sal said. "If I couldn'a beat them, I woulda quit on the spot." The date was marked by one in the seemingly endless series of storms that had plagued New York that spring. In the morning, the topping-out beam—

painted white so the men could sign it with marker pens—was laid out on chocks in the muddy yard on Broadway. Shortly after lunch, men began to gather in the gloom. Around two in the afternoon, a couple of ironworkers hooked chokers to the beam; someone tied a small potted evergreen to it and Jimbo stuck on "Elsie," a six-inch-high plastic cow. The cow is a sacred animal to ironworkers. As the end of a project approaches, they attempt to stretch out the last few weeks of work into an equal number of months of paychecks, a practice known as "milking." There were a lot of jokes about this, and all the ironworkers posed several times for pictures with Elsie, comically bulking their already impressive biceps. Sal considered this in very poor taste. "Get that goddam cow off my beam," he muttered.

Finally, John Gray of Turner spoke into a radio, and the engineer in the crane above lifted the beam a dozen or so feet off the ground, stretching out a huge American flag to its full length. There were more pictures, and then the beam ascended swiftly into the gray sky. As the flag cleared the low setback the wind caught it for a moment and sent it billowing out into the fog. There was a cheer, which died down quickly as the men headed into the atrium and lined up at buffet tables the length of a Union Pacific gondola. The food was industrially sized, with meatballs the diameter of tennis balls and ziti as big as cucumbers, stiff with congealed cheese and grease. "This is Sal's kind of food," said Negrycz dryly, eyeing a tray of linguine in oil and more oil. "If you lit one strand of that spaghetti, it would burn for a week."

It was a somber party. Although Turner's crack industrial-safety forces had spent the day before erecting barricades and wires and netting around the atrium itself and every shaft, drain, or depression that could pose a threat to a celebrant in an accident-prone mood, no alcohol was served. There were no speeches; the only person who might have given one, Bruce himself, was in France on holiday that week. "Saves me the trouble of having to order him off the job," muttered Sal. The ironworkers, who live and die by the economy no less than developers, didn't think they had much to celebrate. A few of the supervisors took their plates up to the American Erectors shanty on the second floor and sat around on office chairs that looked as if they'd been shot at. The conversation consisted of each man naming as many places as he could think of where there was no work. After a while a tired-looking man got up heavily from a chair, ground his cigarette into the concrete underfoot, and shambled off into the gloom. "That's Frank," said one of the foremen to no one in particular. "Twenty years with Bethlehem Fabricating, then he went to Lehigh when they went out of business, and now Lehigh is closing their plant. Time for him to pack it in."

With the topping out, the focus of everyone's attention shifted again toward the lower floors, especially those that would be someday occupied by Hahn. The terms of the Hahn lease provided that BSP started collecting rent six months after the space was completed and "accepted" by Hahn. A prerequisite for Hahn's acceptance was a TCO, a temporary certificate of occupancy from the Department of Buildings. Despite its name there was nothing "temporary" about a TCO. It authorized the space to be occupied by civilians tripping around in high heels and short skirts, with nothing protecting their precious heads, which for safety purposes are presumed to be as fragile as light bulbs, and as empty. Buildings could be occupied for years on a TCO, and although every building eventually got one, the construction industry and the city had turned it into a rite of passage only slightly less grueling than a doctoral dissertation in fractal geometry.

Bruce pushed Mitchell, and Mitchell leaned on Sal, and Sal called in his subcontractors, and the subs responded with their own individual mixtures of solicitude, bluster, and deviousness. In the end the building was built by workers, and they worked at their own speed. For reasons that no one could fathom, that speed varied greatly from job to job, and even on the same job from worker to worker. One gang of curtain-wall erectors would set twelve panels on a given day, and another crew would set three. The elevators, which were critical to a TCO, were caught in an obscure predicament involving the timing of the arrival of certain door parts. John Ellis, Sal, Gary, and Bob Fee convened an all-morning meeting at the site with the elevator foreman and three Otis executives, in white short-sleeved shirts and ties with tie clips.

"We really need to push the retail part of the building, guys," Sal said. "We're shooting for a TCO in November. Can we get the inspectors signed off on the service car?"

"They still have a list," the foreman replied with a sigh.

"Can we make the list go away?"

"Only if you pay them off," the man said matter-of-factly.

Sal shuddered. "We're Turner, we don't do that," he mumbled quickly, with a nervous glance at Scott Lewis.

"There's another problem," the foreman said. "You Sheetrocked the bottom of the shaft, you musta forgot to light a candle that week because it rained for seven days straight. Now you don't got Sheetrock down there anymore, you got blue cheese."

He was right; the spring of 1989 was one of the rainiest in the history of New York City. This being a fast-track building, the bottoms of the elevator shafts were closed in with wallboard while the tops were still open to the elements. Rain cascading down the shafts soaked the wallboard and turned it into an ideal medium for cultivating a fuzzy and fast-growing black and green mold.

"It's gonna cost you around $70,000," Sal said, addressing Scott Lewis. "You gotta face the music. It's a reality. There's no way around it."

"How fast is the drywall going up in the rest of the building?" Mitch asked.

"Not fast enough," Ellis replied glumly. "He's supposed to have ninety-seven guys, we tried to find them and we can't."

"Neither can he," Negrycz put in, "and he's paying them."

"No," Bob Fee corrected him, "he knows where they are. It's just that one guy's the shop steward, one guy's in the toolroom, the third guy is the brother-in-law so he doesn't work, either."

Still, the building was now, in the final months of its gestation, changing rapidly, almost overnight. The lines that Jerde and SOM had drawn on their plans years before were now taking form in the trackless expanses of the lower floors, dividing them into rooms, corridors, and stairwells. In random and disconnected spots, a low sill would appear on the floor, just high enough to catch one's heel on, then a parallel one on the ceiling above, and they would be linked by a fence of vertical studs. The skeleton and sinews of the building were disappearing into obscure closets and corners where no one would ever have to look at them again. On the bottommost cellar, where the massive columns and diagonals came down to the ground, you could glimpse a furry-coated knuckle of thick, heavily bolted steel inside a cage of flimsy studs, and then it would be gone, as all around slabs of drywall were fastened to the studs in a daylong shrilling of power screwdrivers.

Where the ceilings had not yet been hung overhead, the maze of hardware had achieved almost biological complexity. It included not just obvious stuff like HVAC duct and electrical conduit and water and sewer pipe, but a whole separate network of plumbing for the fire sprinklers, vents carrying sewer gases to the roof, steam lines, gas pipe for the food-court kitchens, and miles of thin plastic tubing, which carried compressed air to operate the valves and shutters of the HVAC system.

An electrician was installing downlights in the ceiling. He had a stack of fixtures, which were black open-ended cylinders around a foot high, a pile of thin metal rods about two feet long, and a coil of wire. The job was to attach two metal rods to the fixture. Then the rods would be lashed to a grid of metal channels already in place, suspended from the ceiling. He took a rod, located the centerpoint by balancing it on his forefinger, then cut a length of wire, doubled it, lashed the rod in place with a few bends of his lineman's pliers, snipped off the excess, and repeated the process, giving rise to the inevitable question: couldn't this have been done on an assembly line in Malaysia by factory workers making seventy-five cents an hour?

Near where the electrician was working, when he was working, a couple of steamfitters were checking a joint in the two-and-one-half-inch pipe that supplied the fire sprinklers. The joint was sealed with a rubber gasket held in place by a heavy steel collar, but something had clearly gone wrong with the system; water was dribbling from the joint into a large wheel-mounted plastic trash receptacle on the floor below.

"I can't see nothing wrong with this pipe," said one of the men, slender, with a neat dark goatee.

"I couldn't neither," said his colleague—blond, with a modest overhang of hairy shirtless belly poking between colorful striped suspenders.

The water trickled out a little more quickly and the trash can started to overfill.

"We'd better get a bucket or something," the first one muttered. He located an empty cardboard box that had held the electrician's lighting fixtures—a highly unsuitable container for liquids as a plumber ought have known. In a few seconds, water was running out a seam in the bottom of the box. "Shit," he exclaimed mechanically. His partner found a plastic bucket of joint compound lying around and brought it over. "Be careful taking the top off," the dark one warned. "Those plasterers are all immigrants, they use those buckets to shit in."

"Nah."

"It's true. I heard about it from Artie. He needed a little caulking at home, so he swiped a bucket. On the train it all of a sudden started to smell, he realized he had a bucket full of shit."

The thin steamfitter climbed back up on the ladder. "Wait a minute, I feel it," he said. "It's right here at seven o'clock. The whole seam is split."

The two men looked at the pipe, one end of which disappeared into a hole cut in a Sheetrocked wall. On the far side of the wall, the ceiling had also been Sheetrocked, so the pipe was covered there.

"Shit," the blond one said. "That whole wall's gonna have to come down."

"Yeah," said his partner, shrugging. "They just put that rock up this morning, too. Too bad."

They both laughed.

Outside the building, on the Broadway side, Terry Bell and Scott Lewis were standing together in the yard and looking up at the gray metal storefront, taking turns pointing out dents to each other.

"I guess the only place that's really pretty clean is right here where the movie marquee is supposed to go," Scott said glumly. "And that's where it doesn't matter."

"Maybe we ought to ask Turner to move some of the dents," Terry suggested.

"They keep trying to tell me those aren't dents, they're dirt," Scott said. "But they don't want to try and wash them off."

They were there in part to check on a recaulking operation on a storefront column cover. There was a gap of a half inch or so between the metal panels, which was filled with a rubber gasket and caulked over, and Terry on one of his earlier visits had observed that the caulking was as wavy as a washboard. He insisted it be redone. A workman with a luxuriant curly brown beard picked up his tool—an old steak knife—and prepared it by stropping it on the curbstone a couple of times. He climbed aboard a scissorlift, a wheeled vehicle with a platform that rises and descends on a system of hinged, folding steel tubes. There was another man to operate the lift, who pressed one button for up and another for down. Hoisted into position, the man stuffed a length of gasket between the panels and then traced the joint with a caulking gun.

"Couldn't ask for it better than this!" he called down happily to the dark-suited men peering up at him. "Michelangelo couldn't do no better."

"Another Mannerist," Terry muttered. "If he can't get it right with the owner and the architect watching, I guess he'll never get it right."

"Nah," said one of Ellis's assistants passing by. "These are union guys. It wouldn't make no difference to them if the Pope was watching."

The date for the TCO slipped past November, and then slipped again. The fall of 1989 was anomalous; it snowed on Thanksgiving for the first time in memory, ushering in six weeks of bitterly cold weather; the first twenty days of December averaged nine degrees below normal. Extreme cold slowed the building process down in two ways. First, it interfered with the "wet" trades, those involving concrete, cement, glue, joint compound, or any other substance with water in it. Second, because the areas in which those occupations were being pursued were of necessity heated by portable kerosene heaters (called "salamanders"), nothing got done anywhere else in the building because all the other workmen would spend their days huddled around the nearest salamander, warming their fingers.

The cold especially slowed work in the lobby, where more than 100 stone panels had to be arranged on the walls and floors, held in place with intricate goosenecks of brass wire, dabs of epoxy cement, and large globs of plaster. If the plaster were to freeze before it hardened, it would expand, knocking the stone pieces out of alignment.

On a blustery day in December, a Turner laborer in a scissorlift was struggling to close in the lobby entrance with a heavy plastic tarpaulin. Outside a man on a truck was unloading bundles of cedar planks, which would be used to build the water tank on the roof; for insulation against freezing, resistance to leaks, and even cost, no other material had ever been found to substitute for wood. The man had improvised a cloak from a large sheet of white foam packing insulation, with a hole cut for his head, stapled together under his arms. The wind caught the tarp as it was stretched halfway across the entrance, and sent it billowing inward; the man on the lift pushed a lever, and the machine groaned and rolled a few feet to the left, almost knocking over a sizzling salamander. "Hey! Watch where you're going with that thing," a man working on the ground called up cheerfully. "Didn't ya go to laborer school?"

This was Joe Mingoia, a marble-setter. There actually wasn't any marble in the building, but members of that particular union had jurisdiction over interior stonework of any description—not to be confused with stone-setters, who work on exteriors, or their own assistants, marble-*helpers*. Mingoia was thirty-eight and had been in the union for approximately half his life; his father had been a superintendent with the same company since 1954. "I got into it at just the wrong time," he said. "In 1970, none of my friends in college could find work, and I was making $5,000 a summer doing construction, so I said, hey, this is for me. And now here I am." He considered himself an artisan because his work would be viewed by thousands of people a day, and any defects would be immediately noticed. The blocks of granite, three feet nine inches by two feet two and three-eighths inches, had to be square, true, and flat as they went up the wall. Otherwise the artificiality of the whole construct would be laughably obvious: stone, eternal unyielding stone from the depths of the earth, was being applied like a façade in a fragile layer less than an inch thick. Stone, when it ceased to be a solid, load-bearing material, became a lie, an offense to the true esthetic of architecture—but for all that, it would be worse if it were crooked.

Mingoia and his helper, Chris Guy, hoisted a slab of black Cambrian granite from a pile on the floor and threw it down on a worktable. Mingoia carefully inspected the edges. He grabbed a length of brass wire and with a few deft movements of his pliers put in six intricate bends to form a gooseneck anchor, which he inserted into a hole along one edge of the stone and crimped down with several taps of a heavy mallet. Then the two men hoisted the stone into place alongside its fellows, attached the wire to an anchor in the wall, and in an intricate sequence of adjustments, wedged and shimmed and levered the stone into a perfect fit.

Inside the building, things were not going quite so well, according to Sal. "The weather is killing me, and the owner would like to," he said glumly. "I told Scott we don't look so good for a January 15 TCO [the most recent in a series of missed dates], and he told me that was 'inconceivable.' Inconceivable. It's inconceivable to have two fucking weeks of twenty-degree weather in December, that's what's inconceivable. The men don't want to work. I told Scott, if you want to speed things up, we can turn the heat on in the building. But it will cost $10,000 a day, so you know what the answer was to that."

The answer, according to Scott, was that they would be almost as far behind if the weather had been mild, and they'd have some other excuse.

There was a small Christmas party that year in the office in the job site. "Our third Christmas on the job, and I hope our last," Sal said somberly. "If it's not, we're in trouble." Ellis's responsibilities were winding down, and he was looking ahead. He wanted to go to Taiwan, where Turner was supposed to build one of the tallest buildings in Asia for a big Chinese bank, but, as he said, "in this business you never know, you can be all packed for China and the next week find yourself in Brooklyn for the next three years."

The day of the party, Audrey announced her resignation from SOM. She was leaving to become director of design for the New York office of Perkins and Will, a large Chicago-based firm with a specialty in schools, hospitals, and other institutional buildings. Audrey had been planning to leave since the middle of the year, when she had been passed over for a promotion. This meant she was spared the big round of layoffs that were only months away at this point.

The Broadway sidewalk was reconstructed. The old shed, which had been protecting passersby since the first bricks began dropping off 1540 Broadway, was rebuilt over the sidewalk, meaning that pedestrians no longer had to detour into the street. Within two days the fresh concrete was as gum-specked and litter-strewn as a carnival midway. January 15 came and went without a retail TCO. In deciding, so long ago, to decentralize the building's air-conditioning, JB&B made what was undoubtedly a cost-efficient decision, except for the minor issue of vastly multiplying the number of units that had to be tested, adjusted, inspected, repaired, and reinspected before the building could be occupied. When the atrium units were turned on in the third week of January, they didn't work. Crews worked through the night, every day for two weeks, to get ready for an inspection on January 29. The plan was for the building inspector to visit that day, deliver an informal critique, and then return two weeks later for a reinspection. On the morning of the twenty-ninth, Scott Lewis came to the site office and found Sal and John locked in a room with the inspector. "I'd better stay out here," he joked, "in case they're getting his Swiss bank account number."

After a few minutes John Ellis came out. "Is Jerry Gillman [the expediter] in there?" Scott asked.

"Uh, no," John muttered.

"Don't you need him?"

"Uh, he couldn't make it today, we'll be all right," John said.

A minute later Sal came out and pulled Scott over to a corner. "Uh, the inspector couldn't make it today," Sal whispered.

"So who's that in there?"

"Ah, he's a guy from another job, a guy we know. We're gonna walk him around the job for everybody to see. They've all been working for this TCO night and day, we told them it was the twenty-ninth or bust ... so we're gonna let them see this guy. He's been in the business thirty years, he knows what to say if some foreman comes around."

On Friday, February 16, Ellis was sitting in his office when the phone rang; he answered it briefly, hung up, and announced, "We'll have the TCO Monday." The last week and a half had been spent shuffling paper; the final inspection had been that morning, the third inspection by a plumbing inspector on the pipe that carries diesel fuel for the emergency-power generators. There wasn't actually anything wrong with the pipe; he just needed the contractor to sign a form. In fact, the TCO was not actually, finally in hand until the middle of the week. The elevator inspector had approved the elevators and given copies of his report to Gillman and to Turner, but when they presented their copies to the chief inspector for his signoff, he said he had to have the original from the inspector. Since the inspector only visited his office on alternate days, spending the rest of his week in the field, this actually set the process back by forty-eight full hours.

And why should forty-eight hours have mattered, in a process that began with the first hammer blows of demolition, two and a half years earlier? Because from the time the mechanical systems are turned on in a building, until a TCO is actually in hand, the unions require standby crews of electricians, operating engineers, and similarly redundant personnel around the clock, on overtime wages, an expense that in round numbers can be as much as $10,000 a day.

33

Obtaining the TCO was a necessary—but, it turned out, not a sufficient—condition for Hahn's acceptance of the retail space, which in turn would start the six-month countdown to the longed-for moment when the building would start producing rent. Not long after the TCO was in hand, the senior project manager of the Bridgewater mall, William Jackson, came to view the place on behalf of Hahn. Jackson was a heavyset, dour executive who had made little secret of his disdain for Eichner Properties, 1540 Broadway, Times Square, and New York City in general. He found a loose faceplate on a thirty-amp socket, nudged it disdainfully with a shoe, and said to Scott Lewis:

"Who did you pay off to get a TCO on this place?"

"There is nothing here that is inconsistent with a TCO," Lewis replied stiffly.

"Maybe in New York," Jackson said sourly. "You couldn't get away with loose socket plates in any state we do business in."

This was, it turned out, just the opening shot of a protracted struggle to get Hahn to accept the space Jerde had designed for them, Turner had built, and BSP had paid for. Appointments were made for inspections, and the appointments weren't kept. Or they were kept, and resulted in objections. The specifications for the retail space were so detailed, it was easy to find things to object to, but it was also obvious that something was bothering Hahn. What was bothering them, naturally, was the Whiz Bang.

By 1990, the Whiz Bang was no longer the mind-expanding holistic electronic environment dreamed up by Orne and Jerde. Three years of unremitting toil by Eichner had kept its estimated cost unchanged, which meant, naturally, that its scope had been shrinking steadily. The exotic lasers and special effects were gone; the wall of 360 TV sets had been replaced by four large-screen Panasonic "Astrovision" panels, each twelve feet by fifteen. Long hours of negotiation had gone into obtaining these screens and in convincing Panasonic that the honor of placing them in the world's first Whiz Bang should be counted part of their price. Orne had almost persuaded the puzzled Japanese engineers to leave open the back panels of the machines so that passersby could view their electronic innards, in homage to Jerde's rapidly disappearing notion that walking into the atrium should be like stepping into the inside of an old vacuum-tube radio. The Astrovisions were one of several competing large-screen video technologies developed in the late 1980s. Jerde was right about the intrinsic appeal of giant video images. In early 1991 a twenty-three-foot-high Sony "Jumbotron" went into operation on the outside of a building at the southern end of Times Square. The Brobdingnagian commercials it exhibited were so riveting that the AAA warned of a threat to the concentration of taxi drivers trying to hit as few pedestrians as possible heading south on Seventh Avenue. So the attention-getting value of the Whiz Bang was proven; but on the other hand, if you could watch one giant TV screen from the sidewalk of Seventh Avenue, would four of them be enough to draw you inside the building, around the curve of the atrium, and up an escalator to buy a frozen yogurt you didn't want in the first place?

And Bran Ferren was gone. As the Whiz Bang became steadily less otherworldly, the one thing that didn't change was the $2.5 million cost of the computerized controls that would make it all go. This was partly because Ferren was faithful to Jerde's vision of a single demented genius orchestrating lights, sound, and video in headlong real time. This obviously would require computers of a high sophistication. The alternative was to preprogram the Whiz Bang with a series of recorded effects, and have someone sit in a booth and change the tapes. Ferren explained this once to a somewhat puzzled Al Corti:

"This video wall can display 16 million colors, if you care to count them. It can change in real time, between video frames, in a thirtieth of a second. That's why we need our own computer. We have to put out 150 megabytes a second to keep the video wall updated. The idea is to create an interactive system that can respond to the time of the day, the weather, the energy level in the environment, so that the person walking in has a feeling of immediacy. It's the difference between a series of set pieces interrupted by commercials, and a continuously changing, seamless, organic experience."

"I don't visually see the difference," Corti objected. "I've got a clown giving a kid a balloon as he walks in the door. What does your computer do that the preprogrammed one doesn't?"

"It can show the clown, the kid, wipe from one to the other, flip them, put the clown in the middle with the kid all around and then go to a reaction shot of someone else watching."

"And the other can't?"

"It's not that it can't, it's that it can't do it in real time. It would have to be programmed in ahead of time, instead of spontaneously, in relation to the actual events as they take place."

"I'm still not sure ..." Corti began.

"Let me put it this way," one of Ferren's associates interrupted. "You couldn't cut away to something else if the kid threw up."

That was true as far as it went, but as the display elements of the Whiz Bang were whittled down, spending half the budget on controls obviously made less sense. Bruce came to suspect that the reason the computer, the software, and the human interface never got any cheaper was because they were the components that Ferren himself would build. Nor could he get Ferren to agree to the one thing Bruce felt was essential in dealing with high-technology suppliers, a guaranteed maximum price. A series of increasingly acrimonious meetings in late 1989 ended with Ferren being kicked off the job and replaced by a San Diego outfit called SAIC.

Each of these decisions had been taken with Hahn's knowledge and concurrence. But together they seemed to throw the company into a neurotic crisis, characterized by an inability to make any permanent decisions about its participation in the Broadway State Project. True, Illes had been making progress on the leasing front, although in part the progress consisted of defining the tenants he *didn't* want. A video consultant had produced a four-minute video to explain the Whiz Bang to potential renters. When Illes showed it to a couple of guys from a leading shoestore chain, they chuckled nervously and clicked their mechanical pencils and fiddled with their twenty-five-year-man tie clips and walked right out. Which was okay; he wasn't sure they were "right for the space." He wanted tenants with a concept. He showed up at the site one day with a short, plump woman with frizzy red hair and vivid purple lipstick. "She has a Mexican concept," he explained cheerfully, as they surveyed a slice of dusty concrete on the "International Style" level. A chain of bars that featured sweet, violently colored rum drinks sloshing in glass-doored vats had a frozen-rum-drink concept. Another entrepreneur had a nostalgia concept, built around a famous 1950s rock-and-roll personality, which Illes thought would really bring the entertainment concept alive.

Unfortunately, it would take a great deal of money for these concepts to be realized. Hahn's lease included a $7 million work letter—money that BSP was supposed to give Hahn to be passed along to retail tenants in the form of improvements to their space. Before Hahn accepted their space, they wanted to see proof that the $7 million existed, but the bank was refusing to acknowledge any responsibility for it. They insisted that the sum was not covered by the construction loan. Unless BSP could raise the money some other way, it would become part of the continuing negotiations over a loan increase. This meant that nothing could be done while scores of documents were translated into Japanese and sent in a seemingly endless circle between New York and Tokyo.

In the spring, Scott sent Hahn a three-page letter, gone over three times by the lawyers. "We continue to be disturbed by your apparent disinterest in working with us to resolve the issues you claim support your position that the Retail Unit is not substantially complete," he wrote circumlocutiously. "You are arguing that you cannot lease (a position we strenuously disagree with) because you still have not made up your mind as to what you want the [Whiz Bang] to be and what you want to spend ... yet you expect us to bear the financial responsibility for your inability to finalize the parameters of the [Whiz Bang]."

While this was going on, though, something else was happening that would make it all moot. From a secret chamber in the innermost heart of the Broadway State Project, where the Riese brothers had been serving their unspeakably lucrative interment, came a sudden tapping, like the stirring of a ghost welder sealed between the hulls of a ship. A lot had happened in the four years since Bruce, by waving $3 million under their noses, had induced Irving and Murray Riese to temporarily loosen their grip on the corner of Broadway and 45th Street. Architects had come and gone, zoning changes had ensued, plans had been revised a hundred times, but the Riese brothers had held fast to their dream, a dream of a 5,000-square-foot restaurant on two levels, with thirty-inch crawl spaces and the kind of kitchen exhaust and HVAC supply that would make this location the Versailles of Pizza Huts.

Which they couldn't have, at least not in the precise form specified in the lease. In late 1989, several officials from the Riese Organization had visited the site and observed what had been obvious from the street for a year, that the space on the 45th Street corner, bounded by the curved border of the atrium, did not correspond to the rectangular dimensions described in the lease, although the total square footage was about the same. And while the lease called for fifty feet of Broadway frontage on the mezzanine level for a restaurant sign, the building provided only about half that amount. Murray Riese wrote Bruce to call his attention to these facts and inquire what he proposed to do about it. Since changing the shape of the atrium was out of the question, Bruce proposed to pay Riese some extra money to take the space he was given and shut up about it, an arrangement known to lawyers as "liquidated damages." He assumed, in fact, that the Pompeiian specifications in the lease had been drawn up precisely with this situation in mind. Five million dollars would probably have solved the problem right then. Six months of negotiations went by in this fashion, until in April Murray Riese decided to turn up the pressure. Without any warning, there arrived at Eichner's offices a temporary restraining order freezing all leasing activity in the atrium. Murray Riese had struck again.

Naturally, given the impossibility of physically altering the atrium, that was precisely the remedy Murray Riese demanded from the court. Mere money could never compensate him, he averred, for the lost opportunity to establish "an elegant tablecloth restaurant" at this cynosure corner of Manhattan:

> With the premises as demised in the Lease, instead of the Astor Bar or the clock at the Biltmore, the meeting place of choice could well become Tenant's restaurant at 45th and Broadway.
>
> This is the location where the classic New Year's Eve picture of New York City is taken. Panning out from the dropping ball, the camera brings the corner of 45th and Broadway into millions of homes across the nation.
>
> With the premises as demised in the Lease, with the fifty-foot Broadway frontage and signage, it is the name of Tenant's restaurant that would leap into view. Millions of Americans all around the country, even before ever coming to New York City, would have in their minds the name of a restaurant to come to when they visit New York, Tenant's restaurant at 45th and Broadway.

This is what I bargained for. This is what I got in the Lease—and this is what defendants have now robbed me of!

The harder Riese protested that liquidated damages couldn't possibly do him justice, the more money it was assumed would be required to buy him off. The substance of Riese's complaint was dismissed as sophistry pure and simple. "Elegant tablecloth restaurants" were not what the Riese organization was known for. Their main contribution to the dining landscape of New York up to this point had been the mini food court, which clustered three or four fast-food franchises around a common seating area. This helped defeat satiety, the notorious enemy of fast-food profits; a customer could purchase pizza, french fries, and doughnuts all at once while he was still hungry. The Rieses ran numerous such establishments in the Times Square area, on Fifth Avenue in the Forties, around Grand Central Terminal, and elsewhere in the city. There was no obvious reason why the Broadway State space couldn't accommodate one more.

Bruce had new lawyers, from the firm of Stroock & Stroock & Lavan. A partner and two young associates came to Eichner Properties one afternoon in May to plot strategy. They went over Riese's complaint item by item.

"They say, with respect to their vacating the space in the old building, that you obtained substantial benefits by being able to build a bigger building," one of the Stroock lawyers read. "Is that true?"

Howard looked at her incredulously. "We *paid* them for that," he exclaimed.

With respect to the frontage issue, the lease called for Riese to get twenty-five feet on the ground floor and fifty feet on the mezzanine. As built, Riese's space on the corner of Broadway and 45th Street had a swath of glass twenty feet wide on each floor. Adjacent to that was a column enclosure, fortuitously measuring exactly five feet wide, and on the other side of that, the glass wall of the atrium proper. Howard observed that you could, if you were willing to stretch a point somewhat, call the column enclosure "frontage" and argue that the ground-floor requirement at least was technically met.

"That's not stretching a point," one of the other lawyers said. "Stretching a point would be if it were *two* feet wide and you made the same argument."

That still left unmet the requirement for fifty feet of frontage on the mezzanine. Howard found a section of the zoning code that limited the "ground level frontage" of any one business in Times Square to forty feet. Howard adduced several paragraphs of technical reasons why the mezzanine could actually be considered *part of the ground floor* for the purpose of calculating frontage. He therefore was able to argue that if Riese got twenty feet on the street level and twenty feet on the mezzanine, they would get exactly the forty feet that they could be given under the law.

Of course, in order to make that argument, they would have to *exclude* the column enclosure, because otherwise they would have *twenty-five* feet on each floor, for a total of fifty. But they had just counted the column enclosure *in*, to show that Riese got the twenty-five feet at street level. Everyone hoped that anomaly would pass unnoticed.

"It's kind of a contrived argument, isn't it?" one of the young associates murmured tentatively.

The partner looked at him with amusement. "That's what lawyers do," she replied emphatically. "They contrive arguments."

Bruce, who had been at another meeting, bustled in and listened impatiently to the dry rustle of hairs being split. It seemed to him that the resolution would not ultimately lie in the strength of the legal arguments that could be constructed on this obscure point. "There are three possible outcomes," he said briskly. "They take the space and get compensated, they don't take the space and get more compensation, or they get the space revised, and that's not going to happen, so it's A or B, and I don't think B is going to happen because why should they walk away from this great deal they made for themselves? So they will take the space we built for them and they'll get some more money and the only question is when and how much. But I'm perfectly willing to go in there and shout and pound the table and say, 'Go ahead and walk away and we'll meet in court. If you're gonna be a chazzer [Yiddish for "pig"], I'll be a lunatic.'"

Meanwhile, 868,000 square feet of office space were sitting vacant upstairs. That is, 868,000 *leasable* square feet, a hypothetical figure that would be used only to calculate the rent. The difference between that figure and the number of square feet Pythagoras would find in the building was approximately 20 percent, the so-called loss factor, and the "carpetable" area, on which a tenant could actually conduct gainful business (excluding lobbies and corridors) was smaller still. But even, say, 600,000 square feet was an enormous amount of space, space for 3,000 desks at the standard ratio of one office worker per 200 square feet; if each of those desks had a fifty-wpm typist sitting at it, they could type all of *Moby Dick* in two minutes.

Of course, no one expected that the building would be completely occupied as soon as it was finished. Back in the summer of 1987, when the Broadway State Building consisted of a thick stack of drawings and a shallow hole, the brokers Cushman & Wakefield had prepared a two-hundred-page appraisal of the projected development for the benefit of prospective investors and lenders. Even this document, as radiant with optimism as a junior high school yearbook, predicted that only about a third of the office space would be preleased when the building opened on July 1, 1990; the rest would fill up over the next two years, to be fully occupied by July 1992.

Preleasing a third of the building to one tenant was the ideal. Some tenants were just too small to bother with at this stage. The world was full of 5,000-square-foot travel agencies and insurance brokers, but it made no sense to court them for an empty building. Others, paradoxically, were too large, even if, from a strictly geometric point of view, the building had space for them. The first tenant to go into a new building usually got the best deal, and the landlord exacted stiffer terms as the floors filled up. If the first tenant took the whole building, though, the landlord would have nothing left. That was the problem with what otherwise might have been a promising tenant for One Broadway Place, News America Corporation. This was Rupert Murdoch's American publishing and broadcast arm, including a television station, the Fox network, HarperCollins publishers, and sundry magazines. They had been reported on the point of taking space in 1585 Broadway, a Solomon Equities building; late one Friday afternoon Turchin had called Bruce in high excitement to report that the deal had fallen through and he was setting up a meeting with Murdoch's broker, Ken Laub.

Bruce met right after the weekend with Turchin and Laub. He came back excited by the possibilities but sobered by the facts. News America wanted a million square feet, including around 150,000 square feet for their television studios. The only way to get that much space in One Broadway Place, clearly, was to fill in the atrium floors, and even if that were done Murdoch would have virtually no expansion space in the building.

"Tell him not to buy any more companies," Maria Cheng suggested.

"We'll remeasure the building every five years," David Levinson put in.

But even so the deal made questionable sense for BSP. Turchin reported that Murdoch's failed deal with Solomon had been for $28.50 a square foot, net after operating expenses and real estate taxes. If Bruce made a comparable offer, he would be giving up $100-a-square-foot retail space to put in studios at less than a third that rent. Fifteen eighty-five Broadway was a much bigger building than 1540, and Solomon could make a cheap deal for a million square feet and still have several hundred thousand feet left. But if Bruce gave away practically his whole building at $28.50, the game would be over.

Not that he didn't try to make it work. On the vanishing ground between his cost, now approaching $400 million (counting the future work letter), and market rent, sliding below $30 a square foot, he constructed fabulous castles of debt. If the building's income wouldn't support a conventional mortgage, he would try a "convertible" one, in which the lender traded a lower return now for a share of the equity in twelve or fifteen years, when the rent would be higher. Brainstorming in his office one afternoon with Maria Cheng, he proposed a scenario in which the rent increased three dollars per square foot after five years, and again after ten, then jumped six dollars in year sixteen, when the bank's equity kicked in.

"You have to look at the bank's internal rate of return," Maria mumbled, punching numbers on her calculator.

"No, I think that's exactly the wrong way to look at it," Bruce interrupted, waving the calculator away. "If you look at the IRR, it's not that much. The bank has to be able to get out, that's all. I have a very clear game plan."

"But what's the present value of the six dollars in year fifteen …"

"No, forget it, that's not what the deal is about," Bruce said sharply. "Or, no, okay, the present value is negligible, so okay, *give it to me.* I think it makes terrific sense, a privately held company, a sixty-two-year-old guy … how old is Murdoch, anyway, he's got to be sixty-two, right?"

"I can't talk at this level," Maria said, throwing up her hands. "I need to sit down and see if the numbers work."

A month or so later, Bruce met again with Turchin and with Murdoch's broker. Murdoch himself, Bruce learned at this meeting, had driven past the building, and didn't like it very much. Bruce accepted this fact stoically, since Laub assured him that it didn't matter what Murdoch thought of the building, as long as it was a nickel cheaper than the competition. Other than that, nothing was even remotely clear. "It's like dealing with the Bulgarian KGB," Bruce lamented to Tung the next day.

"You don't know how much of what they're telling you is disinformation and how much is just that they're Bulgarians. There are several elements here. The office space requirement, the studio space, and space for expansion. On the studio space, A, what are their actual requirements, and B, is it really necessary they be situated in the building? I can't get a firm answer on this. Laub says, 'For now let's just focus on the offices.' I know that's stupid, because an hour after you make a deal on the offices, you'll be back in court on the studios.

"My suggestion was, why don't you go back across the street and put the studios in Solomon's building? This was met with shocked silence. These are not guys with a big sense of humor."

Tung went the next day to show the building to a delegation from News America. He came back in a bad mood. "The only thing they're interested in is what we don't want to do. They want to take over the retail for their studios, and they want to pay office rents for it. This is a waste of time."

Turchin had a few other suggestions. The most intriguing was Condé Nast, the magazine publishing company. Condé Nast owned their own headquarters building, a drab heap of brick at 350 Madison Avenue, three blocks due east of Times Square. Turchin thought Si Newhouse, the billionaire owner of Condé Nast, might be persuaded to spend a little more on rent in exchange for giving his company a glamorous new image. He could consolidate his other properties, *The New Yorker* and *Parade,* in one building, he'd be closer to the fashion industry … it was easy for Turchin to convince himself that a move to Bruce's building made terrific sense for Newhouse. The only problem was Newhouse himself, a businessman legendary for reticence and caution. He would have to be persuaded to leave the security of his own building and run the risk of leasing it out on the open market.

"I've already thought of that," said Bruce, when Turchin reached this point in his analysis. "We'll have to do a takeover." In other words, to induce Newhouse to lease space in Bruce's building, Bruce would lease Newhouse's building. Then he could sublease it on the open market. Sound crazy? Often this was the only way to get a tenant, and sometimes you could even make money on the deal. But it meant that having built X square feet of space, you had to go and rent it, in effect, twice.

There was the New York office of Dentsu, a giant Japanese advertising agency. Turchin thought Dentsu was a strong candidate. They liked the building. They didn't mind the garish billboards across the street; on the contrary, they found them inspirational, since most were for

Japanese electronics companies. There was Ketchum Communications, Inc., a big advertising and public relations agency with headquarters in Pittsburgh, seeking to consolidate two separate offices in midtown; there were the usual suspects among the law firms—Squadron Ellenoff; Dewey Ballantine; Phillips, Nizer, Benjamin, Krim & Ballon. Phillips, Nizer was looking for around 100,000 square feet to replace several floors on which leases were expiring in the Squibb Building, on West 57th Street near Seventh Avenue. "We're around a dollar apart on the rent," Turchin reported, "and I think we can close that gap, but they want 1991 free."

"If we're one dollar apart, and the free year," Bruce said, "we'll make that deal. We'll split the dollar with them at the end of the lease, and the year, we'll do."

"I'm meeting with them tomorrow," Turchin said. "If you want to come …"

"No, no," Bruce said quickly. "You go. Because then …"

"If they're too hard on me …"

"You can say, 'I've got to check it with Bruce.'"

"Exactly."

"I'd like to get Dentsu in the bottom of the building," Bruce mused, "Squadron in the top and then play off Phillips, Nizer against Ketchum in the middle."

"You just filled up the building," Tung said.

"It's a multitenant strategy," Bruce said, sounding slightly chagrined, as if caught daydreaming. "You've got to have one."

"We're not going to get all of them," Leslie Eichner said.

"We might not get any of them," Tung said.

Bruce turned to Turchin.

"What's our strategy then? Suppose we can't finance the takeover of 350 Madison, and we don't for some reason do a deal with Dentsu. We don't do a deal with Dentsu because the Ministry of Finance decides to put a hold on Japanese firms going into Japanese-financed buildings in America, or something … then where are we?"

"Then," said Turchin briskly, "we have to reexamine the situation in terms of rent. If you drop five dollars a foot, you're in a whole new area."

"By five dollars, you're talking …"

"Twenty-five dollar net."

"I don't know if we can do that," Bruce said somberly.

Turchin for once had nothing to say.

"So I guess we have to hold our breath," Bruce said after a moment. "We don't have much breath to hold."

Of them all, they came closest to making a deal with Ketchum. Ketchum was represented by a broker named Philip Perrone, who was president of his own small firm, and whom Turchin was sure he was going to eat alive. "You should see their proposal to us," Turchin told Bruce. "It looks like a National Science Foundation grant application. I didn't answer most of their questions. Let them think what they want, I didn't do it." In a subtle form of one-upsmanship, Turchin swept aside Perrone's request for sixty dollars a foot in tenant work and actually offered ten dollars more. But he balanced that generosity with a demand for a rent of $31.50 a square foot, with five-dollar increases every five years. That was a net figure, meaning the tenant would pay in addition a proportionate share of the building's real estate taxes and running expenses. Turchin explained that he had divined Ketchum's complicated tax and accounting requirements, and that a high nominal rent, offset by a large upfront concession by the landlord, would actually meet their needs better than the deal that was proposed by their own broker.

Turchin probably was right. He was a very smart man. But Tung couldn't suppress the suspicion that Turchin was helped in arriving at this conclusion by the fact that his own commission was based on the size of the rent.

Slowly as the winter of 1990 wore on the deal with Ketchum took shape. Ketchum needed around 85,000 square feet, which could be obtained in a variety of configurations around the building; eventually they settled on the top three floors of the low-rise elevator bank, twenty-one through twenty-three, plus part of twenty-four. On at least twenty occasions, Tung or one of the brokers or both showed the building to Ketchum's officers and board members. The building showed well. The floor plates were large and open, and the views were exactly as David Childs had described three years earlier. Invariably, standing in the prow on a winter afternoon and looking south straight across at the top of One Times Square, someone would think of the ball dropping on New Year's Eve and remark on what a great place it would be for a party. As for the architecture … Tung at one point made discreet inquiries whether they were troubled by the fact that some offices might have two different colors of glass in the windows. "Really?" one of the Ketchum executives exclaimed in surprise. "What are the two colors?"

Turchin had to assess the costs of taking over Ketchum's existing space, in two different buildings in midtown. The leases didn't begin expiring until 1994, and some ran until the year 2000. The total rent obligation had a net present value of over $11 million, of which at most half would be recouped by subleasing the space to new tenants. Dozens more questions had to be resolved before the brokers could even begin the work of reducing their agreements to a lease. Only Bruce was impatient, but he knew it was futile to try to hurry things. Turchin as a matter of strategy refused to give the appearance of eagerness. Perrone's methodical approach suited his client; Ketchum had, if not all the time in the world, at least until 1992 before it had to get serious about making up its mind.

The first exchange of letters between Turchin and Perrone took place at the end of January 1990. At this point, with a TCO almost in hand for the retail floors, there were still more than 300 men at work in the building. The office lobby was only partly finished. The core was still being enclosed with drywall, sheet-metal workers were attaching duct to the air-conditioning units, and plumbers were installing fixtures in the toilet rooms. Then Anthony Sabbatiele, the building's first engineer, would go through the floors removing most of the plumbing hardware so it wouldn't be stolen by other construction workers.

"It's not even that they have a use for it," he explained to Tung; "they just love anything shiny. They're like hamsters."

At Eichner Properties, at this time, Henry Miller had left and been replaced by a young man named Patrick O'Malley. Henry regarded his three years with Bruce as a detour in what had been, and he hoped would again be, a Wall Street career of great promise and no small success. He had been seduced by Bruce's ambitions, which fed his own, in that period of general insanity that reigned in the mid-1980s, when making a million dollars a year seemed like the slow way to get rich. He left to become a managing director of Prudential-Bache, which was trying to become a power in investment banking. A few months after he arrived, the chairman of Prudential-Bache announced that the effort had been a mistake and the firm would return to its roots as a retail brokerage, but Henry stayed on. He developed a specialty in bankruptcies and led the team that represented the unsecured creditors of Pan Am.

Two days after Perrone wrote to Turchin with an offer, the *Wall Street Journal* ran a long, page-one article about grave problems at VMS, and two weeks after that, on February 13—the day Drexel Burnham Lambert filed for bankruptcy—the partnership suspended dividend payments to its publicly traded funds. There were eight of these, capitalized at more than $1.2 billion—money that had been raised by the sale of shares to the public and invested exclusively in VMS's projects. One of the eight was the VMS Strategic Land Trust, which had contributed $10 million toward BSP's equity in the form of a loan. The loan by now with accumulated interest amounted to almost $14 million. The *Journal* story went into great detail on the mistakes that had led the Xerox Corporation, which controlled VMS through its credit subsidiary, to fire two of VMS's name partners. These included overpaying for properties, overvaluing them once they were bought, and a curious web of self-dealing relationships that seemed to route every dollar through the partners' hands two or three times. While it was apparently legal, VMS's relationship to the funds—it created them, "advised" them, and borrowed from them for its own projects—struck many of the people the *Journal* spoke to as self-serving even by 1980s standards. Shares in the Strategic Land Trust, which had been issued at ten dollars (and sold as safe, fixed-income investments suitable for personal pension plans) were then trading at around three dollars. "What you are getting now," said a lawyer involved in one of the suits brought against VMS, "is a snapshot of a firm that is unraveling."

VMS's problems immediately reflected on BSP. Within hours of the *Journal's* article, Turner's subcontractors were calling Sal and Gary, asking whether to pull their men off the job. Turner was particularly sensitive just then to the question of client finances, because in December they had been abruptly told to halt work on Americas Tower, the forty-eight-story building at the other end of the block from 1540 Broadway. The problem stemmed from a dispute between the partners in the project, New York Land Company and the Japanese construction giant Kumagai Gumi. From the reported facts, it was easy to deduce what the dispute was about. Two years earlier, faced with the same vesting deadline as Bruce, Kumagai Gumi had rushed into construction without waiting to arrange a construction loan. Their error was now becoming apparent, because there still was no construction loan, and Kumagai Gumi, after pouring the best part of $100 million of its own money into the project, was getting tired of writing checks.

The brief history of Japanese investment in American real estate is characterized by many such moments of revelation. Despite the obsessiveness with which the Japanese negotiated every comma in a contract, despite their preoccupation with gathering data on the number of bolts in the job, they never grasped why they were invited to participate in these projects in the first place. Their role was to relieve everyone else of having to think about where the money would come from. This is not to say that anyone was cheating them, just that everyone assumed that once the Japanese were involved in a deal, their resources would prove equal to any contingency. Americas Tower, topped out but only partially closed in, sat derelict for the next twelve months, offering Bruce only the grim satisfaction that this was one less building competing for the same known roster of potential tenants.

VMS's problems, however, didn't portend imminent disaster for BSP. VMS's equity had already been put up, and, essentially, spent. The $10 million borrowed from the Strategic Land Trust either would or wouldn't be repaid, and if it wasn't, the SLT shareholders would bear the loss, along with the losses from the trust's other failed investments. The other $30 million in equity had been borrowed against a letter of credit, subsequently replaced by a direct loan from European-American Bank. VMS had provided the collateral for the loan. Now the time was drawing near when that loan was supposed to be repaid out of the permanent financing, and if there was no permanent financing—because there were no tenants—European-American would have the right to collect against the collateral. The collateral consisted of interests in hotels, shopping malls, and commercial developments around the country. Anyone reading the newspapers in 1990 could have guessed that those properties were probably worth a lot less than they were in 1986. But again, this wasn't BSP's problem.

But VMS also had a repayment guarantee to Citibank (as did Bruce); that is, they pledged to make good a portion of the loan if it couldn't be repaid out of the proceeds of refinancing. The only collateral for the guarantee was VMS's good name, and its value was now obviously open to question, or, as Bruce said bluntly, "Nil." VMS's problems therefore would provide sufficient excuse for Citibank to declare the loan in default, should they choose to. To complicate things further, BSP was asking for more money from Citibank. It was now nine months after their request for an additional $75 million, and the only thing certain was that any such increase in the loan would require substantial additional guarantees and/or equity. The Japanese, evidently still chagrined over their late discovery that all the original equity in the project had been borrowed, appeared to want the partners to put up cash. At one meeting a Japanese banker had even suggested that Bruce invest his own money, a suggestion he regarded as totally out of order. "I said nothing doing," he recounted later to Tung. "I did my part, I built the building." But clearly there would be no increase in the loan until VMS's troubles sorted themselves out.

Bruce returned on February 13 from a hectic and frustrating trip to Japan, and immediately confronted this new crisis. The newspapers were full of end-of-the-eighties talk. Drexel's bankruptcy would cost 5,000 jobs in the city and dump a million square feet of office space on the market. Millions of bottles of Perrier had been recalled in a scare about benzene contamination. Donald and Ivana Trump were divorcing, and cracks were starting to appear in Trump's Potemkin castle of debt. Bruce plunged ahead. Characteristically, he chose to look on VMS's disaster as a great opportunity. VMS, desperate for cash, obviously would be seeking to liquidate its position in the Broadway State Project. This was Bruce's chance to replace his crippled partner with a strong one. If VMS settled, for, say, a loss of 50 percent on their equity, somebody else could pick up almost half of a $400 million project for around $20 million. Citibank obviously would have to approve this new partner, and in effect the bank could set whatever conditions they chose for the transaction. They could demand new collateral, additional guarantees or cash equity. All Bruce had to do was make sure that this mysterious Mr. Moneybags did what was necessary to support the $75 million loan increase, and—presto!—out of the seeming disaster of VMS's default, salvation for the project, and for him. A day after he stepped off a plane from Tokyo, Bruce picked up the phone and started calling Japan all over again.

Turchin was still negotiating with Ketchum as these momentous events took place in February. After two days during which Bruce's calls were not returned by Citibank, he finally got through to one of his contacts, who assured him that the bank would fund BSP's next draw request. "The building has to be finished, it has to be rented, it has to be financed," the bank told Bruce. This confirmed Bruce's belief that the last thing in the world Citibank wanted was to take over a partly finished (and partly paid-for) project. The building was now entering its "punch-list" phase. This meant that Scott, the architects, and engineers would walk through the building several times a week making lists of things the workers had installed upside down, painted the wrong color, scratched their initials in, or neglected to do altogether. Then someone would have to convince the subcontractor to fix it, by slamming down the phone the next twenty times the sub called to ask for the rest of his money. Compared to 1540 Broadway, it would have been easier for Citibank to foreclose on Brazil. The bank needed Bruce as much as he needed them.

Still, the time was clearly in sight when there would be no money left in the construction loan, and the time was nowhere in sight when there would be permanent financing to repay the construction loan. BSP clearly was fighting a defensive battle. The partners' goals were the following: One, to hold off foreclosure as long as possible. Two, to have enough money left in the bank to pay off the trades and creditors. Three, to achieve this without having to come up with any additional money of their own, under the guarantees Eichner and UMS had issued to the banks.

On his side Bruce had essentially two weapons, apart from his own indomitable personality and will. He could retreat, by trading away his equity, or he could attack, by threatening to put the project into Chapter 7 liquidation. This would probably wipe out his own interest, but also create such legal turmoil that it might take years for the bank to recover any of its money. Moreover, in a Chapter 7 filing the bank would be liable for a New York City real estate transfer tax, which would amount to nearly $8 million on the property for obscure tax reasons, the bank would escape the tax only if the title were conveyed in a Chapter 11 reorganization. Therefore just the threat of Chapter 7 gave the partnership leverage. The precise balance between these tactics and the timing of the inevitable retreat became a point of contention between Bruce and Tung. Tung now occupied an increasingly central and complex role in Eichner Properties. He was Bruce's employee, of course, and he loyally served his interests. But Tung also had wide-ranging social and business contacts in the financial world, and a certain detachment that came from growing up in a wealthy family. Tung came to regard part of his role in the Broadway State Project as saving Bruce from himself. As February turned to March and March to April, he began to see signs that Citibank's patience would not be infinite. He was getting calls almost every week from headhunters seeking property managers for banks, which suggested that banks were expecting to come into a lot of property soon. But Bruce was sure he had the rest of the year at least. And if Tung thought it was time to push the panic button … well, Bruce didn't have a panic button. He just negotiated harder, that was all.

Turchin was still negotiating with Ketchum in April, when Turner began dismantling the sidewalk shed on 45th Street to make the office entry more attractive. The shed on Broadway was left up, mostly to avoid calling undue attention to the lack of activity inside the atrium, which was beginning to mock the predictions of a 1990 opening. In that same month Citicorp, the parent of Citibank, announced that its first-quarter earnings had fallen 56.3 percent, largely due to bad real estate loans. The bank reported that it now had $1.3 billion in real estate loans that were not paying interest. (The Broadway State loan was not yet one of them, but it would be, forecasts showed, by the end of the year.) The vacancy rate for midtown office space was reported at 16 percent. A real estate research firm reported that, in defiance of common sense and almost universal perception, real rents for Manhattan office space had actually declined in the 1980s, when inflation and the cost of landlords' concessions were taken into account.

Turchin was still negotiating with Ketchum in May, when Phillips, Nizer—which had seemed very close to making a deal for 100,000 square feet—abruptly ditched BSP in favor of Harry Macklowe's new building, ironically just down the block from Cityspire on West 56th Street. "A bunch of old lawyers," Tung said dismissively. "They wanted to stay in the same neighborhood. The younger guys were interested." (But then in the end Macklowe would be disappointed as well; the firm ended up taking an eight-year sublease in what had been the E.F. Hutton building four blocks further south. They were gambling that rents wouldn't go up much before they had to renew or move again.)

By this time a number of potential equity partners had looked into the deal and decided to pass on it. That left one party as the logical successor to VMS—Hazama-Gumi, the Japanese construction and real estate giant that had already purchased a 5 percent share of the equity with a $20 million letter of credit. Now it was time to bring them to center stage.

Turchin was still negotiating with Ketchum in June, when *Business Week* used a picture of 1540 Broadway to illustrate an article entitled "The Walls Keep Closing In on New York Developers." The magazine noted that Manhattan had 25 million square feet of office space vacant, twice the total space in Atlanta. Bruce, who had usually been happy to talk to the press when business was going well, and even during the occasional setbacks in the past, "did not respond to phone calls," according to *Business Week*. There wasn't much he could have said, except to point out that he wasn't alone. Around the same time, *Crain's New York Business* profiled the troubled real estate empire of David Solomon, which included three buildings with a total of nearly 2.5 million square feet of space, of which approximately 1.8 million were vacant. "Unlike the Rudin family, which has stayed viable by doing only one building every two or three years, developers like the Solomons wanted to do too much too fast," the magazine said, quoting a prominent broker. Not even

Bruce had attempted to build three large speculative buildings at once. But he was caught in the same squeeze.

But June was also the month that 1540 Broadway actually began generating income. Early on the morning of June 1, a sunny Friday, the building's first paying tenant arrived. It was a car. Bruce's old friend Darryl Mallah, the garage operator who had brought him the site, had been awarded the parking concession. Bruce was quick to point out that others had bid on the contract and Mallah offered to pay the most, a base rent that began at around $500,000 a year. Mallah himself was on hand for the opening, supervising his crew of white-shirted, black-bow-tied attendants. Mallah had arranged to open the garage just as he had to close another in a building nearby which was being renovated. He had invited all his regular customers to move with him, with the result that by mid-morning you couldn't have squeezed a skateboard into the space between the cars. A sign near the entrance quoted the rates, scaled from $5.50 for one hour, to $13.53 a day and $232.56 a month, not including New York City parking tax, which had just been increased to 18.25 percent. "Maybe we should have just built a parking garage," Tung said.

In June, John Ellis, who had been on the job for Turner since the beginning, finally left, although not, as he had hoped, for Taiwan. Instead he was transferred exactly five blocks east to an office building that was being audaciously erected over the tracks just north of Grand Central Terminal. The columns had to be threaded through the shell of an existing post office building that would be preserved as its base. "You can take every problem we had on Broadway State and multiply it by ten," he told Sal a few months later, "and you won't approach what this job is like."

Also on June 1, Tung walked the CEO of Ketchum around the building, the final preliminary, he hoped, to an actual deal. Soon the parties began reducing six months of letters, phone calls, and meetings to a written contract, which eventually comprised 113 legal pages, plus exhibits.

"1.01a: Landlord hereby leases to Tenant, and Tenant hereby hires from Landlord," it began, in magisterial evenhandedness, "the premises described in Section 1.02 in the Building (herein called 'Building') known as One Broadway Place and located at 175 West 45th Street in the City, County and State of New York." Every imaginable contingency that might occur in the course of occupancy was provided for. In the event of a fire, Landlord could forcibly enter Tenant's premises for the purposes of putting it out. Tenant could place a sign on each floor of the premises, if it was "in a location and of a design, size, materials and dimension and method of adhesion, reasonably acceptable to Landlord." The premises amounted to 85,000 rentable square feet; as for the rent, it was $3,272,500 per annum, plus "additional charges" representing real estate taxes and operating costs of the building, "all to be paid in lawful money of the United States to Landlord at its offices." This amounted to an impressive $38.50 per rentable square foot. That figure was deceptive, however; the real value of the rent was diminished by a number of factors. Ketchum would get the first fourteen months of occupancy free. The rent would stay the same for the entire twenty years of the lease, whereas most commercial leases called for increases at (typically) five-year intervals. BSP would take over Ketchum's existing space, and as an added insult pay Ketchum $800,000 for their fixtures, which otherwise would probably just have been thrown away. BSP's "tenant improvement" cost was left blank in the draft, but the figure that was being discussed was eighty dollars a square foot—or nearly $7 million.

Negotiations continued on the lease all summer. During that time Eichner Properties, which had expanded so optimistically three years earlier, began to contract. A development company has to develop, or it dies. Bruce had tried to bring along two projects after 1540 Broadway—another big office building in midtown, and an ambitious mixed-use development on the Brooklyn waterfront. Neither had reached the point of generating any revenue for the company. Cityspire also was in trouble with its lenders, and taking up more and more of Bruce's time. Over the summer Lydia Robinson was let go, and then Patrick O'Malley left, and several others who had been working on projects that were now complete. The staff, reduced to fewer than twenty, consolidated in half the space it had previously occupied, leaving a wing of offices in Cityspire dark and empty.

Shortly after Labor Day, Bruce sat in his office and took stock of matters. A summer's worth of toil had achieved what he considered, with his characteristic optimism, the basis for a framework for an agreement to make a deal for Hazama to purchase VMS's interest. The price, for equity worth $30 million going in, was to be somewhat less than $10 million. Hazama would also contribute additional cash to the project, amount to be determined, and Bruce's position would be diluted in a manner to be specified. "But for the prospect of eventually coming to terms with Hazama," he said, "we would have given the deed back to the bank four months ago. I'm the only one holding this together and now even I don't go to the meetings. Hazama and the bank meet. I get four phone calls a day. Hazama calls me first thing in the morning to tell me their version of what happened. Then Citibank calls to tell me what they think happened, and then each of them calls back in the afternoon to see if I know what the other side is thinking."

Around this time Ketchum came up with an added demand: a "most favored nation" clause in their lease, providing that if BSP subsequently made a more favorable deal with another tenant, Ketchum would get to share the benefits. Negotiations over how to word that provision consumed additional weeks. But by the middle of October, *Crain's* reported that Ketchum Communications Inc. "is on the verge of consolidating its New York City offices in One Broadway Place, Bruce Eichner's new development on Broadway and 45th Street." And not a moment too soon, because there was just enough money left in the loan to cover one more draw. In practice, the loan had been in default for months, in the sense that there was no realistic expectation that it would be repaid on schedule, but everyone had agreed to look the other way; after November that would no longer be possible.

The sidewalk in front of the atrium entrance had been repaved, so that for the first time in three years pedestrians no longer had to make a detour into the street while walking down Broadway, in gratitude for which they immediately pockmarked the fresh concrete with blackened blobs of chewing gum. The lobby was now essentially complete, the security desk running, with a bored security guard behind it, and (one day in late autumn) Terry Bell standing alongside it, staring hard at a wall of plain, uniform, gray granite blocks. It wouldn't seem possible that there could be anything of interest in this blank expanse, except to an architect, and then probably only a Skidmore, Owings & Merrill architect. Bell noted a small stain at approximately waist level on one of the blocks. He found three instances of "lipping," blocks that failed to meet at a plane of Euclidean perfection, creating a barely discernible shadow at their joints. The flamed finish was rougher on some blocks than others, so they reflected light differently. Bell made notes of these things in a notebook he always carried, then shrugged and turned to the woman standing next to him. Audrey Matlock no longer worked at Skidmore. Her office was downtown in the West Twenties, but she couldn't resist another look at this building, which was the biggest she had ever designed and the one she felt most attached to, even though the world knew it as a David Childs building.

"The wall washers show up every imperfection in the stone," she said, indicating a row of bulbs set into the ceiling above the security desk. "Couldn't we just get a filter up there over that fixture to mute the shadows a little?"

"Yes," Terry Bell answered.

"Will you talk to them about it?"

"No."

"Why not?" she demanded.

"They don't have a dime, Audrey," Terry said.

They rode an elevator upstairs to Turner's office; being in the elevators always made Audrey feel better. Inside, files were being packed into boxes. Sal was preparing to leave 1540 Broadway behind. He had been promoted to "project executive"—Gary Negrycz's rank—and rewarded with the unpleasant assignment of restarting work on Americas Tower. Kumagai Gumi had resolved their dispute with their partners by buying them out for an undisclosed sum, and work was supposed to resume by the end of the year, if Sal could corral the forty or so subcontractors who had stalked away in high dudgeon and were still waiting for the money they were owed for the work they had already done.

As for Bruce's Japanese partner, Hazama was, according to Tung, "on board, but squeezing up to the last minute. Kohsaka [Hazama's New York representative] didn't call for a week and Bruce was going stir crazy. So we had to call him and threaten that we would take everybody down with us."

"You wouldn't do that," Kohsaka said.

"You're forcing us to," Tung replied.

"But we're working with the lenders," Kohsaka remonstrated.

"Yeah," Tung said, "but we've got to pack up or we'll never get out of here alive."

"It's a poker game," said Luk Sun. "And they're gonna turn over the last card and we'll see if they're bluffing or not. Whether they're just squeezing us down to the wire, and they're really gonna do it; or they don't have the board's approval and they're gonna walk away at the last minute. Because they could. They've done that before."

"They're always saying, they'll get back to us soon, they haven't studied the papers," Tung said. "I told Kohsaka, I know perfectly well that every piece of paper we send them gets put under a microscope within an hour, and this is intentional. He didn't want to hear that. This morning he came to the building with twelve Japanese. He's always bringing them around, we don't know who they are. I told the guards nobody comes in without our approval. We just want him to know he doesn't own the building yet."

Turchin was still negotiating with Ketchum in early November, when the bank sent Bruce a notice of monetary default, giving him ten days to "cure" the default—a joke, under the circumstances—or face the possibility of a foreclosure. Over the phone, they assured Bruce this was just a legal formality. But that was over the phone, Tung noted darkly. Turchin was still negotiating in December. He was negotiating almost up until the day, in the issue dated December 24, 1990, when *Crain's* reported that "Another large business has decided to shelve plans to lease office space. Ketchum Communications Inc. ... has decided to postpone a decision until 1992, a spokeswoman said.

"She adds that the company decided it was 'more prudent to wait' because of uncertainty in the real estate market and because the new space was more expensive than Ketchum's existing space."

And so 1990 ended. By then it didn't matter that much about Ketchum. Given the cost of putting them into the building, it would have been a marginally profitable lease at best. It certainly wasn't about to rescue Bruce. His fate was now almost entirely in the hands of Hazama, which operated by its own rules and in its own good time. For Bruce, though, time was running out.

34

In the last days of December 1990, Turner as one of its final acts took down the sidewalk bridge on Broadway, because the year before people had been climbing all over it to watch the ball dropping at One Times Square on New Year's Eve. Now one could look straight up from the sidewalk and see the spire poking into the low, sallow clouds that seemed to hang over Manhattan most days. On the fourth-floor setback roof, a huge superstructure of black steel could be seen taking shape, to hold the first of the big supersigns that would contribute a calculated measure of eccentricity to the area, as required in the zoning text. And where the building met the street, the new perspective afforded a view of several large dents in the metal storefront, some furtive and incomprehensible graffiti, and a man sitting on an upturned carton with a sign advertising the fact that he was homeless, but "not a drinker." The holiday tourists hurried by, chased by the low waves of slush thrown up by passing buses.

It was a gloomy season. A *New York* magazine article, "Hard Times," quoted state controller Edward Regan: "By any measure, the New York City economy is in a recession [and] the economic situation will get worse before it gets better." The securities industry had lost 40,000 jobs since its peak in 1987, and salaries at some firms had been cut by as much as a third. It would later be determined that the first two years of the 1990s had wiped out all the job gains of the preceding decade. Department store sales, restaurant profits, newspaper advertising—all were dropping. Commercial real estate was in a virtual depression. The vacancy rate in the financial district would hit nearly 25 percent in the spring—exceeded only by the 27 percent rate in Times Square and the surrounding West Side. Judging by the experience of the 1970s, a report by Salomon Brothers said, the city was less than four years into a decline that could last as long as eight years. "Now you see law firms struggling," the *Times* was told by a leading broker, badly shaken by the spectacle, as who wouldn't be? Lawsuits were what the city ran on.

New office construction was at a virtual standstill. For five years, the state-sponsored 42nd Street Development Project had pressed ruthlessly forward with plans for four monumental office towers at the southern end of Times Square; suddenly, mysteriously, the project stalled on a minor legal glitch just before construction was supposed to start. Mort Zuckerman, whose two-million-square-foot project at Columbus Circle had been held up by an environmental lawsuit, gave the appearance of a man struggling to move ahead while being held back by a strand of dental floss. He was overheard, at one of the East Hampton celebrity softball games he frequented, remarking that he ought to send flowers to Jacqueline Onassis, without whose timely opposition the project might actually have been built. Among architectural preservationists, the feeling was that the recession had come just in time. The buildings were up, but, mostly empty, at least they didn't inflict the dreaded plague of yuppie bankers on the neighborhood. The big signs still radiated defiance of good taste at the heavens, and the tourists still came to gape. "It looks as if financial services will turn out to be a lot more ephemeral in the history of Times Square than Camels," Kent Barwick of the Municipal Art Society said cheerfully. "All the brokerage houses that were going to leave New York if they couldn't get a million square feet of space in Times Square seem to have been relieved of their problem."

But at Skidmore, Owings & Merrill this was no cause for celebration. Layoffs pared the New York office from its 1986 peak of around 400 to 270. Bill Hellmuth, who had worked with David and Audrey in the early stages of the project, was one of the victims; the New York office all but closed its structural engineering group, and Bob Halvorson, the partner in charge, was dispatched to London. But David Childs not only survived, he thrived. In 1991 the partnership reorganized itself on more hierarchical lines, and Childs emerged as chairman of the whole 1,100-person firm, the first one it had ever had.

At Citibank, Alan Rosenstein, who had made the original construction loan, left in February 1991 to take a job in the New York offices of Fuji Bank. In more than three years since the Broadway State loan was made, he had looked at between twenty and thirty deals totaling several billion dollars, but not one of them was ever closed. Broadway State was the last loan he made for Citibank.

At Eichner Properties, the turn of the year seemed to crystallize Bruce's own thinking about his future. If he once imagined that he was founding a real estate empire to rival the Rudins' or the Dursts' … well, his life seemed not to be going down that road at present. Bad luck played a part in this outcome. Bruce's association with European-American Bank, which had provided key funding for the Broadway State project and still held the mortgage on Cityspire, was turning into a curse. EAB was emerging as the most aggressive of the major lenders in dealing with problem real estate loans. The way it dealt with them was by foreclosing. In 1991 EAB would move to take over both Cityspire and one of David Solomon's Times Square buildings. Cityspire had been a ruinously expensive building to complete. Rising costs had passed condominium prices going the other way. Bruce gave up his ambition to live in the triplex under Cityspire's dome, an apartment that, Luk Sun had once calculated, would have cost $20,000 a month in taxes and maintenance charges alone. Leslie was relieved. She had always believed that Brooklyn was a better place to raise children anyway.

But mostly Bruce was a victim of his times. He had been caught up in the explosion of values in the 1980s, and had ridden it as high as he could. Now the fall would be hard in proportion. He had lunch around this time with another young developer who had come from out of nowhere to amass a large fortune, which the banks were now gobbling, a zero at a time. He had just sold his boat. Bruce had let his driver go. "Look," Bruce said, "we had a pretty good ride while it lasted. Who ever promised *us* we'd be worth a hundred million dollars?"

It remained to be seen whether the skills that had brought Bruce such wealth once would be useful in his changed circumstances. "The interesting part will be battling back," he mused. "I've done it before, when the hotel burned down, and I had a lot less resources to fall back on. If we're back to 1975, then everyone starts out the same, for better or for worse. And the next fortunes will be made by the ones who have the next big idea. It might not be me … but maybe it will be."

Meanwhile, of course, there was a project to run. At the end of January, Bruce sat for a fourteen-hour day of meetings with lawyers from

Stroock & Stroock & Lavan. Present were representatives of every legal discipline that might conceivably be relevant to Bruce's situation: real estate partners, bankruptcy partners, and, ominously, litigators. It was clear that if bankruptcy was to be avoided, time was running out for Hazama to buy the building. Bruce together with VMS devised a strategy to force Hazama's hand. The following Monday an interest payment was due on a $20 million loan from Marine Midland Bank, secured by Hazama's letter of credit. If the interest were not paid, then in due course Midland would call the letter of credit, and Hazama would have to come up with the $20 million. Hazama would presumably lay claim to a bigger share of the project's equity, from their present 5 percent to 40 percent. When that formula was arrived at, three years earlier, it seemed fair, but now it was a dubious honor at best, since if they succeeded they would be going from 5 percent of nothing to 40 percent of nothing. As for Bruce, he once would have had himself lashed to the mast of the building and stayed there without food or drink before submitting to such a dilution of his own share. But desperate times call forth desperate remedies. Bruce and VMS resolved not to pay the interest; they would pay creditors instead with the money.

If the intent was to shock Hazama, they succeeded. Kohsaka, Hazama's New York representative, was stunned into virtual incomprehension.

"Midland?" Kohsaka responded when Tung called him the next day to advise him of their intentions. "Who is Midland?"

Tung told him. He added that he knew Hazama's board was meeting later that day and Kohsaka had better get to work and put this on the agenda and call them back on Monday with what had been decided.

"We're like Saddam Hussein in the bunker, firing off Scuds," Tung told Howard later. "Sooner or later we'll hit something."

The following Tuesday, a letter arrived from Hazama, saying the deal under discussion was not satisfactory, but they were interested in pursuing further negotiations. Bruce said his door was always open to negotiations. After a week of frantic letters and phone calls between New York, Tokyo, and Chicago, the parties met again. By the end of that day, Wednesday, January 13, there was an agreement for Hazama to take over the project. Hazama would increase its investment in the project to $45 million. The bank group would forgo interest on the existing construction loan for three more years, on top of approximately four months already owed, and advance an additional $60 million. VMS would get essentially nothing, except release from their guarantees, which were worthless anyway.

Bruce would retain an equity share, much diluted to be sure, and the threat that he would have to come up with $35 million under his guarantee to the bank would be removed. The next day Bruce authorized Tung to pay the interest to Marine Midland.

It was too late. Friday afternoon Kohsaka called Bruce in a state of agitation. Midland had called the loan and presented the letter of credit, which meant that Hazama was out $20 million.

"We were playing chicken," Tung said, "and we didn't turn in time."

The actual consequences of this event were not necessarily fatal. If Hazama were going to wind up with all the equity anyway, it didn't change matters much if they got 40 percent of it in advance. As for the $20 million borrowed from Marine Midland, that would have had to be repaid eventually in any event. But the episode left a certain residue of suspicion that may or may not have affected the deliberations of Hazama's board when in due course they came to take up the deal as presented to them by their New York office. One day that spring, Bruce was summoned out of a meeting to take a call from Dennis Diczok of Citibank.

"I just heard from Tokyo," he told Bruce funereally. "It's all over. Hazama's board turned down Hazama's proposal." The deal was dead.

The exodus from Eichner Properties now accelerated. Scott Lewis left to take over the practice of a retiring structural engineer who specialized in outdoor signs and billboards. Howard and Mitchell departed, one amicably, the other with bitterness. Mitchell claimed that Bruce owed him a bonus equivalent to several months' salary that had been promised years earlier. That was technically true. But Bruce had also kept Mitchell on the job long after many others had been laid off, and long past the time that Eichner Properties had need of a vice president for construction. For several weeks after he was taken off the payroll, Mitchell kept coming to his office, scowling and lurking outside Bruce's door. Then, abruptly and without good-byes, he stopped showing up.

Howard left to join the politically connected law firm of Fischbein Badillo Wagner, where he was to "continue his practice in the area of land use regulation and the government regulatory process." (The Wagner in the firm name was former New York City mayor Robert Wagner, who died shortly afterwards.) Bruce hosted a farewell dinner for Howard at a restaurant in Chinatown. It was a sentimental occasion, as Bruce went down the table, listing what everyone had done over the years, the deals they'd made, the money they'd saved, the close calls they'd survived together. Luk Sun, characteristically, stayed dry-eyed through it all. "Bruce has it wrong," he observed. "He thinks everyone did this for him. They did it because they're professionals. He was lucky to have these people working for him."

In April, Citibank served formal foreclosure papers on Broadway State; they came in six sets and had to be wheeled into the office on a luggage cart. The complaint listed as either defendants or "nondefendant parties" Broadway State Partners, Ian Bruce Eichner, and VMS, plus any individual or entity that had the remotest connection to the building and might still think it was owed some money.

Bruce's lawyers served Citibank in turn. The standard response to a foreclosure action is a barrage of countercharges under the doctrine of "lender liability." As far as lawyers are concerned, all failures can be ascribed to someone else's bad faith and willful, premeditated treachery. There is no accounting for the ambiguities of risk, no category for honest judgments that were overtaken by events. Citibank was accused of forcing BSP into a "highly disadvantageous" lease with Hahn. It was charged with pretending to negotiate a restructuring of the loan while intending no such thing, "part of a continuing pattern of unconscionable and unreasonable conduct by Citibank in negotiating with BSP and its partners in bad faith in order to lull them with false assurances. ..." Citibank was indicted for "sabotage" of the sale of the building to Hazama, although the sale was presumed to have been in Citibank's interests as well. In sum, the response described a pattern of behavior not merely deleterious to BSP's interest, but so obtuse and self-defeating that the wonder is that Citibank's parent company, Citicorp, which lost $324 million in the first nine months of 1991, didn't lose ten times that much.

This is not the place to determine the truth of these allegations. Bruce contends that if the bank had succeeded in restructuring the loan in 1989, the atrium could have been finished to Hahn's specifications, money appropriated for the retail work letter, and the project generating enough income to survive until the office market improved. Former Citibank officials—the only ones who will talk about it—contend that Broadway State failed to come up with a concrete offer of additional equity. Bruce has letters in which such offers were in fact made. But on the specific point of the competence of the management of Citibank's real estate division, in October 1991, Citibank undertook the third major restructuring of its real estate division in a year—something that, as

Crain's pointed out delicately, "will likely fuel the perception among some Citicorp customers that the bank has lacked a coherent strategy in its response to its real estate problems."

BSP still owned and ran the building while the foreclosure made its leisurely way through the wheels of justice, and Tung had his hands full with it. In the last year or so before the old 1540 Broadway was torn down, numerous pedestrians claimed to have injured themselves on the sidewalks outside, and these cases (known generically as "slip-and-falls") were now making their way toward trial. Periodically Tung, who hadn't even been around in 1986, would be called away for several hours to give a deposition disclaiming any conceivable responsibility for the accident. He had to keep the building running, too, as well as he could on whatever money he could extract from Citibank. On one of his last days in Eichner's employ, Mitch stalked down Broadway in a dark blue three-piece suit and a pink baseball cap, his luxuriant curls blowing in the brisk March breeze. At the lobby entrance he yanked forcefully on the handle to one of the swing doors, and it came off in his hand. Handing it, with a look of disgust, to the uniformed brute lounging behind the security desk, he rode an elevator up to the fourth floor to say his good-byes.

Here Tony Sabbatiele, the building manager, had a small, windowless office. From his desk, Tony could call up on his computer real-time readouts of the performance of every major building system. He could see the temperature of the water in any of the cooling towers on the roof or measure the volume of steam passing through the mains in the cellar, check the status of the innumerable pumps, valves, and switches that made the building function. The displays on his screen indicated an accelerating trend toward things going awry. The building was designed to be run by a staff of ten to twelve engineers, mechanics, and porters, not counting the people who cleaned and maintained the tenants' premises. But Tony had only himself and his assistant, and in some ways an empty building required more maintenance than an occupied one. The cooling pumps had to be switched on and off periodically to circulate the chemicals in the pipes. The elevators had to make one trip a week, or the cables and relays would freeze; this was a two-person job, one to ride the elevator and the other to rescue him in case he got stuck between floors. The plumbing had to be run regularly or the valves would stick and the bowls would stain. Every day Tony and his assistant went through the building, a few floors at a time, just flushing the toilets.

But this could not substitute for money to fix things. There were roughly fifty steam traps in various locations, whose function was to drain accumulated condensation from the heating system; several of them had begun to leak, and, for want of replacements, were wasting hundreds of dollars in steam a month. The smoke detectors kept going off inexplicably, at odd hours, summoning Sabbatiele from his home in Long Island. Driving west on 45th Street he would see the building pulsing against the horizon, as the state-of-the-art life-safety system flashed its stroboscopic alarm at the ghost tenants. Then he would hunt up the source of the disturbance, reset the alarm, set a weary course back to the Midtown Tunnel.

Sal LaScala called while Mitch was there. Sal was over at Americas Tower, where work was finally recommencing after a shutdown of more than a year. It had taken Sal three months to overcome the reluctance on the part of the subcontractors to set foot in the building ever again, except to kick anyone from Turner off a high floor. "They wanted to kill somebody, but it shouldna been me," he complained to Mitch. "I was getting screwed just like they were." Working at the other end of the block, he noticed every broken piece of glass in 1540 that was patched with plywood, every scribble of black graffiti. "Ain't it a shame?" he rasped. "I hate what they're doing to my building."

That spring, a new tenant appeared: the Qlinn (pronounced Cue-lynn) sign on the Broadway setback. This was a slab nearly seventy feet long and forty high, holding a matrix of 84,000 small plastic cubes. Each cube was capable of revolving independently to display one of four colored sides—red, white, blue, or green—from which huge and surprisingly detailed pictures could be built up. The idea was to sell time on the board to advertisers who might not be able to afford such a huge sign themselves, interspersed with artwork and a variety of messages and news. The concept had been successful in Asia and Europe, although Tama Starr of Artkraft Strauss pointed out that similar time-sharing arrangements had been failures in Times Square. Signs had to justify themselves on the basis of corporate "presence" and "image," which required, she believed, a permanent, neon-blaring, smoke-puffing, water-spouting kaleidescopic spectacular. Still, this wasn't BSP's problem, because the base rent on the sign was guaranteed—almost as much per month as the garage, which took up an entire floor of the building. As Richard Schaps, president of Van Wagner, remarked: "It's the most expensive real estate in the world, if you figure it on a square-foot basis."

And even as the market crumbled around him, Bruce continued, doggedly, to seek tenants for the building. "A year ago," he noted, "we were talking about deals in the high twenties [dollars per square foot, net]; six months ago, in the mid-twenties; today the numbers being thrown about are in the low twenties." At those numbers, he recognized, nobody would come out of the project whole, but he went ahead anyway. He got a call from a broker named Peter Friedman, who was representing Bertelsmann A.G., the German publishers whose American holdings included RCA Records, *Parents* magazine and the publishers Bantam Doubleday Dell. Bertelsmann was seeking around a half-million square feet in which to consolidate their 1,750 New York employees. More than that, they were looking for a visible presence in New York, commensurate with their status as the second-largest media company in the world, after Time-Warner. Which led Bruce to the idea that Bertelsmann should buy the building, rather than merely rent it. There was every reason for Bertelsmann to do this, in Bruce's opinion. Interest rates were falling through 1991, making financing attractive; they would get the benefits of depreciation, which presumably they could make better use of than Citibank, which was losing money anyway; and they would escape the commercial occupancy tax, a nuisance levy New York City exacts from all rent-paying commercial tenants. You didn't need three degrees from Heidelberg to recognize how much sense that made.

Of course, Bruce could not at this stage make a deal on his own to sell the building, even though he and VMS still nominally owned it; in effect, the building was the banks' to sell. On the other hand, it was clear to him that without his intervention, there would be no deal at all. Bertelsmann was looking for office space and had no intentions of going into the real-estate business. But if they bought 1540 Broadway, they would be responsible not just for their own space, but several hundred thousand additional square feet of offices that would have to be leased, plus a garage, movie theaters, the retail atrium—and the leases for their existing space on Fifth and Sixth Avenues. (If Bertelsmann were to rent space from a commercial developer, the landlord as part of the deal might take over their old space, as Bruce had considered doing for other tenants. But the banks weren't likely to do the same; they were seeking to limit their exposure to the real-estate market, not prolong it.) Bruce, together with Friedman, had to overcome these objections. On the bank side, they had to nudge Citibank into accepting a staggering loss, of money and, perhaps, face. In late August, the Broadway State Project was in the news again, as the *Wall Street Journal* reported that Bertelsmann had made a "stunningly low" offer of around $100 million for the building. This was roughly two-thirds of the hard cost of building it, only about 40 percent of the mortgage, and less than a third of the roughly

$320 million that had been spent on the project altogether. "This building is the litmus test of the whole market," Friedman told the *Journal.* "The market can't recover until the empty buildings lease up. The question is, how low can it go?"

For the next two weeks, people Tung hadn't spoken to in years called to ask what he knew about the Bertelsmann deal, either out of curiosity or to see if they could cut a deal for the building for $100,000,001. One day at the end of the month Tung got a call from Citibank and was told to have the building ready for an inspection at nine the next morning. When Tung got there he discovered John Reed himself, the chairman of Citicorp, along with Robert Laughlin, the head of Citicorp Real Estate. Reed seemed in good spirits. He praised the views, the floor plates, the clever way the retail and office spaces had been kept separate, and in the end turned to Tung and said, "Well, Bill, what do you think it's worth?"

"At least $145," Tung replied, meaning dollars per square foot, which was about what it ended up costing to build.

To William, this visit implied that Citibank wasn't about to give the building away at a loss of $150 million. You don't have to go look at something you're going to sell, he mused; you look at something you're going to keep. A few weeks later, the *Journal,* in one of its periodic roundups of the troubled real estate market, mentioned 1540 Broadway again. This time they quoted a broker who passed on a rumor that Citibank, rather than take a nine-figure loss on the project, would consider putting the whole project into mothballs until values came up again. And when might that happier time be? In September, Reed spoke to a business group in Chicago and predicted that write-offs of the bad real estate loans made during the 1980s might last into the mid-1990s. Citibank, at the time, had around $12 billion in commercial real estate loans on its books.

During 1991 Tung managed to pick up a few dollars now and again for the project by renting out a bit of space to people who wanted its dramatic setting as the backdrop for photography of some kind. One day a production company came and set up in one of the toilet rooms to shoot a commercial for men's suits; they used a ladies' for the purpose, because they didn't want urinals in the shot. And somebody eventually did get to sit at a desk in the prow, three hundred feet high on the imaginary axis around which all New York, and therefore the whole civilized world, rotates. It was an actor portraying a talent agent in the movie, *Mr. Saturday Night.* An office of some pretension was constructed on the sixteenth floor, and for a few days this one corner of the building was filled with the factitious sounds of modern business, the electronic burble of the telephone and the swish of secretarial pantyhose. Audrey was outraged when she heard about it. All along she believed someone would want to put her building in a movie someday, but she hadn't designed it for some dopey Billy Crystal comedy. *Robocop 3* would have been more to her taste.

And then it was quiet again, the building subsiding into a kind of industrial hibernation, the dark windows on Broadway reflecting the immense apple-cheeked children in the Kodak sign across the street. It was never completely still, of course. In the distant cellar, lights were always on in the garage, and cars came and went at all hours. From the street, in those rare moments when the traffic was still, someone standing on the sidewalk outside the Marriott could hear the Qlinn making a little shuffling sound six times a minute as its 84,000 pixels miraculously aligned themselves into flags and pinwheels, then dissolved into an advertisement for fuel additive. The mechanical rooms sporadically were filled with the rumble of fans and pumps striving to maintain the empty floors at a minimum of forty-eight degrees. And in front of the entrance to the atrium, a tall man in a brightly colored African skullcap stood behind an upturned cardboard box and impassively scanned the passersby. He, at least, had figured out how to make money from the building. He was selling Rolexes for forty dollars.

AFTERWORD

The building stayed empty for a long time but, then, it was built to last a century. In early 1992, Broadway State Partners entered Chapter 11 reorganization, and Bertelsmann bought their sole asset, 1540 Broadway. The price was $119 million, an increase from their "stunningly low" offer of $100 million the previous summer, but not by much. This amount was actually less than the cost of construction alone. It was less by far when you added in the price of the land, and (including accumulated interest on the loan) represented a loss of around $130 million to the banks that made the construction loan. Taking into account the partnership's vanished equity, the total amount that disappeared in the transaction was approximately $200 million. The deal was struck on February 28, which was a fateful date for Bruce; it was the anniversary of the day the Margaret Hotel had burned down a decade earlier, almost putting an end to his career just as it was beginning.

On March 3, there was a press conference at City Hall to announce the sale. Bertelsmann was planning to move its U.S. corporate offices, its publishing and music divisions into 1540 Broadway, accounting for about two-thirds of the office space. The rest would be put on the market; a portion of it was pledged as subsidized "incubator space" to foreign companies opening offices in New York for the first time. By threatening to move 500 of its 1,750 jobs to Chicago and Indianapolis, Bertelsmann had won additional tax concessions from the city worth an estimated $11 million. New York's mayor, David Dinkins, made the announcement himself, treating the sale as a hopeful sign for the city's economy, although the story in the next day's *Times* might have been more accurate in describing it as "indication of the weakness of the city's real-estate market." One astute reporter noticed a curious omission in the press release: There was no mention of the identity of the seller. In response to his question, a city official replied that Bertelsmann was buying the building from "Citibank, basically." After years as the Broadway State Building and One Broadway Place, the building was back to being called by its address. But in the summer of 1992, a sign would go up on Broadway with its new name: the Bertelsmann Building.

About the architecture, the object of so much sweat and passion for so many arduous months, the new owners were noncommittal. "I think it looks nice," said Chris Alpers, the Bertelsmann executive who handled the purchase, "but a decision like this is numbers-driven. As long as you don't hate the building it doesn't matter. The location is a good one. When we set out looking, originally if we could have gotten the same deal on Sixth Avenue, we would have taken it in a minute. Now, we're not so sure. Times Square is a great location if you're in the media business, the entertainment business. We see it turning around already." Perhaps so, although sometime later *New York* magazine carried a gossip item to the effect that Doubleday editor Jacqueline Onassis was planning to work at home rather than move into 1540 Broadway. (The publishing group was assigned the lower third of the building. The music people got the top.) From her existing office at 666 Fifth Avenue, Onassis was two short blocks from The Four Seasons. Within the same radius from 1540 Broadway were several kosher delicatessens, a cluster of Brazilian lunch spots, and the many fine restaurants of the Marriott Marquis, whose guests would have been only too thrilled to have the former First Lady appear in their dining room.

One feature of the building Bertelsmann found noteworthy was, of course, the prow. From the moment the prow was conceived, the architects had been sure it would make a terrific executive office for someone someday, but that just showed their ignorance of how giant corporations work. Bertelsmann had a complicated corporate structure comprising music, magazine, and book groups, all reporting separately to headquarters in Germany. Undoubtedly, no one in Germany had an office to compare with the prow. By corporate decree, Alpers said, no single individual in New York was to sit in the prow. The Bertelsmann Building would have instead the world's greatest set of conference rooms.

One name that wasn't mentioned at all in the press conference was Bruce Eichner. Which was fine with him; he had no reason to be ashamed of his association with 1540 Broadway, but he didn't especially crave publicity about it either. Shortly after the bankruptcy plan was approved by the court in May, Peter Grant of *Crain's* wrote that Bruce had managed to salvage something from the disaster: a consulting contract directly from Bertelsmann that would pay him personally a million dollars over the next ten years. Grant wrote that a few of the parties, including Hazama, objected to this payment; its only purpose, they contended, was to buy Bruce's cooperation in the sale. It is true that Bruce, had he chosen to be difficult, could have steered the project onto the rocks of a liquidation, from whose crevices the banks would still be picking out nickels in the year 2000. But that was never his intention. Once the idea of the sale arose, Bruce and Bertelsmann's broker, Peter Friedman, had six hard months of work to convince the skeptical Germans that it was a risk worth taking. Absent those efforts, he says, the banks might have been stuck with the building indefinitely.

"I guess," Bruce said modestly, "I was lucky and smart enough so that when I saw a body on the doorstep I figured out how to do something with it."

VMS ended up in the position of someone who flees a burning airplane on the runway and can't believe that he's still alive. They kept expecting their $35 million guarantee to blow up in their faces, but it never did. VMS at least got something for investors in the Strategic Land Trust, the public REIT that held a $14 million note (including interest) on the project. They got $1 million, ten cents on the dollars they had invested five years earlier.

William Tung went to work for Bertelsmann as "director of real estate," supervising the company's move into the building and the leasing of the remaining space. He made his office in the old marketing suite, and therefore became the first bona-fide office tenant of 1540 Broadway.

Hahn's great experiment in New York retailing seemed to have ended in failure. Out of the wreckage of Broadway State Partners they extracted a token payment of something over $1 million, as partial compensation for their out-of-pocket expenses on the project. In May of 1992, exactly five years after Bruce at his first meeting with Vernon Schwartz pressed him to make a deal right away, Tung and his new bosses from Bertelsmann flew to the shopping-center convention in Las Vegas to look for new retail partners. There they had a meeting with John Gilchrist, who said Hahn might someday be interested in coming back to 1540 Broadway, but on one condition: under no circumstances would there be a Whiz Bang.

The Riese Organization took one final payment of $1 million and said goodbye to the corner of Broadway and 45th Street, which it had sworn it would never leave.

Mitch Mailman returned to his electrical contracting business, which was thriving; utilities have to replace their power lines whether there's a recession or not.

Luk Sun Wong was one of the last employees to leave Eichner Properties, around the end of 1991. He wasn't sure what he would do next; his wife, a flight attendant with a bankrupt airline, was pregnant.

Audrey left her new job after a little more than a year. She taught a course at the University of Texas while she was starting her own practice, with some of her friends who had also left Skidmore. One of the first people she talked to about work was …

… Bruce, who had come up with an ambitious plan to buy a well-known New York City hotel, in a deal involving …

… VMS.

INDEX